Situated Meaning

Situated Meaning

INSIDE AND OUTSIDE
IN JAPANESE SELF, SOCIETY,
AND LANGUAGE

Edited by
Jane M. Bachnik
and
Charles J. Quinn, Jr.

PRINCETON UNIVERSITY PRESS
PRINCETON, NEW JERSEY

Library of Congress Cataloging-in-Publication Data

Situated meaning : inside and outside in
Japanese self, society, and language / edited by
Jane M. Bachnik, Charles J. Quinn, Jr.
p.   cm.
Includes bibliographical references and index.
ISBN 0-691-06965-4 — ISBN 0-691-01538-4 (pbk.)
1. Japan—Civilization—Philosophy.
2. Japanese language—Social aspects.
I. Bachnik, Jane.   II. Quinn, Charles J., Jr., 1948– .
DS821.S59   1994   952—dc20   93-8956

Publication of this book has been aided by
The Ohio State University Institute for Japanese Studies

This book has been composed in New Baskerville

Princeton University Press books are printed on acid-free paper
and meet the guidelines for permanence and durability of the
Committee on Production Guidelines for Book Longevity of
the Council on Library Resources

Printed in the United States of America

1   3   5   7   9   10   8   6   4   2
(Pbk.)
1   3   5   7   9   10   8   6   4   2

To our parents

CONTENTS

Foreword, *by Donald L. Brenneis*   ix

Preface   xiii

Note on Romanization   xv

Key to Abbreviations and Orthographic Conventions   xvii

Contributors   xix

PART ONE: *Indexing Self and Social Context*

CHAPTER ONE
Introduction: *uchi/soto:* Challenging Our Conceptualizations of
Self, Social Order, and Language
   Jane M. Bachnik   3

CHAPTER TWO
The Terms *uchi* and *soto* as Windows on a World
   Charles J. Quinn, Jr.   38

CHAPTER THREE
A Movable Self: The Linguistic Indexing of *uchi* and *soto*
   Patricia J. Wetzel   73

CHAPTER FOUR
Indexing Hierarchy through Japanese Gender Relations
   Nancy R. Rosenberger   88

CHAPTER FIVE
Uchi/soto: Choices in Directive Speech Acts in Japanese
   Robert J. Sukle   113

CHAPTER SIX
Indexing Self and Society in Japanese Family Organization
   Jane M. Bachnik   143

PART TWO: *Failure to Index: Boundary Disintegration and Social Breakdown*

CHAPTER SEVEN
Uchi no kaisha: Company as Family?
   Dorinne K. Kondo   169

CHAPTER EIGHT
The Battle to Belong: Self-Sacrifice and Self-Fulfillment in the
Japanese Family Enterprise
Matthews M. Hamabata   192

CHAPTER NINE
When *uchi* and *soto* Fell Silent in the Night: Shifting Boundaries
in Shiga Naoya's "The Razor"
Michael S. Molasky   209

CHAPTER TEN
Uchi/soto: Authority and Intimacy, Hierarchy and Solidarity
in Japan
Jane M. Bachnik   223

PART THREE: *Language as a Form of Life:*
Clines of Knowledge as Clines of Person

CHAPTER ELEVEN
Uchi/soto: Tip of a Semiotic Iceberg? 'Inside' and 'Outside'
Knowledge in the Grammar of Japanese
Charles J. Quinn, Jr.   247

Index   295

FOREWORD: SITUATED MEANING

DONALD L. BRENNEIS
PITZER COLLEGE

THIS REMARKABLE volume adds a new dimension, both literal and metaphoric, to our understanding of Japan. Turning from the vertical axis of hierarchy and subordination, an organizing trope in much of the literature on Japan, these essays draw our attention to the horizontal, mapping a surprising and stimulating range of cultural practices and orientations in terms of such relational concepts as *uchi* 'inside' and *soto* 'outside'. Subtle, insightful, and very effectively informed by multiple disciplinary perspectives, *Situated Meaning* takes us deeply inside fascinating aspects of Japanese language, literature, daily life, and social experience. It also speaks powerfully to the outside, raising broader questions of language, meaning, and cultural analysis.

Guiding this volume is the notion of Japanese social order as situated, that is, that what analysts see as "social order" inheres in the very specific circumstances of its particular enactments. *Situated Meaning* dramatically extends our understanding of this general insight, which has informed much recent scholarship on Japan. It does so in several ways: first, by exploring the highly significant pairs of relational terms through which "situation" is shaped and construed (for example, *uchi/soto* 'inside/outside' and *omote/ura* 'in front/in back'); second, by considering such terms—and the relationships they imply—not as manifestations of a fixed social framework but as "indexical coordinates," deictic locational practices necessarily centered on an "I"; and third, by considering with great subtlety the experiential implications of such a perspective. This volume takes the often assumed general "context" of Japanese society as problematic, forcing attention to a constantly reconstituted and person-centered set of particular relationships. Further, through its subtle and insightful discussions of personal experience—whether in novels, in domestic life, or in business—*Situated Meaning* successfully conveys the lives of individuals in a complex and remarkably flexible social world.

In its focus on the central role of social indexicality *Situated Meaning* directly challenges the primarily referential view of linguistic and social "meaning," an implicit assumption in much work in linguistics, anthropology, and cultural analysis. Basically, such a view implies the notion of an external "world" which is referred to and reflected in language, whether it be a physical world ("This is a table") or a social one ("This is a social superior"). The central role of language lies in conveying such messages *about* an external, nonlinguistic world; consequently, the core problematic of language lies in how well it reflects this world. The indexical approach at the heart of this volume demands a new perspective, one taking the situationally located relationships among speaker, hearer, and scene as a starting point. Meaning becomes located, rather than being "about" the external. Social life is not, therefore, so much reflected in linguistic practice as it is constituted through it, with speech and its implications being necessarily entangled with situation. "Context," the old warhorse of sociolinguistic writing, takes on a new flavor here; it is not external to speech but reciprocally shaped by it, a point central to the essays in a provocative new volume edited by Duranti and Goodwin (1992).

This volume speaks in stimulating ways to another recent collection, *Unwrapping Japan: Society and Culture in Anthropological Perspective* (Ben-Ari et al. 1990). Central to this book is the importance of wrapping in Japan; themes of elegant presentation, disguise, and concealment are considered in a variety of Japanese social practices, from gift-giving to conversation. Joy Hendry's contribution (1990) speaks directly to the processes of wrapping and unwrapping, suggesting that presentation and an almost literal embedding of the "contents," whether of a gift or of talk, may well be more significant than the contents themselves. Locating the gift within its wrapping—or the talk within its honorifics and allusions—and penetrating the layers of concealment as they shape and locate what they contain is central. As with *Situated Meaning*, the process of linking context and message is necessary and reciprocal.

This book clearly offers a great deal to scholars of Japan. At the same time, it speaks very effectively to a range of questions at the heart of contemporary wranglings with language, culture and social experience. I want briefly to note several provocative points at which such theoretical and comparative concerns are directly implicated.

First, in taking issues of social inequality as flexible and situationally shaped practices, that is, ones that are constructed and negotiated rather than operating in some mechanistic way, *Situated Meaning* reverses what is usually taken for granted in studies of Japan and other apparently hierarchical societies. For those of us working in communities with explicitly egalitarian ideologies (see, for example, the Pacific island communities represented in Brenneis and Myers 1984), the negotiation of social relations is seen as a given; what is often less commonly recognized are those moments in which hierarchical practice is consequential. Bachnik and Quinn's volume makes the assumed problematic for Japan and, in so doing, illuminates the specifics of personal and social negotiation at the heart of quotidian life in an explicitly stratified society.

Second, there are remarkable resonances with emerging discussions in the broader western Pacific literature. The work of Frake (1964, 1975) in the southern Philippines prefigured these discussions, bringing questions of social space and its implications for communicative and cultural practice to the fore. Clare Wolfowitz's recent (1991) monograph on Suriname Javanese, for example, challenges the usual "fixed hierarchy" model of Javanese language style, reorienting an understanding of language use in terms of social space. As with the *uchi/soto* dimension, the situational elements of interactional practice become central, taking precedence over apparently fixed hierarchical distinctions. Similarly, recent work in Melanesia and Polynesia stresses the role of situation and event in shaping both behavior and local theories of personal experience (Watson-Gegeo and White 1990). Within this broader region, issues of interpretation, social practice, and "emotional" life are being linked in increasingly convincing ways to an implicitly indexical, situation-based perspective. This may represent shared cultural orientations within the western Pacific; it may also reflect, in part at least, an emergent regional discourse among Pacific anthropologists and other scholars working in the area. In contrast with the literature on the Mediterranean and the Middle East, for example, where the paradigm of relatively fixed public and private places—and of their consequences for an interpretation of gender relations—shaped arguments not only about those areas but worldwide, *Situated Meaning* makes a compelling case for considering space as socially, situationally, and flexibly defined. The implications of this perspective go far beyond Japan.

Finally, this book contributes both to a refinement of our understanding of how linguistic and cultural meaning works and to a new view of the linguistic ideologies held by both social scientists and those whose lives they seek to understand. *Situated Meaning* is one of the most effective discussions of a socially located approach to culture and communication I have read; the themes of deixis and indexicality are brilliantly teased out, providing a productive and finely wrought exploration of Peircean theory. It joins such works as Silverstein's germinal essay on shifters and indexical meaning (1976), Hanks's magisterial consideration of deixis in Yucatan (1990), and Gumperz and Levinson's reconsideration of linguistic relativity (1991), in mapping a new view of linguistic practice and its complex relationship to cultural meaning.

Situated Meaning provides new maps of territory long recognized as central within Japanese studies. Household, business, aesthetics, and individual experience appear in new and revelatory light. Beyond the regionalist audience, however, this work also brings these new maps together with what is relatively unknown territory for many anthropologists and linguists. Remarkable in its thoughtful attention to the particulars, the volume makes a compelling case for rethinking some of the basic understandings central to anthropology. It speaks with grace and insight to both the "inside" and the "outside" of scholarship in and about Japan.

REFERENCES

Ben-Ari, Eyal, Brian Moeran, and James Valentine, eds. 1990. *Unwrapping Japan: Society and Culture in Anthropological Perspective.* Honolulu: University of Hawaii Press.

Brenneis, Donald, and Fred R. Myers, eds. 1984. *Dangerous Words: Language and Politics in the Pacific.* New York: New York University Press.

Duranti, Alessandro, and Charles Goodwin, eds. 1992. *Rethinking Context: Language as an Interactive Phenomenon.* New York: Cambridge University Press.

Frake, Charles O. 1964. "How to ask for a drink in Subanun." *American Anthropologist* 66: 127–32.

Frake, Charles O. 1975. "How to enter a Yakan house," in Mary Sanches and Ben G. Blount, eds., *Sociocultural Dimensions of Language Use,* 25–40. New York: Academic Press.

Gumperz, John J., and Stephen C. Levinson. 1991. "Rethinking linguistic relativity." *Current Anthropology* 32: 613–22.

Hanks, William F. 1990. *Referential Practice: Language and Lived Space among the Maya.* Chicago: University of Chicago Press.

Hendry, Joy. 1990. "Humidity, hygiene, or ritual care: Some thoughts on wrapping as a social phenomenon," in Eyal Ben-Ari, Brian Moeran, and James Valentine, eds., *Unwrapping Japan: Society and Culture in Anthropological Perspective,* 18–35. Honolulu: University of Hawaii Press.

Silverstein, Michael. 1976. "Shifters, linguistic categories, and cultural description," in Keith H. Basso and Henry A. Selby, eds., *Meaning in Anthropology,* 11–56. Albuquerque: University of New Mexico Press.

Watson-Gegeo, Karen Ann, and Geoffrey M. White, eds. 1990. *Disentangling: Conflict Discourse in Pacific Societies.* Stanford: Stanford University Press.

Wolfowitz, Clare. 1991. *Language Style and Social Space: Stylistic Choice in Suriname Javanese.* Urbana: University of Illinois Press (*Illinois Studies in Anthropology,* no. 18).

PREFACE

THIS PROJECT developed out of a "homestay" the co-editor, Jane Bachnik, made with a Japanese farm family, while traveling in Japan after graduating from college. The purpose of her homestay was to learn Japanese, and in the process of teaching her the language the family members managed to convey something deceptively simple but nonetheless profound: that language is lived. This book is a product of that experience; its focus on 'inside/outside' or *uchi/soto* is a product of glimpsing *how* language is lived, and how this lived perspective is equally important for social life.

All the contributors to the volume shared a similar insight—that 'inside/outside' coordinates are fundamental to Japanese self, society, and language—and that these coordinates have to be grasped and used in experience. The idea of the volume arose spontaneously from conversations—in the field, in academic corridors, and at meetings—that made us aware we were exploring something that crossed disciplinary boundaries, and made us decide to pursue our ideas in a book project. Charles Quinn became a co-editor with Jane Bachnik because he had completed an extended study of epistemology in Japanese grammar, which complemented Jane Bachnik's project on self and society in the Japanese family. Included in the volume are three specialists in linguistics, three in anthropology, one in sociology, and one in comparative literature. All of us focus on Japan.

The volume was conceived as a means of exploring the important parallels we discovered between the use of *uchi/soto* in language and in social life. Most intriguing to us were the ways in which *uchi/soto* revealed deep-seated notions of the Japanese social universe—as located in time and space; as encompassing human beings and requiring *their* perspectives and actions. Yet human beings were also part of an ordering process, so that "structuring," and ordered continuity *over* time, were equally crucial with human beings *in* time. In fact, the balancing of these two perspectives—of specific human beings engaged *in* social situations with a general order that *transcends* situations is the crux of *uchi/soto* organization. This is played out in everyday life in the constant attempts to balance individual will against social norms or obligations; or to weigh self-interest against self-sacrifice for a greater social good. We wanted to portray the centrality of *uchi/soto* issues to Japanese social participants in their everyday lives.

A panel was organized as a first step toward realizing the book volume, and Matthews Hamabata, Patricia Wetzel, Robert Sukle, Dorinne Kondo, Charles Quinn, and Jane Bachnik presented papers for "*uchi/soto:* Shifts in Language and Social Boundaries," at the Association for Asian Studies meetings in Washington, D.C., in 1988. The panel served its purpose of providing a forum to help us focus our ideas. A series of themes emerged—focusing on the indexing of *uchi/soto* and its relation to language, self, and social organization, including the organization of gender, hierarchy, family, and family business. An 'underside' to *uchi/soto* indexing also emerged—in the form of violations of appropriate indexing, which had surprisingly serious consequences. All the papers from this panel were then rewritten and incorporated into the volume, and Nancy Rosenberger and Michael Molasky were invited to contribute to the volume.

Early on, we realized that the issues raised by *uchi/soto* linked our volume to endeavors outside Japan, especially those that involve performative approaches to language, self, and social life, and focus on indexical or 'situated' meaning. We are grateful to Donald Brenneis for his intellectual support in assisting us in working out this linkage, and for his suggestions in reading the manuscript. We are thankful to A. L. Becker and Eleanor H. Jorden for their continuing example in insisting that linguistic and social forms have some relationship to social activity, and to Stanley Cavell for his lectures on Wittgenstein, which unknowingly shed much light on Japanese society. All of us have Japanese friends, informants, and mentors, such as the family mentioned above, to whom we are profoundly grateful, and who shed much light for us on perspectives elaborated in our chapters.

We are grateful to Margaret Case, Rita Bernhard, and Director Walter Lippincott, of Princeton University Press for their considerable support in assisting in the publication of the volume. Finally, we owe a debt of gratitude to Bradley M. Richardson, Director of the Institute for Japanese Studies at The Ohio State University, whose timely assistance gave this book a second lease on life. We hope we have made it clear that all the contributors helped in the creation of this volume. We thank them all for making this a genuinely collaborative intellectual experience, of which this volume is the product.

NOTE ON ROMANIZATION

WE ARE USING a hybrid system of romanization for Japanese terms. Consonants are based on the Hepburn system, while vowel length is indicated by doubling the vowel.

Japanese vowels are pronounced approximately as follows:

The symbol:	approximates:
a	'a' in 'father'
i	'i' in 'machine'
u	'u' in 'put'
e	'e' in 'bet'
o	'o' in 'horse'

The occurrence of the same vowel symbol twice indicates a long vowel, for example, aa, where each vowel retains its original quality and length, but the sequence is pronounced as a continuum (Jorden, *Japanese: The Spoken Language*, Part 1 [New Haven: Yale University Press, 1987], p. 2).

KEY TO ABBREVIATIONS AND
ORTHOGRAPHIC CONVENTIONS

ACC	ACCusative
AFF	AFFirmative (i.e., opposite of NEG)
CAUS	CAUSative
COND	CONDitional (-*tara* form)
CONF	CONFirmative sentence particle *ne*
COP or CP	COPula
COPtent	COPula, tentative (*daroo*)
D	Directive, Imperative
DIR	DIRectional particle *e* 'to, toward'
EP	Extended Predicate (/clause + *no* (*da*)/): Jorden, *Japanese: The Spoken Language*, part 1, 1987
EXTP	Extended Predicate (same as EP)
FACT	modal suffix of established fact ("recall" -*keri*)
G	Gerund (= a perfective infinitive)
GEN	GENitive
HON	HONorific (↑)
HUM	HUMble (↓)
I	Imperfective
ID	IDentifying focus (= "nominative" *ga*)
IF	Inclusive Focus (particle *mo*)
INF	INFinitive
INST	INSTrumental
LOC	LOCative (particle *ni*)
LOC$_{ii}$	LOCative of accompaniment (particle *to*)
MID	MIDdle voice (inflecting suffix -(*r*)*areru*)
NEG	NEGative
OBJ	OBJect
PAST	PAST tense (now-extinct inflecting suffix -*ki*)
PF or P	PerFective (-*ta* form)
PFinf	PerFective infinitive (= the "gerund", V-*te*)
PL	PLural suffix (-*ra*, -*tachi*)
PL+	Polite PLural (-*kata*)
POT	POTential
PROV	PROVisional (-(*r*)*eba*)
Q	Question particle (*ka*)
QUOT	QUOTative *to* (< LOC$_{ii}$)

R	Representative (*-tari* form)
RF	Restrictive Focus (particle *wa*)
S	Stem (= verbal infinitive)
SP	Sentence Particle (e.g., *yo, ne,* etc.)
SUBJ	SUBJect
SUP	SUPpositional modal
TOP	TOPic
UI	Unique Identification (focus particle *koso*)
V	Verb
CAPS	emphasis, usually contrastive
' '	translation of Japanese
( )	optional
[ ]	meaning not signaled in original
/ /	to be taken as a unit (e.g., grammatical construction, formula, etc.)

CONTRIBUTORS

JANE M. BACHNIK
Associate Professor of Anthropology
The University of North Carolina at Chapel Hill

MATTHEWS M. HAMABATA
Dean of Haverford College

DORINNE K. KONDO
MacArthur Associate Professor of Women's Studies and Anthropology
Pomona College

MICHAEL S. MOLASKY
Ph.D. Candidate in Japanese Literature
University of Chicago

CHARLES J. QUINN, JR.
Associate Professor of Japanese
The Ohio State University

NANCY R. ROSENBERGER
Assistant Professor of Anthropology
Oregon State University

ROBERT J. SUKLE
Senior Lecturer in Japanese; Director, FALCON Japanese Program
Cornell University

PATRICIA J. WETZEL
Professor of Japanese
Portland State University

Indexing Self and Social Context

Chapter 1

INTRODUCTION:
UCHI/SOTO: CHALLENGING
OUR CONCEPTUALIZATIONS OF SELF,
SOCIAL ORDER, AND LANGUAGE

Jane M. Bachnik

INSIDE and outside have far more dimensions than appear at first glance. For example, in English, whether one is "looking *in*" or "looking *out*," depends on where one is looking from. Whether one "zooms *in*" or "*out*" depends on the direction of the camera lens in relation to oneself. "Reaching *in*" may refer to putting one's arm inside a container, "outreach" is a metaphorical arm outside one's normal sphere of influence. We manage a rather complex set of directional vantage points, in the course of everyday conversations (which may include take-outs, sit-ins, infields, and outpatients), and we do this without taking much notice.[1]

In this volume we focus on this taken-for-granted process in the everyday use of 'inside' and 'outside'—*uchi* and *soto*—in Japanese society. Although usually unnoticed, these distinctions are crucially important: *uchi/soto* is a major organizational focus for Japanese self, social life, and language. In *uchi/soto*, the 'inside/outside' orientations are also specifically linked with another set of meanings, denoting "self" and "society." Thus the organizing of both self and society can be viewed as situating meaning, through the indexing of inside and outside orientations. But inside/outside distinctions are not limited to Japanese; they are used by people in every society to situate meaning, as illustrated in the above English examples of "looking," "zooming," "reaching." These directional movements are part of a broad system of basic orientations through which all of us—in every known language and society—constantly locate ourselves in relation to the world. Through them we define not only our physical orientations in space but our social and psychic orientations as well. Inside and outside, like a drop of water in a pool, move in ever-widening circles to encompass a broad series of issues, both inside and outside Japan.

More specifically, approaching the organization of self and social order as indexical, or situated, meaning addresses longstanding issues in the formulation of Japanese social life—and links these to theoretical issues that are important beyond Japan. These include (1) defining the organization of a Japanese self, long characterized as "relational" (Araki 1973), (2) approaching Japanese social order as "situationally defined" (Lebra 1976), "organic" (Smith 1983), and "shifting" (Doi 1986).

These issues, in turn, can be related to: (1) the "interdependent" self, acknowledged as having a worldwide existence (Markus and Kitayama 1991); (2) perspectives on context as a central, organizing focus for social life (Duranti and Goodwin 1992); and (3) relationships between self and society, as mutually constitutive, such as Bourdieu's perspective on "habitus" and "practice" (1977, 1990); Giddens' focus on agency and structure (1979, 1984); Merleau-Ponty (1962) and Heidegger's (1962) focus on social life as "lived," and C. S. Peirce's formulations of indexes and indexical meaning (1931–1958). This volume will take up all three sets of issues, and will focus particularly on indexes and indexical meaning.

Joy Hendry's argument on "wrapping" in Japanese society (1993, 1990, 1989) provides an excellent illustration of indexical or situated meaning. Hendry points to the extreme care and attention the Japanese take in wrapping objects—from groceries to gifts—and she draws parallels from the wrapping of material objects to wrapping in language, in the frequent use of polite and respectful language (*keigo*). Architecture wraps as well: "[P]aper room partitions still commonly found in Japanese houses may be described as wrapping architectural space and even a smallish house will have inner and outer layers to which visitors are permitted entry according to their social proximity and status" (Hendry 1989, 627). Ritual wrapping, exemplified in the heavy rope that wraps a shinto shrine, can be linked to transitions from the mundane to the transcendent, or in the other direction, from the highly polite and formal to the mundane. Wrapping of the body also takes place through donning the multiple layers of garments involved in wearing the formal Japanese kimono. Wrapping pervades Japanese society; but how does this help us to characterize the Japanese? In this regard Hendry cautions that attempting to penetrate a labyrinth of layers to reach the content behind the form is to utterly miss the point.[2]

At issue here is no less than the impenetrability by which Japan has long been characterized. Wrapping is much more than a "cover-up" of the meaning inherent in objects, social activities, and linguistic communication. Two approaches to meaning are at issue: one that views the meaning of gifts, language, social order, and rituals in terms of a "center" or "core" beneath the wrapping, and a second approach that focuses on the activity of wrapping itself, and the relations wrapping defines between social participants and their context.

In the first approach wrapping obfuscates content, as paper covers the gift, and must therefore be removed and discarded to reach the gift, as core meaning. But Hendry's point is that for Japanese, wrapping as a form of polite language, ritual, dress, architecture, hierarchy, and so on—is itself closely linked to meaning. This approach regards meaning not as the core behind the wrapping but as linked with the wrapping itself; not as a "thing"—a gift, a speech "level," a "layer" of clothing—but "as an almost literal embedding of the 'contents,' whether of a gift or of talk [that] may well be more significant than the contents themselves" (Brenneis, p. x). Wrapping focuses on the process of locating the social participants in the social context, and *of delineating the context itself in terms of the "wrapping."* Wrapping can also be closely linked to inside/outside, and to indexical perspectives on meaning.

In this volume we focus, not on *the* inside, as a means of penetrating the core of Japanese society, but on *uchi/soto* as uncovering the process of indexing that is crucial to the delineation of a "situated" social order—and a relational self—both highly embedded in social context. Through this volume we attempt a shift of focus in a larger sense. We consider that grasping the significance of *uchi/soto inside* Japan links the volume to important issues *outside* Japan. Viewed as a society where indexing is an *organizing focus* for self, society, and language, Japanese society should provide us with the opportunity for a sustained perspective on an "ordering" that is closely tied to the way in which participants locate themselves in context. In proposing that both self and social order are reciprocally—and indexically—defined in Japan, we are also proposing that the organization of a "contextually defined" self and an "interactionally" approached context *can be linked as two sides of the same coin.* The sustained focus on indexing "self" and "social order," as well as the relationship between the contextually defined self and the contextually defined social order, are therefore highly significant beyond Japan as well.

At stake here is a constitutively oriented approach toward social life. In other words, the organization of self or society is not reducible to a "core" of patterns or structures; or even a "core" of person that is found "behind" social contexts, like the object lies "behind" its wrappings, and social order "behind" its participants. Nor is order itself discarded as a concept. Instead, the approach to order is embedded in social context, and includes the process by which participants constitute social situations, *and thereby participate in a dynamic that includes the mutual process of their constituting and being constituted by social order.* This process *is* the order, and this order includes the organization of self and society, since it is mutually constitutive of both. This dynamic speaks to "practice" (Bourdieu 1977, 1990); to relationships between agency and structure (Giddens 1979, 1984); to phenomenological perspectives (Heidegger 1962; Merleau-Ponty 1962); to Vygotsky's perspective on language and consciousness as both lodged within a matrix of social activity (1962,

1978), and Bakhtin (1981) and Vološinov's (1973) perspectives on language as embedded within a matrix of human interaction, as well as formulations on indexical meaning by Peirce (1931–1958), Jakobson (1960), Lyons (1977), Silverstein (1976), Ochs 1990, and Hanks 1990.

INSIDE AND OUTSIDE AS ORIENTATIONS TO THE WORLD

I will now briefly explain 'inside/outside'—and the Japanese counterparts *uchi/soto*—in more detail. The meaning of inside and outside is remarkable for two reasons: it is largely assumed, and it is practical, or situated. In other words we understand inside and outside, not intellectually, but largely through use, and we use these terms constantly in English. As Mark Johnson traces out the first few minutes of a waking day:

> You wake *out* of a deep sleep and peer *out* from beneath the covers *into* your room. You gradually emerge *out* of your stupor, pull yourself *out* from under the covers, climb *into* your robe, stretch *out* your limbs and walk *in* a daze *out* of the bedroom and *into* the bathroom. You look *in* the mirror and see your face staring *out* at you. You reach *into* the medicine cabinet, take *out* the toothpaste, squeeze *out* some toothpaste, put the toothbrush *into* your mouth, brush your teeth *in* a hurry, and rinse *out* your mouth. At breakfast you perform a host of further *in-out* moves—pouring *out* the coffee, setting *out* the dishes, putting the toast *in* the toaster, spreading *out* the jam *on* the toast, and on and on. Once you are more awake you might even get lost *in* the newspaper, might enter *into* a conversation, which leads to your speaking *out* on some topic (1987, 31–32).

"You" in this scenario is the reader who empathetically takes the position of the waking person. Inside/outside are defined by the movement of our bodies in space, as evident in your empathetic imagining of pulling yourself *out* from under the covers, climbing *into* your robe, stretching *out* your limbs, and walking *out* of the bedroom and *into* the bathroom. Inside/outside also involves more abstract nonspatial relations (Johnson 1987, 32), such as entering *into* a conversation.

As indicated above, the Japanese have specifically linked 'inside' and 'outside' to meanings that specify "self" and "society." These multiple meanings are represented in paired sets of terms, which include *uchi* 'inside' versus *soto* 'outside'; *ura* 'in-back', 'what is kept hidden from others' versus *omote* 'in front', 'surface appearance' (Doi 1986); *ninjoo* 'the world of personal feelings' versus *giri* 'social obligation'; *honne* 'the inner life of feelings' versus *tatemae* 'the surface world of social obligations' (Hamabata 1990, 134). Nor is this list exhaustive.[3]

Doi (1973b, 1986) points out that the meanings of each of these paired terms overlaps, so that aspects of self cluster at one pole, as *uchi*, *ninjoo, ura,* and *honne*; while aspects of social life cluster at the other pole, as *soto, omote, giri,* and *tatemae*. Doi's observation is important, since it directly links aspects of self and society with degrees of insidedness and outsidedness.

These double sets of terms have been widely observed and discussed as occurring throughout Japanese society; for example, in political hierarchy (Ishida 1984), large enterprise organization (Gerlach 1993; Hamabata 1990), small enterprise organization (Kondo 1990); family/household organization (Bachnik, in press), marriage (Edwards 1989), gender (Rosenberger this volume; Kondo 1990; Hamabata 1990), health and illness (Ohnuki-Tierney 1984), and religion (Hardacre 1986).

It is also worth noting that several Japanese specialists have considered these terms as organizational "keys" to various realms of society. Thus Doi uses *omote* and *ura* as central concepts for the organization of a Japanese self, which is characterized by situational shifting between the two modes.[4] Lebra (1976) considers *uchi/soto* and *omote/ura* as central to her treatment of "situationalism" in Japanese culture and behavior. Nakane utilizes *ie/uchi* (*ba* 'field' or 'frame') as a central organizational facet of Japanese society, according to which "Japanese stress situational position in a particular frame" (1970, 2).[5] In fact, Nakane states that the corporate group based on 'frame'—from the household to baseball teams and political factions—is *"the basic principle on which Japanese society is built"* (emphasis mine) (1970, 7).

In this volume we focus especially on *uchi/soto* (although we include the other paired terms as well). We propose that the significance of *uchi/soto* extends beyond the directional coordinates of 'inside' and 'outside'; and that, specifically, these terms link the directional coordinates with self, society, and language; moreover, they provide an organizational dynamic for this linkage. To put this another way, we propose that the *universally defined* orientations for inside/outside are linked with *culturally defined* perspectives for self, society, and language in Japan. Consequently, the organizations of all three have striking parallels, derived from the directional orientations of inside/outside. Moreover, the directional coordinates of *uchi/soto* are basic to the other paired sets of terms as well, making *uchi/soto* the most fundamental of all the terms.

UCHI/SOTO: VIEWING THE RECORD

Consistent problems exist with the present delineation of *uchi/soto* and the other paired terms. It is important to examine these issues, in order to specify how this volume constitutes a shift in perspective from those that precede it. In a nutshell, we agree with the virtually unanimous

characterization of Japanese self and social life as "contextual." Our goal
is to illuminate more specifically *how the organization of context is closely
linked to the organization of both self and society*. The difficulties involved in
this focus can be examined through five sets of issues.

The first problematic issue involves the Japanese social order, which
has been linked to "relativity," "situationalism," and "situational shifting," all of which are regarded as basic "structural principles" of Japanese society (Nakane 1970; Lebra 1976). Smith puts this succinctly:
"[This] is a social order of a decidedly curious kind." It is both ordered
and highly situational. "In so diffuse a system, where could authority
possibly lie?" (1983, 47–48).

More precisely, terms such as "situationalism," "situational ethic," or
"situational position in a frame" (Nakane 1970, 2) are deeply problematic as "structural principles." The latter should convey general meanings that carry beyond situations; instead these terms convey that ethics,
morality, and possibly even social order are defined *by* the situation. The
terms seem patently circular: how can they explain anything about context if they *require* context to mean that they mean? (Bachnik 1989, 240).[6]

The second problematic issue, hierarchy, is also linked closely with
social order. Hierarchy is widely regarded as one of the central organizing parameters in Japanese society. In one of the most influential books
on modern Japan Nakane posits a single ranking order, defined by a
"vertical principle" that exists irrespective of situations (1970, x, 29).
The result is a rigidity, a fixedness that Nakane fully acknowledges in
what she calls the "rigid vertical system."

As a "structural principle," the "vertical principle" should convey
general meanings about hierarchy in specific contexts. Yet, according
to Nakane, hierarchical ranking (accomplished via parameters such as
age, sex, and status) *must be grasped from the situational context* (1970,
30). She also notes that ranking order is perceived from an *egocentric*
perspective and consistently uses the term *relative* to qualify ranking
order. "The *relative* rankings are thus centred on ego and everyone is
placed in a *relative* locus within the firmly established vertical system"
(1970, 28; emphasis mine). Rather than applying a "principle" to define
conduct in situations, hierarchy seems to work in reverse, displaying the
same difficulties as "situationalism" and "social order" above. Thus situational parameters, formulated by relationships between participants,
seem essential to define hierarchy appropriately.[7]

The third problematic issue in the delineation of Japanese self and
social order concerns Doi's comment that "point of view" is important
for both *uchi/soto* and *omote/ura*. "[S]ince *soto* and *uchi* are different for
each individual, what is *soto* for one person may become *uchi* for a
person included in that *soto*. Clearly, the former's *omote* becomes the

latter's *ura*" (1986, 29). *Uchi* involves a point of view, as Doi notes, and this viewpoint "locates" social life in space and time. But how can such a point of view be accounted for in the organization of self and social order?

Furthermore, if point of view is important to *uchi* organization, Nakane's definition of *uchi* (*ba* or 'frame') as a "structural principle," becomes problematic. If Japanese use *uchi* (*ba*) to "stress situational position in a particular frame" (1970, 2), how can *uchi* (and *ba*) as "principles" ignore the point of view embedded in the frame? How can we reconcile the fact that Nakane's definition of this "basic principle"—as a "structural principle"—excludes context, while *uchi* (*ba*) *revolves around the organization of context?* (Bachnik 1989).

The fourth problematic issue involves the characteristic of shifting, which is closely related to point of view discussed above. Doi's statement that "*[S]oto* and *uchi* are different for each individual, [so that] what is *soto* for one person may become *uchi* for a person included in that *soto*" (1986, 29), includes a shifting of perspective. But Doi also relates shifting to the organization of self, when he comments that the organization of self does not hinge on *omote* and *ura* per se, but on the ability *to shift between them.* "The ease with which one shifts from *omote* to *ura* and back again . . . is regarded as the measure of social maturity. . . . [One's] integrity rests upon the complete mastery of *omote* and *ura*" (1973b, 259). Shifting also occurs frequently in language, in the use of register (speech "levels" or politeness) and in social organization, where Lebra (1976) notes the same kind of shifting, and "relativity."

But how do Japanese gauge the shifts from *omote* to *ura* and back again to demonstrate their "social maturity"? How do they gauge the shifts of language register, both within and between contexts? How can shifting be included in the organization of self and social order? Many of the terms used to define and describe Japanese society, including "situationalism," "relational self," "social relativism," evidence a frustrating circularity. These terms inform us that specific situations are key features of Japanese social order. Yet the terms themselves—as general labels abstracted *from* context—contradict *what* they tell us we need to know about specific situations in the way (or *how*) they inform us about these situations.

The fifth problematic issue involves the Japanese self, commonly discussed as highly contextual, "relational" (Araki 1973), and social; meaning that it is defined in interaction with self and other. "There are no fixed points, either [for] 'self' or 'other'. . . (Smith 1983, 77). [B]oth . . . can be expressed only in relational terms" (Smith 1983, 49). Person terms are also highly unstable in Japanese (Fischer 1964; Suzuki 1978, 1977, 1973; Bachnik 1982; Wetzel 1984). Problems with the organization of Japanese self *include most of the issues noted above:* thus self (1) resembles the social order in being "situationally defined"; (2) is "embedded" and encompasses a "point of view"; (3) is characterized by shifting, both in the instability of person terms, and the lack of "fixed points." Kondo notes that a "relational" self challenges the unity and coherence of the Western subject, along with the dualistic perspectives that create distinctions between "self" and "(social) world" (1990, 34). But if so, doesn't "self" then share the same kind of circularity as terms such as "situationalism" noted above? How can we identify self analytically, *as self*, without losing the very aspects of context that seem crucial to its identity? Do the very connotations of self, with its sense of general identity independent from social context, contradict what we need to know about the relatedness of self to context for Japanese? And if so, how do we get at the organization of "self" without either denying the existence of what we are looking for, or becoming embedded in a contradiction-in-terms?

All of the five issues outlined above present different facets of the same problem. The "relational" self, "situated" social order, "vertical principle," embedded "points of view," and "shifting" all pose the same general question for the organization of Japanese self, society, and language use: namely, how can these aspects of context that are particular, situated, embedded—or identified with "uniqueness"—be identified with general "principles," or patterns that *transcend* context?

DELINEATING THE ISSUES IN *UCHI/SOTO*

As mentioned before, two ways of perceiving meaning are at issue here. A semantic (referential, ideational, or propositional) construal of meaning views language (and social life) in terms of *what* is communicated, rather than a set of contextual relationships that locate this particular reference in time and space. The latter construal of meaning addresses the question of *how* something is communicated (through indexical, or pragmatic meaning), as well as *what*. For example, all of the in/out moves in the wake-up scenario gave indexical information as the person waking up was reoriented in myriad ways to time and space.

We can speak of the first meaning perspective discussed above as semantic or propositional—where the semantic value of a sign is considered to have the meaning it has apart from contextual factors. This follows a tradition in logic and linguistic semantics, in which meaning can be treated as an inherent property of a proposition regardless of its context of use. The second kind of meaning is pragmatic, whereby a relationship is stipulated between reference and context, detailing spatiotemporal contiguities (such as distance). Here a reference is related to its context of use. Note that this use of "pragmatic" differs from that in everyday use, and is derived from Peirce's semiotics; here pragmatic meaning is dependent on context, since meaning is derived from relating something to its context.[8] I emphasize that it is impossible to use language without describing *both* general meaning *and* relating what we describe to social context; the foci of both these construals must be taken into account. The question here is how these perspectives are prioritized.

Pragmatic meaning is far less obvious to the English-speaker than semantic meaning, although this has nothing to do with the existence or nonexistence of indexes. Rather, it has to do with what Silverstein calls an "ideology" of language; meaning assumptions—explicit and implicit—about the nature of language that determine its usage and the attitudes taken toward it (Crapanzano 1982, 181). The strong tendency to focus on reference (on words like *chair*, *table*, and *television*), rather than words like *I*, has a long history (Silverstein 1979; Crapanzano 1982), and "a linguistic ideology, going back at least to Aristotle, that gives priority to the naming, referential, denotative function of language (over such other language functions as the indexical)" (Crapanzano 1982, 181). Indexes have been treated by linguists largely as a residual category: "All of our analytic techniques and formal descriptive machinery have been designed for referential signs, which contribute to referential utterances in referential speech events" (Silverstein 1976, 15).

Yet Silverstein argues that cultural meaning should be viewed as pragmatic, rather than semantic meaning (1976, 54); and that " 'pragmatic' analysis of speech behavior—in the tradition extending from Peirce to Jakobson—allows us to describe the real linkage of language to culture, and perhaps the most important aspect of the 'meaning' of speech" (1976, 11–12).

In this volume we present considerable evidence that pragmatic meaning *is* closely linked to cultural meaning for the Japanese. This can be illustrated, for example, by the relationships between indexical meanings such as 'inside/outside' and the meanings for self and society contained in the paired terms, *uchi/soto*, *omote/ura*, *tatemae/honne*, and *giri/ninjoo*. Links with indexing can also be made for the cultural focus on wrapping delineated by Hendry (1993, 1990) and Ben-Ari, et al. (1990).

Even the common definitions of the Japanese as "preoccupied" with relationships (Lebra 1976), and involved in a group 'frame' (*ba*) or context (Nakane 1970), can be linked to indexing. Peirce considered that indexes signal spatiotemporal relations between two points in a context; so that indexes are instrumental in creating contexts. Indexical signs are thus defined by two important parameters: (1) relationships, linking the index with an interpretive "ground" (Hanks 1992); and (2) context, which is partially constituted by such relationships. Lebra's statement— "[T]he Japanese are extremely sensitive to and concerned about social interaction and relationships" (1976, 2)—and Nakane's identification of the Japanese group organization as based on "situational position in a given *frame*" (1970, 1) identify *the same two parameters*, namely relationships and context, as crucially important in Japanese society. Thus the Japanese "preoccupation" with social relationships may actually be a preoccupation with relationships that are indexically defined; group organization based on "situational position in a given 'frame'" may actually refer to the group as a context constituted through the process of indexing.

We can also ask whether "situationalism," and "situational position within a frame" are terms referring to indexing, and thus pragmatic meaning rather than "structural principles"; and whether embedded "points of view" are examples of deixis and deictic reference points, rather than "extreme relativism." Is "shifting" another example of pragmatically defined meaning? Are the "vertical principle" (and the "horizontal principle") examples of indexes, rather than structural principles?

To address these issues, we need to elaborate further the notions of indexing, deixis, and pragmatic meaning. Indexes have been briefly defined above as signaling spatiotemporal relations between two points in a context. The relationships between the points are actual: thus smoke is an index of fire; a rap on the door is an index of someone seeking entry (Peirce 1931–1958, vol. 3). "Peirce's term 'indexical' . . . [is] based upon the idea of identification, or drawing attention to, by pointing" (Lyons 1977, 2:637). Peirce further specifies that indexes do not name objects; they are used to identify and measure degrees and magnitudes. Thermometers, rules, scales, and wind gauges work by indexing, and all these examples include the important specification that "gauging" or pointing must be carried out in relation to a located reference point.

Ordinary discourse is also organized through indexing, which is a major function of deictic devices such as tense, demonstratives, personal pronouns, and particularly the pronoun *I*. In English discourse *I* functions as *the* indexical reference point—the zero point from which all the conversational indexes are anchored. *I* thus points to features of the surrounding context, such as *here* and *over there*, and "anchors" such pointing by providing a location in reference to which the pointers can be understood. This kind of indexing is known as deixis.

Jesperson ([1924] 1965: 219) and Jakobson (1957) have identified the deictic terms discussed above, such as *I, you, here, there, now, then,* and so forth, as "shifters," because the referents of these expressions constantly shift as the relationship between utterance and context changes—for example, when the person identified as *I* changes as the speaker changes. Thus if we cannot trace the speaker who shouts "I'm here!" in a cavernous, echoing building, we cannot understand where *here* is.

The discussion above may seem elementary, but this is because indexing is so familiar to us that we accomplish it without thinking much about it. Moreover, indexing occurs not only with thermometers, rulers, and wind gauges, but throughout social life as well. Thus, for example, choices of politeness register or hierarchical ranking or kinship distance can index the social status of the speaker or the social relationship between speaker and addressee. Yet this indexing is not a mechanical kind of process. As Ochs notes: "Indexical relations are more complex than one-to-one mappings between linguistic forms and contextual features" (1990, 293). One reason for this is that "[indexical relations] cannot be fully understood without additional mappings—between a particular contextual dimension and sets of linguistic forms, and between a particular linguistic form and several contextual dimensions" (Ochs 1990, 293). Thus single linguistic forms—for example, in honorific register, can index a variety of sociocultural dimensions in context, including emotional and social relationships between speaker and addressee, or speaker and referent.

Hendry indicates how this works in wrapping: "Appropriate attire may well correlate with other elements of wrapping, so that in a formal(ly wrapped) environment when participants in an event are wearing kimono or even formal Western dress, people who would otherwise use very little polite language to each other will adopt a more formal level and gifts presented would also need to be properly wrapped. On the other hand, informal occasions, such as those associated with sporting activities . . . may reduce the level of formality in speech, too" (1989, 628).

But indexical relations are more complex than one-to-one mappings for other reasons as well. Thus language socializes not only through relying on explicit practices, or propositional content; by far "the greatest part of sociocultural information is keyed *implicitly*, through language use" (Ochs 1990, 291). This information is conveyed by the *manner* in which the utterances are delivered, as messages about the message that are conveyed along with the direct message (Bateson 1972). Thus the vast majority of these messages about acts and activities, identities and relationships, feelings and beliefs must be inferred (Ochs 1990, 291). For such reasons Ochs considers language socialization to rest on a theory of indexicality, and Lave's focus on studies of apprenticeship and children's math practice (1990, 310) also considers learning (and culture) to rest on pragmatic meaning.

The implications of a cultural focus on pragmatic versus semantic meaning are worth commenting on. While semantic (or referential) meaning is a way of focusing on culture as an accumulation of lexical, or general knowledge (as "what"), pragmatic meaning focuses on establishing general meaning through cultural practices that are learned, and carried on, through a process of doing (or "how"). In this sense, pragmatic meaning forms a kind of "ground" (the habitualized practices) for which reference is a "figure," although this is a bit too tidy. Yet the two facets of general meaning established through habitualized practice and openness are both crucial to pragmatic meaning. Sudnow's ethnography on learning to play improvised jazz (1978) aptly illustrates how such practices are a combination of "the way we do things," and openness or improvisation.

Finally, the creative or performative aspect of meaning expressed in practical understanding also helps to structure the ongoing events. For example, Silverstein remarks that in some cases the speech signal is the only overt sign of the contextual parameter, and "Under these circumstances the indexical token in speech performs its greatest apparent work, seeming to be the very medium through which the relevant aspect of the context is made to 'exist'" (1976, 34).[9]

The way in which practical understanding constitutes events includes the ongoing relationship between the social participants and the structuring of their social context (Gumperz 1982, 1992), which takes place constantly, in social interaction. At issue are two perspectives toward social life, exemplifying the two perspectives toward meaning discussed above, and illustrated by the two perspectives toward learning reported by Lave: one in which the subject matter envelops the learner in a "world" that is empty of context; the other in which the child's understanding gives significance to and envelops the subject matter.

The first view makes it seem as if the problem contains the learner, and results from viewing schooling "as the institutional site for decontextualizing knowledge [and formal, or 'context-free' learning] so that, abstracted, it may become general and hence generalizable, and therefore transferable to situations of use in the 'real' world" (Lave 1990, 310). The second view—which includes, for example, apprenticeship—results from viewing learning as "generated in practice, in situations whose specific characteristics are part of practice as it unfolds" (Lave 1990, 310–11). In this view the learner's understanding encompasses and gives meaning to the subject matter; thus the learner, *and the context in which the learning is accomplished,* envelops the subject matter and becomes *an integral part of the process of learning.*

The two perspectives on social life parallel those on learning, with a bit of modification. In the first, or "context-free" perspective, the organization of "social order," and "self," are abstracted from situations, identified as structures, patterns, traits, and so forth, and in turn utilized to identify a general, context-free "self" and "social order." The circularity in this process comes from failing to acknowledge the facets of situation that are inevitably embedded in both (Bateson 1972). The second view, in which self and social life are defined in practice, considers the context and the process by which each is constituted as integral to the organization of both self and social order. This is a complex dynamic, for social life is both structured and open; participants face ambiguity, potential misunderstanding, and conflict in the practice of social life; yet the habitual nature of the practices, and their associated "mappings," also constitute the social "world"—and even the selves—of the participants.

It is worth elaborating briefly on the issues of semantic versus pragmatic meaning in relation to "self." Both "person" and "self" are regarded as comprised of identities that are bounded off from the fluidity of context, and are therefore fixed and stable. The "fixedness" of self is supported by naming and, in particular, by proper names, just as the identity of person is supported by personal pronouns in English and other Indo-European languages. Here the organization of person is closely linked to that of self, since person is identified via referential indexes (as *I, you,* etc.), differentiated from context and viewed as a stable entity. Person and personal pronouns are also based on the *individual* as the locus of discourse since, in Indo-European languages, the distinction between *I* and *you* in first- and second-person pronouns is that between self and not-self (Bachnik, in press).[10]

The identification of self through referential meaning makes it difficult to view self as constituted in practice, since the very practices by which the "fixed" self is identified, for example, through internal attributes such as traits, abilities, motives and values (Markus and Kitayama 1991), proper names and personal pronouns, incorporate sharply defined distinctions between self and not-self. Such distinctions are also sharply demarcated along inside/outside dimensions.

Japanese terms for *self* and *person*—like those of many other languages in the world—are unstable over time, constantly shifting and contextually dependent in use.[11] This is true even for the usage of proper names (Smith 1983), and suggests that the distinctions between self and social context are not drawn as sharply for Japanese as they are for us—that self is not viewed as "fixed." Another way of viewing the relation between self and context is via a cline, or gradient, which extends from "self" to "world." Becker and Oka have considered person in language in terms of such a cline extending from the speaker and ordering language in terms of degree of distance from the speaker. Rather than considering person by way of referential indexes explicitly specifying person, their perspective allows a broad spectrum of linguistic communication to be included in the definition of person. It is worth pointing out that Becker and Oka (1974, 229) consider the "cline of person" as central:

[P]erhaps *the* central thread in the semantic structure of all languages is the cline of person, an ordering of linguistic forms according to their distance from the speaker. Between the subjective, pointed, specific pronominal 'I' and the objective, generic common noun, between these poles *the words of all languages* . . . are ordered and categorized according to their distance—spatial, temporal, social, biological, and metaphorical—from the first person, the speaker. [emphasis mine]

This cline can extend beyond language to the communication of distance in social conduct (Leach 1964; Bachnik 1986)—including distinctions of formality and various kinds of wrapping behavior discussed by Hendry. Such a cline can be linked to pragmatic, rather than propositional meaning, produced through a process of doing social activity, which would define self, or person, through the communication of distance gradients linking the speaker to a context.

As both Becker and Oka and Lave's foci indicate, pragmatic meaning defines a different perspective on self and social life than semantic, or propositional, meaning. Pragmatic meaning can even be viewed as a constitutive dynamic between self and social life, in which each constitutes and is constituted by the other. Thus the "socially defined" self and a perspective on structure that includes "agency" can be viewed as two sides of the same coin. We propose that this dynamic is central to Japanese self and social order as well, and that it is exemplified in the organization of *uchi/soto*. Approaching the organization of self and society through pragmatic meaning can explain the heretofore problematic characterization of both self and society for Japanese as "relational," "shifting," and "situational"; and it allows all five of the problematic issues concerning the organization of self and society raised above to be addressed.

Consequently, we argue that the ideology of language (Silverstein 1985) "that gives priority to the naming, referential, denotative function of language (over such other language functions as the indexical)" (Crapanzano 1982, 181), and that makes indexing into a residual category, *needs to be turned around.* As exemplified in the Japanese case, indexical meaning should be the primary focus, so that referential, denotative functions of language—or, the "patterns" and "ordering" of social life—can be viewed as indexed by social participants interacting in social context.

Specifically, approaching Japanese society through indexical meaning suggests the following:

1. The organization of self should be approached through its linkage to social context. Rather than viewing self, or person, through a set of specified terms, which differentiate self from context, as a "fixed" entity, self should be approached through a cline of distance from self to "world," extending Becker and Oka's concept to social life as well as language. Here self would be redefined in relation to situation.

2. The organization of a "situationally defined social order" must be approached through linguistic communication and social practice in context, rather than principles, norms, structures, and so on, abstracted from use (Silverstein 1976). Moreover, hierarchy must be reexamined and defined in terms of social practice in context, rather than through indexes such as "vertical" and "horizontal," which lose their points of reference when abstracted from context.

3. "Points of view" and "shifting" can be included in the organization of social life. Here deixis, which has primarily been associated with language, should be investigated for its relationships to the organization of both self and social order.

4. The dynamic by which self and social order are mutually constitutive can also be investigated through the organizational dynamic evident in viewing self, social life, and language as generated in practice. This dynamic speaks to issues that are extremely important for conceptualizating social order, including the way in which social participants both structure and are structured by their social context, and the way in which factors such as contingency, agency, process, chaos, and openness can be integral to the conceptualization of order.

INDEXING: INSIDE AND OUTSIDE OF JAPAN

In reorienting the focus on Japanese self, social life, and language, each of the four issues outlined above must be related beyond Japan. I will now briefly spell out four kinds of foci that do this.

1. The "relational" or "interdependent" self is increasingly reported to be widespread, existing in virtually every area of the world, as acknowledged by psychologists (Markus and Kitayama 1991).
2. Incorporating "context" as a central, organizing focus for social life, has become a subject of attention, for example, in the essays collected in Duranti and Goodwin (1992).
3. Increasing concern has been expressed about the importance of incorporating "emotional aspects" of self-organization in a way that is integral to "social" aspects (Lutz 1988; White 1992), and of relating deictic organization to social organization (Hanks 1990, 1992).
4. There is considerable theoretical interest in including social participants anchored in time in the organization of society, and in developing rela-

tionships between self and society, as mutually constitutive. Examples include Giddens (1979, 1984); Bourdieu (1977, 1990); (Merleau-Ponty 1962; Heidegger 1962); Vygotsky (1962, 1978); Bakhtin (1981), Vološinov (1973); and Peirce (1931–1958). I will now briefly elaborate these issues.

The organization of a "relational," contextually defined "social" self is hardly peculiar to Japan (Bruner 1990; Shotter and Gergen 1989). For example, in a recent review article in psychology, Markus and Kitayama delineate an "interdependent" self as representative not only of Japan and other Asian cultures but of Africa, Latin-America, Island Pacific cultures, and southern Europe as well (1991, 224–25). Markus and Kitayama note striking contrasts between "interdependent" construals of self and that of the "independent" self, "the so-called Western view of the individual as an independent, self-contained, autonomous entity" (1991, 224).[12] Specifically, the "interdependent" conceptions of individuality insist on the "fundamental relatedness of individuals to each other," so that the organization of an "interdependent" self "cannot be properly characterized as a bounded whole, for it changes structure with the nature of the particular social context" (Markus and Kitayama 1991, 224–27), and therefore involves constant shifting. Not the individual, but the *relationship*, may be viewed as "the functional unit of conscious reflection" (Markus and Kitayama 1991, 226) (emphasis in original).

The "interdependent" self described here strongly resembles the Japanese self; moreover, the characteristics attributed to it link the "interdependent" self to indexical meaning as well. Thus self is characterized by embeddedness in context and "shifting," so that relationships between individuals and interactively defined meaning are prioritized over the individual self and "private" meaning. Moreover, as described earlier, inside and outside constitute basic orientations in social life, by which all of us define the world in relation to our embodied selves. They are part of a human orientation to the world that is largely practical and assumed. They are also part of a wider set of spatiotemporal orientations that include up/down, front/back (necessary for upright posture), and left/right (Straus 1967). These orientations are extremely basic to human existence, and are found in every known language and society.

Because of the commonness of both the inside/outside orientations and the "interdependent" self, it should not be surprising that terms which resemble *uchi/soto*, and in fact relate self and society to an inside/outside axis, are important organizational parameters in other societies besides Japan. For example, Shore (1982) explores the relationship between self and society in Samoa, communicated in the categories of *aga*, action that is controlled and appropriate to socially defined statuses, and *amio*, action that is willful and aggressive. In Java, Geertz and Keeler describe the Javanese as moving on two axes: between the realms of external actions (*lair*) and inner experience (*batin*), and between rough and impolite (*kasar*) and pure and polished speech and behavior (*alus*) (Geertz 1960, 232–33; Keeler 1987).

R. Rosaldo (1980) describes the Philippine Ilongot as shifting between *beya* and *liget*—"between a state of sociality and one of opposition and withdrawal, between a self at ease with its environment and one that stands apart" (1980, 44). And Abu-Lughod (1986) describes Egyptian Bedouins in terms of two aspects of self and society, one embedded in honor that is closely related to power, social constraint, and the "outside realm" of males; the other characterized by autonomy, deference, and a strong tradition of emotion and romantic love expressed in the "inside realm" of females through spoken poetry. In fact, Andrew Lock (1982, 32–33) speaks of two prominent axes in society, which move respectively between inner and outer and control and lack of control.

At the same time a series of efforts have focused on reframing issues of emotion and feeling, to move them from residual categories to become a central focus in the organization of self, politics, and social life (M. Rosaldo 1984; White and Kirkpatrick 1985; Lutz 1988; Lutz and Abu-Lughod 1990; White 1992). It is worth noting that these issues are consistently cast within a rubric of inner and outer (as, for example, White's 1992 title).

It is also worth examining M. Rosaldo's perceptive discussion of these issues: "What is important here is, first, the claim that meaning is a fact of public life and, second, the view that cultural patterns—social facts—provide a template for all human action, growth, and understanding" (1984, 140). Rosaldo indicates two problems central to social theory, each the inverse of the other. First is the separation of social order (as "structure," "principle," and so on) from persons interacting in social life. "Culture is, then, always richer than the traits recorded in ethnographers' accounts because its truth resides not in explicit formulations of the rituals of daily life but in the practices of persons who in acting take for granted an account of who they are and how to understand their fellows' moves" (140).

Conversely, the divorce of self from relationships to others divorces one from anchorage in social context as well. In other words, immaculate distinctions between "inner" and "outer" spheres create Cartesian distinctions between mind and world, private and public, and emotional and social. "Thus, for ethnographers in the field, a set of rules that tells them what the natives do can never show them how and why a people's deeds make psychological sense because the sense of action *ultimately depends upon one's embeddedness within a particular sociocultural milieu*" (M. Rosaldo 1984, 140; emphasis mine).

The issues of "public meaning" and "embeddedness within a particular sociocultural milieu" have been raised as major philosophical issues by Wittgenstein (1958), phenomenologists such as Heidegger (1962) and Merleau-Ponty (1962), and ethnomethodologists influenced by Husserl and Schutz (including Garfinkel 1967 and Cicourel 1973). These issues have also been raised recently in perspectives on context as performatively constituted (Duranti and Goodwin 1992; Duranti and Brenneis 1986; Hanks 1990, 1992). "Meaning is collectively defined on the basis of recognized (and sometimes restated) social relationships" (Duranti 1986, 241). Similar issues are involved in recent attempts at locating the events of talk, and of "self" in the broader spectrum of communicative practice, including, importantly, politics (Brenneis and Myers 1984; White and Kirkpatrick 1985; White and Watson-Gegeo 1990). The authors in these collected volumes focus on the interactive role of situation and event in shaping both behavior and local theories of personal experience.

Two broad sets of issues are involved here: (1) the widespread existence of an "interdependent" self, and of patterns of relating inside/outside to self/society in a range of cultures besides Japan; and (2) the relation of meaning to context, as "public," defined in a "we relationship." Such meaning is defined through social practice, as "cooperative work between speaker and hearer"; and exhibited in linguistic communication and shared human interaction.

These two issues, in turn, can be linked to the separation of self from social life discussed by M. Rosaldo. The problem has two sides: the separation of social order (as "structure," "principle") from persons interacting in social life; and the divorce of self from social relationships, by a lack of anchorage in social context. The double problem actually results from a single deficiency: *lack of relation of either self or structure to context.*

In fact, the organization of an "interdependent" self, by the "fundamental relatedness of individuals to each other," bears certain marked similarities to the organization of contextual meaning defined in use, through a "we relationship" and shared human interaction. Each is defined through human relationships, through meaning that moves between "us," in action and in context. At issue here is a perspective on "self" and "context" as two sides of the same coin, each being the recto or verso for the other. The difficulty is that we do not ordinarily consider "self" and "context" as a single subject—moreover, we do not even pursue them within the same academic disciplines. This is because academic distinctions themselves reflect a series of pervasive dualisms, as Lutz points out, "includ[ing] especially the sharp opposition of the individual to the social which is reflected in the existence of the separate disciplines of psychology and anthropology; the concern with a subjective versus an objective reality . . . the analytic separation of thought and action" (Lutz 1985, 38).

At stake in the distinction between *independent* and *interdependent selves* is more than a mere categorization. Rather, these terms represent a set of dualisms formed around a radical separation between inside and outside that developed out of the scientific revolution in Europe. The separation of the physical universe, with its laws of gravity and motion, from the social universe, and ultimately even from the divine (Burtt 1932; Koyré 1957), effectively eliminated the social world from the cosmological universe, which was entirely physical, or "natural." Thus the ordering of the Newtonian universe was based on a delineation of dualities that separated both nature and self from the social world. These dualities included individual/social order; mind/world; ideal/material; objective/subjective; "outside" world/"inner" self; constancy/flux; unity/multiplicity. Nor is this list exhaustive.

These dualities have had a considerable impact on the way we view theory and everyday life (Luckmann 1973). Both the "autonomous" individual and the separation of individual (and consciousness) from "structure" or social order can be related to these perspectives on dualities. The Japanese perspectives on self and social order, which were considerably influenced by China, form a distinct counterpoint to those of the West and reveal a perspective on human nature that defines society as profoundly human, and self as quintessentially social. In the Japanese reading of Confucianism, "the centerpiece of the cosmos is human society and its manifold human relationships" (Smith 1983, 103). Moreover, the cosmos is moral as well as social, since there is "no recognized separation of the moral order from the actual" (Hall 1968, 29, cited in Smith 1983, 25). Both morality and social order are found in the phenomenal, actual world (Nakamura 1964, 362). Thus constancy is found in the flux of human existence; order in the midst of human feelings.

Nevertheless, focusing on the difference between these two perspectives should not make us overlook a crucial similarity: both focus on tensions basic to human existence in all societies (Evens 1990). The relationship between self and society speaks to a fundamental paradox, that each and every social formation is at the same time a multiplicity and a unity (Stark 1962). Social life is carried on by concrete individuals, existing in time and space, yet cannot be ultimately reduced to the individual self, since society includes dimensions they do not originate, in the form of shared traditions (including those that produce and define the self *as* self). By the same token, social life is not reducible to shared traditions or normative order, since individuals define situations that are inherently ambiguous; make choices that have consequences; and attempt to remake their traditions. The tensions that exist between individual and society are ontological and are widely manifested in balancing such conflicting demands as self-expression versus self-sacrifice, individual desire versus social obligation, and even choices of formal versus informal modes of expression.[13]

In approaching these tensions between self and society, two perspectives can be formulated, which in fact parallel the two formulations of self—as independent and interdependent—and the two kinds of meaning—semantic and pragmatic—outlined above. In other words, we can approach self and society as distinct entities, resulting in an analytic separation of self from social order, which differentiates the "subjective" aspects of self from the "objective" aspects of political economy and social order. Another focus is also possible, which goes beyond mere shifting from one polar duality to the other: to consider both self and society by focusing on the *relationship* between them. This relationship includes "the significance of the social in constituting the self, and the significance of the self in bringing shared social constraints to bear on actual events" (Bachnik, in press). This alternate focus replicates the relationship between the "interdependent" self and contextually defined approaches to meaning at another level, by focusing on the relationship between self and society as ontological dualities.[14]

Considerable attention in Western philosophy and social theory in the past century has focused on reorienting the dominance of dualistic legacies, leading to attempts to develop a dynamic of a constitutive self and social order, outlined above, from a number of theoretical perspectives. These include Nietzsche's discussion of the "eternal return," as well as the theoretical perspectives of "agency" and its relation to social structure (Giddens 1979, 1984); conceptualizations of "practice" and "*habitus*" (Bourdieu 1977, 1990); phenomenological approaches to being-in-the-world (especially Heidegger 1962); lived perspectives on time and space (Merleau-Ponty 1962); Vygotsky's focus on language and consciousness as lodged within a matrix of social activity (1962, 1978); Bakhtin (1981) and Vološinov's (1973) perspectives on the relation between language and context; and approaches to indexical or pragmatic meaning, from Peirce (1931–1958). Yet the subject matter of such theoretical approaches mandates a sustained focus on self, social life, and language in context—a focus on theory *and* practice that can be provided by examining *uchi/soto* in the Japanese context.

INSIDE/OUTSIDE AS BASIC HUMAN ORIENTATIONS

We can now relate the 'inside/outside' dynamics of *uchi/soto* to the independent/interdependent approaches to the organization of "self" and the relationships between self and social order presented above. All the complex issues concerning relationships of self to context, and self to society discussed above are embedded in the organization of *uchi/soto*. The issues can be approached on three levels. It is necessary to clarify here that "levels" do not refer to a stacked, nested set of dependent relations, but literally to issues stemming from different "levels" of social reality. These levels of issues include: (1) the process of indexing that produces an "interdependent" self, a "situated social order," and creates and sustains the interactional context; (2) the constitutive dynamic of the relations between self and society, in which each mutually constitutes and is constituted by the other; and (3) the delineation of relationships between what have largely been considered as polar dualities in the West. These include individual/society; subjective/objective; emotions/social order; "inner" mind/"outside" world; unity/diversity; empirical/ideal; constancy/flux; content/form, to name a few. Any instance involving *uchi/soto*—no matter how seemingly simple—*encompasses all these levels*. Thus simple situations are themselves "wrapped" so that they have much more meaning than appears at first glance. Moreover, *uchi/soto* addresses virtually the entire range of issues involving the relationship of self and social life *in* time and their continuity *over* time.

The implications of *uchi/soto* are that we must thoroughly reformulate our conceptualizations of self and social order, to acknowledge the facets of Japanese organization that otherwise resist classification. What is perhaps most central to *uchi/soto* organization is its incompatibility with the notion of an external "world" which Brenneis notes "is referred to and reflected in language whether it be a physical world ('This is a table') or a social one ('This is a social superior')" (p. x). The focus on an "external world" creates a perspective of social life as a scripted stage in which human beings perform the equivalent of "reading" lines or "following" norms. But a focus on indexes like "this" requires a location in a particular situation, with relationships among speaker, hearer, and scene as a starting point. Such a focus also defines a perspective that inverts the "external world" focus—where people interacting in context do not "reflect" a world already created, but participate in the ongoing dynamic of a social world literally constituted in action.

But by the same token, the lack of compatibility of *uchi/soto* with the notion of an external "world" must be extended to its lack of compatibility with the notions of "self" as a bounded, inner, reflective psychological essence. The bounded self reflects an "internal" world that is distinct from an "external" world, thereby replicating polar distinctions between self and world. As such self is constantly differentiated from the world as a distinct entity, rather than being defined through relationships to the world via indexes such as deference and formality/informality distinctions.

It is necessary to spell out more carefully how indexes work, and the parallel ways in which *uchi/soto* works, in order to proceed to delineate the organization of this volume. We approach the range of issues developed above through Peirce's formulation of indexical signs, and his particular focus on pragmatism as a movement between dualities. Peirce developed the index as part of a comprehensive philosophical system, which is of specific interest because of his concern with escaping the Cartesian legacy of mind/matter and subject/object dualism. His system included both a set of phenomenological categories and an equally comprehensive sign system, based on three irreducible sets of relationships, which were in turn related to three kinds of signs: the icon, index, and symbol.[15]

Each of Peirce's three different kinds of signs—icon, index, and symbol—is characterized by different relations of the sign to its referent: "resemblance, contiguity, and association by convention, respectively" (Singer 1980, 491). An iconic sign resembles its referent (in the form of a diagram or an image, which may even momentarily make us forget the distinction between the real and the copy). Examples of icons range from the eucharistic bread and wine to maps, diagrams, word order in a phrase, and onomatopoetic utterances such as "quack quack." An indexical sign has a direct relation to its object and qualifies its referent by really occurring along with it (Quinn, personal communication, 1992). Smoke and fire, fever and mercury in a thermometer, a pointing finger and what it points to, and deictics in language are all examples of indexical signs.

Peirce defines symbols as triads because they have a joint relationship between the object denoted and the mind. The relationship is established by convention (e.g., the word *dog*) and the relationship is arbitrary. Examples of symbols are nouns such as "dog," "woman," or "tree," as well as things we acknowledge as symbols, like the American flag (which, as a diagram, is also iconic). For Peirce, symbols are the residual class of signs, where neither physical similarity nor contextual contiguity hold between sign vehicle and entity signaled.

Indexes are highly contextual, signaling spatiotemporal relations between two points in a context. Indexes do not name objects; they are used to identify and measure degrees, magnitudes, and numbers of specific observations. "The [readings registered by] barometer, plumb line, spirit level, weather vane, pendulum, and photometer are cited by Peirce as respective indices of observed specific pressure, vertical and horizontal directions, wind direction, gravity, and star brightness" (Singer 1980, 490) used to identify and measure degrees, magnitudes, and numbers of specific observations. What makes all these indexical is the zero point or reference point from which they are "placed" (or "read").[16]

Thus indexes work by gauging positions along a scale. This can operate, for example, between high and low (in gauging wind velocity); hot and cold (a thermometer); short and tall (a measuring rod); fat and thin (a scale), and so on. But these points are always gauged *against a located reference point.* The logic involved in indexing relates the terms at each end of the scale inversely to each other. Being hot is inversely related to being cold; so that being hot means being *not* cold. Moreover, hot is defined according to degrees along the temperature scale, so that each degree of being hotter varies inversely (and precisely) with the corresponding degree of *not* being colder. The closer the reading is to 220° on a Fahrenheit Scale, the hotter it is, and the less cold (because the farther from zero) it can be.

We can now relate this discussion of indexes to *uchi/soto* organization. For Japanese 'inside/outside' operates as a basic scale or axis, along which relationships can be indexed via degrees of "more" or "less." Virtually any kind of communication can be mapped in relation to this scale, including bowing, gift-giving, politeness or formality in speech, social space, choice of topic, and dress. In fact, virtually all of Ochs' list of pure indexes are included in the focus of *what* is indexed by the Japanese; meaning that *a wide range of phenomena are indexed,* including (but not limited to) social distance, status, relationships, settings, topics, affective and epistemological stances of social participants.

Moreover, this entire variety of communication is broadly organized along an axis that can be related to Becker and Oka's distance "cline of person." The axis is produced by indexing self, in relation to society, as well as the converse: society in relation to self. The communication that produces this axis is organized by means of linking 'self' with 'inside' at one pole, and 'society' with 'outside' at the opposite pole of the cline. Any number of qualities can then be associated with the 'self/inside' pole (including, for example, engaged, intimate, spontaneous), while the opposite qualities (such as detached, disciplined, ordered) are associated with the 'society/outside' pole. The social participant must "gauge" the appropriateness of a particular characteristic (such as self-restraint), which also inversely indexes the opposing characteristic (spontaneity).

Linked in this way, intimacy and socially required discipline are inversely related so that the more discipline (or self-restraint) that is gauged as appropriate, the less intimacy that can be expressed. To put this another way, one is constantly constraining or expressing 'self', in relation to the degree of social constraint, or relaxation of constraint, that is perceived appropriate. 'Self' is inversely indexed vis-à-vis 'social order' in the same manner. Consequently, the gauging of self expression along the person cline involves a double dynamic in which the degree of self-expression is inversely related to a lack of social constraint.

As mentioned before, *uchi* has at least two basic meanings as listed in the dictionary, Sanseido's 1982 *Kokugo-jiten* (Wetzel 1984, 9). One meaning for *uchi* is 'inside', which is juxtaposed to 'outside' or *soto.* This can be related to the continuum outlined above. The other meaning for *uchi* is 'we', 'us', 'our group', 'me', 'my', 'my group', 'I'. *Uchi* here is also identified as a term that means *ie* (translated as 'family', or 'household'), and that specifically signifies one aspect of the *ie*—the living group of household members—this generation. In this sense *uchi* is located *in* social life (as 'we', 'our group', 'this generation'). *Uchi* has been closely linked to Japanese group organization (Nakane 1970). But *uchi* is not "the" group, but "our" group; another term, *otaku*, is used for "your" group. The embedded viewpoint of *uchi* can thus be linked to deixis: *uchi* is a deictic anchor point.

The English *I* is another deictic anchor point. This means that *I* functions in discourse as the indexical reference point—the zero-point from which all the conversational indexes are anchored. For example, to understand "That one!" two points are necessary: an indexical reference ('that'), and an anchor point from which one locates 'that' out of all the other possibilities on the horizon. Another way of putting this is in terms of a figure/ground relationship (Hanks 1992). 'That' is made comprehensible (as a figure) by the relationship of the speaker's anchor point which "backgrounds" the statement and makes the reference comprehensible. If we cannot find the reference point—the equivalent of "you are here" on a map—we literally cannot "read" the map indexically.

'That' indexes a spatial relationship between the speaker and a person or object, while 'now' directs the attention of the addressee to a particular point in *time*. 'Now' also presumes an axis—of temporal orientation which in English spans from 'now' to 'then', but may also include 'three days ago', 'last week', as well as 'next week' and 'three days from now'. Verb tense indicates a temporal axis that requires two points as well: the speaker's position at the time of the utterance, and the time he or she is pointing out ("I saw it yesterday") (Fillmore 1975).

I thus anchors the discourse, allowing the participants to follow out the pointers. The process by which *I* defines these spatiotemporal relationships by anchoring them is called *deixis*, from the Greek word *deiknumi* 'to point', or to 'indicate'.[17] John Lyons's definition of *deixis* is a handy one: "the location and identification of persons, objects, events, processes and activities talked about, or referred to, in relation to the spatiotemporal context created and sustained by the act of utterance and the participation in it, typically, of a single speaker and at least one addressee" (1977, 2:637).

As a deictic reference point it is extremely significant that *uchi* is *not* an individual, but a speaker *located within a collectivity* (so that the meaning shifts contextually from an 'us' at the upper limit, to a 'me' at the lower). Although it is recognized that all languages have deictics (Benveniste 1971; Kurylowicz 1972; Lyons 1977) little in-depth description of actual usage exists (Levinson 1983; Harré and Mühlhäusler 1990). More-over, attempts at comparative accounts of deixis have often assumed too many of the deictic features of English and Indo-European languages, particularly that of the individual reference point, 'I' (Wetzel 1984).

While *uchi* can signify the individual 'I' as well as the collective 'we', the contextual usage of the same term for both indicates clearly that the individual is identified within the backdrop of the collectivity. *This in no way eliminates the individual*, but merely specifies that the former are al-ways identified within a social context. Moreover, *uchi* is also closely iden-tified with the *ie*, the basic "unit" of social organization—the family. *Uchi* as a collectively defined deictic anchor point therefore raises important questions about the relationship between deixis and social organization, specifically those of family, small groups, and work organizations.

Soto provides a relational contrast with *uchi*, so that each is defined in relation to the other. From the vantage point of the deictic anchor *uchi* and *soto* may be reckoned from different "points of view," just as Doi says, for what is outside (*soto*) for one person becomes inside (*uchi*) for a person included in that outside (which to that person is inside [*uchi*]) (1986, 29). The locatedness of a "point of view" in *uchi* results in differ-ent orientations to the 'inside/outside' coordinates. This gives a basis for both the "relational" aspect of meaning and the constant shifting involved in creating it. Yet inside and outside are linked, and Doi makes this clear for *omote/ura*: "although *omote* and *ura* are clearly distin-guished conceptually, they are in fact closely related. Without *omote* there is no *ura*, without *ura* no *omote*—they are literally two sides (as-pects) of a single entity" (1986, 26).

Although other paired terms exist in addition to *uchi/soto*, including *omote/ura*, *giri/ninjoo*, and *tatemae/honne*, which can also function as in-dexes, *uchi/soto* is more basic in delineating indexical organization, for two reasons. First, *uchi* as 'us', 'our group', and so forth, is explicitly associated with the deictic anchor point, which is not the case for the 'inside' term of the other sets. Second, *uchi/soto* is explicitly linked to the axis indexed by inside/outside distinctions, through gauging de-grees of insidedness and outsidedness. For these reasons we focus on *uchi/soto*, rather than the other paired terms as identifying the organiza-tion of pragmatic, or indexical meaning.

FORMULATION OF ISSUES IN THIS VOLUME

We can now relate the two basic meanings of *uchi* in the discussion above to define a basic paradigm for the organization of self and society in Japan. *Uchi* as 'we', 'us', 'our group', 'me', 'my', 'my group', 'I' is a deictic anchor point that "anchors" the collectivity, giving it an embedded "point of view." *Uchi* as 'inside', assumes a juxtaposition with 'outside' or *soto*, since *uchi* is defined in relation to *soto*. The 'inside' members constantly define *uchi/soto* relationships, by gauging insidedness and outsideness. The juxtaposition creates a continuum of inversely related positions, gauged by the indexing of degrees of insidedness versus degrees of outsidedness, and by the inverse relationship between 'inside' and 'outside', so that the more inside something is gauged to be, the less outside it can be, and vice versa.

As the locus of the "self," *uchi* is thus linked to the *organization of self*, which is defined within a collectivity, even in modern Japan (Rosenberger 1992; Bachnik 1992a, 1992b; Kondo 1990; Hamabata 1990; Edwards 1989; Smith 1983; Lebra 1976; Nakane 1970). Because the deictic locus revolves around engagement, *uchi* involves its members in the indexing of their participation in social life. Juxtaposed to *uchi* is *soto*, and a cluster of characteristics such as 'detached', 'disciplined', 'ordered'. These represent the public 'outer' 'ordered' aspects, which characterize social life, and also "index" it as 'abstract' or 'detached' in relation to the contextual, engaged, "located" placement of self.

To examine these meanings more closely, they account for both the 'inside/outside' axis and a tilting of the axis, because *uchi* as 'we', 'us', 'our group', 'me', 'my', 'I', as a deictic reference point is therefore anchored, while *soto* is abstract, objective, and unanchored. The "tilt" or bias of the axis thus anchors it at one end (*uchi*) in a specific social situation. *Soto* is detached, and nonspecific—in other words, general. Thus the relationship between *uchi/soto* also allows it to move between the occupied, embedded context, and the more general focus that carries beyond context.

The "tilted" axis, then, creates two sets of inverted relationships: between self/society and engagement/detachment. These, in turn, allow *uchi/soto* to be related to all three of the levels previously outlined (p. 23). Keeping in mind that all levels are encompassed in each *uchi/soto* distinction, a discussion of the levels must proceed in a circle. We begin with the most basic or third level—the process of relating ontological dualities, such as self/society and engagement/detachment—carried out by indexing them inversely in relation to each other. This relationship is continually being redefined in interactional contexts, where a variety of communication is indexed along a distance cline, then mapped, by additional indexing, for example, in terms of degrees of formality/informality. The entire range of this communication is crucial in defining self, which is thereby related in multiple ways to context; this communication mutually defines both a "relational" self, and a "contextually defined" social order. Both self and social order are thus mutually defined by means of the interactional context. The mutual definition of self and social order constitutes level 1.

Level 2 is constituted by the tilting of the axis and the resulting relationship between engagement and detachment. Through this relationship, the participants (as agents) are involved in the constitution of social life. The tilting of the axis is what allows a different organizational level of relationships to be indexed: linking concrete with abstract, and the specific context with what is carried beyond that context. This elaborates the dynamic through which self and social order are mutually constituted, for "selves" are constituted by an "ordering" which they themselves do not create, and "social order" encompasses the qualities of existence in time, openness, and ambiguity, which the linkage with self brings. The indexically defined dynamic by which self and social order are mutually constituted forms the second level of self and society in *uchi/soto* organization.

Level 3, the most basic level, revolves around the relationships between ontological dualities. Since these dualities are gauged from an anchored perspective in social life, they also provide a means of indexing "perspective" itself. Perspectives are gauged by epistemic distinctions; meaning that degrees of sharedness/nonsharedness can be indexed, differentiating between knowledge that is familiar, known, experienced in common—or *uchi*—versus the unfamiliar, unknown, not experienced in common—or *soto*. Such distinctions differentiate my/our *cultural* perspective (as *uchi*) from yours (as *soto*), thus enabling indexing of degrees of cultural shared/nonsharedness by gauging degrees of *uchi/soto* from the perspective of each deictic anchor point. This perspective on indexing addresses a conceptual problem arising from a dualistic focus, revolving around difficulties in portraying culture in terms of unity *and* multiplicity (which parallel the difficulties of relating individual and society). At the third level, then, *uchi/soto* defines relationships *between* unity and diversity which allow dualistic perspectives that have crept into theoretical approaches—namely, culture-as-unity versus cultural relativism—to be addressed by the native indexing of inverse relationships between cultural unity and diversity, which parallel the way in which self and society are indexed.

This volume is organized in three parts, which exemplify the three levels of *uchi/soto* organization discussed above. In each part we attempt a shift in perspective, to reformulate the organization of Japanese self, society, and language, by focusing on indexical, or situated meaning. The volume is organized as a series that builds; although each chapter can stand alone, within the volume each is linked to build closely on the discoveries of the previous chapter(s). Moreover, the close relationship between indexical meaning and context makes the inclusion of detailed explications of contexts essential to the volume. Narratives are useful because they evoke situatedness, as no detached summary can, by engaging the reader in the narrator's *uchi*. Quantitative or systemic analyses provide a *soto* kind of complement to this, with their abstracted and generalized views. Yet these quantitative analyses must also address context (*uchi*) just as situated narratives must address generality (*soto*).

The contributors in part 1, "Indexing Self and Social Contexts," elaborate the first level of *uchi/soto* organization by focusing on the role of indexing *uchi/soto* in the constitution of a variety of interactional contexts in language and social life. The themes in part 1 include the delineation of *uchi* as a deictic anchor point, both in language and family/household organization, and detailed empirical explorations of how participants constitute their constantly shifting social contexts through the indexing of relationships between self and other, including guest/host; husband/wife; vender/customer. These papers begin the delineation of self and social order, including dimensions of gender and hierarchy, and develop important relationships between the organization of deictic anchor point, indexing, agency, and practice in social life.

Just as the papers in part 1 focus on the mutual construction of self and social context, the papers in part 2, "Failure to Index: Boundary Disintegration and Social Breakdown," explore the second level of *uchi/soto* organization—the dynamic by which self and social order are mutually constitutive. But because the construction of self and social order is much more embedded and difficult to access than that of social context, the papers in this section all focus on conflicts producing breakdowns and destruction of social order and even self. They present a new focus which relates Japanese conflict to the process of indexing. Each of the chapters in part 2 examines a mistake or failure to index appropriately, and explores the conflict-producing imbalances that result, in a variety of family-business settings, ranging from large to very small scale. In each instance the destruction results from abuse of personal power, and lack of acknowledging collectively defined goals—or, in other words, from imbalances in the indexing of self in relation to society. These conflicts represent failures on the part of social participants to act appropriately as agents in the constitution of social life, and the consequences are disastrously real, including interpersonal tensions, family disintegration, business bankrupcy, and self-destruction.

Part 3, "Language as a Form of Life: Clines of Knowledge as Clines of Person," explores issues in the third level of *uchi/soto* organization, of indexing relationships between dualisms. This section puts together the themes of the volume by demonstrating the remarkable consistency between the organization of *uchi/soto* in language and in social life. Here epistemic distinctions basic to Japanese are explored, including the indexing of perspectives on knowledge as *uchi/soto:* ranging from *uchi* as firsthand, engaged, detailed, and individuated, or 'inside', to *soto* as secondhand, detached, communicated from others, and generic, or epistemically 'outside'. This section develops a cline of engaged and detached perspectives, considered to be the most widely indexed epistemological distinction in the language. This cline is then linked to the cline developed for self and social life in parts 1 and 2, tying the volume together, and bringing the reader full circle back to the beginning.

NOTES

1. I am very grateful to the Institute for the Arts and Humanities, and a Pogue Fellowship, both from the University of North Carolina at Chapel Hill, for support while working on this chapter. I also wish to thank my co-editor Charles Quinn for his insightful help, both theoretical and editorial, in reading and discussing the several drafts of this chapter. Any remaining shortcomings are my own.

2. Wrapping is also the focus of a collected volume by Ben-Ari, Moeran, and Valentine, eds. (*Unwrapping Japan*, Manchester University Press, 1990.)

3. The list of paired terms also includes *ooyake-goto* 'public matters' and *wata-kushi-goto* 'private matters'; *hare* 'sacred, extraordinary, formal' and *ke* 'profane, ordinary, informal'. For additional discussion of these paired terms see Bachnik (1992a, 1992b, 1989, and in press).

4. In fact, the Japanese title of Doi's work, translated as *The Anatomy of Self*, is *Omote to Ura* or "*Omote* and *Ura*." *Uchi/soto*, which Doi regards as "corresponding" to the distinction of *omote/ura*, is introduced even earlier, in his work on the concept of *amae* (1973a, 40–44).

5. Nakane equates *uchi* with *ie*, as a colloquial form of *ie* (1970, 7). She regards *ie* 'household' as a corporate group, and 'frame', which is the English translation for *ba*, as a "criterion which sets a boundary and gives a common basis to a set of individuals who are located or involved in it" (1970, 1). *Ba* is also translated as 'location', or 'field' in physics. Problems with these definitions will be discussed in this chapter and in chapter 6.

6. The specific contradiction is brought out clearly in Lebra, who states: "First, the Japanese distinguish one situation from another according to the dichotomy of *uchi* and *soto*. . . . [Then they] . . . differentiate their behavior by whether the situation is defined as *uchi* or *soto* (Lebra 1976, 112). Here the terms provide an underlying or structural organization for the empirical situation. But Lebra also notes that: "the essential point . . . is that the *uchi/soto* distinction is drawn not by structure but by constantly varying situations" (1976, 112). This makes her explanation circular, "since she first specifies that *uchi/soto* defines the situation, but then argues that the terms are defined *by* the situation" (Bachnik 1989, 240).

7. In fact, Nakane notes that the "vertical principle" is not calculated by a

single criteria, but by multiple social axes, including relative age, sex, and status. Smith (1983) and Maraini (1975) also characterize both Japanese hierarchy and social order as "diffuse." They link "diffuseness" to social relationships: "it is through the measured and considered response of all, as givers in some and receivers in other relationships, that the social order is in part maintained" (Smith 1983, 47).

8. For further discussion of the scope of pragmatics, which has a number of distinct usages, see Levinson (1983) and Silverstein (1976).

9. "Certainly, the English indexical pronouns *I/we* and *you* (vs. *he/she/it/they*) perform this creative function in bounding off the personae of the speech event itself" (Silverstein 1976, 34).

10. Boas points out: "Logically, our three persons of the pronoun are based on the two concepts of self and not-self, the second of which is subdivided, according to the needs of speech, into the two concepts of the person addressed and the person spoken of," or addressed/proximate versus referred to/distal (in Forchheimer 1953, 5). Greenberg states: "All languages have pronominal categories involving at least three persons and two numbers" (1963, 96). But Becker and Oka disagree: "I is not I, you is not you, and we is not we from one language to the next" (1974, 230).

11. The instability of Japanese "pronouns" has long been a subject of discussion, both in linguistics and anthropology (Befu and Norbeck 1958; Fischer 1964; Neustupný 1977; Suzuki 1978, 1977, 1976; Smith 1983; Wetzel 1984; Kondo 1990).

12. Markus and Kitayama acknowledge that differences exist among the "interdependent" construals of self among the above cultures; their point is that conceptualization within the interdependent category is derived along similar premises, which allows them to be juxtaposed to the "independent" construals.

13. I do not mean to imply that the "independent" individual exists in all societies, but rather that "even in societies where relational tensions are emphasized, a social being is somehow differentiated from the social whole. And even in societies like the United States where the individual is highly differentiated, relationships between self and other are both explicitly and implicitly acknowledged in communication" (Bachnik, in press).

14. The term *ontological dualism* is from T.M.S. Evens, n.d.; I am indebted to him for the distinctions made in this paragraph.

15. The triadic structure of the semiotic sign is significant, for it allows Peirce to combine a theory of signification with a theory of communication. This is in marked contrast to Saussure's semiology, "which defines the sign-function as a dyadic relation of signifier and signified that dispenses with both independent objects and subjects" (Singer 1980, 491), yielding a view of culture as "hermetically sealed" (Daniel 1984, 15). For Peirce the triadic relation of sign, object, and interpretant includes the speaker and interpreter as well, making the relation dialogical.

16. I wish to acknowledge Charles Quinn's contribution formulating this section on Peirce's signs.

17. I am grateful to Steven Klein (personal communication, 1990) for this information.

REFERENCES

Abu-Lughod, Lila. 1986. *Veiled Sentiments*. Berkeley: University of California Press.

Araki, Hiroyuki. 1973. *Nihonjin no koodooyoshiki* (Japanese behavioral patterns). Tokyo: Kodansha.

Bachnik, Jane. 1982. "Deixis and Self/Other Reference in Japanese Discourse." *Working Papers in Sociolinguistics* 99: 1–36. Austin, Texas: Southwest Educational Development Laboratory.

———. 1986. "Time, Space and Person in Japanese Relationships," in J. Hendry and J. Webber, eds., *Interpreting Japanese Society: Anthropological Approaches*, 49–75. Oxford: JASO.

———. 1989. "*Omote/ura:* Indexes and the Organization of Self and Society in Japan," in C. Calhoun, ed., *Comparative Social Research* 11: 239–62. Greenwich, Conn.: JAI Press.

———. 1992a. "The Two 'Faces' of Self and Society in Japan." *Ethos* 20 (1): 3–32.

———. 1992b. "*Kejime:* Indexing Self and Social Life in Japan," in N. Rosenberger, ed., *Japanese Sense of Self*, 152–72. Cambridge: Cambridge University Press.

———. In press. *Family, Self, and Society in Contemporary Japan*. Berkeley: University of California Press.

Bakhtin, Mikhail. 1981. *The Dialogic Imagination: Four Essays.* Translated by C. Emerson and M. Holquist. Austin: University of Texas Press.

Bateson, Gregory. 1972. *Steps to an Ecology of Mind*. New York: Ballantine Books.

Becker, A. L., and I Gusti Ngurah Oka. 1974. "Person in Kawi: Exploration of an Elementary Semantic Dimension." *Oceanic Linguistics* 13 (1 and 2): 229–55.

Befu, Harumi, and Edward Norbeck. 1958. "Japanese Usages of Terms of Relationship." *Southwestern Journal of Anthropology* 14: 66–86.

Ben-Ari, Eyal, Brian Moeran, James Valentine, eds. 1990. *Unwrapping Japan*. Manchester: Manchester University Press.

Benveniste, Emile. 1971. *Problems in General Linguistics*. Coral Gables: University of Miami Press (Miami Linguistic Series No. 8).

Brenneis, Donald L., and Fred R. Myers, eds. 1984. *Dangerous Words: Language and Politics in the Pacific*. New York: New York University Press.

Bourdieu, Pierre. 1977. *Outline of a Theory of Practice*. Cambridge: Cambridge University Press.

———. 1990. *The Logic of Practice*. Stanford: Stanford University Press.

Bruner, Jerome S. 1990. *Acts of Meaning*. Cambridge, Mass.: Harvard University Press.

Burtt, E. A. 1932. *The Metaphysical Foundations of Modern Science*. Garden City, N.Y.: Doubleday.

Cicourel, Aaron V. 1973. *Cognitive Sociology: Language and Meaning in Social Interaction*. Harmondsworth: Penguin.

Crapanzano, Vincent. 1982. "The Self, the Third, and Desire," in Benjamin Lee, ed., *Psychosocial Theories of the Self*, 179–206. New York: Plenum.

Daniel, E. Valentine. 1984. *Fluid Signs: Being a Person the Tamil Way.* Berkeley: University of California Press.

Doi, Takeo. 1973a. *The Anatomy of Dependence.* Tokyo: Kodansha International.

———. 1973b. *Omote* and *Ura:* concepts derived from the Japanese 2-fold structure of consciousness. *Journal of Nervous and Mental Disease* 155 (4): 258–61.

———. 1986. *The Anatomy of Self.* Tokyo: Kodansha International.

Duranti, Alessandro. 1986. "The Audience as Co-Author: An Introduction." *Text* 6 (3): 239–47.

Duranti, Alessandro, and Donald Brenneis, eds. 1986. *The Audience as Co-Author, Special Issue of Text* 6 (3).

Duranti, Alessandro, and Charles Goodwin, eds. 1992. *Rethinking Context: Language as an Interactive Phenomenon.* Cambridge: Cambridge University Press.

Edwards, Walter. 1989. *Modern Japan through Its Weddings.* Stanford: Stanford University Press.

Evens, T. M. S. 1990. *Transcendence in Society: The Comparative Study of Conflict and Sacrifice in Social Movements.* Greenwich, Conn.: JAI Press.

———. n.d. *Anthropology as Ethics or Anti-Dualism: Reason and Human Agency in a Postmodern Universe.* Unpublished manuscript.

Fillmore, C. J. 1975. *Santa Cruz Lectures of Deixis* (1971). Bloomington: Indiana University Linguistics Club.

Fischer, John L. 1964. "Words for self and other in some Japanese families." *American Anthropologist* 66 (6): 115–26.

Forchheimer, Paul. 1953. *The Category of Person in Language.* Berlin: Walter de Gruyter.

Garfinkel, Harold. 1967. *Studies in Ethnomethodology.* Englewood Cliffs, N.J.: Prentice–Hall.

Geertz, Clifford. 1960. *The Religion of Java.* Chicago: University of Chicago Press.

Gerlach, Michael. 1993. *Alliance Capitalism: The Social Organization of Japanese Business.* Berkeley: University of California Press.

Giddens, Anthony. 1979. *Central Problems in Social Theory: Action, Structure and Contradiction in Social Analysis.* Berkeley and Los Angeles: University of California Press.

———. 1984. *The Constitution of Society.* Berkeley: University of California Press.

Greenberg, Joseph H. 1963. *Universals of Language.* Cambridge, Mass.: MIT Press.

Gumperz, John J. 1982. *Discourse Strategies.* Cambridge: Cambridge University Press.

———. 1992. "Contextualization and Understanding," in A. Duranti and C. Goodwin, eds., *Rethinking Context,* 229–52. Cambridge: Cambridge University Press.

Hall, John W. 1968. "A Monarch for Modern Japan," in R. E. Ward, ed., *Political Development in Modern Japan.* Princeton, N.J.: Princeton University Press.

Hamabata, Matthews. 1990. *Crested Kimono: Power and Love in the Japanese Business Family.* Ithaca: Cornell University Press.

Hanks, William F. 1990. *Referential Practice: Language and Lived Space among the Maya.* Chicago: University of Chicago Press.

———. 1992. "The Indexical Ground of Deictic Reference," in A. Duranti and

C. Goodwin, eds., *Rethinking Context*, 43–76. Cambridge: Cambridge University Press.

Hardacre, Helen. 1986. *Kurozumikyoo and the New Religions of Japan.* Princeton, N.J.: Princeton University Press.

Harré, Rom, and Peter Mühlhäusler. 1990. *Pronouns and People: The Linguistic Construction of Social and Personal Identity.* Oxford: Basil Blackwell.

Heidegger, Martin. 1962. *Being and Time.* Translated by John MacQuarrie and Edward Robinson. New York: Harper and Row. *Sein und Zeit.* Tübingen: Neomarius Verlag, 1926.

Hendry, Joy. 1989. "To Wrap or Not to Wrap: Politeness and Penetration in Ethnographic Inquiry." *Man* (N.S.) 24 (4): 620–35.

———. 1990. "Humidity, Hygiene, or Ritual Care: Some Thoughts on Wrapping as a Social Phenomenon," in E. Ben-Ari, B. Moeran, and J. Valentine, eds., *Unwrapping Japan.* Manchester: Manchester University Press.

———. 1993. *Wrapping Culture: Politeness, Presentation and Power in Japan and Other Societies.* Oxford: Oxford University Press.

Ishida, Takeshi. 1984. "Conflict and Its Accomodation: *Omote-ura* and *Uchi-soto* Relations," in E. Krauss, T. P. Rohlen, and P. G. Steinhoff, eds., *Conflict in Japan*, 16–38. Honolulu: University of Hawaii Press.

Jakobson, Roman. 1957. "Shifters, Verbal Categories, and the Russian Verb," 1–14. Cambridge, Mass.: Russian Language Project: Department of Slavic Languages and Literatures, Harvard University.

———. 1960. "Concluding Statement: Linguistics and Poetics," in T. Sebeok, ed., *Style in Language*, 350–73. Cambridge, Mass.: MIT Press.

Jesperson, Otto. [1924] 1965. *The Philosophy of Grammar.* New York: W. W. Norton.

Johnson, Mark. 1987. *The Body in the Mind.* Chicago: University of Chicago Press.

Keeler, Ward. 1987. *Javanese Shadow Plays, Javanese Selves.* Princeton, N.J.: Princeton University Press.

Kondo, Dorinne. 1990. *Crafting Selves: Power, Gender, and Discourses of Identity in a Japanese Workplace.* Chicago: University of Chicago Press.

Koyré, Alexandre. 1957. *From the Closed World to the Infinite Universe.* Baltimore: The Johns Hopkins Press.

Kurylowicz, J. 1972. "Universaux Linguistiques," in L. Heilman, ed., *Proceedings of the Eleventh International Congress of Linguists.* Bologna.

Lave, Jean. 1990. "The Culture of Acquisition and the Practice of Understanding," in G. Herdt, R. Shweder, and J. Stigler, eds., *Cultural Psychology: Essays on Comparative Human Development*, 309–27. Cambridge: Cambridge University Press.

Leach, Edmund. 1964. "Anthropological Aspects of Language: Animal Categories and Verbal Abuse," in E. H. Lenneberg, ed., *New Directions in the Study of Language*, 23–63. Cambridge, Mass.: MIT Press.

Lebra, Takie. 1976. *Japanese Patterns of Behavior.* Honolulu: University of Hawaii Press.

Levinson, Stephen C. 1983. *Pragmatics.* Cambridge: Cambridge University Press.

Lock, Andrew. 1982. "Universals in Human Conception," in P. Heelas and

A. Lock, eds., *Indigenous Psychologies: The Anthropology of the Self.* London: Academic Press.

Luckmann, Thomas. 1973. "Philosophy, Science, and Everyday Life," in M. Natanson, ed., *Phenomenology and the Social Sciences*, Vol. 1, 143–85.

Lutz, Catherine A. 1985. "Ethnopsychology Compared to What? Explaining Behavior and Consciousness Among the Ifaluk," in G. M. White and J. Kirkpatrick, eds., *Person, Self, and Experience: Exploring Pacific Ethnopsychologies.* Berkeley: University of California Press.

————. 1988. *Unnatural Emotions.* Chicago: University of Chicago Press.

Lutz, Catherine A., and Lila Abu-Lughod. 1990. *Language and the Politics of Emotion.* Cambridge: Cambridge University Press.

Lyons, John. 1977. *Semantics*, Vols. 1 and 2. Cambridge: Cambridge University Press.

Maraini, Fosco. 1975. "Japan and the Future: Some Suggestions from *Nihonjinron* Literature," in Gianni Fodella, ed., *Social Structures and Economic Dynamics in Japan up to 1980*, 15–77. Milan: Institute of Economic and Social Studies for East Asia, Luigi Bocconi University.

Markus, Hazel Rose, and Shinobu Kitayama. 1991. "Culture and the Self: Implications for Cognition, Emotion and Motivation." *Psychological Review* 98 (2): 224–53.

Merleau-Ponty, Maurice. 1962. *Phenomenology of Perception.* Translated by Colin Smith. London: Routledge and Kegan Paul.

Nakamura, Hajime. 1964. *Ways of Thinking of Eastern Peoples: India, China, Tibet, Japan.* Honolulu: East-West Center Press.

Nakane, Chie. 1970. *Japanese Society.* Berkeley and Los Angeles: University of California Press.

Neustupný, J. V. 1977. "The Variability of Japanese Honorifics," in *Proceedings of the Symposium on Japanese Sociolinguistics*, 125–46. Honolulu: University of Hawaii.

Ochs, Elinor. 1990. "Indexicality and Socialization," in G. Herdt, R. Shweder, and J. Stigler, eds., *Cultural Psychology: Essays on Comparative Human Development*, 287–307. Cambridge: Cambridge University Press.

Ohnuki-Tierney, Emiko. 1984. *Illness and Culture in Contemporary Japan: An Anthropological View.* Cambridge: Cambridge University Press.

Peirce, Charles Sanders. 1931–1958. *Collected Papers*, Vols. 1–8. Edited by C. Hartshorne and P. Weiss. Cambridge, Mass.: Harvard University Press.

Rosaldo, Michelle Z. 1984. "Toward an Anthropology of Self and Feeling," in R. Shweder and R. Levine, eds., *Culture Theory: Essays on Mind, Self and Emotion.* Cambridge: Cambridge University Press.

Rosaldo, Renato. 1980. *Ilongot Headhunting: A Study in History and Society.* Stanford: Stanford University Press.

Rosenberger, Nancy R., ed. 1992. *Japanese Sense of Self.* Cambridge: Cambridge University Press.

Shore, Bradd. 1982. *Sala'ilua: A Samoan Mystery.* New York: Columbia University Press.

Shotter, John, and Kenneth J. Gergen, eds. 1989. *Texts of Identity.* London: Sage.

Silverstein, Michael. 1976. "Shifters, Linguistic Categories, and Cultural Description," in K. Basso and H. Selby, eds., *Meaning in Anthropology*, 11–55. Albuquerque: University of New Mexico Press.

————. 1979. "Language, Structure, and Linguistic Ideology," in P. R. Klyne et al., eds., *The Elements: A Parasession on Linguistic Units and Levels*, 193–247. Chicago: Chicago Linguistic Society.

Singer, Milton. 1980. "Signs of the Self: An Exploration in Semiotic Anthropology." *American Anthropologist* 82: 485–507.

Smith, Robert J. 1983. *Japanese Society: Tradition, Self and the Social Order*. Cambridge: Cambridge University Press.

Stark, Werner. 1962. *The Fundamental Forms of Social Thought*. London: Routledge and Kegan Paul.

Straus, Erwin. 1967. "On Anosognosia," in E. W. Straus and R. M. Griffith, eds., *The Phenomenology of Will and Action*, 103–26. Duquesne: Duquesne University Press.

Sudnow, David. 1978. *Ways of the Hand: The Organization of Improvised Conduct*. Cambridge, Mass.: Harvard University Press.

Suzuki, Takao. 1973. *Japanese and the Japanese: Words in Culture*. Translated by Akira Miura. Tokyo: Kodansha International.

————. 1976. "Language and Behavior in Japan: The Conceptualization of Interpersonal Relationships." *Japan Quarterly* 23: 255–66.

————. 1977. "*Hito* as a self-specifier and *otaku, kare* and *kanojo* as other-specifiers," in *Symposium on Japanese Sociolinguistics*, 195–204. Honolulu: University of Hawaii.

————. 1978. *Words in Context: A Japanese Perspective on Language and Culture*. Translated by Akira Miura. Tokyo: Kodansha International.

Vološinov, Valintin Nikolaevic. 1973. *Marxism and the Philosophy of Language*. Translated by L. Matejka and I. R. Titunik. New York: Seminar Press. Original publication in Russian, 1929.

Vygotsky, Lev Semenovich. 1962. *Thought and Language*. Translated by E. Hanfmann and G. Vakar. Cambridge, Mass.: MIT Press.

————. 1978. *Mind in Society*. Edited by M. Cole, V. John-Steiner, S. Scribner, and E. Souberman. Cambridge, Mass.: Harvard University Press.

Wetzel, Patricia Jean. 1984. *Uti and Soto (In-Group and Out-Group): Social Deixis in Japanese*. Ph.D. dissertation, Department of Linguistics, Cornell University.

White, Geoffrey M. 1992. "Emotions Inside Out: The Anthropology of Affect," in M. Lewis and J. Haviland, eds., *Handbook of Emotion*. New York: Guilford.

White, Geoffrey M., and Karen Ann Watson-Gegeo, eds. 1990. *Disentangling: Conflict Discourse in Pacific Societies*. Stanford: Stanford University Press.

White, Geoffrey M., and John Kirkpatrick, eds. 1985. *Person, Self, and Experience: Exploring Pacific Ethnopsychologies*. Berkeley: University of California Press.

Wittgenstein, Ludwig. 1958. *Philosophical Investigations*. Translated by G. E. M. Anscombe. New York: Macmillan.

Chapter 2

THE TERMS *UCHI* AND *SOTO* AS WINDOWS ON A WORLD

Charles J. Quinn, Jr.

Fuku wa uchi! Oni wa soto!
'Good fortune inside! Demons outside!'

Editors' Introduction

Charles Quinn explores a wide range of expressions that use the word *uchi* 'inside', and the word *soto* 'outside', or both, from the earliest extant texts down to the present. Distinctions drawn over the centuries with the words *uchi* and *soto* have shaped a broad range of domains of human experience, from the spatial and temporal to the social, psychological, and even grammatical. In domain after domain, *uchi/soto* reappears as a flexible, lived schema, whereby a boundary tacitly or explicitly separates an inside from an outside. While the particular "content" of these insides and outsides varies with the domain, and while domains come and go, the Japanese proclivity to structure experience in this way has remained rather constant. Not every use of the word *uchi* has a *soto*-based counterpart and, in fact, the lexical evidence suggests a tendency to elaborate the world more in terms of *uchi* than of *soto*. Such skewing is perhaps only to be expected, given the human tendency to scrutinize and elaborate the nearby in greater detail than the distant. In the aggregate, *uchi* expressions depict a world that is ENCLOSED, CONCAVE, INDOORS, FAMILY, LINEAL, "US," SHARED, FAMILIAR, INFORMAL, PRIVATE, EXPERIENCED, KNOWN, IN CONTROL, SACRED, and PRIMARY. *Soto* expressions, by contrast, see the world as OPEN, CONVEX, OUT-DOORS, NON-FAMILY, EXTRALINEAL, "THEM," NOT SHARED, UNFAMILIAR, FORMAL, PUBLIC, OBSERVED, UNKNOWN, UNCONTROLLED, PROFANE, and SECONDARY. As a lexical resource, *uchi* and *soto* expressions are at once the historical products of a patterned way of living and interpretations adaptable for patterning life anew.

These same opposed values permeate the usage of verbs that assume an 'inside/outside' frame, such as transitive *ireru* 'insert' and *dasu* 'put/take out', or intransitive *hairu* 'enter' and *deru* 'emerge'. These verbs are typically used in relation to 'insides' that are known, private, controlled, and primary, and 'outsides' that are unknown, public, outside one's control, and secondary. Moreover, the opposed values or conceptual contrasts associated with the words *uchi/soto* and 'in/out' verbs like *hairu/deru* and *ireru/dasu* are congruent with epistemological distinctions indexed by a number of basic grammatical devices, as Quinn argues in the volume's concluding chapter.

The lexical evidence Quinn presents and analyzes in this chapter suggests that Japanese people have long practiced an *uchi/soto* lifeway, or *habitus*, to orient themselves and others, in the business of their daily lives; the habitus continues to be remade somewhat in each occasion it shapes. By elaborating the range of experience that has been construed as *uchi/soto*, this chapter sets the stage for the remaining chapters of part 1, each of which delineates particulars of contexts inhabited as 'insides' and 'outsides'.

THE TERMS *UCHI* AND *SOTO* AS WINDOWS ON A WORLD

THIS ESSAY[1] explores the ways in which *uchi/soto* 'inside/outside' orientations are expressed in words, in particular, the more established combinations in which the words *uchi* and *soto* have been used. That there is social behavior understood by the Japanese to be patterned in an *uchi/soto* kind of way is abundantly evident in the vocabulary of their language. The lexical evidence indicates that *uchi/soto* orientations constitute a *lifeway*, a socially learned way of construing, approaching, and moving through one's world, in domains of experience as different as perception and interpersonal relations. The *uchi/soto* lifeway is thus a kind of *habitus*, or "system of acquired dispositions functioning on the practical level as categories of perception and assessment or as classificatory principles as well as being the organizing principles of action . . . constituting the social agent" (Bourdieu 1990, 13).[2] As the wide range of lived contexts surveyed below suggests, the *uchi/soto* habitus is anything but a rigid, fixed, template, but rather is adapted and remade somewhat in every particular encounter it informs.

Focusing on the words *uchi* and *soto* as a lexical resource not only facilitates access to the concepts that go by those names, but will also complement the other essays in this collection, by providing a glimpse at the most clearly labeled practice of the 'inside/outside' habit, the widespread use of words that mean just that. If the more ethnographic essays in this collection, with their experiential detail, are stories that illustrate the lived, indexical quality of what is tagged "*uchi/soto*," the present chapter is a summary about the tags themselves. It asks what varieties of experience each term is used to label and how different uses might be related to one another. It surveys informally, but at some length, the varieties of other words with which *uchi* and *soto* combine, in combinations that are both lexical (i.e., compounding) and collocational (separate words in a single, somewhat idiomatic construction),[3] as items in a larger web of other words. Under the working assumption that "the meaning of a word is its use in language" (Wittgenstein 1958, 20), it sketches an outline of such *uchi/soto* expressions as have emerged and continue to evolve. Their place in the lexicon looks to be as broadly and deeply established as the orientational habit is in social life. The expression of this orientational habit with the words *uchi* and *soto* is in fact one guarantee of that habitus's continued survival, for once people incorporate such terms into the physical, social, and psychological activities they engage in, use of those terms is no longer simply reflective of such behavior, but constitutive of it as well.

The expressions in which we find the word *uchi*, the word *soto*, or both, are *orientational*. With these expressions, people get a fix on the world: themselves, other people, reports; in space, in time, in relation to other people; in the waking world and in their dreams, ad infinitum. They also use these expressions to project an orientation onto *other* people and things as *they* relate in space, in time, and with one another, even to the extent that there are grammatical constructions that have employed the words *uchi* and *(so)to*. Like other words, the words *uchi* and *soto* are at once the historical products of a patterned way of living and tools for patterning life anew. The striking fact about them is the breadth of domains of human experience in which each is used, from the spatial and physical to the social and psychological. As we shall see, *uchi* has been used more widely and variously than *soto*.[4]

Whichever of these experiential domains is described with the terms *uchi* and *soto*, the crucial feature is that of "in relation to." Like other basic orientations, such as "up/down," "front/back," "on/off," or "deep/shallow," the *uchi/soto* opposition is grounded in "the fact that we have bodies of the sort we have, and that they function as they do in our physical environment" (Lakoff and Johnson 1980, 14). While the *uchi/soto* habitus cannot be reduced to the fact of embodied existence, there is no denying the body's informing role in basic orientational schemata. Just how true this is for speakers of English, for example, is illustrated in a telling way by the following passage, an account of "only a few of the many *in-out* orientations that might occur in the first few minutes of an ordinary day" (Johnson 1987, 31–32):

> You wake *out* of a deep sleep and peer *out* from beneath the covers *into* your room. You gradually emerge *out* of your stupor, pull yourself *out* from under the covers, climb *into* your robe, stretch *out* your limbs, and walk *in* a daze *out* of the bedroom and *into* the bathroom. You look *in* the mirror and

see your face staring *out* at you. You reach *into* the medicine cabinet, take *out* the toothpaste, squeeze *out* some toothpaste, put the toothbrush *into* your mouth, brush your teeth *in* a hurry, and rinse *out* your mouth. At breakfast you perform a host of further *in-out* moves—pouring *out* the coffee, setting *out* the dishes, putting the toast *in* the toaster, spreading *out* the jam on the toast, and on and on. Once you are more awake you might even get lost *in* the newspaper, might enter *into* a conversation, which leads to your speaking *out* on some topic.

As Johnson notes, some of these uses of *in* and *out* involve physical orientation in space, while others have to do with nonspatial relations, such as entering *into* a conversation. But whether the domain is physical, social, or psychological, essential to all these expressions is some establishing of relations: among physical objects, among social entities, among events. There is no "in" and no "out" except in *relation* to some "this" or "that," some "here" or "there," that is, to some *context*. What is more, the relation implies a boundary of some kind, insofar as it indicates an "inside" and an "outside." The boundary may be crossed (in the more dynamic predicates, such as "pour *out* the coffee") or it may simply separate the observer from the observed (as in the more static predicates, such as "peering *out*," "*into* the room"). The same essentials of relation and boundary are implicit in the epithet that provides the subtitle to this essay.

Metaphor, according to Aristotle, is "the application to one thing of a name belonging to another" (*Poetics* 1457b). This definition entails no absolute opposition of metaphorical meaning to literal meaning, and it is quite compatible with a view that takes literal meaning as simply conventionalized, "denatured" metaphor. As Dwight Bolinger has remarked, any experience that is not expressed in terms unique to itself is known, in some sense, metaphorically. And insofar as no sign is identical with its referent—so long as "the map is not the territory"—the use of any sign is to some extent metaphorical. Understood in this sense, the metaphorical act is of interest to us because it is the most common way in which words come to participate in new meanings. Many expressions like the English ones above with "in(to)," "out(of)" and those in Japanese that we shall examine, such as *uchiki* 'shy' and *soto-waribiki* 'real discount', can be understood as products of metaphor,[5] insofar as a word or phrase that has functioned in one domain of experience (say, spatial, social) is applied in another realm (e.g., psychological, economic). In fact, it is well documented that naming in new semantic fields, such as portions of a computer disk, and less directly perceptible aspects of our experience, such as subatomic particles, is commonly done by borrowing from more familiar fields and more perceptible phenomena.[6] Not only are there a good many *uchi* and *soto* expressions to be found outside the realm of the physical and spatial, but most of the basic ones are in evidence in the oldest extant written records. Others were clearly added as new domains emerged, such as those relating to financial transactions. The social domain is particularly rich in *uchi* and *soto* expressions, which place another person 'inside' or 'outside' the same bounded area as oneself. To judge from usage, the smallest social *uchi* is the individual; the largest, entities such as the Japanese nation, "the major industrial nations," or even planet earth. But social life is still but one room in a larger household, in which the words *uchi* and *soto* serve to structure a variety of experiential domains.

While it is well nigh impossible to single out points in time when the use of *uchi* or *soto* was extended to a new dimension, it is nevertheless significant that the same terms are found in such a wide variety of semantic fields. This in itself bears testimony to the proclivity of the Japanese to construe much of their experience in ways that have 'insides', 'outsides' and, implicitly, boundaries. The *uchi/soto* orientation does not play out in the same way in every domain of meaning, but these are the three features we can expect to be shared, the aspects of *uchi* and *soto* on which analogies and extensions across domains will be based.

If a survey is limited, as this one is, to the record preserved in dictionaries, it is important that those consulted go beyond the listing of meanings as definitions, identify distinct contexts of use, and illustrate these with examples from authentic sources. Attested contexts of use provide a surer foothold than explanations alone when one is reaching hard for contemporary meanings, but there is nevertheless no discounting their selectivity.[7] In the largest unabridged Japanese dictionary, while there are approximately 405 entries for lexical (including compounds) and collocational uses of the noun *uchi*, there are but 157 listed for *soto* (including eight for its earlier form *to*). The evidence suggests that ever since the earliest written texts, *uchi* has been used in a greater variety of contexts than *(so)to*. There are many more expressions based on the application of *uchi* to nonspatial domains, such as the social and psychological, than there are for *(so)to*. The relative morphonological stability over time of the words themselves suggests that *uchi* has remained the more solidly established of the pair: while *soto* is developed from an earlier form, *to*, which is found in Nara (710–784) and Heian (794–1192) period texts, *uchi* has apparently always been *uchi*. This asymmetry in the degree to which each term has endured, developed, and been extended to new contexts of use is probably a consequence of the natural human proclivity to develop and elaborate that which is nearby and accessible, and to leave unelaborated the removed, distant, or inaccessible. Indeed, that which is significant in our biological and social lives is to a large extent that which is close enough to impinge on us.

When the two are mentioned together, whether the scope is as large as a proverb or as narrow as a compound word, *uchi* invariably precedes *soto,* as "in" precedes "out" in English "ins and outs," as "near" precedes "far," *omote* 'front' precedes *ura* 'back', and so on. The order in which *uchi* and *soto* appear together is an example of what Cooper and Ross (1975) have called the "Me First Principle," whereby semantically related but contrasted elements are frozen into a syntactic order that reflects a proximate-distal semantics. There are also phrasings which come in both an *uchi* version and a *soto* version, such as that illustrated by the epithet quoted at the outset of this chapter, or in such pairs of complementary terms as *uchi-mawari* 'inner [train line] loop' and *soto-mawari* 'outer loop' or *uchi-sen* 'concave drawknife' and *soto-sen* 'convex drawknife'.[8]

Any beginning apparent to an observer will of course have its own beginnings, somehow inaccessable to the observer, and thus not recognized as such. The earliest attested tokens of *uchi* available today appear in texts compiled in the eighth century, and imply established usage that antedates the texts. A wide range of uses for *uchi* is evident by the tenth century, but for all we know, this too may have already been long established, common practice. One of the larger dictionaries of earlier stages of the Japanese language lists ten separate meanings for the word *uchi,* and cites an illustrative example or two for each, in effect claiming that the word was used in ten different ways. The earliest of these uses are from the eighth century collection of poetry, *Manyooshuu* (completed 759), while others date from the ninth, tenth, and eleventh centuries.[9] Even by the rough gauge of dictionary entries, by the eleventh century *uchi* is attested in all of the primary domains in which it is used today: spatial, temporal, quantitative, social, and psychological. It appears unlikely that there was a time in recorded history when *uchi* was restricted to one, two, or even three domains.

While *to* 'outside' is not attested in the numbers that *uchi* is, it too was also used in a variety of domains, such as *tokata* 'away, other direction' (= *to* 'outside' + *kata* 'direction'); *tozama* 'outside alternative, other direction' (= *to* + *sama* 'appearance, style'); *tosaburai* 'outer guards' (= *to* + *saburai* 'serving man'); or *totsukuni* 'foreign country' (*to* + genitive *tsu* + *kuni* 'land'). There is a construction /verb-negative + *to*/ 'before [verb], while-not-[verb]' attested in *Manyooshuu* (*yo no fuke-nu TO ni* 'before the night grows late'), which appears to have contrasted with /verb-affirmative + *uchi*/ 'during [verb], while [verb]' (*tamakiharu UCHI* 'interval while alive'). Furthermore, *to* is used contrastively with *uchi* in a variety of domains of human experience, spatial and social, from the eighth through the fourteenth centuries. Some uses straddle two domains, as when a physical barrier enforces a social one.

Uchi and *to* were also used together contrastively in a single phrase or clause from the earliest texts on, in a wide variety of genres, written down as early as 759. Although from the time of the earliest texts there were several words that could be considered to be semantically opposed to *uchi* (e.g., *yoso* 'other', *hoka* 'outside'), only *to* appears to have been paired with it as systematically as *soto* is today. Even so, paired contrastive *uchi/to* expressions are not in evidence to anywhere near the extent we observe today of *uchi/soto*. While the domains of experience in which the word *uchi* was used run the gamut from spatial to social to psychological, much as today, the term *to* was probably not nearly so widely used as either its contemporary *uchi* was or its descendant *soto* is. At the very least, it is clear that as a handle on various aspects of experience, the concept of *uchi* has been employed in Japan from well before the first written records. While the core constellation of meanings expressed with *uchi* is in evidence from early on, the range and productivity of its later contrastive pairing with *(so)to* seems less in evidence.

TURNING A PHRASE INSIDE OR OUT

The uses of *uchi* and *to* attested from the early texts are, in terms of sign types, *indexical* or *symbolic*, depending on the actual context of use.[10] This remains just as true today. The compound words (e.g., *uchi-mawari* 'inner [train] loop') and constructions (*san-nin no uchi* 'among the three [people]', *hon o yonde iru uchi* 'while reading a book') that include *uchi* and/or *soto* are most often used symbolically, which is to say as common nouns meaning an 'X kind of inside' or a 'Y kind of outside', and are not anchored in the speaker's time or place of uttering them. Compound nouns in which *uchi* or *soto* specifies a second noun, such as *uchi-mawari*, represent a lexicalized kind of deixis, in which ground zero is some place or time other than the speaker's here-and-now, and is fixed by the semantic frame implicit in that word or phrase. If, on the other hand, *uchi* or *soto* is the head noun modified by a clause, as in *hon o yonde iru uchi*, the clause identifies the zero point. Such phrases are commonly used to ground an act or event described in a superordinate predicate, as in *hon o yonde iru uchi ni omoidashita* '[I] remembered [it] while [I] was reading'. But insofar as that ground zero is not the moment of speaking or writing, the expression does not signify in a basic indexical way. The 'inside' or 'outside' in some of these expressions can be anchored in the speaker's own location, and thus used indexically, but this is a matter of the occasion of use, and is not a feature of the words and phrases themselves.

Since it is the central contention of this volume that much social behavior in Japan is *indexed* in an *uchi/soto* schema, the question naturally arises as to why we need to paint a picture of the *symbolic* uses of the same schema. One reason is the general theoretical point that Peirce's three sign types (indexes, icons, and symbols) are better understood as *perspectives, modalities,* or *uses* than as unchanging, invariant entities. A particular word, or sign vehicle, may be used in different modalities at different times, so that a word that was a motivated icon for a community in the past may come to function as an unmotivated, arbitrary symbol for their descendants. This is true, for example, of many *kanji* 'Chinese characters', the component parts of which, while once transparently iconic ("pictographic"), are no longer so. For Americans, the Stars and Stripes was once a diagrammatic icon, in that the numbers of stars and stripes correspond to the numbers of present and original states, but for many today it is simply a symbol of the United States. Conversely, erstwhile symbols often come to be used indexically. Several of the so-called personal pronouns of present-day Japanese, for example, are symbols-turned-indexes. The provenances of words like *wata(ku)shi* 'I' (formerly 'personal, private'), *boku* 'I' (formerly 'humble servant'), *kimi* 'you' (formerly 'gentleman, prince'), *kisama* 'you [rude address]' (formerly 'exalted person'), are fairly well known, but the process by which these erstwhile symbols came to function indexically seems little appreciated.[11]

The main reason for examining the symbolic side of *uchi/soto*, however, is because a catalog of these uses will suggest just how many aspects of Japanese life are routinely and overtly symbolized as 'insides' and 'outsides'. As several of the early examples show, symbolic uses of these two terms have been there all along. An examination of the lexical evidence will now reveal the extent to which *uchi/soto*-oriented indexical behavior has been informed and supported by symbolic uses of the words *uchi* and *soto*. The lists include a number of uses of each that did not survive the three centuries preceding this one, but I shall not pause to identify them, since my main concern has been to suggest, however roughly, the range of domains in which the distinction has served an orientational function in a tradition, or culture, over time. Even those uses that are no longer au courant are nonetheless part of the story of how Japanese society is patterned, just as the heartwood or knots of a tree contribute to its present and future form. The following taxonomy of *uchi*-based words and phrases is representative of what some Japanese lexicographers have seen as warranting separate entries and examples of usage, no more, no less; the validity of conclusions drawn here is necessarily constrained by this fact.

UCHI: A CATALOG OF USES BY DOMAIN

The spatial domain refers simply to bounded areas, physically separate from their surroundings. (See *Uchi*, Table 1.) The words and phrases listed describe acts that occur or conditions that obtain in some relation to that bounded space: it can be 'entered' (*uchi e hairu*), 'worked on' (*uchisakuji*), experienced as 'dark' (*uchikura*, presumably because no light can 'enter'), or it can serve as the origin or ground from which

uchi e hairu 'go inside'
uchi kara kagi o kakeru 'lock from inside'
uchi kara hiraku 'open from inside'
uchikura 'dark inside'
uchisakuji 'interior work, repair'
uchiniku 'endoplasm'
uchipasu 'inside calipers'
uchinori 'inner measurements (from inner edge to inner edge)'
uchizura 'interior surface' ('at-home visage')
uchimawari 'inner (beltway, train) loop'
uchisarugaku 'noh performed indoors'
uchiburo 'indoor bath'
uchiniwa 'inner garden, courtyard'
uchishirasu 'white pebbles inside the apron skirting a noh stage'
uchichootsugai 'inner hinges (on body armor)'
uchibori 'inner moat'
uchipoketto 'inside pocket'
uchiido 'inside well'
uchiniwa 'courtyard, enclosed garden'
uchigooshi 'inside lattice'
Uchi Mooko 'Inner Mongolia'
uchisen 'convex drawknife' (named for its con*cave* cut)
uchimata 'pigeon toed'
uchigama 'inside of legs turned inward'
uchihachimonji 'inside of legs turned inward'
uchisanzun 'inner part of ankle area'
uchiguri 'hollowed inside (sculpture)'
uchikatagiri 'cut with graver facing inside of cut' (metal engraving)
uchiumi 'bay, gulf'
uchitsu 'inlet'
uchiyama 'settled mountains (= around one's village)'
uchimuki 'facing inward'
uchigake 'inside leg *sumoo* throw' (There are many more such terms, and some are used in *juudoo* as well.)
uchibutokoro 'inner "pocket" in folds of *kimono*'
uchisumi 'inner corners' (seating positions at tea ceremony)
uchisetsuin 'inner toilet' (for a tea room)
uchiroji 'inner garden' (for a tea room)
uchibari 'paper or cloth stretched inside a frame'
uchibe 'inside part'
uchimisu 'inner boxes at *kabuki* theater'
uchimiyoshi 'inner timbers of bow of boat'
uchidoi 'inner (concealed) roof gutter'
uchiwaku 'inside frame'
uchisogi 'cutting inward (tips of protruding shrine rafters)', 'shrine rafters cut inward on their tips'

Note: Others listed in "*Uchi* with *Soto*, Table 1: Spatial."

such acts as 'opening' or 'locking' the boundary (a door or window) are staged (*uchi kara hiraku/kakeru*). An *uchinori* 'inside measurement' describes the shortest distance between two bounding edges. *Uchinori* and *uchipasu* 'inside calipers' are so named because of their focus on this interval between bounding edges. The image of a container with a boundary separating an interior from an exterior is clearly evident in expressions of this domain. The other domains are also configured along the lines of a container schema, but they differ from these spatial uses in that while they assume an enclosed space, they are about more than that, too, in ways peculiar to each.

The four compound words beginning with *uchibori* 'inner moat' are so named for the position of the second element in each compound, *uchi-X*. *X* here is implicitly located within a larger, bounded frame. An *uchibori* is so called because it is inside, with the castle it encircles, in relation to a *sotobori* 'outside moat'. The deictic zero point is thus the castle. An *uchipoketto* 'inside pocket' is a pocket that is enclosed or attached inside a piece of clothing, which is construed as a container with contrasting inside and outside; the deictic anchor point for this expression is the wearer, who is 'inside' the clothing. *Uchiido* is a 'well' 'inside' the household enclosure, and an *uchiniwa* is an 'inside garden', enclosed in the same space. *Uchi Mooko* 'Inner Mongolia' is south of the Gobi Desert and closer to China, the zero point implicit in this name; *Soto Mooko* 'Outer Mongolia' was further out from the same center, beyond Inner Mongolia. In keeping with its name, *Uchi Mooko* remains under control of China, but *Soto Mooko* is now its own 'People's Republic' (*Mongoru jinmin kyoowakoku*). Such names of things, activities, conditions, and places are instances of *uchi*-as-symbol; they come with an understood zero point that is not necessarily dependent on the speaker/ writer's own, present-time zero point.

Other words used as symbols in the spatial domain specify the shape of some object. They fully or partially describe an outline with a containing shape, a bounded space with an inside and an outside. An *uchisen* 'convex drawknife', for example, is named for the con*cave* hollow it cuts in wood; the knife creates a shape that approximates the canonical container, since the hollow forms a partially enclosed space. *Uchimata* 'inward-turned legs' is one of several terms that the Japanese have devised to describe the stance assumed when the toes of both feet point inward, thus creating a partial enclosure. An *uchiumi* 'bay', like an *uchitsu* 'inlet', is a body of tidal water that is surrounded to some extent by land, and thus enclosed (as *sotoumi* 'open sea', for example, is not). *Uchiguri* 'hollowed-out carving' is likewise named for its enclosed shape. All of these compounds are instances of aspect-for-whole naming, or synecdoche.

In this way, acts, states and objects have been named for the way in which they approximate, in their own particular manners, the canonical

UCHI, TABLE 2
Social, Domestic

---

uchi de asobu   'play at home/indoors'
uchigirai   'be loath to stay indoors; person with such a disposition'
uchi o motsu   'maintain a household'
uchi o deru   'leave home'
uchi o akete iru   'be away from home'
kane o uchi e ireru   'contribute (financially) at home'
uchi e kaeru   'return home'
uchi no hito   '[my] husband' (lit., 'inside person') ⎫
uchi no mono   'person/people in [my] family'   ⎬ typically used deictically
uchi no shujin   '[my] husband'   ⎪
uchi   '[I]' (female, primarily Western Japan)   ⎭
uchigenkan   'side entrance (not main; for household members)'
uchigi   'casual clothing (for wear at home)'
uchiburo   'bath taken at home'
uchigoshirae   'home made'
uchimago   'grandchild who is child of successor couple'
uchi-kerai   'longtime/principal vassal'
uchi-shuu   'household employees'
uchi-shigoto   'piece work done at home'
uchi-kosaku   'tenant farming (by servant or otherwise in-service people)'
uchi no kaisha   'our firm (corporation)'

---

uchi/soto pattern: enclosed, encircled, inwardly curved, and/or closer to a center. The flexible schema of a container, with its boundary and outside, is basic, but is approximated to varying degrees, in different ways, depending on the domain and other concept(s) brought to bear in an individual lexical expression. Let us turn next to a somewhat less physically enclosed kind of space. (See *Uchi*, Table 2.)

Under this second domain, social/domestic, are listed words and phrases that express aspects of the bounded spaces in which people shelter themselves and anchor their social lives. Some of these uses, such as *uchi de asobu* 'play at home/indoors', *uchigirai* 'be loath to stay indoors; person with such a disposition', or *uchigenkan* 'inside = side/ back/non-main entrance', might also be placed under the spatial category of Table 1, since they relate to some located aspect of the *uchi*. But they also relate to the notion of a *home*: not just any 'indoors', but indoors in a house in which a family dwells; not just any 'inside entrance', but one used by the members of that household and their familiars, while outsiders are greeted and admitted at the *omote genkan* 'front entrance'. It is in this frame of reference that phrases like *uchi no hito* 'my husband' ('person of the household') and *uchi o motsu* 'maintain a household' have their significance. Some of the activities that characterize an *uchi* as a family or a home are described by the language collocated with this word: playing there, managing it, leaving, returning, belonging to it, and so on. There is thus a tendency to treat *uchi* as a thing, an entity that can be 'held' (*motsu*) and 'left empty' (*akeru*), a location to which one 'returns' (*kaeru*), from which one 'departs' (*deru* 'separates'), or into which one 'deposits money' (*o-kane o ireru*). The homely images of *uchigi* 'casual clothing' and *uchigoshirae* 'home made', like the proverbs at the end of Table 3, remind us that *uchi* is a space to which people can retreat and (as an American might say) "be themselves," free from the restraints and obligations of nondomestic society outside. These kinds of feelings are expressed in many of the phrases of the psychological domain, which is taken up next.

In the social/domestic domain, then, we have the *uchi* that is succeeded to and managed, departed from, returned to, handed down to the next generation, and so on. While it is often not without physical attributes, such as a shared dwelling or land, *uchi* as social space is structured by certain roles and activities its inhabitants perform, a point made in detail by several essays in this volume. The last five items on this list, beginning with the phrase *uchi no kaisha* 'our company/firm', remind us that households are corporate enterprises and that membership may be had in a variety of roles other than those one is born to. These phrases thus provide a bridge to the commerce-related expressions listed in Table 4 below, the domain of social/nondomestic. But first, let us explore the psychological domain. In the experience of such invisible phenomena as feelings, attitudes, and beliefs, metaphor and metonymy provide the means for the expression of some rather basic meanings. (See *Uchi*, Table 3.)

A *futokoro* is the space, or natural pocket, between the outer and inner layers of a *kimono*, and the *uchibutokoro* 'inner *futokoro*' is the space between the inner layer of *kimono* and the wearer's chest. The *futokoro* is reached into most easily by the right hand, which enters just over the heart (*kokoro*) and above the stomach (*hara*), seats of one's true feelings and thoughts. If metonymy is based on contiguity, *futokoro* was in just the right place to be applied in the expression of feelings and thoughts. The words *futokoro* and *uchibutokoro* have presumably been extended into the psychological domain because what is inside this pocket is accessible only to the wearer of the clothing, and hidden from people outside. Thus, one can 'conceal' (*shinobaseru*) information in the *uchibutokoro* or suffer someone's 'seeing into' it (*misukasareru*). *Uchikabuto* 'inner helmet' refers to 'inside' the outer shell of the *kabuto* 'helmet' that one wears to protect one's head, or seat of strategic planning. To have the 'inside' of one's 'helmet' 'seen into', then, is to have one's martial in-

UCHI, TABLE 3
Psychological/Attitudinal

---

uchibutokoro 'open space under innermost layer of *kimono*', 'one's inner feelings, thoughts'

uchibutokoro ni shinobaseru 'conceal evil intent'

uchibutokoro o misukasareru 'be seen through'

uchikabuto o misukasareru 'have one's designs seen through' (lit., 'be seen through inside the helmet')

uchiki(mono) 'retiring, withdrawn (person)'

uchi ni kaerimite, yamashiku nai 'have a clear conscience' (lit., 'looking within, nothing to be ashamed of')

uchi hadaka de mo soto nishiki 'even if naked at home, brocade outside'

uchi-hadakari no soto-subori 'bossy at home, meek outside'

uchi-benkei no soto-beso 'a lion at home, a bellybutton (= the opposite) outside'

uchi-hirogari no soto-subomari 'expansive/outgoing/bossy at home, closed tight when outside'

sotozura wa yoi no desu ga, uchizura wa warui '[S/he] is affable outside,' (lit., 'outside demeanor is good'), 'but is difficult at home' (lit., 'at-home demeanor is bad').

soto-mizu no uchi hirogari 'naive of the world, expansive/outgoing/bossy at home'

---

tents or schemes found out. Casting the psychological in terms of clothing and other items in which one's body is enclosed provides a way to speak of one's inner feelings and attitudes as things that can be 'concealed' or 'seen into'.

The proverbs that conclude this list of uses in the psychological domain contrast 'inside' attitudes and personal character with their 'outside' counterparts, and suggest again that *uchi* is an enclosed space where one can admit to his or her inner feelings and "have a bad attitude." Different components of the spatial schema of *uchi/soto* thus come to be associated with the meanings and values of different domains. The words *soto-subori*, *soto-beso*, and *soto-subomari* are compounds that describe a person's behavior *out*side the home (*soto-*) in inverted imagery: *subori* and *subomari* describe inwardly puckered shapes, as does *-beso* (< *heso* 'navel'). This image is a metaphor for a retiring, withdrawn personality, and is in each of these idioms contrasted sharply with the same person's behavior inside the home, viz., *-hadakari* 'very expressive, "loud"', *-Benkei* (a large, courageous, and voluble folk-hero), and *-hirogari* 'expansiveness'. The ironic humor in these proverbs follows from the way they reframe values assumed for social 'insides' and 'outsides', so that *uchi*'s openness is brash, and *soto*'s quality of closed up is timidity.

Uchi-based expressions used in the next domain show clearly that

UCHI, Table 4
Social, Nondomestic

---

uchikata 'your wife', 'living quarters (back of shop in same building)' (lit., 'inside direction')

uchiguruma 'rickshaw for private use'

uchiuchi de 'in private'

uchimaku 'inner workings/inside dope' (lit., 'inside' + 'curtain')

uchimaku o shitte iru 'know the inside story'

uchimakubanashi o suru 'give someone the lowdown'

uchiwa 'inside circle, familiars, insiders'

uchiwa o nozoku 'peek inside, obtain inside information'

uchiwa o abaku 'expose, uncover, blow open'

uchiwa no koto 'private matter'

uchiwa dooshi de 'between/among fellow insiders'

uchiwa de kaiketsu suru 'solve [a problem] inside' (i.e., without outside mediation)

uchiwa no hi o sarakedasu 'wash one's dirty linen in public'

uchiwa ni iu 'understate'

nanigoto mo uchiwa ni yaru beki 'Whatever one does, it should be done within bounds'

uchikenchi '*han* (fief)-internal surveying'

uchikemi 'internal estimate of crop yield'

uchiwaribiki 'insider's (i.e., banker's) discount'

uchikehai 'inside (estimated) stock price (before market opens)'

uchikashikari 'lending and borrowing for insiders only'

uchikanjoo 'insider bookkeeping, false receipts'

uchikoo 'in-house proofreading'

uchizata 'lawsuit handled privately', 'out-of-court settlement'

uchimome 'inside strife'

uchigiki 'love poem'

uchi-otori no to-medeta 'inferior in substance, impressive in appearance'

---

when *uchi* refers to 'family', that 'family' routinely extends beyond the nuclear one. (See *Uchi* Table 4.)

As Nakane Chie pointed out two decades ago, corporate enterprises in Japan have long functioned as a kind of *uchi*, and we find considerable use of the term *uchi* in commercial society. Some of these expressions relate to both domains, such as *uchikata*, literally 'inner [of two] side[s]', which was used in two rather different senses: (1) to refer to another's wife (identified with the 'inside' of that household), and (2) to refer to a dwelling attached to a shop (the residence was 'inside', opposed to the shop 'outside'; see Molasky's chapter below). In the rickshaw business, there was also *uchiguruma* 'rickshaw for private (not public) use', and in publishing, *uchikoo* 'in-house proofreading'. Two older words, *uchikenchi* '(fief-) internal surveying of acreage' and *uchikemi* 'internal estimate of crop yield', refer to local matters, close to home, distinct from those involving the national government, the Tokugawa shogunate.

The rhetoric of the next two sets of phrases, those built on *uchimaku* 'inside curtain' and *uchiwa* 'inside ring/circle', resembles that of *uchibutokoro* (Table 3, just discussed). Like the *futokoro* of clothing, *maku* 'curtain' and *wa* 'ring/circle' refer to an enclosed space, albeit in different ways. While *futokoro* names the enclosed space itself, *maku* and *wa* are more like *kabuto* 'helmet' in that they name only the bounding or separating entity. Thus, one can establish the image of an enclosed self by metonymy, as we saw in the use of *uchibutokoro* to refer to one's innermost feelings, or by synecdoche, in which part of the enclosure (the boundary or divider) stands for the whole. This synecdoche of using the bounding entity to refer to the enclosure (which is then a metaphor for 'inner thoughts') works as well as it does because insofar as someone encounters a boundary, there exists an 'inside' and an 'outside'. *Uchi/soto* is one of those "tight" (cf. Rumelhart, McClelland et al. 1986), "basic" (cf. Lakoff 1987) schemata in which the presence of any component strongly predicts the others; put conversely, the components do not occur without one another. The dividing and concealing typically accomplished by 'curtains' and 'rings' or 'circles' of people make *uchimaku* 'inner curtain' and *uchiwa* 'inner ring' particularly apt in expressing the proprietary side of information, as something privately familiar to those who are inside either the 'curtain' or the 'ring', but concealed from those on the outside. *Uchiwa-dooshi* 'fellow insiders' uses the word *uchiwa* 'inner circle' to refer to individuals who belong there. The last two examples of the *uchiwa*-based expressions, *uchiwa ni iu* 'understate' and *nanigoto mo uchiwa ni yaru beki* 'Whatever one does, it should be done within bounds', utilize the word *uchiwa* 'inside circle' in an expression of manner to indicate the range or degree of the behavior specified in the final predicate. By these expressions, then, what one 'says' or 'does' is said or done within the bounds of an implicit *uchiwa*.

In the same group of words, there is a series of terms for activities that have to do with producing and marketing goods (*-kenchi* 'surveying acreage', *-kemi* 'estimation of crop yield', *-waribiki* 'discounting', *-kehai* 'hint', *-kashikari* 'lending and borrowing', *-kanjoo* 'bookkeeping') that are conducted by insiders on their side of the boundary. The *uchi-*variant of any of these has the common characteristic of being information that is accessible to those engaged in handling it, but not to outsiders. Words in this domain that do not carry a nuance of willful concealment at least denote a sense of the personal or private, as with *uchigiki* 'love letter' and *uchizata* 'private (out of court) settlement'.

A summary of the features of these first four domains—spatial, social-domestic, psychological, and social-nondomestic—yields a composite image of a bounded area that is enclosed, nearby, accessible, and familiar, which is not generally visible to those outside the boundary, and inside which one is free to feel relaxed and act in a relatively unconstrained manner. When outside, by contrast, one is in less familiar and less controllable territory, and so in more careful control over oneself.[12] Viewed from without, *uchi* is shut off, inaccessible, and concealed. Being inside the boundary gives access to information that is familiar, shared, and—because it is not accessible outside—valuable. An 'inside' position is privileged; it brings with it a sharing of the space with the others who inhabit it and a shared detachment from those who do not. All of these values may be seen to follow from focusing on this or that feature of the spatial schema implicit in *uchi* as it applies in a particular domain. In that all four domains are structured with reference to the spatial characteristics of *uchi*, the spatial is basic; through abduction[13] and analogy, it provides a means whereby social and psychological experience are conceived and talked about. The image schema associated with the term *uchi*, with its enclosure, boundary, and exterior, is of course not the only one that serves to structure these domains, but it is a major one.

UCHI, TABLE 5
Temporal Intervals

jippun no uchi (ni)	'within ten minutes'
ichinichi, futsuka no uchi (ni)	'in a day or two'
sono hi no uchi (ni)	'in the course of the day'
kotoshi no uchi (ni)	'some time this year' (i.e., before next year)
wakai uchi (ni)	'while young'
hon o yonde iru uchi (ni)	'while reading a book'
tokaku suru uchi (ni)	'in the meantime' (lit., 'while doing this and that')
hi ga denai uchi (ni)	'before sunrise' (lit., 'while the sun has not risen')
ichikiro mo ikanai uchi (ni)	'before having gone even a kilometer'
sono uchi (ni)	'before long' (lit., 'in the interval')
hakushu kassai no uchi (ni)	'amidst applause'
hinkon no uchi ni seijin suru	'grow up in poverty'
ichinen no uchi de sankagetsu shika inai	'is absent but three months of the year'

Let us turn now to a pair of substitution frames based on the term *uchi*, delineation of bounded temporal intervals (*Uchi*, Table 5) and bounded sets (*Uchi*, Table 6). The second of these covers just about any domain in which countable items figure, and thus differs markedly from other, single-domain tables. If this use can be said to belong to a domain of our experience, it is the cognitive one of nonce categorization. The

UCHI, TABLE 6
Bounded Sets

---

sono uchi (de) 'among them' (lit., 'being among them')
ano sannin no uchi (de) 'of those three people' (lit., 'being among . . .')
shitte iru Amerikajin no uchi (de) 'among Americans [I] know'
daikoogyookoku no uchi ni haitte iru 'is among the major industrial nations'
daihyoosaku no uchi ni hairu 'is among his major works'
uchiwake 'breakdown (of particulars)'
uchihyoo 'itemized table'
gookei gohyakuman-en, sono uchi wa tsugi no toori 'a total of five million yen, the
    itemized details of which are as follows'

---

expressions listed within "bounded temporal intervals" and "bounded sets" of items are notably less value-laden than those of the first four tables, since the spaces they demarcate can apply equally to virtually any social group, natural event, or human activity. These expressions share the function of grouping, clustering, or otherwise joining aspects of socially meaningful experience into bounded units.

It is significant that in most of these uses, *uchi* functions as an independent lexical item, and does not form compound words. The structure here is periphrastic (or syntactic, that is, words related to one another), not lexical or morphotactic (morphemes joined to form words). There is good functional reason for these meanings to be expressed in syntactic constructions rather than lexical compounds: as a substitution frame, a syntactic construction allows great flexibility with regard to what is framed as an interval or set. By contrast, having a separate compound word for every conceivable interval or set to be created with *uchi* would mean a rather large number of compounds which, if theoretically possible, would be unwieldy. Compound words are not substitution frames and are not amenable to regular, habitual recomposition. Indeed, that is what makes them words. Lexicalization can be thought of as a kind of minting—pressing into a compact, hard form—so that the sign so minted is handily used and retains its shape over many uses, in many contexts. When *uchi* combines with another term to form a compound lexical item, this is a function of the currency in social discourse of the corresponding compound concept as a regularly isolable and referrable entity. The genius of syntactic expression, on the other hand, allows for freer substitution of all manner of units which may in other contexts be conceptually unrelated to *uchi*. A looser frame, in which many different kinds of referents can be freely substituted, works better for handling the vast number of concepts that are *not* so regularly conceived in terms of bounded containers as to warrant their own *uchi-*

compound. The looser the structure, the less the need for semantic relevance among the terms that are joined.[14]

Grammatical constructions built around the word *uchi* take that word as syntactic head in a noun phrase of the form /specifier X + *uchi*/ 'interval-set X'. The preceding specifier takes the form of one of the three major predicate types, viz. nominal (*sono hi no uchi* 'interval of that day', *sannin no uchi* 'set of three people'), adjectival (*wakai uchi* 'interval of being young'), and verbal (*hon o yonde iru uchi* 'interval of reading a book'), as well as bound demonstrative determiners like *kono* (e.g., *sono uchi* 'that interval-set'). Whether it is an interval or a set that is specified is established with the meaning of the specifier and/or the larger context. This meaning is further clarified in the frame within which this /specifier X + *uchi*/ construction is employed, so that for intervals, we often find the construction marked with locative particle *ni* 'in', to specify the point at which something occurs, for example, *Yonde iru uchi NI wakatta* 'It came clear to me while I was reading'.

While intervals are spaces within which events occur, sets typically are not. Instead, sets are referred to as the range within which some other condition is attributed or some action described. A set is often subordinated to the gerund of the copula, *de*, as in *Ano sannin no uchi DE, Tanaka ga ichiban ii*, literally 'being the set of those three people, Tanaka is best' (= 'Of the three, Tanaka is best'). Or, *A to B to C no uchi DE, dore o toru?* 'Inside of [= 'among'] A, B, and C, which will you take?' The metaphor implicit in /*uchi* X + *de*/ is that X is a container with an internal structure of members, 'given' (*de*) which, something holds true of or happens to one or some of those members. Sets can also be 'entered', as illustrated by expressions like *daihyoosaku no uchi NI hairu* 'is among [her] representative works'.

The last domain listed for *uchi*, that of "partitive," is actually a subtype of the use that demarcates a bounded interval or set. Each example here indicates a subinterval or subset of some implicit larger whole. (See *Uchi*, Table 7.) All but the last two of these examples are compound words, shaped for ready use in particular domains. While most of them are neutral with regard to social valuation, there is such value in the notion that the *uchi* portion of a payment or delivery due is the part most under one's control, and it is more basic—a precondition for completing the transaction. There is also value in the two words from the noh theater and the incense ceremony, which employ *uchi* to indicate that this subset ('ten incenses', '100 noh plays') is primary, principal, and more important than others outside it. In sum, then, objects, events, people, and information described as *uchi* tend to be conceived of as *enclosed, nearby, accessible, familiar,* and *controlled,* in an engaged realm in which *informality* is the rule. That which is contained is valued

UCHI, Table 7
Partitive (Bounded Subintervals/Subsets)

uchibarai	'partial payment, money partly paid'
uchikin to shite juuman-en	'¥10,000 as down payment'
uchiage	'partial payment for goods/of a loan'
uchiwatashi	'partial delivery'
uchiiri	'partial payment of a bill'
uchigashi	'cash advance'
uchigawa	'tributary (of a river)'
uchitokumi	'primary ten incenses' (incense ceremony)
uchihyakuban	'primary 100 noh plays'
juunin no uchi kunin made	'nine out of ten people'
kyuuryoo no uchi kara chokin suru	'put part of one's income into savings'

as *important*, more so than what exists outside. Someone else's *uchi* is one to which one has not gained entry, and thus *soto*, typically *detached, inaccessible, concealed*, and *uncontrolled*.

Now that we have seen a bit of the inside story, let us have a look on the outside. Again, the catalog is not exhaustive and the categories or domains are informally defined.

Soto: A Catalog of Uses by Domain

The way in which the term *soto* is used in the spatial domain resembles what we observed of *uchi*: it describes a *position* relative to some frame or other entity, or it describes a *shape*. As with *uchi*, when *soto* is the first element in a compound noun, it indicates the position or shape associated with what the second element names. For example, *sotokazari* 'exterior decorating' is *kazari* 'decorating' on the 'outside', as *sotomata* 'inside of the leg outward' is *mata* 'inside of the leg' held in an outward-facing posture, and *sotosen* 'concave drawknife' is a *sen* that creates a convex cut, a surface that resembles part of the 'outside' of a container.

The first five examples in the list in *Soto* Table 1 contrast 'indoors' to 'outdoors' in the context of a house, and are perhaps representative of the first uses learned by children. Some examples that follow, beginning with *soto kara* 'from [the] outside', indicate that *soto* is one's starting point in approaching an *uchi*; in *soto kara nagameta dake da* 'I've only seen it from the outside', it is clear that gazing on something from without does not measure up to seeing it from within. Not all these expressions have counterparts in *uchi-*; there is, for example, no **uchikasa* 'inner penumbra' of heavenly bodies, and no **uchiera* 'concealed gills', presumably since these are either contradictory or the unmarked, normative case, and not in need of a morpheme that overtly specifies position.

Spatial

uchi no soto de   'outside the house, outdoors'
soto de asobu   'play outdoors'
soto de matte   'Wait outside.'
soto wa samui   'It's cold outside.'
soto wa moo kurai   'It's dark outside already.'
ana kara soto e hikidashita   '[We] pulled it out of its den.'
soto kara akeru   'open from the outside'
soto kara to ni kagi o kakeru   'lock the door from the outside'
soto kara nagameta dake da   'I've only seen it from the outside.'
sototsunagi   'outdoor hitching (post)'
sotobenjo   'outhouse'
sotonagashi   'outdoor (washing) sink'
sotobiraki ni naru   'opens out'
soto-omote   'folding [material] so that outer surface is exposed'
sotobari   'cloth or paper stretched over a frame'
sotoage   'outside hem'
sotonori   'outer measurements (from outer edge to outer edge)'
sotopasu   'outer calipers'
sotobei   'outer wall'
sotogaki   'outer brush wall'
sotogooshi   'outer lattice'
sotogakoi   'outer walls'
sotojiro   'outer part of castle'
sotowa   'outer circle'
sotobori   'outer moat'
sotoroji   'outer garden' (tea gardens)
sotowaku   'outer frame'
sotoi   'outer boundary, periphery'
sotopoketto   'outer pocket'
sotobutokoro   'outer "pocket" in folds of kimono'
sotochootsugai   'outer hinges on body armor'
sotoguruma   'outside wheel(s)', i.e., 'sidewheeler' (steamboat)
sotoumi   'open (not enclosed) sea', 'deep sea'
sotoiwashi   'fish caught on open sea (off mid-Honshu)'
sotomawari   'outer (train, beltway) loop'
sotoido   'well located off one's own land'
sotokasa   'outer penumbra (of sun, moon)'
sotoera   'exposed gills'
sotomomo   'outer thigh'
sotogama   'inside of legs facing/exposed outward'
sotomata   'inside of the leg outward' (toes pointed outward, standing 'ten to two')
sotogawa   'outer side' ('other party')
sotoire   'outer of two nested containers'
sotokazari   'exterior decorating'
sotogamae   'outside appearance'
sotogakari   'external appearance'
sotosen   'concave drawknife' (named for its con*vex* cut)
sotomuki   'facing outward'

Note: Others listed in "*Uchi* with *Soto*, Table 1: Spatial."

SOTO, TABLE 2
Social, Domestic

---

metta ni soto e denai '[S/he] almost never goes out [of the house]'.
shokuji wa taitei soto de sumaseru '[I] usually eat out [away from home]'.
sotogirai 'is loath to go out [of the house]', 'person of such a disposition'
soto o ie ni suru 'be rarely at home' (lit., 'make the outside one's house[hold]')
sotosuzume 'someone who never stays at home' (lit., 'outside sparrow')
sotomawari o yaru 'make business rounds (outside home)'
sotomago 'grandchild of a daughter (who lives *out* of the household)'
sotoburo 'taking a bath outside the home'

SOTO, TABLE 3
Psychological/Attitudinal

---

uchi hadaka de mo soto-nishiki 'even if naked at home, brocade outside'
uchi-hadakari no soto-subori 'bossy at home, meek outside'
uchi-benkei no soto-beso 'a lion at home, a bellybutton (= the opposite) outside'
uchi-hirogari no soto-subomari 'expansive/outgoing/bossy at home, closed tight
   when outside'
sotozura wa yoi no desu ga, uchizura wa warui '[S/he] is affable outside' (lit., 'outside demeanor is good'), 'but is difficult at home' (lit., 'at-home demeanor is
   bad').
soto-mizu no uchi hirogari 'naive of the world, expansive/outgoing/bossy at
   home'

As in the list of spatial uses in *Soto* Table 1 (and with *uchi*), the fact
that space is so often defined according to social criteria makes for some
overlap and blurring of domains. Since the first several examples here
take the home as *uchi* and use *soto* in contrast to it, I have listed them
under "social/domestic," despite the fact that they are *soto*, that is,
non-*uchi* expressions. (See *Soto* Table 2.) In the use of *sotogirai* 'is loath
to go out [of the house]' to refer to the *person* who holds that attitude,
we have a common metonym, in which the name of the attitude is used
to refer to the person who holds that attitude; this has already come up
in the corresponding *uchigirai* 'is loath to stay at home'. As these examples suggest, *soto* too is used in the expression of attitudes. (See *Soto*,
Table 3.)

These examples describe attitudes and personal character in terms of
the domestic and nondomestic sides of social behavior. We have already
discussed the rhetoric of their nuances for *uchi* in *Uchi*, Table 3, above.
It is interesting that every psychological/attitudinal expression that uses
the term *soto* also uses *uchi*. In other words, there are apparently no non-
contrastive uses of *soto* in this domain.

In contrast to *Soto* Table 3, none of *Soto* Table 4's items save *sotogawa*

SOTO, TABLE 4
Social, Nondomestic

sotomezurashii	'unaccustomed to going out'
sotogawa	'other party'
soto goyoo	'business outside, on master's orders'
sotoaruki	'wandering about town'
sotode	'going out'
sotonagashi	'making (guard's) rounds'
sotomawari	'make rounds of corporate customers (leave office)'
sotodomari	'staying overnight somewhere other than home'
sotomachi	'*un*regulated, unofficial redlight district'
sotodaka	'taxation on land cultivated *after* tax reforms'

SOTO, TABLE 5
Partitive (Bounded Subsets)

sototokumi	'secondary ten incenses' (incense ceremony)
sotohyakuban	'second 100 noh plays'

'other party' (which is also used in the spatial sense of 'outer side') has a corresponding *uchi* expression. They are all unique to *soto* used in the social domain. If we contrast the "social/nondomestic" list shown in *Soto* Table 4 with the corresponding list for *uchi* (*Uchi*, Table 4), we note that many of the items that lengthen the *uchi* list, such as the compounds with -*maku* 'curtain' and -*wa* 'ring, circle', are missing here, no doubt because those expressions are employed in talking about acts done exclusively for or by people on the *in*side. The reason that the *soto*-based expressions listed here lack any *uchi* counterparts is presumably the same principle cited in reference to *soto-era* 'external gills' in *Soto* Table 1 above. In such instances, *soto* is used to indicate the off-norm, marked case (e.g., *sotonagashi* 'outside sink', *sotodomari* 'staying overnight outside the home', *sotomachi* 'unregulated redlight district'). Apparently no special term exists for the normative, unmarked correspondents of these terms, no equivalent for 'indoor sink', 'sleeping at home', or 'regulated redlight district'. The two expressions shown in *Soto* Table 5 correspond to *uchitokumi* 'primary ten incenses' and *uchihyakuban* 'primary one hundred noh plays'. The *soto*- alternant names the category that contains the items (incenses, plays) of less importance.

We are left with two domains in which the term *uchi*, but not *soto*, is attested. These are *uchi* "temporal intervals" (*Uchi*, Table 5) and "bounded sets" (*Uchi*, Table 6), both of which depend crucially on the quality of boundedness for their meaning. I have suggested that the *uchi/soto* habitus, like Lakoff and Johnson's "container" schema, involves three identifiable elements: an inside, an outside, and a boundary that separates them. In the domains in which the terms *uchi* and *soto* are used, the compound words and phrases in which they figure focus on the inside, the outside, or both, as the base concept warrants. The *uchi* domains of *Uchi* Tables 5 and 6, however, depend in their expression not only on the contents of the 'inside' being accessible and familiar, but also on the *boundary* being in focus. In other words, these particular meanings can be created with the word *uchi* not only because its contents are accessible and familiar, but because the boundary or limit is so central to its meaning, as it not with *soto*. For these two sets of uses, the boundary feature of the *uchi/soto* schema is crucial.

That no such concepts are expressed with *soto* can be explained by the fact that an 'outside' is not bounded to the extent that an 'inside' is, and thus is not so clearly defined as an 'inside' is. To be sure, on one level of analysis, *soto* entails an *uchi*, as *uchi* entails a *soto*. And, logically speaking, both entail a boundary that separates them. But of the two, *uchi* depends for its image as what it is—an enclosure—on the presence of a boundary *on most sides*. A prototypical *uchi* space is entirely enclosed, bounded in every direction. *Soto* spaces, on the other hand, have a boundary at the point where they meet a corresponding *uchi*, but in all other directions, bounding is simply not specified. If it were, we would have an enclosure—an *uchi*. In terms of boundary, *soto* is simply not as well defined as *uchi*. Consequently, for expressing images or notions to which the notion of a boundary is crucial—such as limits, bounded intervals, or sets—the image that accompanies the term *soto* is less possessed of the very element crucial to indicating those limits. A boundary is definitive for *uchi* to an extent—literally, on most sides—that it is not for *soto*.

Since the catalogs presented in this chapter depend on just a few dictionaries (albeit one of them unabridged), it is unlikely that *uchi*-based expressions at any time outnumbered those based on *soto* with exactly the ratio that emerges here. On the other hand, if even a dictionary survey reveals this kind of discrepancy, it seems likely that, on the whole, *uchi* has always been the more productive term of the two, by a considerable margin. This is most likely a consequence of the human tendency to cultivate an *uchi* kind of space in the world, to differentiate, categorize, name, and otherwise detail those parts of the environment in which we are closely engaged—that which is nearby, accessible, over time familiar, knowable, and therefore manipulable and controllable. It is no less than a preferred perspective with proven survival value.

Insofar as our bodies are the indexical ground when we first learn to distinguish an inside from an outside, and insofar as taking a perspective that is grounded *outside* the self—imagining that one is standing in another *uchi*—is a skill that is later to develop (e.g., deixis that is not speaker-based and anaphora), looking outward from an inside has a kind of existential and experiential primacy. For this reason, *uchi* is more likely as a place to look *from*, as a person engages and appropriates the world. Insofar as it is in this primal experience that the container schema is first learned and from which it is then projected onto relations in the external world, we identify with an *uchi* perspective and tend to regard *soto* as "out there," observable but less familiar, detached from ourselves and what we know best, and less under our control. As a place to stand, *uchi* is the stable, familiar norm; out in *soto*, the footing is less sure.

The final lists in this catalog of expressions (shown in *Uchi* with *Soto* Tables 1–4) summarize cases in which *uchi* and *soto* are used together contrastively, with a shared third term. In most cases, the contrastive frame is lexical, as when either *uchi-* or *soto-* is the variable first morpheme in compound words in which the second element is invariant, for example, *uchimawari* 'inner (beltway, train) loop' versus *sotomawari* 'outer (beltway, train) loop', or *uchipasu* 'inside calipers' versus *sotopasu* 'outside calipers'. In other instances, they occur as opposed concepts in a single phrase or clause, as in the proverbs that describe people in terms of how they behave 'inside' and 'outside'. As might be expected, many items already surveyed occur in such pairs. Nor, of course, do we find contrastive *uchi/soto* pairs used to express "temporal intervals" or "bounded sets."

UCHI WITH *SOTO*: A CATALOG OF CONTRASTIVE PAIRS

As observed earlier, the primary significance of either *uchi* (or *soto*)[15] as the initial term in a compound is to indicate position or shape of the following head. In the case of position, the head in the compound is 'inside' or 'outside' with reference to its opposite. For example, *uchibori* 'inner moat' is 'inside' the *sotobori* 'outer moat', and closer to the castle that a *hori* 'moat' surrounds. In the case of shape as well, the *uchi-* alternative specifies that its referent (the second element in the compound) faces or is shaped 'inward', in contrast to the 'outward' facing or shaping of the *soto-* alternative, as in *uchikatagiri* 'concave cut' and *sotokatagiri* 'convex cut'. As might be expected, pairs that contrast position outnumber by far those that contrast shape. But compounds that name things outnumber those that name pure positions or orientations, like *uchi-/soto-muki* 'facing inward/outward'. (See *Uchi* with *Soto*, Table 1.)

Why should there be so few contrastive *uchi/soto* pairs in the social, domestic domain shown in *Uchi* with *Soto*, Table 2? There are undoubtedly a few others, but probably few things, people, and behaviors are regarded as equally common to both 'inside' and 'outside' the household.

UCHI with SOTO, Table 1
Spatial

uchisoto 'inside and outside'

doa wa uchisoto ni aku 'the door opens inward and outward'

uchi-/soto-zura 'interior/exterior surface', 'at-home visage/outside visage'

uchi-/soto-gooshi 'inside/outside lattice'

uchi-/soto-mawari 'inner/outer (beltway, train) loop'

uchi-/soto-niwa 'inner/outer garden'

uchi-/soto-bori 'inner/outer moat'

uchi-/soto-gawa 'inner/outer sides', 'our side/their side'

uchi-/soto-gake 'inner/outer leg *sumoo* throw' (There are many more such terms, and some are used in *juudoo* as well.)

uchi-/soto-muki 'facing inward/outward'

uchi-/soto-shirasu 'white pebbles inside and outside apron skirting the noh stage'

uchi-/soto-chootsugai 'inner and outer hinges (on body armor)'

uchi-/soto-buro 'indoor/outdoor bath'

uchi-/soto-wa 'inner/outer ring, circle'

uchi-/soto-momo 'inner/outer thigh'

uchi-/soto-sanzun 'inner/outer part of ankle area'

uchi-/soto-butokoro 'inner/outer "pocket" in folds of kimono'

uchi-/soto-sumi 'inner/outer corners' (seating positions at tea ceremony)

uchi-/soto-setsuin 'inner/outer toilet' (for a tea room)

uchi-/soto-roji 'inner/outer garden' (for a tea room)

uchi-/soto-bari 'paper or cloth stretched inside/over a frame'

uchi-/soto-be 'inside/outside', 'this side/that side'

uchi-/soto-misu 'inner/outer boxes at *kabuki* theater'

uchi-/soto-yama 'settled mountain villages/unsettled mountains'

uchi-/soto-miyoshi 'inner/outer timbers of bow of boat'

uchi-/soto-doi 'inner (concealed)/outer (visible) roof gutter'

uchi-/soto-waku 'inside/outside frame'

uchi-/soto-katagiri 'cut with graver facing inside/outside of cut'

uchi-/soto-sogi 'cutting inward/outward (tips of protruding shrine rafters)', 'shrine rafters cut inward/outward on their tips'

uchi-/soto-sen 'convex/concave drawknife'

uchi-/soto-nori 'measurements to inner/outer edges'

uchi-/soto-pasu 'inside/outside calipers'

uchi-/soto-mata 'inside of legs facing inward/exposed outward'

uchi-/soto-gama 'inside of legs facing inward/exposed outward'

uchi-/soto-wa 'inside of legs facing inward/exposed outward'

uchi-/soto-hachimonji 'inside of legs facing inward/exposed outward'

UCHI with SOTO, Table 2
Social, Domestic

---

uchi-/soto-mago 'grandchild = child of household successor/grandchild = child of child who "married out"'
uchi-/soto-buro 'at home/public bathing'

UCHI with SOTO, Table 3
Social, Nondomestic

---

uchi-/soto no saburai 'warrior allies from our own ranks and without'
uchi-/soto-gawa 'our side/their side'
uchi-/soto-muki 'for inside/outside consumption' (information)
uchi-otori no to-medeta 'inferior in substance, impressive in appearance'

UCHI with SOTO, Table 4
Partitive

---

uchi-/soto-beri 'amount of grain lost in hulling grain/ratio of loss to remainder'
uchi-/soto-tokumi 'primary/secondary ten incenses' (incense ceremony)
uchi-/soto-hyakuban 'primary/secondary 100 noh plays'

For *uchi* X contrasted with *soto* X in the psychological and attitudinal domain, please consult *Soto*, Table 3 (p. 58 above). *Uchi* with *Soto*, Table 3 also repeats expressions and uses already introduced.

Finally, there are a few *uchi/soto* contrasts in the partitive. (See *Uchi* with *Soto*, Table 4.)

Conclusions

If we review the concepts that are specified, described, or otherwise modified with the terms *uchi* and *soto* in the preceding three taxonomies of *uchi* expressions, *soto* expressions, and *uchi/soto* expressions, certain patterns emerge. Judging from the concepts *uchi* participates in expressing, this word has been associated with notions such as FULLY BOUNDED; INDOORS, NEARBY, ENCLOSED, CONCAVE, DARK; DOMESTIC, FAMILY, INTRALINEAL, "US"; CASUAL, COMFORTABLE, INFORMAL, FAMILIAR, PRIVATE, INDULGENT, FREE; CONCEALED, SECRET, PRIVILEGED, DETAILED, KNOWN, SHARED, MUTUAL BENEFIT; LOCAL, LIMITED, CONTROLLED, SPECIFIABLE, ENUMERABLE, PART OF LARGER WHOLE; SACRED, SPECIAL, and PRIMARY. A summary review of *soto* finds it used in the company of such concepts as OUTSIDE AN ENCLOSURE, OUTDOORS, OPEN, PROTRUDING, CONVEX; EXTRALINEAL, NONDOMESTIC, "THEM," SECULAR, PRO-

SUMMARY TABLE
Lexical *Uchi* vs. *Soto*, Regular Conceptual Contrasts

UCHI : SOTO =

INDOORS : OUTDOORS

CLOSED : OPEN

EXPERIENCED : OBSERVED

HIDDEN : REVEALED

FULLY BOUNDED : PARTLY BOUNDED

CLEARLY DEFINED : LESS CLEARLY DEFINED

LIMITED : LIMIT-IRRELEVANT

SACRED : SECULAR (Cf. imperial palace vs. outer buildings, outer shrine vs. inner
          shrine at Ise, etc.)

SELF(-VES) : OTHER(S)

LINEAL FAMILY : EXTRALINEAL FAMILY

FAMILIAR : UNFAMILIAR

"US" : "THEM"

PRIVATE : PUBLIC

INCLUDED : EXCLUDED

KNOWN : UNKNOWN

INFORMED : UNINFORMED

CONTROLLED : UNCONTROLLED

ENGAGED : DETACHED

EARLY/PRIMARY : LATE/SECONDARY

FANE; REMOVED, EXPOSED, VISIBLE; CUSTOMERS, WELL-BEHAVED, RE-STRAINED, MAINTAINING APPEARANCES; "ON THE TOWN"; PERIPHERAL, FOREIGN; LESS KNOWN, LESS DETAILED, UNDIFFERENTIATED; UNCON-TROLLED; and SECONDARY. These associations show regular contrast, and can be arrayed as a single proportion that holds across a variety of domains. (See Summary Table: *Uchi* vs. *Soto*.)

Listing such compounds, collocations, and grammatical constructions as examined above has its tedious side, but doing so reveals affinities and oppositions that might otherwise go unremarked. These are the symbolic values we find inside and outside the boundary in the *uchi/soto* schema, as revealed by representative usage of these two complementary words, recorded in Japan across a variety of lived domains since the eighth century.

It is the *affinities* common to these values to which we turn in conclusion. What has happened over the centuries is that the words indicative of domain, which have combined syntagmatically with the word *uchi* or *soto*, have thereby come to *associate paradigmatically with one another*. In the company they all keep with *uchi*, for example, such concepts as NEARBY, ENCLOSED, DOMESTIC, "US," CASUAL, FAMILIAR, KNOWN, DE-

TAILED, SHARED, LOCAL, CONTROLLED, SACRED, and PRIMARY (as listed just above) themselves constitute a natural, evolved category. Those elements that are used in syntagmatic combination with the term *soto,* too, cluster together in paradigmatic relation, with OUTDOOR spaces associated with OPEN, UNBOUNDED, REVEALED, and PUBLIC, as well as UNFAMILIAR, LESS DETAILED, UNINFORMED, UNSHARED, UNCONTROLLED, SECULAR, EXCLUDED, and SECONDARY. Both these natural categories have emerged, as other social structures do, in a coevolution of cultural tradition and social praxis. Their stability is maintained where received custom is applied in meeting the needs of new contexts.

Some of the items in the preceding catalog are no longer in current use; others, yet to be invented, will no doubt appear. But any new extension of the meanings of *uchi* and *soto* has the foregoing associations to fit in with or to contend against; projections of either concept into new domains will be facilitated or hindered by this historically grown net of relations, which has been woven, rended, patched, and rewoven, in lived communities. New metaphors, metonymies, and synecdoches based on *uchi* or *soto* will emerge from somewhere in this habitus and, like the present members, will be created in abduction and analogy. Some, like those of the domains "social," "temporal intervals," "bounded sets," and "partitive," will be more abstract—which is to say versatile across more domains—than others. Still more removed from the spatial domain are those grammatical meanings that are structured in terms of the *uchi/soto* schema.

The Japanese habitus of *uchi/soto* constitutes for Japanese culture what Gregory Bateson (1979, 8) has called a "pattern which connects," a pattern of patterns. An *uchi/soto* metapattern insinuates itself when a variety of different aspects of communicative behavior appear to pattern homologously. In biology, of course, homology is a sort of anatomical analogy, in which the relations between the parts of one organism resemble the relations between corresponding parts of another organism; "such resemblance is considered to be evidence of evolutionary relatedness" (Bateson 1979, 250). For example, we may speak of a fish's "head" based on the homology we observe between the relative positions of its eyes and mouth and those of our own eyes and mouths. The fish's eyes, mouth, and head resemble our own less in phenomenal detail than in the formal relations that obtain among them. Similarly, in language, we may say that the preposition *in* of "in school this year," "in the kitchen," and "in trouble" is the same *in,* despite these differences in semantic domain. The *relation* expressed between the location and the located, we feel, is somehow the same, analogous. Likewise with "accusative" (actually a kind of scope) marker *o* in *Hon o kaesu* 'return a book', *Hashi o wataru* 'cross a bridge', and *Ima o ikiru* 'Live the present'. Semantically, the scope in each clause differs from the others, as undergoer, path, and range, respectively. Users of the language have nevertheless come to categorize each with the same *o*. In the case of *uchi* and *soto*, too, it is the formal relation that is of definitive importance, so that whether the domain is that of the human body, the physical and spatial world, social relations, or an exchange of information, the relations peculiar to each are related to one another analogically. If this is true of a wide variety of domains—such as social interaction and lexico-grammatical structure— the *uchi/soto* schema qualifies as a pattern that connects other patterns, a *metapattern*. In its lived quality, we refer to it as *habitus*.

I should finally like to point out that values associated paradigmatically with the words *uchi* and *soto* are also regularly expressed in a number of pairs of words that are unrelated to the terms *uchi* or *soto* in any etymological sense. The internal structure of these pairs is analogically *uchi/soto*, for they too assume an inside, an outside, and a dividing boundary and, what is more, associate the same sorts of physical, social, and psychological values just reviewed with their own insides and outsides. Pairs of semantically opposed nouns such as *omote* 'surface, front' and *ura* 'inside, back side' are one type of example, which Bachnik and Molasky touch on in this volume. But the phenomenon is hardly limited to nouns, as is evident, for example, in the many expressions based on intransitive verbs *hairu* 'enter' and *deru* 'emerge'. A few examples of how *hairu* and *deru* are used will suggest how congruent their own opposed uses are with those already observed of the words *uchi* and *soto*.

Omote-zata ni deru, literally 'get out into front-side treatment', refers to inside or private information becoming publicly known. News, too, will 'emerge' into a public place where it is accessible to all (*nyuusu ni deru* 'appear in the news', *shinbun ni deru* 'appear in the newspaper'). To attend a meeting or seminar, or to enter a competition—all public venues—is to *deru* 'go out' into it. The warning expressed in *nanigoto mo uchiwa ni yaru beki* 'Better keep within bounds in all things' has a *soto*-focused counterpart in the well-known proverb *deru kui/kugi wa utareru* 'the peg/nail that protrudes gets pounded'. The moral is that one should stay unobtrusively inside with everyone else. The proverb is all the more coherent and resonant for its links with the many lived, social contexts that are shaped and known in an *uchi/soto* kind of way. Conversely, the verb *hairu* 'go in, enter' is used in expressing many concepts of an *uchi* sort: entering, belonging, fitting in, and so on. It is employed in nonvolitional contexts to express being included in a set, as we saw in *daihyoosaku no uchi ni hairu* 'is among [her] representative writings', and also in a volitional sense, as in *furo ni hairu* 'take a bath' or *kurabu ni hairu* 'join a club'.

The same sort of 'inside/outside' opposition can be found in the transitive verbs *dasu* 'put/take out' and *ireru* 'put in, insert', which are etymologically related to intransitive *deru* and *hairu*, respectively. *Dasu* is used to express such meanings as 'expose' (*hiza o dasu* 'expose one's knees', *sita o dasu* 'stick out one's tongue'), 'send out' (*tegami o dasu* 'mail a letter'), and 'put out' (*hon o dasu* 'put out a book', *shinbun ni dasu* 'publish [it] in the newspaper'). The common feature here is putting something *out* into an area beyond one's body, control, knowledge, *uchi*: into public view, into custody of the postal service, and so on. The same verb is also used routinely in the sense of 'handing in' or 'submitting' things (e.g., *shukudai o dasu* 'hand in one's homework'), of 'exhibiting' a piece of art at a show, of 'serving' a certain dish (e.g., at a restaurant), or 'producing' casualities (e.g., an earthquake). The similarity of such concepts to those expressed with intransitive *deru* are apparent. And as with *deru*, these few sample contexts just scratch the surface.

If *dasu* removes things to an 'outside', *ireru* 'put in, insert' is for getting them 'inside'. *Ireru* can be used to denote 'inserting' one's hand into one's pocket, 'putting' cream into coffee, 'placing' someone into a particular group (as when either 'admitting' or 'placing' a child into a school), or to express 'accepting' or 'acceding to' a view that differs from one's own (literally 'letting it in'). *Ireru* participates in the expression of inclusion, too, as in volitional *nakama ni ireru* 'let/include [someone] into one's circle' or somewhat differently in nonvolitional *watashi o irete, go-nin kazoku desu* 'Including myself, it's a family of five'. *Ireru* is also used when 'paying' interest 'into' an account, and when 'casting' a vote 'in' favor of a candidate. *Ireru* differs from *dasu* as *hairu* differs from *deru*. Etymologically related *ireru* and *hairu* refer to events that take an inside as their goal, while *dasu* and *deru* denote departure *from* an inside for a goal that is outside. Like the terms *uchi* and *soto*, the transitive members of these two pairs of verbs also participate in a variety of compounds and collocations that play major roles in the language of everyday life. As a productive suffix, for example, -*dasu* indicates inceptive aspect, as in *shaberi-dasu* 'start to talk', and -*ireru*, directionality, as in *kaki-ireru* 'enter, write in, fill out' and *kai-ireru* 'purchase, lay in'.

These and many more expressions like them bear a family resemblance to the uses of the terms *uchi* and *soto* surveyed above, and also to certain grammatical distinctions, which are described in chapter 11, the final chapter of this volume. They project the same kind of dual perspective, including the values associated with each side, onto a variety of otherwise unrelated domains, which range from spatial, physical, and social to abstract and grammatical. *Uchi/soto* is, I think, as good a name as any for this family of related concepts, which Japanese people maintain by daily use, in their social lives, particularly in their language. As we have seen in this brief tour of uses of the terms *uchi* and *soto*, metaphor and other tropes have spread this opposition far and wide through the language, from common nouns used in prototypically "nouny" ways, to a number of very basic grammatical uses, such as *kyoo no uchi ni* 'within today' and *ikanai uchi ni* 'before going'.

In the day-in, day-out activity of communication, which is to say, of pointing out, referring, naming, and renaming such aspects of our experience as require it, people are constantly reestablishing, extending, or allowing to atrophy the categories with which they press the flux of phenomenal experience into coherent parts and wholes. The lexicon of a language can thus be understood as the distillate of a culturally and socially negotiated process of categorization. It is not surprising that the orientational habitus of *uchi/soto* should be widespread in the vocabulary with which Japanese society sustains itself. As I shall argue in the conclusion to this volume, the same *uchi/soto* habitus also informs distinctions drawn by the more abstract structures of Japanese grammar.[16] And these lexical and grammatical phenomena themselves, of course, index the dynamic, evanescent dance of social life itself.

Notes

1. This research was conducted in 1990–91 under support from a Seed Grant from The Ohio State University, a Fulbright Grant administered through the Japan–U.S. Educational Commission, and a Research Grant from the Social Science Research Council, for which I am very grateful. Thanks to co-editor Jane Bachnik and to my wife Shelley for their helpful criticisms and suggestions.

The words of the epigraph (*Fuku wa uchi! Oni wa soto!*) are shouted as beans are tossed out of the house, in an exorcism ritual that is performed every year on February 3. For a key to abbreviations and orthographic conventions followed in this and the other linguistically oriented chapters (Wetzel's, Sukle's, and Quinn's closing contribution), see the "Key to Abbreviations and Orthographic Conventions," p. xvii.

2. Bourdieu has said that he developed the notion of *habitus* in order to refer to social life as incorporated in individuals and, at the same time, avoid "the scientifically quite absurd opposition between individual and society" (1990, 31). It is "a system of lasting, transposable dispositions, . . . a matrix of perceptions, appreciations, and actions" (1977, 82–83). William Hanks's (1987, 677) characterization of habitus suggests its relevance for our project:

Habitus has the . . . potential to generate homologous formations across different cultural fields, relating, for example, the calendars of cooking, daily tasks, times of day, and the same set of symbolic relations and modes of practice (rhythm of execution, sequence, duration, and so forth), with respect to which they are schematically equivalent. Bourdieu represents these equivalences as variant realizations of a single type of structure, summarized in his synoptic diagrams (Bourdieu 1977, figures 3–9). Being grounded in cultural schemata that recur across distinct fields of action, habitus is logically prior to any actual event of practice. At the same time, *it is subject to innovation and strategic manipulation in practice, such that it is a product as well as a resource that changes over time* (emphasis added).

A similar idea is explored in contexts chemical and biological, as well as social, in Sheldrake 1988.

3. *Collocations* are phrases and clauses in which a word typically combines with a limited set of other words. Knowing the parts of a collocation is enough to understand it (e.g., "to be worth the trouble, to be worth the bother"), while this is not true of an idiom ("to be worth while"). Cf. Bolinger 1975, 102.

4. Limiting the survey that follows to the terms *uchi* and *soto* restricts our study of the lexical expression of the concepts *uchi/soto* to but one segment of a larger part of the vocabulary. Excluded from consideration, for example, will be Sino-Japanese words that express the same concepts by including as one of their formants the character 内 or 外 , and reading it not as "*uchi*" or "*soto*" but as "*nai*" or "*gai*." Since, unlike the terms *uchi* and *soto, nai* and *gai* are not usually used as independent words, their role in the lexicon is more specialized.

5. In the sense in which George Lakoff and Mark Johnson (1980), among others, use the term, which is to say broadly, in no way restricted to mere rhetorical flourish. From their perspective, the absolute opposition of "literal" meaning to "metaphorical" meaning is the product of too restricted a vision. Certain very common expressions are based on our bodily experience, as we live it, for example, the many based on the metaphors "Up is good," "Down is not," and are thus existentially more basic than others which, while still metaphorical, are perspectively independent of our bodies, for example, "A project is a building," with entailed foundation, exterior, interior, stories, and so on.

6. See, for example, Bates, Camaioni, and Volterra 1979; Givón 1973, 1979; Lakoff and Johnson 1980; Lakoff 1987; Sweetser 1990; Traugott 1982; Traugott 1989; and Volterra and Antinucci 1979, among others.

7. In such a survey, it is necessary to rely on dictionaries, despite their shortcomings. Since even the newest and largest dictionary tells us nothing about frequency of use, and grows quickly out of date, what it reveals of how a word fits into the communicative ecology of its community will be fragmented and partial, as Aitchison notes (1987, 14). Nevertheless, provided one's aims are less ambitious than accounting for how people learn, know, and use words (Aitchison's "mental lexicon"), dictionaries can help. A survey will do nicely enough if the aim is to outline such records as exist of a word's uses.

8. These are named for the shape of the cut they make: a concave scooping cut for the *uchi-sen*, and a convex or rounding-off cut for the *soto-sen*.

9. Earlier attestations were examined in: *Manyooshuu* (759), *Kokinshuu* (907), *Utsuho monogatari* (mid-Heian), *Taketori monogatari* (early Heian), *Toodaiji fuushoo monkoo* (early Heian), *Sanboo e-kotoba* (984), *Genji monogatari* (ca. 1010), *Ookagami* (late Heian), *Rin'yooshuu* (1178), and *Heike monogatari* (a text oral in origin, probably written down in some form between 1219 and 1242).

10. See Bachnik's introduction to this volume for a more detailed discussion of C. S. Peirce's semiotic. In Peirce's conception, a *symbol* is a sign that stands in a relation to its referent that is less obvious than it is with the other sign types, *icons*, and *indexes*. Symbolic signs need not be grounded in the situation in which they are used, in contrast to indexical signs (e.g., the speaker as ground for "this," "that," or her present point in time as ground for "now," "then," etc.). Nor does a symbolic sign mimic in its form perceived features of the concept it represents, in contrast to the icon (e.g., the vowel length in "loooong" is an iconic sign; the word "long" is a symbol). The symbol's abstraction away from the particularities of occasion-of-use and the signified gives symbolic representation its great flexibility, which "can turn reality over on its beam ends beyond what is possible through actions or images" (Bruner 1966, 11).

11. These terms index more than grammatical person, specifically some aspect of the speaker's social (*uchi/soto*) relation to the referent. The indexical use was originally motivated by the term's *symbolic* value. Other terms of personal reference are not only indexical in origin, but extensions from simpler, more purely spatial deictics, such as *anata* 'you' (formerly 'direction away from speaker and listener'), *omae* 'you' (formerly 'honored-in-front'), or *kare* 'he' (formerly 'the one [we know/removed from speaker and listener]') and *kanojo* 'she' (formerly 'that female [we know/removed from speaker and listener]'). And while *anata* and *omae* take the speaker as ground zero, they express an *uchi/soto* indexing. *Omae*, once a distancing polite term, has been reinterpreted ironically to express intimacy or insult, depending on whether the person so addressed is in-group or out-group to the speaker. *Anata* 'you', earlier a distal directional pronoun ('that direction away from us', equivalent to present-day *achira*) was reinterpreted as an indirect means of address and reference.

12. Rosenberger (this volume) cites scholarship that identifies the "poles of meaning for self and social life" among Samoans, Javanese, and the Ilongots (Philippines) with "contexts of bound, concentrated energy that is outer-oriented and contexts of unbound, less controlled energy that is inner-oriented."

13. *Abduction*: in Charles Peirce's sense of the term, the process of grasping new phenomenon B by assuming it can be understood in a way similar to that whereby we understand known phenomenon A.

14. On the significance of this concept for morphology, see Bybee 1985.

15. A slash between a hyphenated *uchi-* and *soto-* indicates that each occurs as the first element in a compound word. For example, *uchi-/soto-zura* means there exist two semantically contrastive compounds, *uchi-zura* and *soto-zura*. When no slash separates them—for example, *uchisoto*—they are both part of the same word.

16. For this latter aspect of *uchi/soto* structuring, see chapter 11, the final chapter of this volume.

REFERENCES

Aitchison, Jean. 1987. *Words in the Mind: An Introduction to the Mental Lexicon.* New York: Basil Blackwell.

Aristotle. 1984. "Poetics," in *The Rhetoric and Poetics of Aristotle.* Translated by Ingram Bywater. New York: The Modern Library.

Bates, Elizabeth, Luigia Camaioni, and Virginia Volterra. 1979. "The Acquisition of Performatives Prior to Speech," in E. Ochs and B. Schieffelin, eds., *Developmental Pragmatics*, 111–30. New York: Academic Press.

Bateson, Gregory. 1979. *Mind and Nature: a Necessary Unity*. New York: Bantam Books.

Bolinger, Dwight. 1975. *Aspects of Language*, 2d ed. New York: Harcourt Brace Jovanovich.

Bourdieu, Pierre. 1977. *Outline of a Theory of Practice*. New York: Cambridge University Press.

———. 1990. *In Other Words*. Stanford: Stanford University Press.

Bruner, Jerome S. 1966. *The Relevance of Education*. Cambridge, Mass.: Harvard University Press.

Bybee, Joan. 1985. *Morphology*. Philadelphia: John Benjamins.

Cooper, William E., and John R. Ross. 1975. "World Order," in *Proceedings of the Annual Meeting of the Chicago Linguistic Society*, 63–103. Chicago: Chicago Linguistic Society.

Givón, Talmy. 1973. "The Time-axis Phenomenon." *Language* 49: 890–925.

———. 1979. *On Understanding Grammar*. New York: Academic Press.

Hanks, William F. 1987. "Discourse Genres in a Theory of Practice," *American Ethnologist* 14 (4): 668–92.

Johnson, Mark. 1987. *The Body in the Mind*. Chicago: University of Chicago Press.

Lakoff, George. 1987. *Women, Fire and Dangerous Things: What Categories Reveal about the Mind*. Chicago: University of Chicago Press.

Lakoff, George, and Mark Johnson. 1980. *Metaphors We Live By*. Chicago: University of Chicago Press.

Nakada, Norio, Wada Toshimasa, and Kitahara Yasuo, eds. 1983. *Kogo daijiten* (Major dictionary of earlier Japanese). Tokyo: Shoogakkan.

Rumelhart, David E., James L. McClelland, and the PDP Research Group. 1986. *Parallel Distributed Processing: Explorations in the Microstructure of Cognition*, 2 vols. Cambridge, Mass.: Bradford Books/MIT Press.

Sheldrake, Rupert. 1988. *The Presence of the Past: Morphic Resonance and the Habits of Nature*. New York: Vintage Books.

Shoogaku Tosho, ed. 1981. *Kokugo Daijiten* (Major dictionary of the Japanese language). Tokyo: Shoogakkan.

Sweetser, Eve. 1990. *From Etymology to Pragmatics: Metaphorical and Cultural Aspects of Semantic Structure*. New York: Cambridge University Press.

Traugott, Elizabeth Closs. 1982. "From propositional to textual and expressive meanings; some semantic-pragmatic aspects of grammaticalization," in *Perspectives on Historical Linguistics*, Winfred P. Lehmann and Yakov Malkiel, eds., 245–71. Philadelphia: John Benjamins.

———. 1989. "On the rise of epistemic meanings in English: An example of subjectification in semantic change," *Language* 65: 31–55.

Volterra, Virginia, and Francesco Antinucci. 1979. "Negation in Child Language: a Pragmatic Study," in E. Ochs and B. Schieffelin, eds. *Developmental Pragmatics*, 281–304. New York: Academic Press.

Wittgenstein, Ludwig. 1958. *Philosophical Investigations*. Translated by G.E.M. Anscombe. New York: Macmillan.

RELATED READINGS

Bennet, David C. 1975. *Spatial and Temporal Uses of English Prepositions: An Essay in Stratificational Semantics.* London: Longmans.

Bruner, Jerome S. 1990. *Acts of Meaning.* Cambridge, Mass.: Harvard University Press.

Givón, Talmy. 1984. *Syntax: a Functional-Typological Introduction,* Vol. 1. Philadelphia: John Benjamins.

Greenberg, Joseph H. 1978. *Universals of Human Language,* Vol. 4: *Syntax.* Stanford: Stanford University Press.

Grimm, H. 1975. "On the child's acquisition of semantic structure underlying the wordfield of prepositions." *Language and Speech* 18 (1975): 97–119.

Labov, William. 1973. "The Boundaries of Words and Their Meanings," in C. -J. N. Bailey and R. W. Shuy, eds., *New Ways of Analyzing Variation in English.* Washington, D.C.: Georgetown University Press.

Miller, George A., and Philip N. Johnson-Laird. 1976. *Language and Perception.* Cambridge, Mass.: The Belknap Press of Harvard University Press.

Ochs, Eleanor, and Bambi Schieffelin, eds. 1979. *Developmental Pragmatics.* New York: Academic Press.

Rosch, Eleanor. 1975. "Cognitive Representations of Semantic Categories." *Journal of Experimental Psychology: General* 104: 192–233.

Rosch, Eleanor, and B. B. Lloyd, eds. 1978. *Cognition and Categorization.* Hillsdale, N.J.: Lawrence Erlbaum.

Talmy, Leonard. 1978. "Figure and Ground in Complex Sentences," in J. H. Greenberg, ed., *Universals of Human Language,* Vol. 4: *Syntax.* Stanford: Stanford University Press.

————. 1985. "Lexicalization Patterns: Semantic Structure in Lexical Forms," in Timothy Shopen, ed., *Language Typology and Syntactic Description,* Vol. 3: *Grammatical Categories and the Lexicon.* Cambridge: Cambridge University Press.

Traugott, Elizabeth Closs. 1978. "On the Expression of Spatio-Temporal Relations in Language," in J. S. Greenberg, ed., *Universals of Human Language,* Vol. 3: *Word Structure,* 369–400. Stanford: Stanford University Press.

————. 1985. "Conditional Markers," in J. Haiman, ed., *Iconicity in Syntax,* 289–310. Philadelphia: John Benjamins.

Tversky, Barbara, and K. Hemenway. 1984. "Objects, Parts, and Categories." *Journal of Experimental Psychology: General* 113: 169–93.

Chapter 3

A MOVABLE SELF: THE LINGUISTIC INDEXING OF *UCHI* AND *SOTO*

PATRICIA J. WETZEL

EDITORS' INTRODUCTION

Patricia Wetzel's seminal paper challenges the assumption that the 'I' of Indo-European languages is the universal deictic ground for all discourse. She argues that in Japanese the deictic anchor point or ground is not an individual ego, but rather a collectively defined vantage point represented as *uchi*. Wetzel focuses on the implications of considering *uchi* as a deictic anchor point, in allowing for the development of a more coherent account of the organization of "person" in Japanese.

Wetzel's reformulations have important consequences: she shows the Indo-European paradigm of first, second, and third persons to be ill suited to describing person in Japanese. Instead, person can be considered to be communicated more broadly than by person terms. *Uchi/soto* 'in-group/out-group' distinctions are much more crucial than pronouns for delineating person in Japanese. Moreover, many 'in-group/out-group' distinctions are signaled not through nominal *uchi/soto* reference but in a variety of other ways, for example, through verbs of giving and receiving, and polite forms. Thus it is significant that reference to 'in-group/out-group' by politeness marking on the verb outnumbers that of pronouns by a ratio of ten to one.

Wetzel's reformulations open up a number of important new avenues for investigation. Do the collectively defined deictic anchor point, and the designation of person via 'inside/outside' distinctions, have implications for the organization of "self"? The designation of *uchi* and *soto*—who is 'in' and who is 'out'—depends on the constant calculations of participants in particular situations. Shifts in their calculations create shifts in group boundaries, which are fluid, rather than static, and therefore differ markedly from Nakane's portrayal of rigid boundaries. But what ramifications does group-based deixis have for the *social organization* of Japanese groups? Does the process of fluid, constantly shifting group boundaries characterize *social* as well as linguistic aspects of Japanese group organization? These questions are pursued by all the papers that follow.

A MOVABLE SELF:
THE LINGUISTIC INDEXING OF *UCHI* AND *SOTO*

UCHI AND *SOTO*

It has become virtually impossible to speak of Japanese social behavior without reference to (or at least recognition of) the importance of *uchi/soto* boundaries.[1] Benedict's 1946 interpretation of the importance of personal ties within Japanese culture initiated Western recognition of Japanese *uchi/soto* 'in-group/out-group' relationships, and this recognition has been expanded and refined by anthropologists (Nakane 1970; Lebra 1976), psychologists (DeVos 1985; Roland 1988), political scientists (Pye 1985), and others, drawing together much of Japanese behavior that is otherwise inexplicable (at least from a Western perspective).

Feelings of group belongingness are nurtured throughout one's lifetime in Japan (DeVos 1985, 165), and are associated with other positive feelings such as *amae* (Doi 1973; Rosenberger, this volume). Each of the papers in this volume provides important evidence of the centrality of *uchi/soto* to our analysis of Japanese culture and behavior: parallels between the behavior of family members (Rosenberger) and office workers (Kondo) make sense only in the recognition of *uchi/soto*; even as simple an interaction as ordering vegetables at a market (Sukle) falls within the analytical scope of *uchi/soto*. The explanatory power of the *uchi/soto* distinction cannot be ignored in our analysis of Japanese behavior—including linguistic behavior and, in particular, Japanese deixis. *Uchi* comes to constitute the central anchor for one's identity in Japan.

NAKANE'S ACCOUNT OF GROUP CONSCIOUSNESS

Nakane's pioneer work on Japanese group formation and structure begins with the observation that for the Japanese there is a tendency to emphasize situational position over individual attribute in any given frame:

> [W]hen a Japanese "faces the outside" (confronts another person) and affixes some position to himself socially he is inclined to give precedence to institution over kind of occupation. . . . In group identification, a frame such as a "company" or "association" is of primary importance; the attribute of the individual is a secondary matter. . . . Such group consciousness and orientation fosters the strength of an institution, and the institutional unit (such as a school or company) is in fact the basis of Japanese social organization. (1970, 2–3)

The main shortcoming of Nakane's work is that it does not go far enough in relating group consciousness to behavior. Group consciousness for Nakane is at most a cognitive category or a matter of ideology that has no real explanatory power when we attempt to apply it to observations of linguistic behavior. Nakane's portrayal of group consciousness results in rigid group boundaries, and this is contradicted by all the papers in this volume. As has been demonstrated again and again, *uchi/soto* involves shifting boundaries that at once include and define the self. "There are no fixed points, either 'self' or 'other' . . . there is no fixed center from which, in effect, the individual asserts a noncontingent existence" (Smith 1983, 77–81). What this means for our analysis of the language is that we need to reexamine categories that have long been assumed to be axiomatic, in particular those that are said to define deixis.

DEIXIS: *UCHI* AS ANCHOR

The *uchi/soto* distinction has far-reaching implications for study of the language. Overwhelming evidence from Japanese language and behavior indicates that in Japanese the deictic center is not in fact ego as understood or intended by those of us who share a Western cultural heritage, but rather a situationally dependent *uchi* with fluid boundaries. This *uchi* must always include the speaker,[2] but its boundaries shift from moment to moment depending on the kinds of sociocultural factors explored in this volume. When we recognize *uchi* in Japanese we open up the possibility of a very different sort of deictic center from that to which we are accustomed.

An early categorization of phenomena that are currently termed *deictic* was developed by Jesperson (1922), who coined the word *shifters* for elements of language "whose meaning differs according to the situation" (123). Jakobson's (1957) expanded treatment recognizes categories of person, gender, tense, mood, and elements like *this/that, here/there*, as deictic. Lyons's (1977) definition of deixis is provisionally adopted here: "The location and identification of persons, objects, events, processes, and activities being talked about, or referred to, in relation to the spaciotemporal context created and sustained by the act of utterance and participation in it, typically, of *a single speaker* [emphasis mine] and at least some addressee" (636). Lyons's definition rests firmly on the notion that ego is the deictic anchor, and much of linguistic as well as philosophical discussion of deixis explores the nature of "I." In Japan however, where the basic unit of society is not the individual self but *uchi*, the deictic anchor point comes into serious question (Bachnik 1982, 11).

A corollary of Lyons's definition is the assumption that first person is primary, and second and third person are somehow derivative (see, for example, Benveniste 1946). Forms that encode person in various languages have come under intense scrutiny in the Western linguistic tradition. The overriding concern with grammatical person is the reason why person deixis has been investigated to the exclusion of deixis encoded elsewhere in Japanese.

PERSON: PERSONAL PRONOUNS, ANAPHORA
AND ELLIPSIS

Whether *person* and all that it implies is a term that can be applied to Japanese is a question that has so far received little or no attention. Japanese linguistics follows the Western lead in assuming the centrality of person to descriptions of Japanese deixis. This approach has resulted in a multitude of analyses of Japanese pronouns and pronominalization (Hinds 1978; Kuno 1973; Kuroda 1967; Miyaji 1964; Peng 1973), anaphora (Farmer 1980; Oshima 1979; Saito and Hoji 1983; Whitman 1982), and ellipsis (Clancy 1980; Hamada 1983; Hinds 1978, 1980; Kuroda 1967).

The single most important argument in favor of recognizing grammatical person within the Japanese language is that the forms *watakushi* 'I' and *anata* 'you' refer uniquely to speaker and addressee. Since the use of both of these forms depends on the participant roles of the speaker and addressee, they fall within Lyons's definition of deixis. Yet the bounds of person as such are problematic in Japanese.

Wolff (1980, 20) mentions uses of *watakushi* such as *watakushi-ritsu* 'private', *watakushi suru* 'take for one's own use, embezzle', and *watakushi no nai* 'unselfish, impartial, fair'. He points out that in these expressions *watakushi* is not used for self reference. But in fact, *watakushi* is not used for reference at all in these examples. As a referring expression, *watakushi* can only be used for the first person, and *anata* for the addressee. Only in nonreferring expressions like those listed above is *watakushi* used in the sense of 'self' or 'private'.

Granted that there are forms reflective of the participant roles of speaker and addressee, as Lyons suggests are necessary for person, the next question centers on what we are to make of the remaining body of terms that are typically included in discussions of Japanese person. In the spoken language alone, among forms for speaker reference Miller (1967) lists *watakushi, watashi, washi, atakushi, atashi, temae, waga-hai, boku, ore, ora, oira* , and for addressee *anata, anta, sensei, omae, kimi, kisama,* and *temae.*

Suzuki (1978, 98–100) adds *kochira* to the list of first-person forms, and notes that all these are specialized uses of definite descriptions whose meanings are:

watakushi 'private, personal'	*anata* 'that direction'
temae 'this side of'	*omae* 'front'
boku 'your servant'	*kimi* 'lord, prince'
ore 'oneself'	*kisama* 'noble person'
kochira 'this direction'	*sensei* 'teacher'

Martin's (1975, 1075–79) list of first-person forms includes *watakushi* (variant forms: *watashi, atashi, atakushi, watai, wate, wai, atai, ate, watchi*), *boku, ore/ora, uchi, jibun,* and *ono/onore* while his accompanying list of second-person forms includes *anata, omae, kimi, otaku,* and *sochira.*

One outstanding feature of these lists of first- and second-person forms is their lack of agreement as to what is to be included. Is *sensei* 'teacher' a second-person form or is it not? There are no criteria offered for putting together any of these lists. Miller (1967, 341) observes that "the multiplicity of these words reflects in an almost one-to-one ratio the many levels into which Japanese society itself is structured." This is remarkably similar to a situation that Lyons (1977, 641–43) speculates about: the possibility of a language lacking personal pronouns as such, but which makes use of a "special subset of definite descriptions (such as 'master', 'servant')" for vocative and referring expressions. These special nominals, he allows, "are indirectly related to participant roles . . . but it does not follow from this fact that they are personal pronouns, or even that they grammaticalize the category of person."

This raises the additional issue of whether person must be encoded via personal pronouns. Accounts of person in Japanese overwhelmingly operate under the assumption that the Japanese forms that encode person can safely be termed *pronouns,* or in Japanese *daimeishi* (lit. 'pronoun').

Arguments over whether the category "pronoun" applies to Japanese focus primarily on the existence of formal features that might distinguish personal pronouns from other nouns in the language. Kuroda (1967) concludes that items such as *watakushi* and *anata* are not to be termed *pronouns,* based on the fact that they do not have characteristic declensions. Contrast English *I/me, she/her,* and *he/him* with the Japanese forms *watakushi* 'I/me', *kanojo* 'she/her', and *kare* 'he/him' in the following examples:

7a. I called her/him.
 b. She/he called me.
8a. Watakushi ga kanojo/kare o yonda.
 b. Kanojo/kare ga watakushi o yonda.

Kuroda also notes that the Japanese forms can be modified in the same way as other nouns; that the distribution of nouns and pronouns is identical in Japanese. Compare the following English examples to the Japanese:

9a. the short man
 b. *the short he
10a. chiisai hito
 b. chiisai kare

Hinds (1971) argues, in contrast, that Japanese does indeed manifest a separate class of personal pronouns. A distinguishing feature of this class, he argues, is that it is obligatory that all its members add a suffix such as *-ra* or *-tachi* in the plural. For all other [+human] nouns this is optional; that is, the sentence *Kodomo wa byooki desu* can be interpreted as 'The child or children are sick'. But *Watakushi wa byooki desu* can only mean 'I am sick'. In order to convey 'We are sick' the plural suffix *-tachi* must be used: *Watakushi-tachi wa byooki desu*. Similarly, for third-person forms, *kare* 'he' can only be singular, while *kare-ra* is plural.

Hinds fails to observe, however, that proper names in Japanese follow the same pluralization pattern as *watakushi*; that is, *Tanaka-san* can only mean 'Mr./Ms. Tanaka'; it cannot mean 'the Tanakas'. In order to indicate that the entire Tanaka family is sick the plural suffix *-tachi* is required: *Tanaka-san-tachi wa byooki desu*.

Hinds also claims that the personal pronouns cannot be modified by demonstratives such as *kono* 'this' and *sono* 'that' as other nouns can. Martin (1975, 1067) provides evidence to the contrary: *kono watashi mo* 'even this person who I am'; *sono kare wa* 'that he'. Thus, there are no morphological or distributional criteria that warrant recognizing an independent class of pronouns in Japanese.

Elsewhere, the search for person in Japanese leads to the analysis of anaphora and ellipsis. In terms of sheer use, it has been observed that Japanese tend not to use person forms to the same extent that, for example, English does. Thus, in one data sample,[3] there were three uses of first- or second-person forms (two *watashi* and one *boku*), and eleven other forms of address/reference that included predominantly use of names and the term *sensei* . Based on figures provided by Allen and Guy (1974) and Goffman (1961), we would expect upwards of 225 pronouns per 1,000 words in a comparable English conversation. The Japanese data do not approach this figure.

There is a good deal of research to the effect that the anaphoric function of pronouns in English corresponds more closely to ellipsis in Japanese (Kuroda 1967; Hinds 1975, 1977, 1978, 1980; Clancy 1980). Clancy (1980, 133) shows that Japanese speakers used ellipsis in 73 percent of the places where a nominal was possible, compared to 20 percent in English. She interprets this as evidence that "the distributions of English pronouns and Japanese ellipsis are more similar than those of nominal references" (140).

Yet underlying the focus of interest on personal pronouns, anaphora, and ellipsis is the assumption that the central deictic distinctions of Japanese are the same as those of English and Indo-European, and that those distinctions are reflected in nominal elements. It is just such an approach that, I think, fails to do justice to the system underlying these elements, and more seriously misses key generalizations about them.

Social Deixis

One of the most recently defined and explored linguistic phenomena for which sociocultural distinctions play a descriptive role is what Levinson (1983) terms *social deixis*. Social deixis refers to "the encoding of social distinctions that are relevant to participant roles, particularly aspects of the social relationship holding between the speaker and the addressee(s) or speaker and some referent" (63).[4]

Certainly Japanese elements such as the polite forms (honorific and humble forms),[5] as well as the verbs of giving and receiving, fall within this characterization of social deixis: they encode social distinctions (*uchi/soto*) that are relevant to the social relationship holding between the speaker and the addressee(s) or speaker and some referent. Yet Levinson's account of social deixis is still clouded by an underlying assumption that social deixis is somehow derivative or peripheral to person deixis. The speaker (ego) is still assumed to be the deictic anchor. But compare his definition of social deixis above with his earlier definitions for pragmatics and deixis:

> Pragmatics is the study of those relations between language and context that are *grammaticalized*, or encoded in the structure of the language. (9)

> The single most obvious way in which the relationship between language and context is reflected in the structure of languages themselves is through the phenomenon of deixis. . . . Essentially, deixis concerns the ways in which languages encode or grammaticalize features of the context of utterance or speech event. (54)

Are we to conclude that deixis is the primary concern of pragmatics? Does this confounding of deixis with pragmatics demonstrate a lack of focus in what we are to take to be the concern of pragmatics? Or of investigations into deictic phenomena? The inadequacy of Levinson's analysis becomes even more evident when he allows that "it is generally (but not invariably) true that deixis is organized in an egocentric way" (63). Levinson fails to follow up on what nonegocentric deixis would mean to our understanding of deixis and our analysis of language in general. When for Japanese we define *uchi*, and not ego, as the deictic anchor point, it has profound implications for our analysis of language. In essence, we erase the division that Levinson has drawn between deixis and social deixis.

LINGUISTIC MANIFESTATIONS OF *UCHI* AND *SOTO*

Nakane observes: "If one listens to a conversation between Japanese one does not have to wait long to hear the words *uchi-no* or *uchi dewa* referring to one's own people and work place. *Uchi* may mean the institution as a whole, or it may mean the department or section to which the speaker belongs" (1970, 125). Yet nominal reference to *uchi* is only one of a number of ways in which the distinction between *uchi* and *soto* is signaled in Japanese. The even more frequent use of Japanese verbs of giving and receiving, as well as polite forms (honorific and humble forms), provides a window on speakers' perceptions of the *uchi* and *soto* of the situation in which they occur. The Japanese data sample mentioned above[6] contained forty-three instances of verbs of giving and receiving and polite forms. If we recognize the deictic nature of the verbs of giving and receiving and polite forms, there is much more deictic reference than first realized: verbs of giving and receiving and polite forms outnumbered person forms by more than ten to one.

A few Japanese grammarians have tried to call attention at least to the directional nature of the polite forms and verbs of giving and receiving. One of these is Mikami (1970, 149–53) who appends a discussion of verbs like *kureru, morau,* and *ageru* to his discussion of the deictic and anaphoric uses of the demonstratives. Although he does not overtly refer to these verbs as deictic, he does refer to their "directional nature" (*hookoosei*). The dichotomy, he says, is between verbs denoting "for me" versus those denoting "for non-me" (he uses the English), and he innovatively calls the former "centripetal" (*kyuushin-teki*) and the latter "noncentripetal" (*hikyuushin-teki*).

Miyaji (1965) also attends to the directional nature of the verbs of giving and receiving in terms of how speaker viewpoint interacts with the grammatical person of the subject, object, or indirect object. This illustrates the tendency, even among Japanese grammarians, to accept person deixis as a point of departure for the analysis of how the polite forms and verbs of giving and receiving function.

Both Martin (1964, 408) and Miller (1967, 273) analyze the verbs of giving and receiving in terms of the speaker's in-group or *uchi*—that is, as 'give to *uchi*' (*kureru/kudasaru*), 'give (from *uchi*) to *soto*' (*ageru/sashia-geru*), and 'get from *soto*' (*morau/itadaku*). In effect, we observe the set of verbs that can be illustrated as follows (the difference between plain and polite forms is discussed below):

kureru/kudasaru

'give to *uchi*'

ageru/sashiageru   <————   UCHI   <—————

'give to *soto*'

morau/itadaku

'get from *soto*'

The use of the verbs of giving and receiving is primarily dependent on what the speaker perceives to be the make-up of *uchi*, and the direction of giving vis-à-vis *uchi*. Thus, in speaking to an acquaintance in class about a professor, I might utter the sentence:

11. Sensei   wa   setumei   o   shite *kudasaimashita.*[7]
    professor TOP explanation OBJ doing gave to *uchi* (honorific)
    'The professor explained [it] to [me/us].'

By using *kudasaimashita* 'gave to *uchi*' I can include the addressee (and/ or possibly other classmates) in those who benefit from the teacher's explanation, but I definitely place the professor outside.

But the next moment, on learning that the same classmate has lost a book, I might turn and say:

12. Watashi no o   kashite *agemashoo*   ka.
    I/my   one OBJ lending give to *soto* (tentative) Q
    'Shall [I] give [you] mine?'

The use of *agemashoo* 'give to *soto*' here signals a group division between myself (the speaker) and the classmate.

The two preceding examples illustrate how the boundaries of *uchi* can vary from situation to situation—in one instance the classmate is part of my (the speaker's) *uchi*, but in the next becomes *soto*. The importance of this variation in the boundaries of *uchi* to our description of the verbs of giving and receiving cannot be overemphasized. In any given context a speaker's perception of *uchi* and *soto* determines the choice of giving or receiving verb. Yet in any given situation, speakers may not always perceive *uchi* and *soto* the same way, and their choice of verb reflects this. Imagine, for example, that a bookstore is giving away copies of a bestseller at its opening. Observing an acquaintance walking away carrying a book, I might ask:

13. Ah, hon o   *kureta*   n   desu ka?
    oh book OBJ gave to *uchi* EXTP COP Q
    'Oh, so [they] gave [you] a book?'

or alternatively

14. Ah, hon o   *ageta*   n   desu ka?
    oh book OBJ gave to *soto* EXTP COP Q
    'Oh, so [they] gave [you] a book?'

Either way of asking is appropriate, but the perspective the two questions take on the event is quite different. In example 13, the acquaintance is *uchi*, while in example 14 the acquaintance is *soto*. In example 13 the speaker takes the perspective of the acquaintance, making the bookstore *soto*, while in example 14 the speaker takes the perspective of the bookstore, making the acquaintance *soto*.[8]

There is an interesting tendency in Japanese grammars to discuss the verbs of giving and receiving in connection with the system of polite forms. Why this should be the case becomes clear only when we recognize that the use of polite forms in Japanese is in large measure determined by perceived boundaries of *uchi* and *soto*; that is, honorific forms are by definition *soto* oriented—they cannot be used in regard to the speaker or the speaker's *uchi*. The subject[9] of sentences like the following must be someone other than the speaker or the speaker's group.

15a. Shichi-ji   ni *irasshaimasu.*
     seven o'clock at go (honorific)
     '[S/he] will go at seven o'clock.'
15b. . . . maa, roosu ka nanka   o   *otsukai ni natte* mo ii . . . [10]
         well roast or something OBJ use (honorific) also good
         '[It] would also be good if [you] used a roast or something . . . '
15c. . . . onaka   ippai ni *meshiagatte*   'masu no de . . .
          stomach full   eating (honorific) will be so . . .
          '[You]'ll be eating till [you]'re full, so . . . '
15d. Maa, kore wa . . . ippan no resutoran ya nanka   de mo
     well this TOP   general   restaurant or something at too
         meshiagaremasu.
         can eat (honorific)
         'Well, this . . . [you] can eat at any restaurant.'

The subject of a humble form, in contrast, must be *uchi* —the speaker or the speaker's in-group.

16a. Hamada-kun ni *okiki-shimasu.*[11]
     Mr. Hamada of will ask (humble)
     '[I] will ask Mr. Hamada.'

16b. Kore . . . nanajuu-hachinen no juunigatsu no nijuugo-nichi no . . .
    this   1978   December   25th
     nikkei   dete   *orimasu.*
    [newspaper] appearing be (humble)
    'This . . . is what appeared in the *Nikkei* [newspaper] on December
    25, 1978.'
16c. . . . futankin no mondai ni tsuite wa   hanashite *itadakitai*
         funds   problem about   TOP speaking want to have (humble)
      to iu koto desu.
      it is a matter of
    '[We] would like to have [him] speak about the problem of funds.'

The subject is not overtly specified in any of the above examples, nor is it specified in the surrounding discourse. Rather, it is implicit in the verb form used and derivable if we have sufficient information about the context. Honorific forms encode an implicit reference to *soto* or 'out-group', and humble forms encode an implicit reference to *uchi* or 'in-group'. The 'we' or 'I' in brackets in the above translations is this writer's interpretation of the boundaries of *uchi* in the discourse.

The polite forms and the verbs of giving and receiving have hereto-fore been vaguely defined as related; recognizing *uchi/soto* allows us to articulate the nature of that relationship. Recognizing *uchi/soto* as the central deictic distinction of Japanese also allows us to compare ele-ments that encode these categories in Japanese (the polite forms and the verbs of giving and receiving) to forms that encode parallel deictic categories such as person in other languages (pronouns). It may be said, in fact, that Japanese verb forms obligatorily "conjugate" for *uchi/soto* in much the same way that Indo-European languages conjugate for person. As Brown and Levinson (1987) observe: "The free deletion of subjects and the nonexistence of proper possessive pronouns can be at-tributed to the pragmatic encoding of person in the kind of honorific chosen" (284). This can now be restated: "The free deletion of subjects and the nonexistence of proper possessive pronouns can be attributed to the pragmatic encoding of *uchi/soto* in the kind of honorific chosen." Similarly, Shibatani (1978) points out the polite language is "highly comparable to subject-verb agreement in that both processes are trig-gered by one particular N[oun] P[hrase] . . . and both involve some kind of marking on the predicate element" (57). The marking that Shi-batani alludes to but does not specify is *uchi/soto*.

Because their description relies on the speaker's point of view with re-gard to group boundaries at the time of utterance, the polite forms and the verbs of giving and receiving must be recognized as deictic. The deictic categories that these forms encode is what is recognized in this volume as *uchi/soto* deixis.

Recognizing *uchi/soto* social deixis in Japanese has wide-ranging implications. It demands a reevaluation of what we take to be the defining feature(s) of deixis and social deixis. It demands a reexamination of what is traditionally assumed to be the universal deictic anchor. It demands that we rethink our preoccupation with forms that occur infrequently (namely, personal or anaphoric pronouns) and attend instead to the data that the language itself offers us.

In the larger scheme of things, recognizing *uchi/soto* deixis provides us with a powerful tool for examining linguistic phenomena that have long been taken to be related but for which existing models are inadequate; observed parallels between the so-called pronouns of power and solidarity (Brown and Gilman 1960) and Japanese polite forms can be drawn together under the rubric of social deixis. At the same time, this calls for reconsideration of the relationship between power and hierarchy in the West and in Japan.

Finally, the linguistic manifestations of *uchi/soto* demonstrate once again the complex interrelationship between language and its sociocultural setting. *Uchi* makes the link between language and social organization explicit. Important avenues for further investigation include: detailed description of group *uchi/soto* boundaries in both language and social life (Quinn [this volume] provides evidence of the wide variety of semantic domains into which the terms *uchi* and *soto* have been extended); descriptions of whether and how shifting in social relations is the same as shifting in language; elaboration of how language and social life are defined situationally, and how this is basic to both; expansion of Molasky's observation (this volume) that *uchi/soto* and *omote/ura* are related (this point is also raised by Lebra 1976); further elaboration of the tie between *uchi/soto* and *amae* that Rosenberger (this volume) examines in some detail, and the relationship of both of these to linguistic behavior. An untouched area of linguistic research is the relationship between linguistic behavior and hierarchy, power and authority that Kondo (this volume) outlines in terms of *uchi/soto*. Similarly, the papers by Rosenberger and Sukle (this volume) raise the question of what role sex or gender plays in perceptions of *uchi/soto* and the linguistic behavior that reflects these categories. Japanese provides a wealth of opportunities for sociolinguistic investigation, much of which may require similar reevaluation of our assumptions about linguistic categories, sociocultural phenomena, and their interrelationships. The papers in this volume provide good examples of how important it is to take culture into account in any linguistic investigation.

NOTES

1. My thanks go to Jane Bachnik and Charlie Quinn for their extensive comments on earlier versions of this paper. All errors remain my own. Much of the material contained herein is from my 1984 Cornell Ph.D. dissertation, funding for which was provided by the National Science Foundation.

2. Apparent exceptions to this are discussed as "deictic projection" (Lyons 1977, 579) in Wetzel 1985, 150–55.

3. A fourteen-and-a-half-minute televised cooking lesson taped in Sapporo in 1980.

4. One kind of social deixis that Levinson treats in some detail is expressed in the world's languages via so-called honorifics. Following Comrie (1976), he distinguishes among referent, addressee, and bystander honorifics. He specifically cites the Japanese language as possessing both referent and addressee honorifics—here taken to be polite forms and *masu/desu,* respectively.

5. Frequently in the literature the term *honorifics* is equivalent to what I call *polite forms.* The term *honorific* is reserved here for those forms that are said to exalt the subject in Japanese (Martin 1975, 331).

6. A televised cooking lesson taped in Sapporo in 1980.

7. Abbreviations used in the translations include: TOP 'topic', suoBJ 'subject', OBJ 'object', EXTP 'extended predicate' (Jorden and Noda 1987, 242–44), COP 'copula' and Q 'question particle'.

8. This is one example of "deictic projection" (mentioned in note 2 above).

9. The question of what sentence role triggers honorification has been addressed by Martin (1964, 1975), Miller (1967), and Harada (1976). This paper assumes that the abstract subject (Wetzel 1984, 51–57) is the trigger for all polite predicates.

10. Examples 15b through 15d are from the televised cooking lesson taped in Sapporo in 1980.

11. These examples are from data taped at a meeting of native-Japanese speaking architects in 1980.

REFERENCES

Allen, Donald E., and Rebecca F. Guy. 1974. *Conversation Analysis.* The Hague: Mouton.

Bachnik, Jane M. 1982. "Deixis and self/other reference in Japanese discourse." *Sociolinguistic working papers* 99. Austin: Southwest Educational Development Laboratory.

Benedict, Ruth. 1946. *The Chrysanthemum and the Sword.* Boston: Houghton Mifflin.

Benveniste, Emile. 1946. "Relationships of person in the verb." (From *Bulletin de la societe de linguistique de Paris* 43.) Reprinted in Benveniste 1971: 195–204.

————. 1971. *Problems in General Linguistics.* Coral Gables: University of Miami Press.

Brown, Penelope, and Stephen C. Levinson. 1987. *Politeness: Some Universals in Language Use.* Cambridge: Cambridge University Press.

Brown, Roger, and Albert Gilman. 1960. "The pronouns of power and solidarity." Reprinted in Pier Paolo Giglioli, ed., *Language and Social Context.* 1972. Hammondsport: Penguin.

Clancy, Patricia. 1980. "Referential choice in English and Japanese narrative discourse," in Wallace L. Chafe, ed., *The Pear Stories,* 127–202. Norwood: Ablex.

Comrie, Bernard. 1976. "Linguistic politeness axes: Speaker-addressee, speaker-referent, speaker-bystander." *Pragmatics microfiche* 1.7: A3. Department of Linguistics, University of Cambridge.

DeVos, George. 1985. "Dimensions of self in Japanese culture," in Anthony J. Marsella, George Devos, and Francis L. K. Hsu, eds., *Culture and Self,* 141–84. New York: Tavistock Publications.

Doi, Takeo. 1973. *The Anatomy of Dependence.* Translation of *Amae no kozo.* Tokyo: Kodansha.

Farmer, Ann. 1980. "On the Interaction of Morphology and Syntax." Ph.D. dissertation, MIT.

Goffman, Erving. 1961. *Encounters.* Indianapolis: Bobbs-Merrill.

Hamada, Morio. 1983. "Referential Choice in Theme, Subject, and Ellipsis in Written Narrative Discourse: A Case Study of Japanese Folktales." Master's Thesis, Cornell University.

Harada, S. I. 1976. "Honorifics," in M. Shibatani, ed., *Syntax and Semantics,* Vol. 5: *Japanese Generative Grammar,* 499–561. New York: Academic Press.

Hinds, John. 1971. "Personal pronouns in Japanese." *Glossa* 5(2): 146–55.

———. 1975. "Third person pronouns in Japanese," in Fred C. C. Peng, ed., *Language in Japanese Society,* 129–57. Tokyo: University of Tokyo Press.

———. 1977. "Paragraph structure and pronominalization." *Papers in linguistics* 10: 1–2, 77–99.

———. 1978. "Anaphora in Japanese conversation," in John Hinds, ed., *Anaphora in Discourse,* 136–79. Edmonton: Linguistic Research.

———. 1980. "Japanese conversation, discourse structure, and ellipsis." *Discourse processes* 3:263–86.

Jakobson, Roman. 1957. "Shifters, verbal categories, and the Russian verb," in *Selected Writings II.* The Hague: Mouton.

Jespersen, Otto. 1922. *Language: Its Nature and Development.* London: George Allen.

Jorden, Eleanor H., and Mari Noda. 1987. *Japanese: The Spoken Language, Part 1.* New Haven: Yale University Press.

Kuno, Susumu. 1973. *The Structure of the Japanese Language.* Cambridge: MIT Press.

Kuroda, S.- Y. 1967, 1979. *Generative Grammatical Studies in the Japanese Language.* New York: Garland.

Lebra, Takie Sugiyama. 1976. *Japanese Patterns of Behavior.* Honolulu: University of Hawaii Press.

Levinson, Stephen C. 1983. *Pragmatics.* Cambridge: Cambridge University Press.

Lyons, John. 1977. *Semantics,* Vols. 1 and 2. Cambridge: Cambridge University Press.

Martin, Samuel. 1964. "Speech levels in Japan and Korea," in Dell Hymes, ed., *Language in Culture and Society*, 407–15. New York: Harper and Row.

———. 1975. *A Reference Grammar of Japanese*. New Haven: Yale University Press.

Mikami, Akira. 1970. *Bunpoo shooronshuu*. Tokyo: Kurosio.

Miller, Roy Andrew. 1967. *The Japanese Language*. Chicago: Chicago University Press.

Miyaji, Atsuko. 1964. *Daimeishi* (Pronouns). *Gendaigo* 6: *Kogo bunpoo no mondaiten*, 200–209. Tokyo: Meiji Shoin.

Miyaji, Yutaka. 1965. *Yaru, kureru, morau o jutsugo to suru bun no koozoo ni tuite* (On the construction of sentences that have the verbs *yaru, kureru,* and *morau* as predicates). *Kokugogaku* 63: 21–33

Nakane, Chie. 1970. *Japanese Society*. Berkeley: University of California Press.

Oshima, Shin. 1979. "Conditions on rules: Anaphora in Japanese," in George Bedell et al., eds., *Explorations in Linguistics: Papers in Honor of Kazuko Inoue,* 423–45. Tokyo: Kenkyusha.

Peng, Fred C. C. 1973. "La parole of Japanese pronouns." *Language sciences* 25:36–39.

Pye, Lucian W. 1985. *Asian Power and Politics*. Cambridge: Harvard University Press.

Roland, Alan. 1988. *In Search of Self in India and Japan*. Princeton: Princeton University Press.

Saito, Mamoru, and Hajime Hoji. 1983. "Weak crossover and move α in Japanese." *Natural language and linguistic theory* 1:2.245–259.

Shibatani Masayoshi. 1978. "Minami Akira and the notion of 'subject' in Japanese grammar," in John Hinds and Irwin Howard, eds., *Problems in Japanese Syntax and Semantics*, 52–67. Tokyo: Kaitakusha.

Smith, Robert J. 1983. *Japanese Society: Tradition, Self and the Social Order.* Cambridge: Cambridge University Press.

Suzuki, Takao. 1978. *Japanese and the Japanese*. Tokyo: Kodansha.

Wetzel, Patricia J. 1984. "*Uchi* and *soto* (in-group and out-group): Social deixis in Japanese." Ph.D. dissertation, Cornell University.

———. 1985. "In-group and out-group deixis: Situational variation in the verbs of giving and receiving in Japanese," in Joseph P. Forgas, ed., *Language and Social Situations*, 141–57. New York: Springer-Verlag.

Whitman, John. 1982. "Configurationality parameters." Unpublished ms.

Wolff, Jonathan Hart. 1980. "Linguistic Socialization, Self and Personal Referents in Japanese." Master's thesis, Cornell University.

Chapter 4

INDEXING HIERARCHY
THROUGH JAPANESE GENDER RELATIONS

NANCY R. ROSENBERGER

EDITORS' INTRODUCTION

This chapter is both innovative and theoretically important: Nancy Rosenberger delineates *uchi/soto* in the communication of individual relationships, linking these in turn to the organization of gender, hierarchy, and conceptualization of the sacred in Shinto. Utilizing the starting point of the collective deictic anchor point, *uchi*, Rosenberger focuses on dyadic *relationships* within the anchor point as the basic unit of analysis, rather than the individual 'I' which is invariably assumed. This has important ramifications, for *in redefining the starting point* for approaching power, hierarchy, and gender, Rosenberger also *radically redefines the way these subjects are approached*.

Rosenberger's paper focuses on the detailed delineation of interaction in ethnographic context—a Japanese family within which she herself lived. Through presentation of densely contextual ethnographic scenes, Rosenberger sketches an orientation to social life that shifts between an outer, *soto*, pole of more distant, authoritative relations, and an inner, *uchi*, pole of more intimate, spontaneous relations. In a more *soto* context, people are self-disciplined, detaching themselves from their personal feelings to focus on "representing" their group in relation to other groups. In a more *uchi* context, they are freer to express ideas and feelings as individual selves within their group. Yet this is also too simple, because the *uchi/soto* continuum defines more than one level of social life—of context as a whole, and of dyadic relationships within a context.

Within a dyadic relationship, the same continuum is also indexed, so that one person is more disciplined (*soto*); the other more spontaneous (*uchi*). Within relationships, *uchi/soto* corresponds to Doi's (1973) and Lebra's (1976) discussions of *amaeru/amayakasu*; to *amayakasu* is to be disciplined (*soto*) and allow the other the indulgence of free expression; to *amaeru* is to be spontaneous (*uchi*) and accept the indulgence offered by another. Since *amaeru/amayakasu* is a dynamic crucial to interpersonal relationships, *uchi/soto* indexing pervades the organization of interpersonal relationships as well.

From here Rosenberger traces the dynamics of hierarchy, based on ambiguities derived from the *amaeru/amayakasu* relationship. Since the focus may be either on the intimacy, *amaeru* (*uchi*) pole of the relationship, emphasizing solidarity, or on the authority *amayakasu* (*soto*) pole, emphasizing hierarchy, a potential for an *uchi/soto* shift is thus basic to the indexing of the *amaeru/amayakasu* relationship. Rosenberger further links authority and intimacy to a Shinto cycle of sacred power that shifts through a dynamic cycle of an outward (*soto*) manifestation that is differentiated and authoritative to an inward (*uchi*) manifestation that is generative and consolidating.

Rosenberger's analysis traces out an intricate, but multileveled indexing of *uchi/soto* relationships, based on widely shared cultural knowledge. In so doing, she formulates a basis for both gender and hierarchy which gives a far more coherent account of a variety of social phenomena than such concepts as "vertical/horizontal" principles, or "equality/inequality." Moreover, the organization of power based on the Shinto notions of the sacred can be linked beyond Japan, especially throughout the Pacific area. Thus women are associated with the generative *uchi* orientation of facilitating solidarity; men with the differentiated *soto* orientation of facilitating authority. Consequently, although both women and men are in *amayakasu* positions with one another, when women *amayakasu* they most often facilitate solidarity, and *give* deference; when men *amayakasu* they facilitate authority and *receive* deference. Moreover, the multileveled indexing of *uchi/soto* results in women most often being in an *amayakasu* (*soto*) position in an *uchi* situation, and in an *amaeru* (*uchi*) position in a (*soto*) situation, meaning that they are under more tension. Yet even this is too simple, since social life consists of constantly indexing *uchi/soto*, even within intimate or restrained situations. Rosenberger details both how this indexing is motivated, and how all of the imaginable permutations of *uchi/soto* relationship positions in *uchi/soto* situations, do in fact occur.

INDEXING HIERARCHY
THROUGH JAPANESE GENDER RELATIONS

WHEN I WENT to Japan to teach English in a public high school in a regional city, I lived with a family whose mother taught home economics part-time at the same school. The father of the family was a doctor rising in the levels of administration at the local teaching hospital. Only one child was living with them at the time, a daughter who had just entered the best high school in town. By the standards of that city in the early seventies, they were wealthy—at least wealthy enough to keep an American foreigner.

In the evenings the daughter, the mother, and I would usually eat before the father arrived home. There was a part-time maid who helped the mother make the food and serve the dinner, so the mother, whom we all called *okaasan*, usually ate with us. The *kotatsu* 'low table with a warmer under it' was cleared by the maid, *okaasan*, and myself. After the dishes were done, the maid would return home and we would settle ourselves around the *kotatsu* again with the daughter doing her homework, me studying Japanese, and *okaasan* sewing. It was a relaxed time with everyone exchanging comments and help on various school and home happenings in informal language.

Around 9:00 P.M., the father—called *otoosan* by all—would return home and instantly the mother began scurrying around helping him change into the kimono he wore at home, giving him his dinner if he had not yet had it, and beginning to draw the bath. Again things would settle down as the *otoosan* finished his meal and his tea. *Okaasan* would sit down beside him in a rather tentative position, not a formal kneeling position but with legs folded to the side on the edge of her *zabuton* 'sitting pillow', ready to jump when he needed anything. She got up and down regularly to bring him tea, cigarettes, newspaper, and drink in response to his informal expression of need "*Oi!*" He spoke in the abbreviated informal style and talked of little except his immediate needs. She alternated between use of verb endings that show semipolite deference and shorter, informal endings during those intervals when she, too, was able to sit and relax as when *otoosan* was eating. If she initiated any conversation, it was usually an entertaining or worried remark about the daughter.

Otoosan rarely talked to me, a young female with poor Japanese. It was to his daughter that he addressed questions about her day and responded with teasing and lighthearted laughter. The daughter would bring a particularly difficult math problem to him and he would tease her into figuring out the answer. When she understood, she would snap her fingers with a big smile and he would give a belly laugh. The mother would look at me and laugh and I would enter in, too.

Okaasan would soon be off to check the bath and call the *otoosan* to enter. She would help him to prepare for the bath, sit for a moment, and then run off in response to his "*Oi!*" from the bathroom. Next was myself, then the daughter, and finally the mother for a brief bath. The baths finished, *otoosan* would lean back in his floor chair with legs outstretched, the daughter reclining on the floor, and I leaning over the table on my elbows. *Otoosan* and the daughter would exchange laughter and informal comments about the actions on television. While we were tingling from the warmth of the bath, *okaasan* would bring the teapot and pour us tea, serve *sembei* (rice crackers) and tangerines, often retrieving these from the coldness of the connected *kura* 'storehouse'. She had little time to partake except for a sip of tea now and then. Lulled by all these signs of relaxation, the daughter and I were not long in getting off to bed, with *otoosan* soon to follow. Sounds of *okaasan* going out to lock the outer gate and the inner door were usually the last sounds I heard.

UCHI/SOTO AXES AND HIERARCHICAL RELATIONS

Japanese would locate this situation toward the engaged end of an *uchi/soto* continuum that orients social life between an outer pole of more distant, authoritative relations, and an inner pole of more intimate, spontaneous relations. While in a more *soto* context, people act in a disciplined way, detaching themselves from their personal feelings to focus on the definition and productivity of their group in relation to other groups. In a more *uchi* context, people are freer to express their personal ideas and feelings as individual selves within their group (Lebra 1976; Bachnik 1987; Rosenberger 1989a). This simple definition serves as a baseline for the complex interworkings of *uchi/soto* in the scene just described.

To grasp the dynamics of *uchi/soto* we must realize that this continuum defines more than one level of social life—the level of a context as a whole and the level of dyadic relationship within a context. The continuum in relationships is judged between two people, one being more disciplined and the other more spontaneous. Thus both the individuals in the scene and the parameters of the scene itself are interwoven into *uchi/soto* distinctions. This means that it is possible for a person like the *okaasan* to be at the disciplined end of a relationship continuum and still be in a spontaneous situation.

This very interplay between *uchi/soto* operating both in relationships and context defines the distinct flavor of the situation. Because any alteration in a relationship or in the more general context shifts the sense of the situation, the meaning is constantly changing and can only be grasped *in situ*. It is through this constant interplay that gender relations and hierarchy are constructed in Japanese society. (Although these *uchi/soto* shifts seem very subtle, their interpretation is widely shared by Japanese.) To understand this, we must look more closely at the dynamics of the scene presented above.

UNDERSTANDING AN EVENING AT HOME

Japanese label the opening vignette an *uchi* situation because it is an informal family setting. My own presence as a guest, albeit a long-term one, keeps the situation from being as informal as it might be in terms of engaged relaxation, but Japanese would recognize signs that contributed to building an *uchi* atmosphere such as the *kotatsu* table, the liberal consumption of crackers and tangerines with papers and skins littered about, the relaxed postures, the bath, the TV, and the impromptu jokes.

Within this relatively intimate, private situation, the context is colored by various shades of interactions along the *uchi/soto* spectrum. For example, the daughter, the father, and I are able to sit back and enjoy the relaxed intimacy of the occasion more than the mother. The mother maintains enough detachment to serve drinks and food and draw the bath. Yet she too shifts from moments when she is making sure the group is satisfied and using semipolite language to moments when she is a laughing, eating member of the group and using the same informal language as everyone else. Those moments last longer when she is with the daughter and myself (both females and both younger than she is) and when she has the maid to help.

When relating to the mother, the father expresses his personal feelings quite freely and is the center of attention. But when relating to the daughter, he keeps his personal feelings back, helping her with her homework in a manner that allows her to appear cute and smart in the process. Once when the father demanded of the daughter, "Glasses!" as he pointed at them, the daughter masqueraded a low bow and handed the glasses up to him with both hands, as if to say this action makes it seem as if I am serving you, but I am still the one who gets the attention (cf. Goffman 1974).

From my own perspective as the guest, I can lean back and enjoy the satisfied feelings of a full stomach, warmth, and camaraderie. Both the mother's service and the father's undemanding silence toward me excuse me from the alert help that would be expected were I a daughter-in-law. On some nights the daughter would need help with English homework, at which time my discipline would tighten and I would become the outside teacher in response to whom the daughter would straighten her sitting posture and talk more politely.

Ignoring these other relations for the moment, I will focus on the relationship between the mother and father. The mother is responsible to everyone for supplying the material objects that help to make the situation relaxing and engaged, but she exhibits special responsibility toward the father's needs. Once he arrives home, she partakes of the objects of enjoyment only sparingly and supplies extras to him that no one else shares in. Most of her actions in relation to the father are characterized by disciplined action—that is, of more *soto* or outer contexts.

The father's actions toward the mother show spontaneous expression of personal need. The father does not hesitate to make demands on the mother, even expecting her to understand his wants nonverbally. He soaks in her attention and plays his role of hierarchical power to the hilt. The father displays engaged *uchi*-like behavior in relation to the mother.

At the level of this relationship, the disciplined actions of the mother are juxtaposed to the spontaneous actions of the father. Furthermore, while the personally oriented demands of the father fit with the sense of the larger social encounter as an engaged, *uchi* context, the group-oriented tasks of the mother are a counterpoint to it.

WOMEN'S TENSIONS FROM AN INDIVIDUAL POINT OF VIEW

What are the feelings of the woman involved in this juxtaposition of a *soto* relationship in an *uchi* context? Further, how does this help us to understand gender relationships in Japanese society?

My experience living in Japan and my research in Japan with middle-aged women from 1980 to 1983 have convinced me that tension and feelings of subordination exist in situations such as the one outlined above. For example, a Tokyo housewife in her early forties, visiting with her neighbor and myself, said, "I can never really relax when my husband is home. I am alert (*ki o tsukau*). I never know if he'll want tea or something. Even when he's in his *futon* reading on Sunday afternoon, I always peek in to see if he needs anything."

This is especially true if elders live in the household. A housewife from a regional city who lived with her husband, daughters, and husband's parents, said, "I am tense '*kinchoo*' when I am home. I always have to be thinking what they [the grandparents] need without being asked. And not so much as a thank-you."

The woman in the original scene is married to a man who is her senior by about ten years. She is his second wife by an arranged marriage, having had two children by him, after his first wife bore two. She would be expected to feel some tension in relation to him who is by age superior. Women who meet their husbands themselves and are quite close in age to their husbands report less feeling of tension.

Thus, from an individual point of view, feelings of tension exist for a woman in an engaged, private situation in which she is with older men and carries responsibility.[1] Women express the need to establish other situations that are even more "inner" (*uchi* of *uchi*) in order to relax (Rosenberger 1987a). My *okaasan* looked forward to doing her wood-carving hobby in the afternoons, teaching several hours a week, and visiting with other women. She enjoyed weekends at hot springs resorts with her friends with whom she had studied home economics before her marriage. When her cousin came to visit, their talk—complaints and laughter—filled the informal areas of the house.

Despite the woman's tension and search for relief of tension, the unequal relationship continues. But let us continue our analysis of meaning at the level of relationship.

FROM THE PERSPECTIVE OF DYADIC RELATIONS

At the dyadic level, the mother's actions can be explained in terms first analyzed by Doi (1973) as *amaeru* and *amayakasu*. Doi has introduced an important basis for dyadic interrelation in Japan in the terms *amaeru* and *amayakasu*. To *amayakasu* another is to allow another the indulgence of free expression, and to give active love; literally, to allow another to be sweet or dependent. To *amaeru* is to be sweet, that is to accept the indulgence offered by another and to receive love passively.

Doi's analysis focuses on the *amaeru* side of the relationship and claims this as a universal need for passive love. In so doing, he emphasizes the aspect of solidarity, of ideally feeling at one with another, epitomized in the mother-child relationship which is sought after between boss and underling or even between two company presidents.

The dyadic relationship of giving and receiving indulgence or dependence is born in and reproduces relations of hierarchy (see Doi 1973, 28; Lebra 1976, 51). These unequal relations can represent solidarity (as Doi has emphasized), but they can also represent authority. The very oneness of the mother-child relationship or the closeness of the boss-underling relationship gives the superior a great deal of potential social authority. The authority is supported by the emotion and obligation that the social inferior feels from having been allowed personal expressions of power in certain contexts.

We can view the *amaeru/amayakasu* level of dyadic relations as one level of a multileveled set of *uchi/soto* continuums. The person who is *amayakasu*-ing or providing for the dependency of the others is to some extent transcending the situation and thus distanced from it. In this sense, the indulger is more *soto* in the dyadic relationship. The person who is *amaeru*-ing or receiving dependency is engaged in the situation—his or her engagement deepened by the objects provided by and actions and speech allowed by *amayakasu*-ing the person. The indulgee is more *uchi* in the relationship. In the opening scene, the mother is transcending the situation to provide for the father's involvement and relaxation.

In relation to an axis of engaged versus detached (*uchi/soto*) a person's situation is affected by a level of relationship and a level of context, both of which carry a pragmatic meaning in the sense defined by Peirce (1931–35, vol. 2).[2] This explains why for the father there is little tension because the levels coincide. Yet, for the mother, tensions exist because levels are juxtaposed. The mother's actions and speech are defined in part by the informality of the in-group context, and in part according to her side of the relationship with the father. Thus her language switches between formal and informal modes.

Part of the tension also results from the hierarchy inherent in the *amaeru/amayakasu* hierarchy relationship. Although in an *uchi* context authority is muted, the *okaasan* still defers to the *otoosan* with semiformal language. Niyekawa has noted the same deference in *uchi* situations in a television drama. She finds that intimacy can be communicated by the content of the speech, although status is maintained grammatically (1984, 77). At the relationship level, the mother communicates her deferential status as an in-marrying wife. Were the father to emphasize the authoritative side of hierarchy in this situation by enforcing his will, he would increase the tension in the situation.

If Japanese women were to interpret their lives only from a viewpoint of the individual as a center of control, they might see themselves as trapped in subordination and tension. Indeed, as I have mentioned above, they do complain to other women of always having to be tense or of being at the beck and call of other adults in the family. However, these conversations are usually encompassed by an assumption that this suffering finally brings satisfaction and pride. On looking back, women reinterpret their suffering as obligations fulfilled and maturity acquired.

GENDER RELATIONS IN HIERARCHY

If we are to understand why *uchi/soto* situations are meaningful for many Japanese women despite feelings of tension and subordination, we need to grasp the meaning of hierarchy for Japanese. First and foremost, hierarchy implies relationship, yet hierarchy may not always necessitate relations of authority, as Westerners tend to assume.

Dumont (1980) has argued for multiple shifting meanings in hierarchical relationships. At one level, a "contrary opposition" can be defined with one component superior and the other inferior. At another level, however, these two components represent a whole by the encompassing of the inferior by the superior—what Dumont calls the encompassing of the contrary. He illustrates this with the example of Adam and Eve. In this example, the man and woman do not relate just as structural opposites. Their opposition is valued and, in being valued, one is superior and the other inferior.[3] This valued opposition of hierarchy points back to the whole, the totality of humanness which they comprise by means of each other (240–42).

In this situation, the *amaeru/amayakasu* relationship of the mother and father taken as a whole indexes the social encounter as intimate and engaged. Even though from the woman's individual perspective the relationship produces subordination and tension, considered as whole, this particular inequality communicates the informality and in-groupness of an *uchi* context. Though hierarchical, this part/whole relationship communicates solidarity. The woman endures tension at the level of the individual for the sake of creating meaning at the level of the relationship and group.

Permutations of Hierarchical Relations

To further our understanding of how hierarchy indexes the *uchi/soto* continuum, let us look at a *soto* situation that will contrast to the *uchi* situation under discussion.[4] Because of my family-centered relationship with the father and mother, I was rarely in *soto* or formal contexts with them. One of the few occasions was my own wedding, a small gathering held in the home of a local missionary. Although nothing like a typical Japanese wedding, the occasion allowed me to see the two of them relate in a formal setting. Now their roles seemed reversed. He was the one who was managing the situation, leading the way in greeting others. She followed. He appeared to know the correct protocol about shoes, coats, and seats, and she conformed, showing small signs of embarrassment (hand over mouth, bent head, slight smile) when she made some small mistakes. He made a formal speech of congratulations in skillful rhetoric and she a short, rather emotional speech in much less polite phrasing and grammar. In short, he appeared to be the one who was managing this situation (*amayakasu*-ing) and she the dependent (*amaeru*-ing).

Japanese would label this situation as *soto*—restrained, with hierarchical relations between groups. Again, the *okaasan* as an individual is in a position of tension and subordination. She is the inferior in status, her dependent or *amaeru*-ing manner juxtaposed with the *soto* situation in which individuals should be highly disciplined, rational, and polite. The *otoosan*'s actions and speech are in sync with the situation.

Once more we must look at the relationship between these two as a complementarity of two people that indicates something. The hierarchical relationship as a whole indexes the *soto* context. Here, hierarchy between husband and wife exists within the framework of hierarchy between households. The reversed *amaeru/amayakasu* relationship now emphasizes hierarchy as authority in display toward other groups. The indulgence of the mother by the father at the wedding represents the proper status of the head male of the group in relation to the wife, and thus of the group itself in relation to other groups.

DYNAMIC SHIFTING OF HIERARCHICAL RELATIONS

Dumont (1980, 242) suggests that the dynamism in a hierarchical system is found in the reversals between hierarchically related pairs or dualities when they switch levels. Developing Dumont's ideas in a detailed study of the Nyamwezi of Tanzania, Tcherkezoff (1987, 56–59) gives an example of reversal in which at the royal level of ritual and divination, black is superior to white (the king derives his power from the black rain) whereas at the commoner level of family ritual and divination, white is superior to black (white sorghum four is given to the ancestors; witchcraft is black). In a hierarchical system, "efficacy is then measured . . . in terms of the relations between levels, and in terms of *changes in level*, which would be the only possible means of measuring a movement" (124). Inequality and reversals are not contradictions, but means of communication between socially differentiated levels.

Thus gender hierarchy gains its dynamic meaning in Japan through fluidity of gender roles in relation to *amaeru/amayakasu* dyads and the *uchi/soto* continuum. At any point in time the hierarchical relationship may appear static and thus meaningless but, when viewed over time, meaning and movement emerge, as individuals within the hierarchical relationship shift roles. The relationship itself indexes different aspects of life—at one time solidarity, at another authority.

Use of different terms for the genders in contexts of *soto* and *uchi* underlines this dynamic shifting. At the wedding, the father and mother were referred to as *okusan* and *dannasan*—words of address and reference that indicate their positions in the household. They would refer to (not address) each other in hierarchical terms of *shujin* 'husband' (literally, master) and *nyoobo* or *kanai* 'wife' (literally, inside the house). These terms signal their hierarchical relationship as operators of the household and representatives to other groups relating to the household.

In the home situation, they refer to and address each other as *okaasan* and *otoosan*: mother and father. These terms indicate solidarity, with the female gender encompassing the male in the *amaeru/amayakasu* relationship. This in no way implies an immature relationship in a Freudian sense (that is, the husband relating to his wife as a mother); these terms signal a type of relationship between the genders.

FLUID CONTENTS

Making a still life of *soto* and *uchi* contexts has its problems because these are always fluid according to the perspective one takes. The two derive meaning only in relation to each other. Like a series of Chinese boxes, what is *soto* in relation to one *uchi* soon becomes *uchi* in relation to a more public, detached level of *soto*. Although I have posited certain regularities in how gender relations are arranged as they index *soto* and *uchi*, analyses can be made definitive only in relation to actual situations.

Returning to the wedding scene, no sooner had the father and mother conveyed the idea of the authority of their group as he guided her through formalities than they shifted their relations, and the context as well. The most formal part of the ceremony finished, the speeches given, the wife, my *okaasan*, hurried to serve her husband in the buffet reception. It would not have been proper for him to get up and serve himself. He sat rather stiffly barking his needs at her, and she was again scurrying in a manner reminiscent of her actions at home in the evenings.

The wedding has moved into a more *uchi* situation, but one that was not as close to the intimate, engaged pole of *uchi*, as the evening at home. This is a public *uchi*—a *soto*-like *uchi*, if you will. The relationship of the woman *amayakasu*-ing or indulging the male could communicate solidarity if seen from an in-group perspective. But in relation to the assembled gathering, this relationship does not carry a message of solidarity so much as of status in hierarchy. The *otoosan*'s status in his group, and thus the status of his group vis-à-vis other groups, is supported by the fact that he does nothing for himself. While this is true as well in the home situation, others do not usually witness it (although such an impression may have been meant for me as guest), and thus the solidarity of the in-group is stressed (see Lebra 1976, 52).

The Last Alternative

We may wonder, however, if the male ever does *amayakasu* in private to an *amaeru*-ing female. In the course of my research on middle-aged women, a doctor in northeast Japan told me the following story concerning a middle-aged couple who had no children. The woman was complaining of various symptoms attributed to menopause. Her husband felt sorry for her and allowed her to rest all the time while he not only did his regular work but also bought the groceries every day and cooked the meals.

From the couple's point of view, this relationship showed extreme solidarity. When the story was told, the women in the room remarked that the husband was certainly gentle (*yasashii*). He had, in a sense, taken on the guise of a female in his nurturing role, and the women appreciated this service to his in-group.

However, the male doctor's evaluation was that the woman was being overly powerful in the sense of authority over her husband. To him, this particular reversal of the gender relation in a private sphere implied that the woman was being weak in the nurturing sense in which she should be strong, and thus not developing a strong psychological defense against her menopausal symptoms. This relationship indexed an *uchi* context, but the gendered roles for a married couple were ill arranged. The next section helps to explain the deeper assumptions of power in gender relations, which will shed light on why this relationship was askew.

METAPHYSICAL MEANINGS OF *SOTO, UCHI,* AND GENDER RELATIONS

The Japanese are only one of a number of cultural groups in the Pacific Region where poles of meaning for self and social life parallel *uchi/soto* poles of meaning in Japan. Among Samoans (Shore 1982), Javanese (Keeler 1987), and the Ilongot of the Philippines (Rosaldo 1980), people move between contexts of bound, concentrated energy that is outer-oriented and contexts of unbound, less-controlled energy that is inner-oriented.[5]

For Polynesia, Shore (1986, 63–66) proposes that the two main contexts between which self and society shift are linked with two basic transformations of the universal power of *mana*, a universal power that inheres in people, objects, and processes. One is a bounded, ordering force, and the other, an unbounded, generative force. In all these societies, people try to achieve the ideal strength by binding the power of the universe through control of people (both self and others) and relationships. Yet they consider that the unbound power of the universe is also necessary as a kind of untamed fuel for life (see Benedict 1972).

Japanese express similar ideas of harnessing and channeling one's energy without direct reference to any power of the universe. The Japanese think that it is necessary to develop spiritual energy (*seishin* or *kiryoku*) in order to have the restraint to be a cooperative, productive member of a group. Meditation or concentrated practice of martial or aesthetic arts can sharpen the ability to control one's spiritual energy. In folk psychology, such spiritual energy is the underpinning of making successful *soto* contexts. At the opposite end of the continuum, *uchi* contexts depend on the ability of at least some people in the group to loosen their restrained energy and express the inner feelings (*kimochi*) of their spirits or hearts (*kokoro*), ideally to enable people's emotions to blend in harmony (Rosenberger 1989a).[6]

Research into the conceptions of the powers of the universe in Shintoism has led me to argue that, like other Pacific societies, a link does indeed exist between the power of the universe as Japanese have conceived of it in the past and the importance of making and experiencing *soto* and *uchi* contexts in Japan today. No one consciously thinks of the link to this power in a religious sense, but ideas about it have been incorporated into common sense assumptions about context and relationship in contemporary Japan.

The power of the universe is understood in Shintoism as a unified force or process with various transformations. In early Japan, all inanimate and animate parts of nature were thought to be imbued with a common sacred *kami* nature (Kitagawa 1987, 120). This sacred nature is often called *tama* in Shinto; for humans it is referred to as *kokoro*, the word that is still used to denote the wellspring of feeling and source of purity in people (Kitagawa 1987, 36, 121; Herbert 1967, 22).

At least two main manifestations of this sacred power have been conceptualized in Shinto meditation—an outer manifestation that is authoritative and differentiated and an inner essence that is harmonious and centralizing (Herbert 1967, 61–62; Kitagawa 1987, 121).[7] These transformations of the sacred power are portrayed in a cyclical relationship like the seasons of the year reflected in a tree's changes. The inner manifestation is pictured as the folding in of the tree upon itself in winter, consolidating its energy in its roots and returning to its inner essence for generativity. The outer manifestation is illustrated in the outward growth of the tree in spring and summer, showing its authority to differentiate the tree's energy into branches, flowers, and leaves, each with its own place and function.

This metaphor for the power of the universe helps us to understand the nature of *soto* and *uchi* and the way that they interrelate. Like the sacred power, *soto* and *uchi* are ways of relating to others and the world that are transformations of a single process of life. Various degrees of discipline and spontaneity along the *uchi/soto* axis relate to a basic energy that people and groups tighten and loosen in order to mature along a path of natural growth (cf. Rosenberger 1989a).

Soto is like the summer process of the tree: concerned with outward orientations, differentiated statuses, even with competition between elements and wholes. It is energy that is bound and channeled and in human company manifests itself in authority that overcomes chaos. *Soto* is a centrifugal force pushing people and groups outward into social configurations that must relate with others.

Uchi is like the winter processes of the tree: closed into itself, concerned with inner processes of centralized growth through harmonious interaction of elements. Energy here is less closely bound and shows itself in the flow of emotions and generative sexuality among humans. *Uchi* is a centripetal force pulling people and groups inward toward likeness and generative reproduction. People risk chaos in this mode, and in some societies it is avoided or discouraged, but Japanese manage to exploit the generative energies of muted hierarchy, loosened emotions, and sexuality, while delicately binding them. Sources of generative power, such as nature and women, are literally roped into human use: the rope around the unique rock on the coast, the *obi* binding the kimono-clad woman, the knot on envelopes containing money.

METAPHYSICAL ORIENTATIONS AND GENDER

Shinto writers also explain the manifestations of sacred power through the metaphor of gender, associating the outward manifestation with the male gender and the inward essence with the female gender (cf. Shore 1981, 200). Humans of male or female gender are not confined to either process, and participate in both.[8] In relations with others, their growth depends on the same cycle of processes as the tree.[9]

Yet by virtue of their gender, real people are identified, and to some extent identify themselves, with certain qualities and actions that are like those of the Shinto powers of the universe. For example, in books written about femininity and masculinity, a popular male television personality advises women to supply harmony and rejuvenation to others, such as by serving tea to thirsty, tired men at work. He tells men to give decisive authority and rational organization, such as by bringing order among women employees who otherwise fritter away their time in bickering and envy (Suzuki 1980, 1982). A public speech given by a principal of a rural high school in the early eighties advised similar behavior: women should be inside the house, gently caring for others, and men should be outside the house, giving brave leadership. Real women and men do not always lead their lives according to these precepts, but they do feel a responsibility to fulfill societal needs that demand such gender-specific behavior (Rosenberger 1989b; Dubisch 1986).

An adult male, such as the father above, often communicates status-based authority when relating to females in a public situation; he stage-manages *soto* contexts and facilitates the participation of females (as well as other males lower in the hierarchy). This is not a nurturing kind of facilitation; it is an ordering and categorizing one. Deemphasizing dominance, Japanese think that good leaders should have self-discipline and that this model will benefit those of lower status as well.

An adult female, such as the mother above, often communicates centralized harmony in relating to males in a relatively private situation. She stage-manages *uchi* contexts and facilitates the participation of males (as well as females). She facilitates group harmony—individual relaxation and freedom being an offshoot of that. Geishas and bar girls are excellent examples of this; in the restaurant or bar, they infuse men's gathering with warmth and good will through their jokes, teasing, and sexual license—all of which they let loose to just the right degree (Rosenberger 1986).

The person who is *amayakasu*-ing or providing guidance and allowing (or forcing) dependence is often the one whose very "nature" (in cultural terms) reverberates with the aspect of sacred power represented in that context. He or she is in charge of the performance that indexes orientations of inner and outer. In terms of hierarchy, he or she encompasses the gender relationship in that particular situation.

In sum, the *amayakasu*-ing person is in charge, and thus should be superior in that context. In the *soto* context of the wedding, the father is superior and encompasses the mother in terms of "power" as authority. Indeed, male-led authority over women helps to produce *soto*-like relationships thought to be necessary for the formation of productive groups and the development of the self-restraint required of group members.

In the *uchi* context of the evening at home, the mother is superior to the father and encompasses him in terms of the "power" of centrality. True, she cannot relax or express herself as freely as he does, and in terms of power as authority remains subordinate to him. But the meaning of the relationship and the context is neither relaxation and freedom, nor authority, but centrality and unity. Her activity should include not only actions that are in accord with the situation, such as laughter, informal language, and relations of relative equality, but also actions that show her as the ritual manager of the situation. As such, she is the facilitator for men (and others) to enjoy the benefits of the *uchi*-type relationships on which the emotional solidarity of groups is based and in which its members are strengthened through nurturance.

As we shall see, these pragmatic uses of gender relations vary according to the specifics of the situation, but people with moral authority often recommend the pattern described above for married people in domestic and public contexts (cf. Edwards 1989). This is the reason that the doctor disapproved of the woman who allowed her husband to do the housework.

World Views Based on Relationship or on the Individual

Returning to a question central to our concern as people of the nineties: what about those who experience tension and subordination in these situations? This question, which at first blocks our acceptance of an explanation in terms of relationship, in fact pushes us to a deeper understanding of it. The question shows us that we are rooted in a world view—and a conception of power—based on individuals and their rights. The conception of "power" described in this essay is based on a world view that privileges relationship.

The ramifications of this difference in world views emerge by briefly comparing the transformations in the *uchi/soto* continuum with transformations that Brown and Gillman (1960) have traced in the French uses of *tu* and *vous*. They find that the uses of *tu* and *vous* vary historically, indicating alternately either "solidarity" or "power" (as authority). At first glance, these transformations seem similar to examples of *uchi/soto* transformations, but salient differences exist. The French usages assume the person as an objective core of meaning; the individual is the prime reality. The concern is to place and control the individual core of the person vis-à-vis other persons. The individual shifts from relationships of opposition ("power") to relationships of alliance ("solidarity").

In the transformations of *uchi/soto*, the core of meaning resides in complementary relations between people. The matter of importance is to place the relationship or group vis-à-vis the processes of society (or of the universe), and thus gain control over these processes.

Thus, in the French usage, "power" (as authority) has the sense of one person's ability to make another person comply. From the perspective of *soto* (which also includes authority), the sense is of people in relationships together controlling societal (or universal) chaos. Authority is inherent in the differentiation among people that is necessary to control chaos, but all are responsible to one another to achieve order. Thus leadership (authority) in Japan depends on compliance with consensus.

In the French usage, "solidarity" implies a personal core brought into relationship with another personal core to form a solid mass, with the implication of opposition by another solidarity. In the case of *uchi*, solidarity exists in the sense of togetherness but not in the sense of solidity of object. In this mode, people come together in an intimate emotionality in which people and the situation are quite fluid. Risking chaos, people open up the generative processes of the world through their complementary relationships.

The question of the individual woman's tensions is important and relevant from a world view based on the individual person as core meaning, and Japanese themselves perceive life in this way at times. However, we must stretch our perceptions to understand the validity of meaning at the level of the relationship and group—a meaning that at times overrides concerns with individuals. At the level of relationship we meet with no trivial matter: people manipulating their social order in order to create world processes as they perceive them.

Our tendency to understand personal relations in terms of inequality or equality is a stumbling block here. No matter what the locus of the situation along the *uchi/soto* continuum, unequal relations exist in the form of *amaeru/amayakasu*. It is important to acknowledge this and

struggle against unequal relations that are exploitative. Yet the complementarity between unequal relations is salient because (1) the relationships are not indicating their individual parts, but a set of meanings beyond themselves, and (2) the relationships go through permutations
that index various aspects of that set of meanings. These relationships
flip around constantly according to the situation, so that inequality is
only one of several concerns.

Complementary relations of *amaeru/amayakasu* have a multiplicity of
forms as they provide orientation along an *uchi/soto* continuum. Authority in *soto* contexts is not the purview of males, nor is centrality the purview of females in *uchi* contexts. The permutations extend to virtually all
the logical possibilities.

AXES OF AGE AND POSITION

Before ending, I will describe briefly some of the possible permutations
of *uchi/soto* and *amaeru/amayakasu* relationships that cross-cut any neat
categorizations of gender relationships. This will augment the reader's
awareness of the dynamism of this world view based on complementary
relationships that index contexts and processes.

Because age and position intersect with gender, both men and
women provide orientation as contexts shift from private (*uchi*) to public (*soto*) and back. Further, same-gender as well as cross-gender relations serve as indexers of *uchi/soto*.

Women can be on the *amayakasu* side of an *amaeru/amayakasu* relationship in a *soto* situation or on the *amaeru* side in an *uchi* situation.
For example, position overcomes gender when women head companies
or political parties, as they successfully do (Lebra 1984).

In the first half of this century, Japanese mothers were representatives
of authority and weavers of more *soto* situations when the son married
and brought home a daughter-in-law. Age allowed the mother a new
location on the *uchi/soto* axis. The stereotype of a mother-in-law is one of
unwielding authority over the daughter-in-law, resented for her lack of
sympathy, yet respected for her self-discipline and toughness. Her role
was to train the daughter-in-law to be a productive manager of the
household, both economically and ritually.

Although nuclear families and working wives are eroding this relationship between female in-laws, my *okaasan* is now experiencing a variation of this shift, with the adoption of a son-in-law into the household
through marriage.[10] The *otoosan* now having died, the *okaasan* has obtained a modicum of authority over this younger in-marrying male of
the household. On informal evenings, the son-in-law usually cannot
relax to the extent of stretching out on the *tatami*; he does small favors

for the mother-in-law, such as handing her the newspaper or her glasses. Thus, to some extent, she takes the *amaeru*-ing or *uchi* role in the relationship as the *otoosan* did formerly with her.

Another example of a similar permutation is the father-daughter relationship in the original *uchi*-scene in which an older male plays the indulging (*amayakasu*) role to a younger female who shines in her cute dependency (*amaeru*). However, the relationship could flip if an issue such as low grades prompted the father to shift into a more authoritarian mode—a relationship which would give the whole home atmosphere a more *soto* cast.

When we discuss multiple permutations of relationships, we are confronted by a mixing of relationships, shifting in various directions. Relationships that highlight *soto* and *uchi* may be juxtaposed within a context. For example, *soto*-type relationships indicating differentation and authority can be embedded within *uchi* contexts and can be participated in by people who are also in relationships indicating *uchi*. These embedded relationships can erode the integrity of a context, as in Kondo's examples (this volume) in which the centralized harmony of the group becomes a facade under the extremely authoritative behavior of the confectionary boss. On the other hand, in Bachnik's paper (this volume), people find a solution to their problems by embedding an *uchi* relationship in a *soto* situation. They use the authoritative, public mode of the *soto* situation to redress the overexpression of negative emotion in an *uchi* context.

Often a counterpoint relationship happens behind the scenes of the obvious context. Bar girls and "mama-san" who seem such perfect representatives of *uchi* are also running a business that is productive through authoritative relationships. Although they create (and sell) centralized harmony, the older women and younger women are clearly differentiated in relation to each other.

Similarly, the *okaasan* in the original scene was aided in her creation of an *uchi* scene by the authority that she held as an employer of a younger female. The maid was a young junior high graduate who had been sent to learn the skills of homemaking from an accomplished older female. Thus the mother had a *soto* relationship embedded in the *uchi* context.

The *okaasan* also occasionally created a more *soto*-like situation within the home when she authoritatively dispatched the daughter off to her room to do homework. However, the more usual feeling of relaxed exchange between the mother and daughter in which *okaasan* felt free to laugh and joke underscored the intimate context of the home. In future years, the mother-daughter relationship would continue to be an important locus for sharing personal feelings.

Amaeru/amayakasu relations between males are indexed as *uchi/soto* and can also index shifts along the *uchi/soto* continuum. At a university department with which I was affiliated, the shifts in the relationship of the department head, Mr. Suzuki, and his right-hand junior professor, Mr. Nozue, puzzled me. When Mr. Nozue first introduced me to Mr. Suzuki, Nozue was quite polite in language and action toward his superior, sitting quietly aside while the head advised me in strongly authoritative terms. I was surprised then at weekly meetings of faculty and graduate students to witness Nozue's authoritarian posture over students and Suzuki's withdrawal. Suzuki, the head, would sit at the head of a long table, with Nozue at his left side, less favored faculty at his right, and students below. Nozue actually ran the meetings, grilling the students mercilessly, shaming them about their shortcomings and lecturing them on the correct methods. He spoke in a disdainful, scolding tone, using the briefest verb forms and pronouns such as *o-mae*, clearly indicating the students' inferiority. Meanwhile the department head would sit at the head of the table smoking, looking off, and often combing his hair. His ostentatious lack of authority surprised me.

One way of understanding this switch in relationship is through the indexing of orientations along the *uchi/soto* continuum. In the formal, clearly *soto*, introduction to me, a new foreign student, the hierarchical status of their relationship was made clear. The regular Monday morning meetings with students were a little farther toward *uchi*—the inner group of faculty and students in a fairly hierarchical setting. In this context, the department head was indulging this favored junior professor by allowing him to impress his views authoritatively on the students in front of his colleagues. By combing his hair, Suzuki gave the impression that he himself was being indulged, and in a sense he was, because the details of the research problems were cared for by his inferior in this somewhat *uchi* context. But the department head was ultimately in control, establishing his position by lending his authority temporarily to an underling (cf. Befu 1977). His presence was important in establishing the extent of hierarchical authority in the meeting.

At departmental parties in local restaurants, the same favored instructor indulged the wishes of his department head. Nozue made sure that Suzuki had his wishes satisfied in food, drink, speeches, and seating arrangements. He defended his superior against students who expressed dissatisfactions to the head, and at the end of the party sent us all home with an enthusiastic feeling of togetherness by leading us in an ear-splitting cheer for the university. In this *uchi* situation Nozue, the inferior male, is the stage manager of the department's harmony, much like the mother at home. His indulgence of Suzuki, his superior, signals an *uchi* context where people are harmonious and engaged.

In short, although relations that differ by gender are important proto-types for shifts in context and universal energies, relations differing by status and age also shift to index subtle changes in *soto* and *uchi* contexts.

In this essay, I have shown that social life in Japan is best understood as a kaleidoscope of relationships and contexts in which patterns are al-ways shifting to create meaning in the here and now of their occurrence. The crystal change within the range of *uchi/soto* axes shows facets of spontaneity and discipline, engaged centrality and distanced differenti-ation. The permutations of relationships are limitless as people of differ-ent ages, genders, and social positions move from indulgee to indulger and back (*amaeru/amayakasu*). These occur in contexts that vary in sub-tle shades between extremes of spontaneity and rigidity (*uchi/soto*), influenced, of course, by the arrangement of relations within them. Jux-taposition, counterpoint, and an overlay of perspectives is inherent in social life that gains meaning from movement among social frames.

Japanese understand relationships and contexts (and their relations) in the specific instance. They assess the orientation and potential shift-ing of situations and relationships along the *uchi/soto* axes at a point in time and space. The process may seem complex to us, but the scenarios described in this essay would be elementary for those raised in Japanese society. Through experience, they have acquired a sense of the range of differences among relationships and contexts and can place new ones easily within that range. Indeed, the only way that *amaeru/amayakasu* re-lationships and *uchi/soto* contexts can gain meaning is through human perception of the differences between them.

Humans link fields of difference at a number of levels: the transfor-mations of Shinto sacred power of the universe are the processes of the *uchi/soto* continua of relations and contexts revisited. People magnify meanings by making transformations that reverberate at a number of different levels (context, relationship, sacred power).

These transformations are signifiers—the part of the sign that people use to represent something. Here, we have signifiers referring to one another in a giant circle. The transformations of relationships refer to transformations of sacred power that refer to transformations of nature that refer to transformations of context, and so on. They are a circle of signifiers referring one another in an endless exchange of voices (Der-rida 1989).

There is no core of meaning (no original center) here except the permutations and transformations of the patterns in relation to one an-other. If we look to Shinto sacred power to furnish a center (as in the West we look to God or the Truth), we find that *tama*, the sacred power (like *mana*), is beyond language, beyond the valued difference that is necessary to symbolic thought. Full of contradictions, it is everything—a "zero symbolic value" that can take on any value required (Levi-Strauss 1950, xlix). It points to the emptiness beyond the fields of differences created by forms and patterns (Barthes 1982, 68).

Neither are *uchi/soto* and *amaeru/amayakasu* centers in the sense of a notion or presence that is of supreme value. They are frameworks that enable differentiation and thus judgment and orientation. They are axes of movement and exist only in relation to moments of human experience measured on the axes. Thus our concern is not with meaning as a product (a tangible notion) but rather with meaning as a process undergoing transformations (Rice and Waugh 1989, 110).

These points challenge the objective use of concepts such as gender, hierarchy, and power. These terms should be used simply as guideposts that alert us to a range of various relationships in which there are differences among people. The meaning of these differences requires constant interpretation in the here and now of experience.

Gender can be understood only within relationships—which themselves are interpretable only from the perspective of a field of differences among multiple relationships in a number of contexts. Further, gender relations are embedded in a field of relationships with other differences such as age and position and must be considered in relation to these (Ortner 1981; Herzfeld 1986). Gender affects individuals, but the effect is fully comprehendable only within a broad perspective of relationships over time and place (Dubisch 1986). Given this broad perspective, one can grasp the meaning of gender differences to any person or relationship only within specific contexts with specific shifts in relationship.

Gender relations do not fit easily into words like *superior, inferior,* or *hierarchical.* From the perspective of individual rights and obligations to have economic and political control, gender relations in Japan are unfair—they subordinate and cause tension for adult women (Pharr 1982). From the perspective of individual rights and obligations to nurture family and self, gender relations are unfair—adult men are deprived. But from the perspective of social rights and obligations to be a person who discriminates powers of authority from powers of consolidation, able to enact and participate effectively in various degrees of both, unequal gender relations are dynamic and useful. I do not intend to understate the existence (and recognition by Japanese women) of tension and subordination in these relations at certain times, but rather to explain the tenacity of unequal gender relations by understanding their indexing functions at levels other than the individual.

Hierarchy as a concept is significant only as a valued difference among people. Within the Japanese social field, hierarchy does not have an opposite. It is a condition that so pervades social life as an assumption that the task is not to define hierarchy as a concept but to understand how actors constantly manipulate this "valued difference between people" in a meaningful way in various contexts and spheres of life. The most we can say about the "nature" of hierarchy in Japanese society is that unequal relations take the form of indulgor and indulgee (*amaeru/ amayakasu*) and that these relationships shift positions as they move along an axis ranging from private to public, spontaneity to discipline (*uchi/soto*). The use of hierarchy is so wide-ranging and flexible that constant redefinition is necessary as to who is valued differently from whom, in what way, and why.

Hierarchy is best understood as a process. The process has energy that people can shape. If they emphasize the differences in hierarchy, they generate a energy of ordered authority, but if they stress the commonalities of the valued difference, they generate an energy of nurturative consolidation. Other processes could be generated at the extremes—uninhibited anger or tyranny, for example. The point is that hierarchy can be perceived as a condition that enables movement and change in social life.

In a similar fashion, the term *power* should be used as an indicator of various permutations of energy. Rather than connoting only authority or influence, power would imply energy in a general sense. We then would have a term that could be used to understand multiple forms and patterns of energy of different spheres, context, and relationships (cf. Mukhopadhayay 1982). This paper amply proves such a need.

In sum, I urge a definition of conceptual terms concerning differences between individuals that enables us to talk about people in social life beyond an objective, individual perspective. Such terms would allow us to perceive social life in terms of its dynamic shifts in meaning and action at levels of relationship and context.

NOTES

1. A Japanese woman would also feel such tension with older females, especially a mother-in-law, just as a man would feel it with older males such as a father-in-law or a superior at work. Unlike women in hierarchical relations between the genders, however, the younger subordinates in a hierarchical relation between people of the same sex have a good possibility of becoming older superiors in the future.

2. Both levels of relationship and context carry a pragmatic message—a message that indexes context and social relations (Silverstein 1976, 20). Pragmatic meaning is defined as "meaning that is dependent on context," whereas semantic meaning has a "notional core" apart from contextual factors (Mertz 1985, 4).

3. Eve in her origin from Adam's rib is encompassed by him; together they make a whole. As a human she is identical with him. When separated from him, she is inferior to him and stands in opposition to him as a different kind of human.

4. Lebra (1976, 60) has made the point that gender relations differ between public and private. I hope to extend her analysis by showing the use of these gender relations as pragmatic signs of context with sacred dimensions.

5. In Samoa the person moves between *amio*, which focuses on individual will or drives, and *aga*, which suggests conformity to prescribed social behavior (Shore 1982, 154). Among the Ilongot, people move between *liget*, the passion of the heart without which life could not go on, and a concentrated form of that energy called *beya*, which represents a human's most potent use of the universal power (Rosaldo 1980, 47–50). The Javanese male self is intent on developing a concentrated energy called *batin* through ascetic practices, while drawing energy with caution from the more emotional chaotic energy experienced when watching a puppet play (Keeler 1987, 39).

6. The basic spiritual energy is called *ki* which in its original meaning in China and Japan conveyed the idea of a power of the universe that inhered in people's bodies as well as other objects. In contemporary Japan, Japanese use *ki* in relation to a person to describe an energy that is of the spirit or heart, rather than the body or universe. The *ki* reaches out and meets with the ki of other people, and is easily influenced by the environment. *Ki* also is used in words to refer to the weather.

7. The most enlightened understand the sacred power of *tama* in four different aspects: (1) *arimitama*, the raw power of outer manifestation that is empowered to have authority over unruly areas of life; (2) *nigimitama*, the mild power of inner essence that leads to consolidation and harmony; (3) *kushimitama*, the power to differentiate, split, or analyze (which gives mysterious transformations); and (4) *sakimitama*, the power to penetrate and centralize (which imparts blessings) (Herbert 1967, 61–62; Kitagawa 1987, 121).

8. For a detailed analysis of how a woman participates in various contexts, giving and taking objects and relations that have a sacred dimension, see Rosenberger 1992.

9. The reader is referred to arguments put forth by Vygotsky (1978) and Bakhtin (Clark and Holquist 1984, chap. 3) that self develops higher mental processes and exists only through the mediation of signs communicated in relationship with others.

10. In Japan, a son may be adopted at the time of marriage to one's daughter in order to have male and female heads of the household who will be responsible for the household and provide an heir.

REFERENCES

Anderson, Benedict. 1972. "The Idea of Power in Java," in C. Halt, B. Anderson, and J. Siegel, eds., *Culture and Politics in Indonesia.* Ithaca: Cornell University Press.
Bachnik, Jane. 1987. "Native Perspectives of Distance and Anthropological Perspective of Culture." *Anthropological Quarterly* 60 (1): 25–34.

Barthes, Roland. 1982. *Empire of Signs.* New York: Hill and Wang.

Befu, Harumi. 1977. "Power in the Great White Tower," in R. Fogelson and R. Adams, eds., *Anthropology of Power.* New York: Academic Press.

Brown, Roger, and Albert Gilman. 1960. "The Pronouns of Power and Solidarity," in T. A. Sebeok, ed., *Style in Language,* 253–72. Cambridge, Mass.: MIT Press.

Clark, Katerina, and Michael Holquist. 1984. *Mikhail Bakhtin.* Cambridge, Mass.: Harvard University Press.

Derrida, Jacques. 1989. "Structure, Sign and Play in the Discourse of the Human Sciences," in P. Rice and P. Waugh, eds., *Modern Literacy Theory.* New York: Edward Arnold.

Doi, Takeo. 1973. *The Anatomy of Dependence.* Tokyo: Kodansha International.

Dubisch, Jill. 1986. "Introduction," in J. Dubisch, ed., *Gender and Power in Rural Greece.* Princeton, N.J.: Princeton University Press.

Dumont, Louis. 1980. *Homo Hierarchicus.* Revised edition. Chicago: University of Chicago Press.

Edwards, Walter. 1989. *Modern Japan Through Its Weddings: Gender, Person and Society in Ritual Portrayal.* Stanford: Stanford University Press.

Goffman, Erving. 1974. *Frame Analysis.* New York: Harper and Row.

Herbert, Jean. 1967. *Shinto: The Fountainhead of Japan.* New York: Stein and Day.

Herzfeld, Michael. 1986. "Within and Without: The Category of 'Female' in the Ethnography of Modern Greece," in J. Dubisch, ed., *Gender and Power in Rural Greece.* Princeton, N.J.: Princeton University Press.

Keeler, Ward. 1987. *Javanese Shadow Plays, Javanese Selves.* Princeton, N.J.: Princeton University Press.

Kitagawa, Joseph. 1987. *On Understanding Japanese Religion.* Princeton, N.J.: Princeton University Press.

Lebra, Takie Sugiyama. 1976. *Japanese Patterns of Behavior.* Honolulu: University of Hawaii Press.

————. 1984. *Japanese Women: Constraint and Fulfillment.* Honolulu: University of Hawaii Press.

Levi-Strauss, Claude. 1950. "Introduction a l'oeuvre de Marcel Mauss," in M. Mauss, ed., *Sociologie et Anthropologie.* Paris: P.U.F.

Mertz, Elizabeth. 1985. "Beyond Symbolic Anthropology: Introducing Semiotic Mediation," in E. Mertz and R. Parmentier, eds., *Semiotic Mediation: Sociocultural and Psychological Perspectives.* Orlando, Fla.: Academic Press.

Mukhopadhayay, Carol. 1982. "*Sati* or *Shakti*: Women, Culture and Politics in India," in J. O'Barr, ed., *Perspectives on Power: Women in Africa, Asia and Latin America,* 11–26. Durham, N.C.: Duke University Center for International Studies.

Niyekawa, Agnes. 1984. "Analysis of Conflict in a Television Home Drama," in E. Krauss, T. Rohlen, and P. Steinhoff, eds., *Conflict in Japan,* 61–84. Honolulu: University of Hawaii Press.

Ortner, Sherry. 1981. "Gender and Sexuality in Hierarchical Societies: The Case of Polynesia and Some Comparative Implications," in S. Ortner and H. Whitehead, eds., *Sexual Meanings.* New York: Cambridge University Press.

Peirce Charles S. 1931–35. *Collected Papers.* Vol. 2. Edited by C. Hartshorne and P. Weiss. Cambridge, Mass.: Harvard University Press.

Pharr, Susan. 1982. "Tea and Power: The Anatomy of a Conflict," in J. O'Barr, ed., *Perspectives on Power: Women in Africa, Asia and Latin America*, 37–49. Durham, N.C.: Duke University Center for International Studies.

Rice, Phillip, and Patricia Waugh. 1989. Introduction. *Modern Literary Theory: A Reader*. New York: Edward Arnold.

Rosaldo, Michelle. 1980. *Knowledge and Passion: ILongot Notions of Self and Social Life*. New York; Cambridge University Press.

Rosenberger, Nancy. 1984. "Middle-age Japanese Women and the Meanings of the Menopausal Transition." Unpublished doctoral dissertation, University of Michigan.

———. 1986. "Japanese Women: Paradoxes of Power and Self." Presented at the Southeast Regional Association for Asian Studies Conference, Chattanooga, Tenn.

———. 1987a. "Productivity, Sexuality and Ideologies of Menopausal Problems in Japan," in E. Norbeck and M. Lock, eds., *Health, Illness, and Medical Care in Japan*. Honolulu: University of Hawaii Press.

———. 1989a. "Dialectical Balance in the Polar Model of Self: The Japan Case." *Ethos* 17:1.

———. 1989b. "Japanese Women and the Debate over Feminity or Feminism." Presented at the Center for Humanities Conference: The Feminine Revolution in Asia: Fact or Fiction? University of Georgia.

———. 1992. "Tree in Summer, Tree in Winter: Movement of Self in Japan," in N. Rosenberger, ed., *Japanese Sense of Self*. Cambridge: Cambridge University Press.

Silverstein, Michael. 1976. "Shifters, Linguistic Categories and Cultural Description," in Keith Basso and Henry Selby, eds., *Meaning in Anthropology*. Albuquerque, N. Mex.: University of New Mexico Press.

Shore, Bradd. 1981. "Sexuality and Gender in Samoa: Conceptions and Missed Conceptions," in S. Ortner and H. Whitehead, eds., *Sexual Meanings*. Cambridge: Cambridge University Press.

———. 1982. *Sala'llua: A Samoan Mystery*. New York: Columbia University Press.

———. n.d. "Polynesian Worldview: A Synthesis." Unpublished ms.

Suzuki, Kenji. 1980. *Otoko ga Yonjudai ni Yatteokubeki Koto* (Things a man should be doing when he hits the forties). Tokyo: Daiwa Press.

———. 1982. *Onnarashisa Monogatari* (The tale of femininity). Tokyo: Shogakkan.

Tcherkezoff, Serge. 1987. *Dual Classification Reconsidered: Nyamwezi Sacred Kingship and Other Examples*. Cambridge: Cambridge University Press.

Vygotsky, L. S. 1978. *Mind in Society*. Edited by Michael Cole et al., Cambridge, Mass.: Harvard University Press.

Chapter 5

UCHI/SOTO:
CHOICES IN DIRECTIVE SPEECH ACTS
IN JAPANESE

ROBERT J. SUKLE

EDITORS' INTRODUCTION

Robert Sukle's chapter complements Rosenberger's in its focus on linking *uchi/soto* to the processes of indexing and shifting—this time in language use. Sukle's approach combines two intersecting research goals: he manages to obtain a large corpus of material covering a variety of situations, while recording natural interaction. Sukle has managed these goals by focusing on a single type of speech act—directive speech, including requests, commands, hints, and so forth—and observing a large number of usage cases. Sukle's paper contrasts with Rosenberger's ethnographic approach, which focuses on intense description of a small number of cases, tracing out the permutations in relationships over a variety of different contexts.

Sukle's extensive corpus of empirical data addresses a question about which surprisingly little is known: how speakers designate *uchi/soto* distinctions in actual speech situations. Sukle's data are taken from four locations: a railway ticket window, a post office window, a neighborhood vegetable market, and a middle-class family, and his cases range across the entire *uchi/soto* continuum. The language behavior he presents ranges from a near-ritual avoidance of addressing railroad and postal clerks as *uchi*, to an almost complete avoidance in the home of speaking to fellow family members as *soto*.

Sukle finds that the situations in which speakers are virtual strangers—the railroad station and post office—are demarcated as *soto* in 100 percent of the directive speech acts, while the interaction at the neighborhood vegetable market—where the majority of participants are known to one another—is markedly different. Speakers at the vegetable market designate *uchi* significantly more than those at the railroad station and post office; they also shift register a great deal. The vegetable vender is known to most of his customers and is therefore more *uchi*. Yet the use of *soto* indicators as well as *uchi*, and the frequency of shifting,

indicate that participants at the vegetable market are negotiating a social definition of the very context in which they are interacting. Sukle
explains the shifts in a way that corresponds to Rosenberger: the frequent marking of the vendor by the customer as *uchi*, and the customer
by the vendor as *soto*, expresses a relationship in which *he* is catering to
them. Just like the *okaasan* in Rosenberger's narrative, the vendor is in a
soto relationship position within an *uchi* situation.

Finally, the family is much more unambiguously defined as *uchi* than
the vegetable market is. Yet shifting of register in directive usage from
uchi to *soto* occurs even within the family, although more rarely. Sukle
shows with humor and insight how occasions occur when one member
feels obliged to take up an 'outside' stance in dealing with another
member who remains 'inside'. In the illustration of how even mothers
and daughters will step 'outside' their shared circle for certain purposes, Sukle's paper again substantiates the indexing of gender and
hierarchy within the family delineated by Rosenberger.

UCHI/SOTO: CHOICES IN DIRECTIVE SPEECH ACTS
IN JAPANESE

THIS ESSAY presents and examines empirical evidence of the linguistic
signaling of *uchi/soto* 'in-group/out-group' boundaries in everyday Japanese interaction.[1] The analysis is based on data taken from four locations: (1) a ticket window at Sugamo National Railway Station in Tokyo,
(2) a counter window at Shinjuku Central Post Office in Tokyo, (3) a
small neighborhood vegetable market in a Tokyo suburb, and (4) the
home of a middle-class, white-collar family residing in a Tokyo suburb.
All locations are representative of settings in which any urban speaker is
likely to interact with others, on a daily basis.

Focus will be on *uchi/soto* indexing in the specific area of directive
speech acts in Japanese. Directive speech acts are those in which the
speaker attempts to linguistically direct the behavior of the addressee by
making a request, issuing a command, hinting, or the like. Such acts are
a fertile area of language to examine for sociolinguistic variation, since
they involve an interpersonal negotiation in which a speaker imposes his
or her will on an addressee and endeavors to get the addressee to do
something for the speaker or to give something to the speaker. This
imposition of the will of one party on that of another is one example of
what Brown and Levinson (1978) call a "face-threatening act," asserting
as it does the power of one party over the other. Brown and Levinson
claim that speakers performing face-threatening acts have available to
them in their language a variety of polite strategies for avoiding conflict
that could arise from the face-threatening act if it were performed with-

out such strategies. According to them, the question of what constitutes a face-threatening act is culture-specific, and strategies for handling them are language-specific. The relationship between face-threatening acts and the employment of polite strategies, however, is claimed to be universal and rationally based. The selection of the directive speech act as a focus for this study was hence motivated partly by theoretical considerations. Linguistic manifestations of directive speech acts will be referred to as "directives."

The study is divided into two parts. The first part treats data collected at the first three locations, the service settings, and isolates a distance-gauging parameter employed there. The second part treats data collected in the family. This two-part division represents speakers interacting with out-group members (*soto*) on the one hand, and with in-group members (*uchi*) on the other hand. However, as we shall see, linguistically signaled group boundaries are hardly isomorphous with this simple division. Rather, it is quite clear that language serves in part as a means for negotiating a social definition of the interaction. A variety of language acts in Japanese index *uchi/soto* boundaries in such a way as to mark the addressee as *uchi* on one occasion but as *soto* on another. The choice depends both on the social relationships presumed between speaker and addressee and the specific kind of interaction being negotiated.

The *uchi/soto* dichotomy is a social phenomenon; the way it is expressed in language is a matter of sociolinguistics and pragmatics. Analysis of Japanese in terms of phonology, syntax, morphology, semantics, or lexicon alone is not sufficient to grasp the linguistic manifestation of the *uchi/soto* concept since, as a phenomenon, it is *lived*, a property of social life. Analysis of the semantics of the Japanese verb system, for example, may reveal that the system is equipped to signal the *uchi/soto* distinction, but this alone tells one nothing about how, when, and to what extent such signals actually occur in language use in society, or by whom, to whom, and for what purpose such signals are transmitted. More important for present purposes, it tells nothing about the insight such signals can provide into the social phenomenon *uchi/soto* itself. To address *uchi/soto* as it is lived in language, one must address questions such as these. In other words, *uchi/soto* signaling must be examined in actual social interaction, such as occurs at the locations where data were collected for the present study. Although interaction at ticket windows or vegetable markets may at first thought seem to be a strange choice for such an investigation, it has first of all the advantage of being a real and natural interaction of the sort that many speakers engage in daily, in some form or other. Second, it is a type of interaction that provides large amounts of data occurring completely naturally and spontaneously in virtually identical pragmatic contexts. This fact means that a natural experimental control of sociolinguistic variables is built into the situation, so that artificiality and intervention do not intrude in the interaction.

Directives Issued to Out-Group or *Soto*

Social Parameters of the Data-collection Locations

Before looking at the patterns of interaction at the service settings, some information about the social character of each institution is in order. Both the railroad station and the post office were large, government-operated institutions located in central Tokyo, not in residential neighborhoods. Both serve thousands of people each day. The railroad station probably deals with many times this number, very likely tens, or even hundreds, of thousands. Interaction in both locations is rapid, impersonal, and perfunctory. There are, however, some ways in which the two institutions differ.

The large Central Post Office was frequented by a wide variety of people—male and female white- and blue-collar workers, housewives, students, foreigners, and retirees—as judged on the basis of behavior, clothing, and other factors. Although many, if not most, customers may have been stopping there for the first time, or even the only time, others were very likely "regulars." In particular, many of the *sarariiman* 'salaried men' or 'white-collar workers' and *ooeru* 'OLs' or 'office ladies' (women employed by companies as secretaries and general office helpers) came in with office business to do—mass mailings, orders for large numbers of supplies like stamps or postcards, and so on. Since Shinjuku is a large center of commerce and banking, as well as shopping and entertainment, most of these people were probably from companies in the immediate area. Some of them were even observed to come several times—or even daily in a few cases—during the period that the data were being collected. It is not unlikely, then, that some vague sense of familiarity with the clerks could develop in a way that would be highly unlikely at the railroad station.

While it is also true that a large proportion of the people moving through any major station in Tokyo may be regular commuters to work or school, they would rarely have occasion to interact with a clerk at a station since tickets are sold mainly by vending machine and since regular commuters generally purchase renewals for their passes as infrequently as twice as year. Others were purchasing a long-distance ticket for a destination to which their daily pass would not take them but this, too, is an activity rarely engaged in.

In social terms, the vegetable market stands in sharp contrast to the station and the post office. It was a small, family-owned business located in a narrow, winding street of a residential suburban area of Tokyo and was frequented largely by neighborhood housewives doing their daily shopping (which generally is, by the way, a *daily* pursuit in Japan). Most of the customers can be presumed to know the vendor. There is, in fact, some indirect evidence in the data that the vendor does know the customers: he is sometimes asked to deliver an item to the customer's house on his way home; he comments on the fact that one woman's baby has broken out in a rash *again*; customers readily leave purchased items with him while they go off to other shops to make other purchases. He interacts with the customers on a very personal and personable level in other ways as well: he gives them hints as to how to prepare unusual items; he talks to their children, often urging them to eat a lot (so his sales will increase); in a jovial manner, he frequently pressures customers to purchase an additional item or offers them the last one at a discount. He jokes with some customers, and some joke with him. Although the interaction is conducted on a commercial basis, it definitely has a personal side as well. Behavior of this type was never observed in interactions at the station or even at the post office, where communication was completely impersonal, efficient, and perfunctory.

COLLECTION AND SELECTION OF THE DATA

Data for this portion of the study were collected at a ticket window of the station, a stamp window of the post office, and at the service area of the vegetable market. They were collected by the investigator accompanied by a Japanese informant at the first two locations and by a specially trained Japanese informant alone at the vegetable market. Although large quantities of data were collected at all three locations, those focused on in the first section of this study include only those items that represented one well-defined type of encounter in terms of pragmatics—one in which the speaker requests a product from the clerk or vendor. For example, at the post office, this product was stamps, cash envelopes, postcards, or the like; requests for special services, such as the weighing of a package, the registration of a letter, or the borrowing of an item, were excluded from analysis here. With these exclusions, the remaining body of data was remarkably homogeneous in nature: all encounters were virtually identical pragmatically, and differed only in the identity of the participants and the type of institution at which the collection occurred. It can be assumed, then, that the range of variation observed in the data is both permitted and constrained mostly by social variables, such as the identities and relationship of speaker and addressee, rather than by pragmatic variables.

In addition to selecting one specific type of interaction from the data, further restrictions were imposed: only items in which the speaker is female and the addressee male were analyzed. This restriction was made necessary partly by the nature of the data itself, since in nearly all cases the addressees (the clerks or vendor at the service settings) were male. The speakers at all three locations included both males and females, but male speakers were rather underrepresented at the vegetable market. For this reason and for the reason of space limitations, it was decided to limit the analysis to female speakers only. Furthermore, the differences in linguistic patterns between male and female speakers proved to be interesting sociolinguistically but unproductive in terms of further elucidating the *uchi/soto* dichotomy.

STRUCTURE OF THE DATA

The structure of virtually all items collected at each of the three service counters can be analyzed as involving the following functional categories.

(A) Specification of the type of goods desired
(B) Specification of the number or amount of goods
(C) Specification of the social relationship obtaining between speaker and addressee.

Specification of the type of goods was represented by the occurrence of a single nominal in most cases and of a more elaborate nominal phrase containing modifiers when a particular variety of the desired goods was specified. Specification of the desired goods is the only one of the three elements listed above that is obligatory under most circumstances; therefore a substantial number of items at each of the three data collection locations consisted solely of this category (with or without further specification as to particular type of goods), as in the following examples:[2]

At the railroad station:
  (1) (a) *nagano.*
            Nagano
            '(A ticket to) Nagano.'
       (b) *chuuoosen no ootsuki.*
            Chuo Line's Otsuki
            '(A ticket to) Otsuki on the Chuo Line.'
At the post office:
       (c) *nana-juu-en no kitte.*
            seventy-yen 's stamp
            'A seventy-yen stamp.'

Example (1a) above is less complex, containing only specification of the desired goods (or, more precisely, specification of the type of de-

sired goods with the goods themselves being understood from context);
(1b) and (1c) are more complex, containing both specification of goods
and a modifier specifying type.

Category (B) of the functional categories above, specification of the
number or amount of goods, is optional when the desired number is
one, and obligatory only when it is more than one. When number or
amount was specified, it was expressed by a numeral-plus-classifier compound.

Functional category (C), which is somewhat cryptically termed here
"specification of relation obtaining between speaker and addressee," refers to the occurrence of some element expressing information like
"give me," "let me have," "I'll take," "I request," or the like. Such information is expressed in this Japanese data by (1) a predicate (that is, a
verb, adjective, or nominal-plus-copula), or by (2) the nominal *choodai*
'receive'. Category (C) is optional, as is made clear by the fact that
speakers failed to specify it in 48.1 percent of the cases at the post office,
22.7 percent at the railroad station, and 24.6 percent at the vegetable
market. These speakers were nevertheless readily understood by the addressee in each case since such information, being present in the context, does not require an explicit mention. The question thus arises as to
what motivation a speaker would have for expressing such information
at all, if it adds nothing that is not already deduceable from the context.
It seems clear that the motivation for such specification is to express
social information concerning the relationship between speaker and addressee. To see that this is so, it will be necessary to examine in some
detail the forms that occurred in specifying this information.

SOCIOLINGUISTIC MEANING INDEXED IN THE DIRECTIVES

Table 1 indicates the extent of specification within category (C) at all
service settings and the type of forms that occurred. The table shows
that out of the 145 items collected at the three locations, 85.5 percent or
124 are accounted for with only three linguistic strategies: (1) lack of
specification, (2) specification with *kudasai*, and (3) specification with
choodai.

The form *kudasai* is the imperative form of the honorific verb *kudasaru* which, in view of Wetzel's (1984) analysis, can be glossed as "*soto*
'out-group' gives to *uchi* 'in-group'." In addition, the verb *kudasaru*,
being honorific, expresses respectful distance between the *soto* giver and
the speaker by elevating the giver; thus, in a sense, it doubly marks giver
as *soto*. Though the imperative form *kudasai* does not carry the Distal[3]
morpheme -*mas*- (as contrasted with *kudasaimase*, the Distal counterpart), the combination of the honorific feature, the feature marking
giver as *soto*, and the feature marking the recipient as *uchi* benefactor

TABLE 1
Degree of Specification of Social Relationship at All Three
Service Locations

Total	100%	(145)
Unspecified	33.1%	(48)
Kudasai	45.6%	(66)
Choodai	06.9%	(10)
Other	14.5%	(21)

render the form quite distant in nature; it is therefore associated with speech to out-group rather than speech within a socially close group, as will be demonstrated. Therefore *kudasai* tends to occur with high frequency in public contexts, such as those under investigation here, on signs directed to the general public, in public announcements, such as those on public address systems, in operating instructions on vending machines, or in brochures and other contexts where the Distal form would occur in other predicates.[4] Henceforth, the term *Distant* will be used to refer to an utterance containing *either* the form *kudasai* or some other predicate in the Distal form.

The form *choodai* contrasts sharply with *kudasai* grammatically as well as semantically. *Choodai* is a nominal that refers to the act of receiving on the part of the speaker. Whereas a sequence ending with an imperative form like *kudasai* is classified as a major sentence[5] in Japanese, a sequence ending with a nominal like *choodai* is, strictly speaking, not a major sentence grammatically but qualifies rather as a fragment (Jorden 1987, 20). Significant for this study, Jorden (1987, 197) observes: "Casual speech is marked by the frequent use of fragments without predicates. . . . Careful speech has fewer fragments without predicates and more major sentences . . . and more distal-style inflected forms . . . at least in sentence-final predicates." While *choodai* is classified as a humble polite item, it is not associated with out-group, public speech as is *kudasai*; it is, rather, somewhat close, intimate, and typical of in-group speech, as will be demonstrated.

Given this background on these forms, the patterns of occurrence of the directives at the three data collection locations show revealing trends, as is demonstrated by Table 2. PO, RR, and VM refer to post office, railroad station, and vegetable market, respectively. If we temporarily suspend discussion of the category "Other" in the table, it is apparent that a speaker at the vegetable market has basically a three-way choice in terms of linguistic strategy: the addressee can be marked (1) as *soto* by selection of *kudasai*, (2) as close, intimate, or *uchi* by selection of *choodai*, or (3) the social relationship between speaker and addressee can be left unspecified.

TABLE 2
Type of Indexing of Social Relationship at Each of the Three
Service Locations

Location	All Forms	Unspecified	Kudasai	Choodai	Other
VM	100% (69)	24.6% (17)	36.2% (25)	14.5% (10)	24.6% (17)
PO	100% (54)	48.1% (26)	51.9% (28)	00.0% (0)	00.0% (0)
RR	100% (22)	22.7% (5)	59.1% (13)	00.0% (0)	18.2% (4)

If this range of choice is compared to that available at the railroad station or the post office, it is clear that *choodai* was simply not available as a choice in these two more distant social contexts: speakers there never marked the addressee as an intimate, as a member of *uchi*. *Choodai* did not occur even once. Instead, the addressee was marked as *soto* in 51.9 percent of the cases at the post office and the marking of social relationship was simply left unspecified in the other 48.1 percent of the cases. No other options occurred in the post office sample. At the railroad station, the addressee was marked as *soto* in an even greater 59.1 percent of the cases. Social relationship was left unspecified in 22.7 percent of the cases, and in 18.2 percent (four cases) other strategies were relied on. As at the post office, in no case was the addressee marked as *uchi* through occurrence of *choodai*.

At the vegetable market, by contrast, the addressee was marked as *soto* in only 36.2 percent of the cases. This is roughly 70 percent of the rate found at the post office and only 60 percent that found at the railroad station. In addition, the addressee at the vegetable market was marked as *uchi* in 14.5 percent of the cases. In 24.6 percent of the cases the social relationship was left unspecified. It is clear that interaction at the vegetable market can be characterized as distinctly "more *uchi*" and at the other two locations as distinctly "more *soto*." This contrast becomes even more marked when the category "Other" is examined.

Only four items consisting of two distinct types occurred in the category "Other" in the railroad station data. These are given in (3) below.

(3) X represents the item requested by speaker.
    (a) *X onegai-shimasu.*   (2 items)
        request/hum-I
        '(I humbly) request X'.
    (b) *X itadakitai*   *n*   *desu ga*   (2 items)
        get/hum-want-I EP Cp-I but
        'It's the case that (I'd humbly) like to get X, but . . .'

Not only do all four items in this category contain humble forms, which mark the speaker as *uchi* and the addressee as *soto*, but they also contain the Distal markings, -*mas*- in the case of (a) and *desu* in the case of (b), which mark the utterances as speech between nonintimates. Thus, these four cases can be added to those that mark the addressee as *soto*, making a total of seventeen out of twenty-two, or 77.3 percent, with the remainder unspecified.

In sharp contrast with this pattern of marking are the seventeen items in category "Other" in the vegetable market data. These are given below as (4).

(4) X represents the item requested.

    (a) *X morau wa.*   (5 items)
        get-I   SP
        '(I)'ll take X.'

    (b) *X moratte [i]ku wa.*   (3 items)
        get-G   go-I SP
        '(I)'ll take X and go.'

    (c) *X itadaku   wa.*   (2 items)
        get/hum-I SP
        '(I)'ll (humbly) take X.'

    (d) *X itadaite   [i]ku wa.*   (1 item)
        get/hum-G go-I SP
        '(I)'ll (humbly) take X and go.'

    (e) *X itadakoo ka sira.*   (1 item)
        get-C   Q wonder
        '(I) wonder if (I) should take X?'

    (f) *X ni   suru   wa.*   (2 items)
        goal make-I SP
        '(I)'ll make it X.'

    (g) *X ga   ii   wa.*   (1 item)
        subj. good-I SP
        'X will be good.'

    (h) *X aru?*   (1 item)
        have-I
        'Do (you) have X?'

    (i) *ja.*   (1 item)
        well then
        'Well then, (I'll take it).' [upon being urged to buy something else]

Every one of the sixteen items represented by (4a) through (4h) are major sentences, ending as they do with a verbal predicate. As such, it is possible to mark them with the Distal -*mas*- signal, but not one of the items in fact exhibits such marking as do the items in the "Other" category from the railroad data. The seventeenth item, given here as (4i), is grammatically a fragment; it thus lacks a final predicate and therefore

TABLE 3
Indexing of Addressee as *uchi* or *soto* at Each of the Three Service Locations

Location	Total	Unspecified	Specified as soto	Specified as uchi
RR	100% (22)	22.7% (5)	77.3% (17)	00.0% (0)
PO	100% (54)	48.1% (26)	51.9% (28)	00.0% (0)
VM	100% (69)	26.1% (18)	36.2% (25)	37.7% (26)

also lacks the Distal marking which may be attached to predicates. In addition, fragments tend to be associated with more casual speech, as was pointed out earlier. In other words, sixteen of these items served to mark the interacting parties as close, or *uchi*, and the seventeenth was left unspecified as to social relationship.[6]

It is clear, then, that consideration of the category "Other" establishes the group of interactants at the vegetable market as even more markedly *uchi* than was previously discovered. Sixteen of the items, like the *choodai* items, signal a close social relationship; the seventeenth can be added to the "Unspecified" category. Table 3 summarizes the reanalyzed findings for the three data collection locations, in terms of specification of addressee as *uchi* or *soto*.

Table 3 shows that interaction at the railroad station was the most Distant, with addressee marked as *soto* in 77.3 percent of the cases, little reliance on the evasive strategy of leaving social relationship unspecified (22.7 percent), and no cases of specifying addressee as *uchi*. Speakers at the post office marked the addressee as *soto* less often, at a rate of 51.9 percent. They also refrained completely from marking the addressee as *uchi*, and relied instead on the evasive strategy of lack of specification at a frequency of 48.1 percent, higher than that of speakers at the railroad station.

Although patterns of interaction at the post office and those at the railroad station differ in these respects, the two resemble each other much more than either resembles those at the vegetable market, where marking of the addressee as *soto* has a much lower rate of 36.2 percent. It is significant that a linguistic option was available here that was missing in the other locales: that of marking the addressee as *uchi*. These strikingly different results are of course attributable at least in part to the social characteristics of each of the three locales, as explicated earlier: in particular, that while the vegetable market is a neighborhood institution, the other two are large public institutions. Furthermore, it is admittedly feasible that "regulars" at the post office may develop some vague sense of familiarity with clerks working behind the counter but quite impossible for the same to happen at the railroad station.

STYLE-SHIFTING AT THE VEGETABLE MARKET:
DEFINING SOCIAL PARAMETERS LINGUISTICALLY

It is not surprising that verbal interaction at the vegetable market should differ greatly from that at the station and the post office. What may be surprising is that 36.2 percent of the speakers at the market actually marked the addressee as *soto*. One might ask why the marking was not as *uchi* or at the very least left unspecified in all cases. There are several possible answers. First, it is possible that the form *kudasai* is not actually as strong a marker of distance as was assumed in the analysis. However, the trends shown in the present data, as well as those in large amounts of other data on directives collected by the present investigator, show compelling evidence for the strength of the out-group signal inherent in *kudasai*. Moreover, this claim is further supported by additional data introduced in the next section of the present study. Second, it is possible that 36.2 percent of the speakers at the vegetable market actually were strangers, who were either rare or first-time shoppers at this location. Direct data on the nature of the relationship between the vendor and the customers are not available, so such a proposal can be entertained. However, many data items involving more extended interaction between customer and vegetable vendor cast doubt on the likelihood of this hypothesis. Consider the following exchanges, where C indicates "customer" and V "vegetable vendor." Numerals following C and V are added for convenience of reference to the data items. Ages given were estimated by the native Japanese informant collecting the data.

(5) A forty-six-year-old female customer speaks to vendor.
   C1 *kore kudasai — ni-hyaku   go-juu-en no.*
       this give/hon-D two-hundred fifty-yen one
       'Give me this—the two-hundred-and-fifty-yen one.'
   C2 *a, komakai no aru   wa.*
       oh small-I one have-I SP
       'Oh, (I) have small change.'
(6) A fifty-five-year-old female customer speaks to vendor.
   C1 *banana kudasai.*
       banana give/hon-D
       'Give me (some) bananas.'
   V1 *erande   kudasai   ne.*
       choose-G give/hon-D ok
       'Please choose (the ones you want), ok?'
   C2 *kore ni   suru   wa.*
       this goal make-I SP
       '(I)'ll make (it) these.'

C3 *fukuro ni   irete   kureru?*
   bag   goal insert-G give-I
   'Will (you) put (them) into a bag (for me)?'

V2 *okusan, hanbun ni   kitte   ii   desu ka.*
   wife   half   goal cut-G ok-I Cp-I Q
   'Ma'am, is it ok to cut it in half?'

V3 *chotto, kore hainnai   ya.*
   a bit   this enter-neg-I SP
   'This just won't go in.'

C4 *doozo,   watte   choodai.*
   go-ahead split-G receive
   'Go ahead and split it (for me).'

In (5), the customer's first utterance, C1, contains the Distant form *kudasai*, which marks the addressee as *soto*. However, the second utterance, C2, is a major sentence lacking the Distant marking and therefore is a Direct utterance that marks the addressee as a familiar, *uchi* member. Similarly, in the more complex, extended interaction of (6), the customer's first utterance, C1, contains *kudasai* to mark the addressee as *soto*, as does V1, the vendor's first utterance. In C2, however, the customer has shifted to the familiar Direct style, as evidenced by the lack of Distant marking on the verb *suru* 'make'. C3 is also Direct, since it ends with the verb *kureru* 'give (to me/us)' without the Distant marker -*mas-*. The second utterance of the vendor, V2, is a major sentence that carries the Distant *desu*, which marks the customer/addressee as *soto*, and thus maintains the style established with V1. V3 shows a shift in distance since it is a major sentence, but lacks the Distant signal -*mas-*. Finally, C4 ends with the request form *choodai*, and thus signals a closer, *uchi* relationship than C1, with *kudasai*.

Not all interactions of more than one utterance show this sort of distance-shifting. In (7) below, the customer's utterances are all Direct, marking the vendor as *uchi*, whereas the vendor's are all Distant, marking the customer as *soto*. The vendor's preference for a *soto* style here may be occasioned by a less-than-intimate relationship with this particular customer, or perhaps by the potentially face-threatening circumstance of disappointing the customer initially and then pressuring her to take an unwanted item.

(7) A twenty-eight-year-old female customer talks with the vendor.
   C1 *gureepu wa   aru?*
      grape   top. have-I
      'Grapes—do (you) have (any)?'
   V1 *nai   n   desu yo.*
      have-neg-I EP Cp-I SP
      '(It's the case that I) don't have (any).'

V2 *suimasen.*
  sorry-neg-I
  '(I)'m sorry.'

V3 *painappuru de   gaman-shite kudasai.*
  pineapple   ins. endure-G give/hon-D
  'Please put up with a pineapple.'

C2 *soo   wa ikanai   wa yo.*
  that-way top. go-neg-I SP SP
  '(I)'m not going to go along with that.'

V4 *ja,   purinsumeron, doo desu ka.*
  well prince-melon how Cp-I Q
  'Well then, how about (some) Prince melons?'

C3 *soo   nee.*
  that-way SP
  'Hmmm, let me see.'

C4 *hito-sara   itadaku   wa.*
  one-plate take/hum-I SP
  '(I)'ll take one plate (of them).'

Example (8) shows both speakers employing the Direct style throughout. All utterances lack Distant *-mas-/desu*; V2 is a fragment that ends
with a non-sentence-final verb form that lacks the Distant *-mas-*.

(8) A sixty-year-old female customer talks to the vendor.

C1 *kore, dore   ga   urete   n no?*
  these which subj. ripe-G be EP
  'These—(it's the case that) which one is ripe?'

C2 *dotchi ga   ii?*
  which subj. good-I
  'Which one is good?'

V1 *kore ii   yo.*
  this good-I SP
  'This one is fine.'

V2 *kore ni   shitara?*
  this goal make-Cond.
  'Why don't (you) make it this one?' [lit.: 'if you make it this one?']

If all major sentences in the data on interaction between female customers and the vendor are tabulated, excluding customers' directive utterances already analyzed, the pattern shown in Table 4 emerges.

Table 4 indicates that in spite of extensive style-shifting, the vendor
still marked the customer as *soto* in 46.5 percent of his utterances. Furthermore, though shifting on the part of customers was observed in examples above, Table 4 indicates that this was confined almost entirely to
their directive utterances. As was shown previously, they marked the

TABLE 4

Degree of Indexing of Addressee as *uchi* or *soto* in Nondirective Sentences of
Vendor and Customer

	All Sentences	*Distant*	*Direct*
Customer	100% (35)	08.6% (3)	91.4% (32)
Vendor	100% (43)	46.5% (20)	53.5% (23)

vendor as *soto* in 36.2 percent of their directive utterances. In fact, one of the three Distant sentences from Table 4 that occurred in the speech of the customers (9 below) was itself a request for a small box. This utterance was not included in the foregoing analysis of directives since it was not a request for *purchased* goods. One other was a request for permission to give the vendor small change (10 below), and it also constitutes an apology of sorts for doing so.

(9) A forty-year-old female customer talks to vendor.
    C1 *chotto, kore kudasai.*
        a bit   this give/hon-D
        'Say, give (me) these (potatoes).'
    C2 *nani ka   chiisai hako itadakemasu ka.*
        something small-I box get/hum-I Q
        'Can (I) get a small box or something?'
(10) A forty-five-year-old female customer talks to vendor.
    C1 *retasu   choodai.*
        lettuce receive
        '(I)'ll take a lettuce.'
    C2 *komakai no   de   ii   desu ka.*
        small   one Cp-G good-I Cp-I Q
        'Would it be ok if it's small (change)?' [lit., 'small ones']
    C3 *go-en   made majitte [i]ru kedo . . .*
        five-yen even mix-G be-I but
        'Even five-yen (coins) are mixed in, but (is that ok?)'

The third Distant sentence in the speech of the customers can probably be discounted as not having much effect as a Distant signal, since it ends in the Distant form of the copula, *deshoo*. This form contrasts in sentence-final position with the Direct equivalent, *daroo*, only in restricted social contexts, specifically, in the speech of males, and particularly when speaking to other males. It is rare in the speech of females. This lack of shift to *daroo* is therefore common even when speakers are employing Direct forms in all other cases. Similar data on *deshoo* appear in the next section also.

Although many of the customer/vendor interactions at the vegetable market consisted of only one utterance each, many other cases consisted of several utterances produced by the customer or the vendor. These make it abundantly clear that a great deal of style-shifting occurred. The carefully selected set of directive utterances recorded at the vegetable market showed a 36.2 percent rate of marking the addressee as *soto*. It must be emphasized, however, that this rate applies only to the *directive* speech act. As examples (5) and (6) above show, some exchanges include speech acts other than directives, which may themselves serve to mark the addressee as *uchi* or *soto* or as neither. Though it is this type of definition and control that gives some meaningful basis of comparison with interaction at the railroad station and the post office, it is clear that this single parameter does not tell the entire story— nor was it meant to. The principle of experimental control in any science is the pinning down of details at the price of the entire picture; it is assumed, nevertheless, that precise information about enough different types of details contributes to and eventually leads to understanding of the entirety.

Negotiation of Social Definition through Style-Shifting

What, then, does all this mean with respect to the concept *uchi/soto*? For one thing, the data have shown so far that degrees of *uchi* or *soto* can be distinguished in a meaningful way on linguistic grounds—if there is a well-defined, controlled parameter against which to compare social contexts. Next, given this parameter, it would appear to be the case that the low rate of the Distance indicator found at the vegetable market (36.2 percent) helped to define a social context characterized by extensive occurrence of style-shifting. Though the vendor was marked as *uchi* by the customers' utterances much more frequently than the customers were so marked by the vendor's utterances, both parties engaged in style shifts of both directions in the body of data. Examples showed clearly that mixing of styles occurred within the speech of a single customer, as well as within the speech of the vendor while waiting on a single customer, rather than settling on one style for one interaction and then shifting to a different style and staying there for another.

Though interaction at the vegetable market stands out as clearly "more *uchi*" in character than that at the railroad station or the post office, it also contains many signals associated with *soto* interaction because of this shifting. It therefore seems apparent that the participants in interaction at the vegetable market are *negotiating a social definition* of the very context in which they are interacting. This type of negotiation is strikingly reminiscent of the description in Rosenberger (this volume) of the manner in which the married couple who were guests at the wedding party shifted their behavioral patterns during the party from the more formal *soto* behavior, with the husband firmly in control of the situation, to a more *uchi*-like behavior, with the wife in control and the husband relaxed, being waited on, and freely expressing personal wants and needs. The point is that a given real-world situation can be imbued with social definition by the participants through negotiated shifts in behavior or language. Language does not merely mirror and conform to a given social reality—it in part defines or even creates it.

Even more significant, it appears clear that customers at the vegetable market indulged in shifting to a more Distant style only in expressing requests—which, as was pointed out earlier, are speech acts of somewhat greater face-threatening import. This pattern of linguistic interaction would imply that the customers living in the neighborhood of the vegetable vendor feel close to him and relaxed around him in general as a fellow member of the neighborhood, but many still feel at times a need to acknowledge more ultimate group boundaries when imposing on him in some way—however slight—or in expressing needs and wants. This is again reminiscent of Rosenberger's study (this volume), in which free expression of needs and wants on the part of the husband at home was one of the behavioral factors that defined the setting as an *uchi* one. Here, by contrast, the caution or carefulness in expression of needs and wants on the part of some customers at the vegetable market defined the interaction and the addressee, at least in that context, as *soto*. While interaction at the market tended to define relationships more toward the *uchi* side of the continuum, it stopped well short of the literal *uchi*, that is, the home. In the next section we shall see that interaction within a Japanese household provides a contrast with interaction at the vegetable market (and, of course, at the post office and the railroad station). We shall see, nevertheless, that the same principles of linguistically defining *uchi/soto* are definitely at work, but on a more microscopic level.

Interaction within a Family: The Ultimate In-group?

The corpus of data for this portion of the study was collected by the same Japanese informant who collected the data at the vegetable market. This setting differs first of all in that interaction in a family group is not nearly as controlled as that for the three locations previously discussed. The other locations were chosen for the high potential for control that comes with interaction of such an extremely specific type to produce a remarkably uniform variety of data on directives.

The Family Members

The family was a middle-class Japanese family residing in a Tokyo suburb. It consisted of the father, the mother, the twenty-one-year-old
daughter, the eighteen-year-old daughter, and the family dog (to whom
a number of the directives collected were addressed). The father was
fifty-two years old, a university graduate, and a white-collar worker employed with a large company in Tokyo. The mother was forty-four years
old, a graduate of a girls' high school, and a housewife. Both daughters
were university students. The family was not wealthy, but they were well
off. The daughters, for example, had the means to go on ski trips, and
the older daughter, who had studied linguistics and Spanish at the university, was saving money for a trip to Spain in the near future. The dog
was a somewhat pampered house pet.

The Corpus of Data

The corpus collected in this family home consisted of 376 directives of a
wide variety of structural types, which occurred under a wide variety of
pragmatic conditions. This is substantially more than double the number of items employed by speakers at the railroad station, post office,
and vegetable market combined. The distribution of directives by family
members is given in Table 5.

As is apparent from Table 5, there is substantial data for each family
member except the father who, in the pattern of Japanese white-collar
fathers, was often absent from home because of his work and frequent
business trips. Even within the limited amount of data on him, however,
the pattern of *uchi* behavior of head-of-household described by Rosenberger (this volume) is evident: most of the father's directives (67.7 percent) are issued to his wife, who is on hand to cater to his freely expressed needs. And even though the wife issued far more directives than
her husband (nearly five times as many), only 8.9 percent are addressed
to him. The daughters also issued far fewer directives to their father
than to their mother or to each other. While these patterns no doubt
reflect the fact that the father was not at home as much as the others, it
seems equally certain that they also express the special status of the father as household head and his special relationship with his wife in that
capacity, as described by Rosenberger.

The 376 directives collected from this family were classified as to
structural type. The types and the speakers using each type are given in
Table 6, which will give the reader a general idea of the types of directives occurring in the family, their relative frequency, and the degree to
which each family member employed each type.

TABLE 5
Distribution of Directives by Family Members

Father		1st Daughter	
To wife	21	To father	18
To 1st daughter	9	To mother	42
To 2d daughter	1	To sister	41[a]
To dog	0	To dog	9
Total	31	Total	110
Mother		2d Daughter	
To husband	13	To father	4
To 1st daughter	95	To mother	39
To 2d daughter	37	To sister	44
To dog	1	To dog	2
Total	146	Total	89

Total for family = 376

[a] One of these is directed to the sister and the mother, and one to the sister, the mother, and the father.

TABLE 6
The 365 Directives from the Family, Classified by Structural Type

	Father	Mother	1st Daughter	2d Daughter	Total
1. Unspecified fragment	4	9	7	22	42
2. *V-te.* 'Do V!'	8	67	44	38	157
3. *V-(a)nai de.* 'Don't do V!'	0	2	3	5	10
4. STEM-*nasai.* 'Do STEM!'	3	15	7	0	25
5. *choodai.* 'Receiving.'	7	16	0	3	26
6. *goran.* 'Look!'	2	3	4	0	9
7. *irasshai.* 'Come/go/be!'	0	7	4	0	11
8. *oide.* 'Come/go/be!'	0	1	4	2	7
9. *kure.* 'Give me/us!'	1	0	0	0	1
10. *kureru/kurenai.* 'Give/won't give me/us.'	0	5	7	7	19
11. *kudasai.* 'Give me/us!'	0	2	0	1	3
12. *kudasaru/kudasaranai.* 'Give/won't give me/us.'	0	2	0	0	2
13. *itadakeru.* 'I/we can receive.'	0	1	0	0	1
14. Other	5	17	30	11	63
Total	31	146	110	89	376

Although limitations of space do not permit discussion of each type, the following points should be noted. Expressions (4) through (8) are all polite items and, except for the humble *choodai*, all are honorific. In addition, (6) and (8), like *choodai*, are fragments, not major sentences. Items (4) through (8) lack Distal marking and are associated with in-group speech, as we have already seen is the case for *choodai*. Expressions (12) and (13) are, respectively, honorific and humble; either may be inflected with Distal marking, though only one of the three occurrences in the corpus in fact was. The category "Other" included such utterances as suggestions, prohibitions, statements of problem, and questions of existence, all of which were interpreted as directives by the informant collecting the data.

In examining the range of choice obtaining in this sample for directives, it is clear immediately that the range is vast indeed compared to that obtaining in the service settings already described. This great difference between the service data and the present data indicates the need to provide for some type of control if one is to isolate specific social messages from individual forms, such as the strong *uchi* marking of *choodai* and the clear *soto* marking of *kudasai* noted earlier. Now that such distinctions have been elucidated, it can be seen that the same principles hold up when tested against this body of less controlled, more complex data.

Social Parameters in the Family Corpus

Table 7 gives the percentage of reliance on *choodai* and *kudasai* for each speaker.

The father's speech shows the greatest reliance on *choodai*, and is followed by the mother's. Since interaction within the family was not controlled in any way, both the types of interaction and the types of linguistic strategies selected in negotiating the interaction are vastly more varied than either was in the service settings. It is not, therefore, surprising that the over-all rate of occurrence here for *choodai* is much less than the 14.5 percent at the vegetable market, where basically only three or four choices were available to speakers. Yet the father uses *choodai* at a rate (22.6 percent) much higher than the one at the market (14.5 percent) and the mother at a rate nearly as high (11.0 percent). Perhaps not too much should be made of these figures since the numbers are small. What is more important is that the rate for *choodai*, as used in the family, is *much higher than* that for *kudasai*, which is all but nonexistent. These rates are compared in Table 8.

While the rate of occurrence of *kudasai* at the market was about two and a half times that for *choodai*, in the family, this reduces to only about

TABLE 7

Degree of Reliance on *Kudasai* and *Choodai* for Each Family Member

Speaker	Choodai	Kudasai
Father	22.6% (7)	00.0% (0)
Mother	11.0% (16)	01.4% (2)
1st Daughter	00.0% (0)	01.1% (1)
2d Daughter	03.4% (3)	00.0% (0)
All Speakers	07.0% (26)	00.8% (3)

TABLE 8

Comparison of Rates of Occurrence of *Choodai* and *Kudasai* at the Vegetable Market and in the Family

Location	Choodai	Kudasai
Vegetable market	14.5% (10)	36.2% (25)
Family	07.0% (26)	00.8% (3)

one-tenth. Though the number of *kudasai* occurrences in the family is very small, the entire body of data on the family is substantial enough to ensure that these results are no accident. They further confirm the roles of *choodai* and *kudasai*, as important indicators of *uchi* and *soto* relationships, respectively. Furthermore, the extremely small ratio of *kudasai* to *choodai* in terms of frequency of usage in the family indicates a very close in-group relationship among the speakers: the speech context is much more clearly defined as unambiguously *uchi* than it was at the vegetable market, where *kudasai* occurrence was two and a half times that of *choodai* and where style-switching occurred readily, especially on the part of the vendor. The *choodai/kudasai* ratio obtaining within the family leads one to expect that style-switching either would not occur in this speech context or would occur only at very low frequency. If the style-switching contained in the data is scrutinized, we find that these expectations are borne out.

All utterances contained in the data for each speaker were classified into three categories: (1) major sentences containing Distant marking; (2) major sentences not containing Distant marking (i.e., Direct-style sentences); and (3) fragments (all utterances other than 1 and 2). The results are given in Table 9.

These figures would indicate that style-switching barely occurred at all in the family. Both "Fragment" and "Direct" utterances must be considered "non-Distant," since neither carries a Distal marker or *kudasai*. This means that 96.2 percent of the utterances of one family member to an-

TABLE 9
All Utterances of Each Family Member, Classified in Terms
of Distance Indexing

	Total	Fragment	Direct	Distant
Father	100% (37)	81.1% (30)	13.5% (5)	05.4% (2)
Mother	100% (167)	66.5% (111)	28.1% (47)	05.4% (9)
1st Daughter	100% (145)	51.7% (75)	44.8% (65)	03.4% (5)
2d Daughter	100% (104)	77.9% (81)	21.2% (22)	01.0% (1)
All speakers	100% (453)	65.6% (297)	30.7% (139)	03.8% (17)

other failed to mark the addressee as *soto*, and only 3.8 percent, or 17 utterances out of 453, exhibited Distant marking. Though this rate is extremely low, the question arises as to why any Distant utterances occurred at all. It is therefore necessary to examine the group of Distant utterances in greater detail.

Table 9 shows that out of 453 total utterances, the entire body of Distant utterances consisted of 2 uttered by the father, 9 by the mother, 5 by the first daughter, and 1 by the second daughter. Both of the father's, all of the first daughter's, and 5 of the mother's were Distant by virtue of the fact that they ended in *deshoo*, the Distal tentative form of the copula, which contrasts with the Direct tentative form *daroo*. However, as mentioned earlier, the form *deshoo* frequently occurs in contexts where speech is otherwise clearly Direct-style. Shifting to the Direct *daroo* in sentence-final position rarely occurs in the speech of females and appears to be highly restricted even in the speech of males. Given this peculiar relation of *deshoo* to *daroo*, none of the women's *deshoo* utterances, and perhaps none of the father's as well, can be properly considered as signaling distance. Thus, only 4 of the mother's utterances and 1 of the second daughter's utterances should be categorized as indicators of distance. The "Distant" column of Table 9 should therefore be revised as in Table 10.

The figures in Table 10 show an almost negligible rate of signaling of distance. When such signals did occur, they occurred only in the speech of the mother (four times) and the second daughter (once). It is significant that *all five of these are directives*. As noted of interaction at the vegetable market, it appears that treating the addressee as *soto* through markers of distance is a strategy employed only in acts that present a relatively greater face-threat to the addressee. However, unlike interactants at the vegetable market, family members used this strategy with extreme infrequency, even though most of their requests were for far more demanding acts on the part of the addressee than mere provision of some

TABLE 10
Revised Rates of Distance Indexing for Each Family Member

Speaker	Distant
Father	00.0% (0)
Mother	02.4% (4)
1st Daughter	00.0% (0)
2d Daughter	01.0% (1)
All speakers	01.1% (5)

item—which would of course even be paid for by the speaker at the vegetable market. This extreme infrequency of distancing is a linguistic index of the degree of closeness of the members in the family group, the *uchi*. At the same time, it is one of the things they do that *constitutes* that closeness: to raise the frequency of distance-marking is to create a different family. But the question arises: if there is such a degree of closeness, when and why is the distancing strategy employed at all? To answer this question, it will be necessary to examine in greater detail the few occasions when family members used the distancing strategy.

Motivation for Distance Indexing within uchi

There were 5 occurrences of distancing utterances, 1 uttered by the second daughter and 4 by the mother. The daughter's is given as (16) below, along with the rather remarkable context which preceded it.

(11) Second (younger) daughter speaks to first (older) daughter, who is sitting near the facial tissue.
    tisshuu totte   kureru?
    tissue   pass-G give-I
    'Will (you) pass (me) a tissue?'

(12) Second daughter speaks to first daughter, who is sitting near the thermos.
    (This is a few moments after 11 above.)
    oyu   totte   kureru?
    hot-water pass-G give-I
    'Will (you) pass me the hot water?'

(13) Second daughter speaks to first daughter, who has gotten the thermos.
    oyu,   kon naka ni irete   kureru?
    hot-water this inside goal insert-G give-I
    'Will (you) put some hot water into this (for me)?'
    [as she holds out her cup]

(14) Second daughter speaks to first daughter, who is pouring water for her.
moo   chotto, moo   chotto.
additional bit   additional bit
'A little more, a little more!'

(15) Second daughter speaks to first daughter, who is filling her cup with
      water.
aa, sutoppu.
oh stop
'Oh, stop!' [i.e., you've poured me enough water now.]

(16) Second daughter speaks to first daughter, a few moments after (15)
      above.
kagami totte   kudasai.
mirror pass-G give/hon-D
'Please pass me the mirror'.

It seems clear that the second daughter is not reluctant to approach her older sister with a request devoid of the Distant strategy, since she readily did this in examples (11) through (15), which followed "in fairly rapid succession," to quote the informant. Thus, use of the distancing device *kudasai*, as in example (16), is for the second daughter a highly marked strategy. This is the only use of such a strategy in eighty-nine directives uttered to the various family members by the second daughter. It seems obvious that the shift here is due to the unusual context, that is, to the fact that it was immediately preceded by five other directives. The speaker's awareness of an increasing imposition on the addressee conditioned the marked choice to back off, to accord the addressee the respect afforded by the honorific *kudasai*. By this act is introduced some separation, in place of the usually assumed solidarity. Brown and Levinson (1978) would consider this an example of a negative-polite strategy—that is, one that accords the addressee greater freedom and deemphasizes the speaker's intention to control or impose on the addressee. An honorific in Japanese signals such information by marking the addressee as superior in status, and therefore not of the same social rank as the speaker; associated implications are that the addressee may be appealed to but not commanded and that the addressee, rather than the speaker, is in a position to exercise will and comply or to refrain from doing so. The strategy was successfully applied in this case, as the first daughter did in fact supply her sister with the mirror.

At the vegetable market the frequency with which *kudasai* was used, in absence of special conditioning, would indicate that selection of *kudasai* was an unmarked strategy in that setting. Within the family, the reverse would be true. In interaction between the two sisters, the same strategy is highly marked since it required special conditioning factors. In such a marked context, use of the same form communicated fear of having imposed too much or fear of possible refusal.

The same sort of phenomenon is observed in the mother's application of distancing strategy. As was mentioned earlier, the mother applied the strategy only 4 times out of a total of 146 directives. One of these is given below with relevant context.

(17) The mother speaks to the first daughter, handing food for the dog
          to her.
       hai,   agete   ne?
       here give-G ok
       'Here, give (this to the dog), ok?'
(18) The daughter responds.
       e?   iya   da.
       huh dislike Cp-I
       'What? No!'
(19) The mother counters.
       chikai n   da   kara, yatte yo.
       close-I EP Cp-I so   do-G SP
       '(You)'re close, so do it!'
(20) The mother speaks to the daughter; no intervening material in
          the data.
       otya kudasaai.
       tea give/hon-D
       'Pleeease give (me) some tea.'

No utterances occurred between items (19) and (20), though it is not known how long a time period intervened. The shift exhibited in the mother's marked use of *kudasai* in (20) is strikingly reminiscent of the shift in the second daughter's speech discussed above. The same elements of increasing degree of imposition of speaker on addressee and fear of possibility of refusal are clearly also involved here. However, there may be another factor involved. As in most Japanese households, the mother usually made and served the tea and this was in general assumed by other family members to be her duty. On one occasion in the data the first daughter is seen to be less than fully cooperative when asked by the mother to make tea. It is thus quite possible that the mother's awareness of her responsibility for making tea and of her family's feeling that this was her responsibility was also a contributing factor in her highly marked use of *kudasai* in (20). This possibility is suggested even more strongly by the fact that one more of the four distancing utterances of the mother was in reference to the first daughter's making the tea:

(21) The mother speaks to the first daughter, while pointing to the tea kettle.
     osoreirimasu ga . . .
     sorry-I   but
     '(I)'m sorry (to bother you), but . . . (would you make the tea?)'

The item *osoreirimasu* is Distant as it carries the Distal -*mas*- marking; but what is more, it is only indirectly interpreted as a directive. It merely expresses apology for imposition on the addressee, with the directive being understood. *Osoreirimasu* is a rather stiff and formal expression of both gratitude and apology. The informant noted that the mother "asked politely intentionally to avoid refusal," which might have been possible "if the daughter were busy."

The entire corpus for the mother contains 7 directives requesting other family members to make, fill, pour, or give her tea. Of the 4 Distant directives occurring in her corpus of 146, 2 of them, (20) and (21) above, involve tea. In addition, the corpus of 7 "tea directives" contains (a) the only example in the entire family corpus of 376 items of a directive with the Direct-style humble verb of receiving, *itadaku*, and (b) 1 of only 2 occurrences in the mother's corpus of directives ending in the negative *kurenai*, which is less direct and more polite than the affirmative *kureru* form. Though neither of these is Distant in the sense being developed here, both represent markedly polite directives in terms of the family corpus. These are given below as (22) and (23), respectively.

(22) The mother speaks to the first daughter, as she hands her a teacup.
     irete   itadakeru   ka shira . . .
     fill-G receive/pot.-I Q wonder
     '(I) wonder if (I) could get (you) to fill (this cup)?'
(23) The mother speaks to the first daughter
     X-chan,   ocha irete   kurenai?
     X-diminutive tea make-G give-neg-I
     'X, won't (you) make the tea (for me)?'

Though the numbers are few, it can be no accident that only 4.8 percent of the mother's directives, the "tea directives," contain 50 percent of her distancing directives, 50 percent of her negative *kurenai* forms, and the 1 and only instance of the humble polite *itadaku* in the entire family corpus.

The other 2 Distant directives in the mother's corpus occur consecutively without intervening material. These are given below, along with a reply from the daughter.

(24) The mother speaks to the first daughter, who is near the drawer
        containing the paste.

nori   o   totte   kudasaimasen?
paste obj get-G give/hon-neg-I
'Won't (you) please get me the paste?'
(25) The mother speaks to the first daughter, who is near the bag.
  chotto, sono iremono   totte   kudasai.
  a bit   that contents get-G give/hon-D
  'Please just get me the stuff in that (bag).'
(26) The first daughter responds.
  jibun de totte   yo.
  self   by get-G SP
  'Get it yourself!'

The data provide little insight into exactly what task the mother is occupied with in (24) and (25) above, but given what has been demonstrated thus far of the application of the Distant strategy in this family, it seems obvious that the mother anticipated the daughter's reaction in (26) or at least sensed that she was bordering on imposing too much to be assured of continuing cooperation.

A final additional example from the mother's speech corpus illustrates the same approach to avoiding refusal. On only one occasion, the mother used a directive based on the Direct-style *kudasaru,* which contrasts with the Distal negative form *kudasaimasen* in (24) above. Like (22) and (23) above, (27) below is not representative of the Distant strategy as developed here, but it *is* a highly marked, very polite directive and the sole use of *kudasaru* in the entire family corpus.

(27) The mother speaks to the first daughter.
  inu   no gohan shite   kudasaru?
  dog 's   food   do-G give/hon-I
  'Will (you) do the dog's food (for me)?'

The informant commented that the mother "intentionally spoke politely because she knew the job was troublesome." Elsewhere the informant had mentioned that the dog was usually cared for by the mother. The mother's corpus contained seven directives requesting the daughters to care in some way for the family dog (two addressed to the second daughter and the remainder to the first daughter). No fewer than five of these were met with some type of refusal by the addressee, one example of which is the sequence (17) through (19) given earlier.

The foregoing examples constitute all cases in the family corpus of employment of the Distant strategy—that is, selection of *kudasai* or shifting to the Distal style. In addition, the only occurrences of the Direct-style honorific *kudasaru* and the Direct-style humble *itadakeru* were examined. Except for items (4) through (8) in Table 6 (page 131), this accounts for all instances of Distal forms or humble and honorific polite forms in the family corpus.

The foregoing examples strongly suggest that even though employment of Distant forms was a highly marked, statistically infrequent strategy within the family studied, this strategy was regularly conditioned by a desire on the part of the speaker to avoid further imposition on the addressee, from whom refusal or lack of cooperation was possible or impending. This strategy is an example of negative politeness in the sense of Brown and Levinson (1978), which stresses the freedom of the addressee to be left alone and the speaker's unwillingness to impose his or her will on the addressee. This is accomplished in Japanese in the present data by marking the addressee as *soto* and thereby indexing the separateness of speaker and addressee. As at the vegetable market, the family members used language to *negotiate a social definition* of the situation at hand. Within the family, it even appears that evocation of the *uchi/soto* dichotomy served in part to define groups responsible for certain household chores. The data reveal a tendency for possible refusal by an addressee to condition the speaker's adoption of a more negatively polite approach. This strategy, in effect, established a group boundary that separated speaker and addressee when the issue at hand was a chore the addressee might have legitimately refused to do. It bears emphasizing that the frequency and directness of *refusal* in the family also define the interaction as *uchi*, which contrasts markedly with interaction at the vegetable market, where even indirect refusal would be unthinkable. Comparison of interaction at the various locations examined shows language at work in all aspects of negotiation of *uchi/soto* boundaries—not only as they are created and maintained, but also as they are removed and redrawn. The situation-specific, negotiated nature of this social indexing is clear even within the supposedly ultimate *uchi*, the Japanese household, where individual members can themselves be identified and distinguished as in-group or out-group.

NOTES

1. I am grateful to the editors of this volume, Jane Bachnik and Charles Quinn, for their many helpful suggestions and criticisms. I particularly thank Charles Quinn for a careful and helpful editing of the manuscript. His suggestions and additions are too numerous to mention individually, but are much appreciated. However, the responsibility for any flaws or errors is my own.

2. In citing examples from the data, the Japanese utterance will be given in

romanization with a literal gloss directly below the Japanese and a more natural English equivalent below that. The literal gloss is to help the reader identify what parts of the Japanese utterance correspond to what features of meaning in the English translation. Glosses for inflected words will consist of a literal equivalent of the word followed by symbol(s) indicating the category of inflection or politeness level as follows:

hon.	honorific	R	Representative
hum.	humble	Pot.	Potential
Neg.	Negative	D	Imperative
I	Imperfect	V	Verb
P	Perfect	Cp	Copula
G	Gerund	SP	Sentence Particle
S	Stem	EP	Extended Predicate
T	Tentative	subj.	Subject
Cond.	Conditional	obj.	Object
Prov.	Provisional	top.	Topic

D refers mnemonically to 'directive' since imperatives are one type of directive. SP designates 'sentence-final particle' only when no English gloss is readily available. EP glosses the nominal *no* 'case, matter' or its contracted equivalent *n* when either occurs in the so-called extended predicate (Jorden 1987, 242–44). The copula *da* or equivalents are glossed as Cp followed by a symbol designating inflectional category. The grammatical particles are glossed by an English equivalent like 'from' or 'to' or 'by' when such a gloss is meaningful or by a more abstract semantic categorization like 'means' or 'goal' when it is not. The other particles will simply be glossed as *o* 'obj', *ga* 'subj', *wa* 'top'.

3. The terminology *Direct* and *Distal* will be adopted here following Jorden (1987); traditionally, this dichotomy has been referred to as *Formal* and *Informal*, respectively. Jorden's terminology seems preferable in that it succeeds in expressing the meaning of distance associated with Distal forms as elucidated by Ikuta (1980). The Distal category is signaled by presence of the morpheme *-mas-* attached to verbs and the form *desu* (or variants thereof) in adjective-type and nominal-type sentences. Absence of a Distal signal on a verb, adjective, or nominal-plus-copula sequence will be termed *Direct* style. The term *Distant* is adopted here to refer to an utterance containing *either* the Distal signal *or* the form *kudasai*, the imperative form of the honorific *kudasaru* 'out-group gives to in-group'.

4. Predicates are verbs, adjectives, or nominal-plus-copula sequences.

5. A major sentence can be defined for present purposes along the lines of Jorden (1963, 47) as a sequence ending with or consisting of a predicate in the Perfect, Imperfect, Tentative, or Imperative forms followed or not by a sentence-final particle or particles.

6. Another independent parameter of *uchi/soto* marking is that signaled by verbs of giving and receiving as in (4)(a) through (4)(e); this parameter is being ignored in this study, where focus is on signaling of distance by employment of Distal forms or *kudasai*. Wetzel (1984) treats the other parameter.

REFERENCES

Brown, Penelope, and Stephen Levinson. 1978. "Universals in Language Usage: Politeness Phenomena," in Esther N. Goody, ed., *Questions and Politeness*, 56–289. Cambridge: Cambridge University Press.

Goody, Esther N., ed. 1978. *Questions and Politeness: Strategies in Social Interaction.* Cambridge: Cambridge University Press.

Ikuta, Shoko. 1980. "Ethnography and Discourse Cohesion: Aspects of Speech Level Shift in Japanese Discourse." Master's thesis, Cornell University.

Jorden, Eleanor H. 1963. *Beginning Japanese,* Part 1. New Haven and London: Yale University Press.

———. 1987. *Japanese: The Spoken Language,* Part 1. New Haven and London: Yale University Press.

Wetzel, Patricia J. 1984. "*Uchi* and *Soto* (In-group and out-group): Social Deixis in Japanese." Ph.D. dissertation, Cornell University.

Chapter 6

INDEXING SELF AND SOCIETY
IN JAPANESE FAMILY ORGANIZATION

JANE M. BACHNIK

EDITORS' INTRODUCTION

Bachnik's paper pursues important issues raised by Wetzel's reformulation of the deictic anchor point in chapter 2. Specifically, what are the implications of deixis for Japanese family, self, and social organization? Here Bachnik focuses on the *ie* 'family' or 'household', long regarded as the basic "unit" of Japanese society. The *ie*-as-family appears throughout the volume: for Rosenberger, Sukle, and Bachnik in part 1; in part 2 for Kondo, Hamabata, and Molasky (via Shiga Naoya) who focus on family-business settings.

In this chapter Bachnik focuses on the relationship between *uchi* as deictic anchor point and *uchi* 'inside' as opposed to *soto* 'outside', exploring how the organization of context, self, and social order is delineated in the *ie* through *uchi* as the deictic anchor point. Through ethnographic vignettes, Bachnik identifies a system of indexing involving a "mapping" (Ochs 1990) of a variety of communication modes—including degree of emotional expression versus social constraint, use of space, bowing, gift-giving, and so on—onto an axis of formality/informality. Indexing along this axis is crucial for virtually every speech utterance and mode of social communication for Japanese. "Mapping" is derived from indexing the relationship distance (*omote/ura*) and deference (*uchi/soto*) between participants in social situations. Household members thus "create" the defining parameters both for self and interactional situations by indexing virtually all their communication along an axis of formality/informality and deference. This axis defines both self and social order via a series of variations along a continuum indexed by inside/outside.

But *uchi* is also specifically linked to *ie* organization. *Uchi*—as a deictic anchor point—identifies a named facet along with *ie*: specifically, the present generation *in time* (*uchi*) of an organization that is defined by its continuity *over time* (*ie*). As a collectively defined anchor point, *uchi* (1) defines self in relation to the collectivity; (2) is crucial in defining the in-group organization of the *ie*; and (3) defines the organization of the

ie by means of the relation between the two facets of *uchi/ie* (respectively, as "agency" and "structure") so that the organizational dynamic
spells out the participation of living members in structuring *ie* structure.
Bachnik links the chapters in part 1 to those in part 2, for she concludes
that the *ie* spells out the dynamic for the "situational self" and "situated
social order" in its own organization.

This reevaluation links *ie* organization to large theoretical issues, involving the organization of self, social order, and the relationship between the two. The *ie* is redefined with flexible, shifting boundaries.
Rather than an organizational "box" defined by form, or structure, *uchi*
and *uchi/soto* define strong two-way links between inside members and
the socioeconomic world outside the *ie* that have considerable implications for household organization.

INDEXING SELF AND SOCIETY
IN JAPANESE FAMILY ORGANIZATION

WETZEL'S ARGUMENT in chapter 3 that the deictic anchor point in Japanese comprises a collectivity, rather than an individual, has profound
implications for the analysis of self and society. If the deictic anchor
point is socially, rather than individually defined—if *uchi* is a collective
counterpart to the English "I"—then questions must be raised about the
relationship of deixis to Japanese self and social organization. In this
chapter I will examine some of the implications raised by Wetzel
through focusing on the *ie*, translated as 'family' or 'household', and
long regarded as the basic "unit" of Japanese society. What ramifications
do the group reference point—and deixis—have for the social organization of Japanese groups? For the organization of Japanese self?

Wetzel notes that social deixis has been considered peripheral to person deixis, and considers this due to assumptions of the egocentric organization of deixis (Levinson 1983, 63). Yet assumptions about meaning
also contribute to the peripherality of social deixis. In other words, the
egocentric organization of deixis is itself a consequence of approaches
that assume meaning to be within ego (or ego's mind), as private, individual, and divorced from context—as code. But meaning can also be
approached as socially shared, and realized through communicative
acts in social contexts, so that "speech (and therefore deictic meaning)
is *public* and intersubjective by nature" (Duranti 1986, 239). As Hanks
puts this:

> [D]eixis, both as a linguistic subsystem and as a kind of act, is a *social con-*
> *struction*, central to the organization of communicative practice and intelli-
> gible only in relation to a sociocultural system. . . . Not only is the speaking
> "ego" a social construction, but the act of deictic reference is in important

ways grounded on the relation between interlocutors. When speakers say "Here it is," he or she unavoidably conveys something like, "Hey, you and I stand in a certain relation to each other and to this object and this place, right now." (1990, 5–7)

In this chapter I argue that social deixis is not only important but crucial in the organization of the Japanese *ie*. The importance of social deixis in the *ie* can be linked to the importance of situated meaning, which can in turn be linked to the organization of a "situationally defined" self and a "situated" social order, both widely characterized throughout Japan.

This discussion stems from a rethinking of *ie* organization (Bachnik, in press, 1983; Hamabata 1990; Kondo 1990), in which the *ie* is redefined to include *uchi* as a named facet of its organization. *Ie* organization revolves around the relationship between these two named aspects: *uchi*, the deictic anchor point, and *ie*, whose main connotation is that of organizational continuity over time. *Uchi* includes the two meanings discussed in this volume: (1) the deictic anchor point: 'we', 'us', 'our group', 'me', 'my', 'my group', 'I', and 'this generation of the household', all of which specify the living group of household members; (2) 'inside', juxtaposed to 'outside' or *soto*.

Ie organization is comprised of the relationship between the facets of *ie* and *uchi* so that *ie* concerns the entire time/space trajectory of the house; *uchi* focuses on the present occupants of the household in close-up. The organization can thus be viewed as something like a strip of movie film. *Uchi* is the "frame" that is now before the camera lens: 'this living generation', 'us', 'our group'. *Ie* concerns the continuity of the organization over time—or, to put this another way, the reproduction of its structure over time.

Translating the *ie* as 'family' or 'household' is inaccurate, for the *ie* incorporates far more than the ordinary connotations of either 'family' or 'household'. I will argue that deixis is a major aspect of *ie* organization, providing an ongoing dynamic in which human beings located *in* space/time mutually interact with social order continuing *over* time, so that each constitutes the other in an ongoing way (Bachnik, in press). The named facets of the *ie* therefore detail relationships between what can be called 'agency' and 'structure' (Giddens 1979, 1984), or habitus and relations of practice (Bourdieu 1977, 1990). They speak to such issues as lived space and time (Merleau-Ponty 1962), phenomenological perspectives on being-in-the-world (Heidegger 1962), and indexical or pragmatic meaning (C. S. Peirce 1931–1958; Lyons 1977; Silverstein 1976).

Furthermore, general agreement exists that the modern Japanese self is defined as an individual within a collectivity (Edwards 1989; Smith

1983; Nakane 1970; Lebra 1976; Rosenberger 1992; Bachnik 1992a, 1992b). Therefore the *ie*, as the basic collectivity, is important, not simply by reason of its "family" or "household" attributes but because its organization defines the basic dynamic of Japanese self and social organization, which is spelled out throughout Japanese society in a series of paired sets of indexical terms, which are the focus of this volume. These include *uchi/soto* (which includes *uchi*, the deictic anchor point), *omote/ura* (roughly glosssed 'in front', 'surface appearance/in-back', 'what is kept hidden from others' (Doi 1986); *tatemae/honne* ('the presented stance/the world of inner feelings' (Doi 1986); *giri/ninjoo* ('social obligation/personal feelings'); *hare/ke* ('sacred/profane'), and so on. The "situationally defined" self and "situated" social order are both situated by means of deixis, through the anchor point of *uchi*. They are two sides of the same coin manifested through the ongoing dynamic between *uchi* and *ie*, of the mutual constitution of self and social order.

In this chapter I will focus on the two facets of meaning for *uchi*—(1) as deictic anchor point, and (2) *uchi* 'inside' as juxtaposed to *soto* 'outside'—and their relationship to *ie* organization. I will develop the deictic organization of the *ie* in two ways: First, I will reconsider two axes, linked respectively to distinctions of address/distance/formality/informality and reference/directional deference. I will then combine these two, viewing them as a single axis by relating the distinctions to the two facets of meaning for *uchi* discussed above. Second, I will explore how the organization of self and social order is delineated in the *ie* through the functioning of *uchi* as a deictic anchor point.

I will proceed by focusing on terms called "shifters," by Jakobson ([1957] 1971) and "referential indexicals" by Silverstein (1976), whose "basic communicative function is to individuate or single out objects of reference or address in terms of their relation to the current interactive context in which the utterance occurs" (Hanks 1992, 47). Referential indexes such as 'here', 'there', 'this', 'that', 'now', 'it') identify an object of reference through relational features ('close' versus 'distant', 'inside' versus 'outside', 'immediate' versus 'non-immediate', and so forth). But terms such as *here* and *there* are made comprehensible by their relationship to an anchor point or "ground," from which the relationship is being gauged. Two points are necessary to understand referential indexes: the anchor point and the reference itself. As Hanks points out, we tend to foreground the reference, yet the anchor point as background is necessary to comprehend the foreground. Both figure and ground, as foreground and background, are necessary to comprehend indexes like 'here' and 'there' (Hanks 1992, 59–60; 62). Thus two kinds of indexing can be differentiated: the referential indexing of relational features, and the deictic indexing of the anchor point.

These two kinds of indexing are pertinent to the *ie*, since they can be related with the two meanings of *uchi* outlined above. *Uchi* is a deictic anchor point, as Wetzel argues in this volume (see also Wetzel 1984 and Bachnik 1982), whereas *uchi/soto* indexes relational features—specifically 'inside/outside'. *Uchi/soto* can be related to figure and the foregrounding that Hanks defines—although these indexes are far more comprehensive than referential indexes—while *uchi* can be linked to ground and backgrounding.[1] Thus two points are necessary to understand *uchi/soto* distinctions: the inside/outside distinction that is made, in any of a number of communication modes, and the anchor point from which inside/outside is understood.

These two kinds of indexing are also pertinent to the two axes acknowledged in Japanese linguistic studies. These were originally termed *reference* and *address* by Martin (1964, 408–409) and Miller (1967, 270) who were focusing on Japanese register (or polite language), and they have also been linked, respectively, with *omote/ura* and *uchi/soto*. The axis originally associated with address involves a two-way distinction between formal and informal (Jorden 1962) or distal and direct (Jorden 1987) styles. Ikuta notes that the social relationship between speaker and hearer is the basis for defining formality/informality, and that distance is the crucial factor: "if the speaker feels very close to his listener 'informal' speech is employed; if not 'formal' speech is used" (1980, 2).[2] Ikuta also links the axis of distance specifically to the use of *omote/ura*. The other axis associated with reference and *uchi/soto* has been linked to distinctions of directional deference by Wetzel (1984). Wetzel notes that the communication of deference can be linked to inside/outside distinctions, and that both are far more prevalent than distinctions of person. Thus she argues that inside/outside distinctions actually function to communicate person in Japanese, through the organization of deixis.

But what have been termed *axes* of *omote/ura* (address-formality/informality) and *uchi/soto* (reference-directional deference) can also be combined into a single axis through the two meanings of *uchi*. Both the indexing of *omote/ura* and that of *uchi/soto* require *uchi* as deictic anchor point to be understood. As Jorden notes, these two sets of distinctions are regarded as extremely important in Japanese: "Almost without exception even single utterances are marked for politeness [deference] and formality, and certainly anything longer than a two-item exchange will be so marked" (1977, 103).

Since *omote/ura* and *uchi/soto* distinctions are widely used and have been associated with the organization of self and social life, the foreground/background perspective allows us to relate indexicality and deixis more broadly to the organization of self and social life. For example, as "ground" the deictic anchor point is more than a spot or "place"—a spatial or temporal reference point; it includes a common frame-of-reference as well, and this is where culture can enter the scene. Hanks also makes these connections: "A central aspect of the indexical [ground] is the degree to which the interactants share, or fail to share, a common framework (1992, 67)." In this sense Nakane's statement that "human relationships within this household group are thought of as more important than all other human relationships" becomes much more comprehensible (1970, 5). *Uchi* as 'inside' always implies *soto* 'outside', and vice versa. The relational feature of 'inside/outside' requires a deictic ground to be interpreted. *Uchi* is also this "ground" in the sense of a common framework of shared meaning or culture.

But how does one define directional deference as *uchi/soto* and relate this to *omote/ura* distinctions of social distance? How does "common ground" affect these distinctions? How is the deictic anchor point related to the organization of an individual self defined *within* a collectivity? Taking the figure/ground relationships of *uchi* and *uchi/soto* as my starting point, I will now examine: (1) how *uchi/soto* and *omote/ura* distinctions are made in the Japanese *ie* and how they are crucial in defining the organization of social contexts; (2) how *uchi* is crucial in defining the organization of self, and in making deference distinctions that create shifting boundaries for the *ie* group.

To address these questions I will develop a set of events in an *ie*, or household, I call the Katoos, which occurred shortly before the wedding of the oldest son and successor, Shigeto. At the time of these vignettes I had known the Katoos for six years and had lived with them for two (which would identify me as 'close'). My fieldwork, based with the Katoos, took place for six years, over the course of a twenty-year period.[3]

TIME AND SPACE: TWO VIGNETTES

Vignette 1.   Setting: The Katoo farmhouse fronting on the house garden which is blooming profusely on a mild September day. The house is opened up all along the front (south) side, and four guests are making their way along the stepping stones through the garden. Beckoned on by the Katoos inside the house, they walk up a stone stairway, remove their shoes, step up to the *tatami* mats and kneel, bowing so their heads touch the floor, as they greet those in the house. They present gifts to the Katoos, who also kneel and bow just as low in return. The guests return the bow of the hosts and then rise, as they are invited over to sit at a low table on *zabuton* 'cushions'.

The guests are Etsuko, the bride-to-be, who will soon marry Shigeto, the oldest son and successor of the house, and her father, her mother, and her father's sister. The hosts for the guests are the sister of the Katoo *otoosan* (the household head), and the *okaasan* (the househead's wife). The otoosan's sister (*obasan*) is visiting for the day. I am also there, greeting them. The *okaasan* and *obasan* bring tea for the guests, and we all sit, quietly sipping tea and enjoying the view of the garden. Then I am left to talk with them in a meandering way, comparing this prefecture with the one they are from in aspects ranging from local dialects to pickle-making.

They have come from a region renowned for its silk-making, and have brought the Katoos (and me), as gifts, pieces of silk and exquisite items made from the silk. Bride-to-be Etsuko, who is short with a squarish face and glasses, talks quietly, seriously, politely. . . . Her mother, very slight, has a wiry energy that makes her the most talkative. The father is heavy-set, calm, and says very little, but his silence is pleasant, a silence of acquiescence.

The room is open to the garden on two sides, and this openness makes it seem as if we are almost in the garden. Insects buzz in and out, and at midday the sun comes part way into the room. At the end of the room farthest from the garden is an alcove which has a flower arrangement—made from flowers in the garden. A scroll, mounted on silk, hangs in the alcove.

Just when I am beginning to become conscious of having to make conversation, the *okaasan* and *obasan* return with the first course of an elaborate meal that is tastefully laid out on the Katoos' best hand-painted porcelain and lacquerware serving dishes. They have taken these out of the storehouse, since the serving pieces are used only for special occasions. Although it is now nearly three o'clock and I am famished, the guests are reserved as they approach the food. They sample a few pieces of each kind of food, eating delicately, and remark on the freshness of the farm vegetables, but do not finish all they are served.

The talk during the meal is also slow, meandering, and punctuated by quiet pauses. We finish with tea, which seems to accentuate the quiet calm of the afternoon, and the laziness heightened by the sunshine coming in from the garden. There is a feeling of calm, as if time has stopped and removed us from the bustle of daily life.

Vignette 2.   Setting: Several hours before Vignette 1, in a different room of the same Katoo farmhouse. The *okaasan, obasan,* and I are sitting in the *kotatsu,* a low table with a charcoal warming fire beneath it. This room has a less impressive view of the garden, and the room is cluttered with everyday things. Holes poked in the paper-covered doors indicate the presence of the Katoos' grandchildren, as do the magazines and children's storybooks lying around the room. An old television set is in the corner. The *tatami* mats are old and worn, and there are cracks in the fittings of the doors and windows.

The *otoosan*'s sister (*obasan*) has come to visit for the day, and she and the *okaasan* are talking about goings-on in their households (the *obasan* has married into another house), as we all sit and drink tea from the brown ceramic teapot we use every day. The *okaasan* has just gotten up to put in new tea leaves, and I am listening to the stories they are telling in extremely informal language, punctuated by howls of laughter from the *okaasan*, as she slaps her sister-in-law on the back. Suddenly the phone rings in the next room, and the *okaasan* goes to answer it. We hear a loud shriek through the walls—then a pause.

The *okaasan* comes back into the room and begins talking more animatedly but in a different tone of voice than before: *"Ah komaru. Tai-HEN komaru!"* 'Ooh no! Are we in a mess!' I gather from what she is saying that Shigeto, who is about to be married, has just arrived at the train station in the next town with the bride-to-be and her relatives, seven hours early. Nothing is ready—nor preparations even started— and they will arrive within twenty minutes.

The *okaasan* is still recounting the conversation and moaning about what she can do, when the *obasan* gets up and begins climbing out of the *kotatsu*, unwrapping a bundle that she has beside her. "Don't worry about a thing! I've brought my work clothes (*monpe*) and am all set to help. No problem. We'll do it in no time."

The *okaasan* protests (rather weakly) that the *obasan* is a guest and certainly cannot be expected to help. The *obasan* responds by pulling on her *monpe*, saying as she does so, "Can't work in a *kimono*—slows you down something terrible." The *okaasan* protests—even more weakly— while they head toward the kitchen, and then, quickly, they are all business, and I am delegated to go to the store. The two women work furiously and manage to have a complete meal ready within a couple of hours, while I am again delegated to occupy the guests during the frantic preparations still taking place after they arrive.[4]

PART 1: *OMOTE/URA* AND
FORMALITY/INFORMALITY DISTINCTIONS AS "FIGURE"

Each of the above two vignettes is characterized by communication in a number of different modes: for example, the greetings, bowing, giving and receiving of gifts and food, spatial communication, speech register, kind of dress worn, and communication content. Each mode has at least two kinds of communication: (1) information communicated by *what* people say or referential meaning ("They're seven hours early!") or what they do (giving presents of handmade silk; or sitting in the *kotatsu*

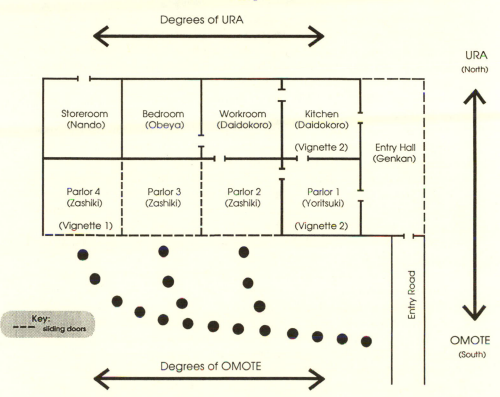

Figure 1. House plan for Katoo household.

in parlor 1), and (2) indexical messages, like that of distance in register usage that communicate *how* people define their relationships with one another.[5]

A close connection also exists between the distance defined in the relationships among participants and *what* the participants say and do in each vignette. The communication that took place in vignette 1 (see Figure 1) was characterized by formality of dress and speech register; by the giving of expensive and aesthetically pleasing gifts by the guests; and by the presentation of a specially prepared and artfully arranged meal by the Katoos. In the scenes in this vignette, relatively small amounts of information (referential) and a large number of relational (or indexical) messages were communicated. In fact, the indexical messages (that the people were distantly related) became *the* messages, so that the focus in this vignette was on form, rather than content, and the primary content message was one of 'emptiness'.[6]

The communication of self and other that took place in vignette 2, in contrast, was characterized by *informality* of dress and use of speech register; by the giving of much simpler gifts (the sister-in-law brought the house ancestors cakes she had made); and by the receiving of ordinary tea and crackers by the guest. The women readily gave much information to each other—in fact, information was the focus of their conversation—exemplified both in the animated talk around the *kotatsu* and even more so at the point of the phone call, since the *okaasan* informed the *obasan* of the content of the phone call. But the scenes in this vignette were striking in their *lack* of aesthetics, as well as etiquette decorum. The room was cluttered; the women were in informal dress, drinking ordinary tea, speaking in informal language, and slapping each other on the back as they howled with laughter. The women paid much less attention to form than to content, and the interaction was that of ordinary, everyday life.

In the first vignette all the modes of communication expressed formality, 'emptiness' of content, and difference from ordinary life. What people did and said expressed their relationship as 'far' (or as outsiders). Communication in the second vignette expressed informality, everyday life-styles, and a high degree of content—what people did and said expressed their relationship as 'close' (or as insiders).

The focus here differs from American social situations in that the relationship the Katoos defined between their own anchor point and those of others is crucial to the subsequent communication, and all the parties are aware of this.[7] Participants in these vignettes acknowledge that what is said and done in each of them (the referential focus on speech and action) is defined by the indexing of distance between anchor points of self and other. Thus, the Katoos indexed each scene by gauging distance from the anchor point(s) of their *ie* and those of the two different sets of guests, and modulated their communication accordingly, along an axis indexed inversely from empty to full, as exemplified in vignettes 1 and 2.

Moreover, the setting within which the two vignettes occurred (including the design of the house, the setting of the garden in relation to the house, and the furnishing of the rooms of the house) was also indexed in the same way by the participants. A series of rooms represented the axis in space. For each situation, the Katoos selected a room whose setting approximated the social distance between the anchor points of host and guests. The "set" nature of physical space required the continuum to be laid out in advance; yet the Katoos still selected the spatial context appropriate to each relationship, which became the backdrop for the situation.

Indexing of knowledge can also be linked to the same continuum, inversely indexed between 'full' and 'empty', and this looks ahead to part 3. Specifically, the distance between anchor points indexes the degree of familiarity, or shared cultural knowledge acknowledged by the participants, producing a range of communication along the same continuum. Thus 'close' is associated with 'full', or greater shared knowledge, while 'distant' is associated with 'empty', or less common knowledge. Moreover, these meanings can be additionally linked to 'informal/formal' distinctions, such that 'full', 'close', and 'informal' are "mapped" together, while 'distant', 'empty', and 'formal' are also "mapped" together (using Och's [1990] terminology).

Omote 'outsidedness', 'form', 'formality', and 'difference from everydayness' and *ura* 'insideness', 'content', 'informality', and 'everydayness' express this 'empty/full' axis, and both are major concepts in Japanese social life and in the *ie*. The communication in vignette 1 is obviously characterized by *omote*, and this word is also used to describe the section of the Katoo house that encompasses the four parlors (see Figure 1). The communication in vignette 2 is characterized by *ura*, the word also used to describe the section of the house that consists of the four 'back' rooms. None of these glosses is adequate as a definition, for I am suggesting that *omote* and *ura* index rather than reference, that they define a distance cline, *between* self and other, rather than primarily 'naming' or describing any characteristic of either.[8]

Thus in vignette 1, in addition to what is said, the indexical messages 'say' (by formality) that the two groups of people (the Katoos and the family of the bride-to-be) are *distant* and this message is similar (or redundant) in each mode—greetings, bowing, giving and receiving of gifts and food, spatial communication, and speech register. In vignette 2, the indexical messages communicate (by informality) that the two women (and their groups) are very 'close'; and this is also similar in a number of modes: the clutter of the room; its poor view of the garden; the informal dress; the informal speech register; the laughter and slaps on the back; and the informal gifts and mode of tea drinking. The basis of defining the bride-to-be and her relatives as 'distant' is that the marriage has not yet taken place; this is the initial meeting of the people in vignette 1. The basis of defining the *okaasan*'s husband's sister as 'close' is that she is the only sibling of the household head. The respective anchor points are crucial to gauging both these relationships.

In order to understand the variation in forms of Japanese social life, we can view each manifestation of communication as if it were placed along an inverted axis, which allows a range of forms, as well as degrees of content, to be indexed. The variations in form are related specifically by *degrees* of difference. For example, a bow is understood to be formal or informal by the degree of incline of the head vis-à-vis the floor; a seating place is understood to be *kamiza* 'higher' or *shimoza* 'lower' by (among other things) calculating the degree of distance from the *tokonoma* 'alcove', and the entryway relative to the other seating places (Hamabata 1990, 11–14). Hamabata warns of the high degree of *precise* variability of the rules in these matters; this precise variability can be understood (and even charted in interactions) if bowing and seating arrangements are viewed as indexed.

Moreover, the arrangement of the Katoo house design itself spells out an axis of formality/informality, which is closely connected to the discussion of *omote/ura*. The house building (Figure 1) consists of two rows of four rooms each, set back to back. One of these (the front set) is considered *omote*, the other (the back set) is *ura*. The front set of rooms, all guest rooms, are used only when members interact with outsiders; the rear rooms—kitchen, workroom, bedroom, and storeroom—are used only by household members.

The rooms within each set are also arranged along an axis of formality/informality. In the *omote* area the axis ranges from parlor 4 to parlor 1; in the *ura* area it ranges from the kitchen to the house storeroom. These two sets of rooms are partially, though not completely, separated. No entryway exists between parlor 4 and the storeroom, or between parlor 3 and the bedroom. But there is access between parlor 2 and the workroom, and between parlor 1 and the kitchen. This allows us to view the two axes as "opened out" like the end of a scissors, so that the most formal *omote* rooms (parlors 4 and 3) and the most informal *ura* rooms (storeroom and bedroom) form the ends of the scissor blades; the kitchen and parlor 1 (and to a lesser extent the workroom and parlor 2) form the point where the blades are joined.[9]

It is crucial to remember that this axis is defined by the interaction between householders and guests. The four *omote* rooms are not used by members unless guests are present (which means parlors 3 and 4 are used much less than 1 and 2). The four *ura* rooms are not accessible to outsiders (especially the bedroom and storeroom). But parlor 1 (an outside room) is often used by householders when they are relaxing, and the kitchen (an inside room) *can* be entered by outsiders when they are participating in household work (as the *obasan* did in vignette 2).[10]

Omote/ura do not define "norms" of situational interaction. Nor are they "categories" that distinguish these two situations from each other, for example, as formal and informal. *Omote/ura* are not meanings applied to already existing situations that label aspects of the situation. They define the situations, through the way in which participants continually specify the *degree of distance* in their relationships.[11] This distinction is important: the *omote/ura* axis is *produced* by participants in the scenes I have just described. Their social distance is what allows them to define appropriate action, dress, greeting, or gift. But social distance is itself directly derived from acknowledgement of the respective anchor points of the interactants. This allows us to make the linkage between the anchor point, deixis, and social agency. Agency is essential to the organization of the *omote/ura* axis, *which cannot be defined in the abstract.* Through agency the participants continually gauge the relationships between form *and* content, and these in turn become basic parameters for production of situation.

Omote/ura consists of more than indexing 'close/far' along a distance axis. Crucial to the organization of *omote/ura* is the fact that form and content are not dichotomies but are regarded as inversely related. Therefore a range of possible *forms* of social, spatial, and language communication can be selected by participants, depending on how distance is gauged between the anchor points of self and other. Moreover, a range of *content* disclosure is also available to them. Finally, the inverse relation of form to content means that the more attention given to form, the less content will be revealed, as I have already pointed out.

While the varied manifestations of *omote/ura* communications may seem to make generalization that transcends context difficult, the "systematic" aspect of indexes can be derived by investigating their rules of use (Silverstein 1976, 25); approaching indexes by "how" rather than by "what" questions. Thus Etsuko and her relatives, coming to the Katoo house for the first time, know how to index and interpret appropriate degrees of *omote/ura,* and how to interpret the Katoos' behavior toward them, even though this is a new context for them. Knowledge of *how to index* is widely shared by Japanese, and is carried over from context to context by them.

As indexes, *omote/ura* outline an approach to the organization of social life as practice. Through indexing of relationships from respective anchor points to create an agreed-upon distance axis, participants construct their social situations by modulating a wide variety of communication modes, from gift-giving to use of space—whose organization can be made comprehensible as a series of variations along a single axis gauged between the two anchor points.

PART 2: *UCHI/SOTO:* (IN-GROUP/OUT-GROUP) AND DIRECTIONAL DEFERENCE DISTINCTIONS AS "GROUND"

"[I]f one listens to a conversation between Japanese one does not have to wait long to hear the words *uchi-no* or *uchi-dewa,* referring to one's own people and work place" (Nakane 1970, 120). In addition to 'inside', the other primary meanings of *uchi,* the words most commonly used to speak about the *ie,* are 'us', 'our group', 'we', 'our', as well as 'I', 'me', 'my', 'my group'. *Uchi* indicates a specific house—'this' one of which I am a member, and because the referential value of *uchi* is based on the speaker's orientation at the time of utterance, it is by definition deictic.

But Nakane's identification of group with *ba* 'field' or 'frame of reference', has not been linked to the deictic meanings of *uchi*. The reference for *ba* is general and abstract, even though *uchi* is particular, immediate, and located; therefore *ba* cannot represent the *particular* social group, or an *immediate* social frame, both of which are crucial to *uchi*. Moreover, the linkage of self to a group that is not deictically defined makes the individual defined within the collectivity seem like a contradiction in terms. How can self *be* individually defined if it is also defined as within the collectivity?

Defining Person in the Ie

The group reference point has major implications for the definition of person in language and self in social life. The question here is whether *uchi/soto* distinctions are more significant for Japanese speakers than distinctions made on the basis of person categories (such as 'I', 'you', 'he', 'she', 'it', and so forth) in English or Indo-European. Wetzel argues, "The group-oriented *uchi/soto* distinction is as strongly encoded in Japanese as the person categories are in English or Indo-European" (1984, 30), and signals of *uchi* and *soto* are more frequent than signals of person. "The deictic distinctions which *uchi/soto* define depend on group identity" (5) . . . yet approaches to person in Japanese language have largely followed Indo-European assumptions of person (42).[12]

Issues of self within *ie* organization strongly parallel those of person in language. If the *ie* is a deictic anchor point, person must be defined in reference to the anchor point as a collectivity, whereas the focus on person terms has assumed the anchor point to be an individual. Here it follows that if the group is "fixed"—an unchanging anchor point—self cannot be "fixed" since self must be identified by location within a group, and this identification will necessarily vary according to the orientation of the speakers. This, in turn, makes sense of Smith's statement: "There are no fixed points, either [for] 'self' or 'other' " (Smith 1983, 77), as well as the variability and instability of person terms within the *ie*.[13] Moreover, deixis also clarifies the meaning of *jibun*, a commonly used word for self, as literally 'self' (*ji*) 'place' (*bun*) (Lebra 1976), which translates as a part/whole relationship between self and group. *Bun* is thus one's part in a larger whole, which is consistent with a collective deictic anchor point.

Uchi, as noted earlier, is translated as 'us', 'our group', 'we', 'our', as well as 'I', 'me', 'my', 'my group', whereas 'your' 'yours' 'your group' is communicated by a different word—*otaku*. *Uchi* and *otaku* thus operate in some ways like the first and second person pronouns in English. But there is an important difference in defining person in Japanese. Both 'I' *and* other members of my group are *uchi*; you *and* members of your group are *otaku*. This means that the other is not defined solely vis-à-vis the self, *but rather vis-à-vis the group to which ego belongs*. The group is the primary background through which figures such as the self are foregrounded and, as such, it is assumed as a common framework or "ground." In terms of this "ground," others can be differentiated in two ways: as "inside others" or "outside others." As a consequence of the collective deictic anchor point, the group boundary thus emerges as an important feature in communicating distinctions between self and other, so that these boundary distinctions replace the distinction between self and not-self in English and Indo-European. Moreover, self is demarcated within a larger "ground" and in a particular situational relationship. Taken alone, self constitutes neither figure nor ground.

Self/other distinctions revolve around the selection of deferential terms used only to refer to others outside one's group, and humble terms used only to refer to self and others inside one's group (Wetzel 1984). In fact distinctions defining inside/outside in relation to the group boundary far outnumber the use of person terms in Japanese—by a ratio of 10 to 1 (Wetzel 1984). From the speaker's perspective, honorific forms communicate a reference outside the group boundary, while humble forms communicate self-reference or reference inside the group boundary. Deferential communication is thus directional, signaling a relationship with the subject, such that the subject is either inside or outside the speaker's group. Thus the "axis of reference relies . . . on the distinction between *uchi* and *soto*, which is calibrated only with reference to the speaker" (Wetzel 1984, 19).

Self/Other and Group Boundaries in Social Life

I will now examine these boundary distinctions more explicitly through discussion of *uchi/soto* distinctions made in the two vignettes above. Here it is essential to focus on the constitution of self through indexing of anchor points in a particular relationship situation. Rosenberger details how two-person relationships, even within the *uchi*, are defined in terms of the indexing of self-restraint versus indulging the other (*amaeru/amayakasu*). The degree of distance between respective anchor points is an important basis for this distinction. Thus the degree of guest indulgence and self-restraint is more marked in the first vignette, since much more distance exists between the Katoos and Etsuko's family, than between them and the *obasan*.

We can also look at the indexing of self-restraint/indulgence in guest/host relationships in terms of the figure/ground relationship by which Hanks characterizes deixis (1992). The foregrounding of the guest (who is indexed by distance and highlighted as "figure") and the back-grounding of self (as host, who is defined by inclusion within the deictic anchor point) explains the dynamics of the directional communication of deference toward the guests and humbling toward self, which epito-mizes *uchi/soto* (and *amayeru/amayakasu*) in dyadic relationships.

The degree of outsidedness is markedly different between the two vi-gnettes, *and this creates the marked differences in behavior* within the two scenes, along the dimensions explained in part 1. We can say that the degree of distance between guest and host also explains the difference in the degree of foregrounding/backgrounding between the host (the *okaasan*) in relating to two different guests. Thus *omote/ura* can be closely linked to *uchi/soto* in the communication of deference toward guests.

To illustrate this point further, each vignette establishes *uchi/soto* rela-tionships for each participant. In vignette 2 (which happened first) the visiting sister-in-law, or *obasan*, is *soto*, and the *okaasan* (and myself) are *uchi*. One could perceive this from the interaction; the *obasan's* bow and greetings were those of an outsider, and she presented an informal gift (ancestor cakes that she had made). The *okaasan* stopped her own work when the *obasan* came, turned her full attention to the *obasan*, and began serving her tea and cookies. The *okaasan* served and the *obasan* sat on the guest side of the *kotatsu*. The foregrounding of the *obasan* in vignette 2 is not nearly as marked as that of the guests in vignette 1, precisely because of the cultural connotations of "ground," which I will explain below.

Here the interaction between the *okaasan* and *obasan* was stopped short by the phone call, which produced a shift for both *okaasan* and *obasan*. After the phone call, the *obasan* changed her clothes (to work clothes); she went to another room (the kitchen, an 'inside' or *ura* room); and she began to work. All these transformations signaled the *obasan's* shift from *soto* to *uchi*. This meant that she had moved from guest to host, and from figure to ground. The phone call produced the boundary shift that brought the *obasan into* the *uchi* or anchor point, because of the information of the imminent arrival of the four new guests, all of whom were visiting the house for the first time. Since this was a "new" relationship (the marriage had not yet taken place) Et-suko's relatives were clearly more *soto* than the *obasan*, and they required much more deference than she did. A crucial factor here was the degree to which the participants shared a common frame-of-reference. As the Katoo househead's only sister who had grown up in the household, the *obasan* shared a great deal of knowledge of the Katoo *ie*—including the knowledge of the dilemma the *okaasan* was experiencing at that very moment. Moreover, the degree of common cultural ground was acknowledged by the *okaasan* in divulging the contents of the phone call to the *obasan*. Note how the guests in these scenes are all defined in relation to their anchor groups.

The response of the *obasan* was immediate. She changed her "place" to accord with the change in situation, which brought her into the "ground" and thereby changed the direction of deference. The Katoo group boundary opened up at the moment the *obasan* changed her clothes, stepped from the parlor to the kitchen, and went to work helping the *okaasan* prepare the meal. Throughout the scene described in vignette 1, the *obasan* acted as part of the *uchi*, in greeting the guests, serving the food, in the place she occupied when she ate, and in helping to clean up—that is, in virtually all her interactions.

The shift may also be closely linked to symmetrical versus asymmetrical distinctions developed by Hanks and related to pronoun usage, for example, in *tu/vous*. This usage of symmetry and asymmetry is consistent with Brown and Gillman's (1960) and Friedrich's ([1966] 1979) classic studies of pronouns of power and solidarity. Thus a central aspect of the collectively defined anchor point is the degree to which the interactants share, or fail to share, a common framework. Here Hanks considers that common ground is pragmatically symmetric, because it joins the speaker and hearer, and "puts them on roughly equal footing relative to the referent" (1992, 67). In contrast, the "grounds" for ego and alter are pragmatically asymmetric, because the speaker is split from the addressee (or the host from the guest in the Japanese case).

Thus at the beginning of vignette 2, the *obasan* was indexed as *soto*, in comparison with the *okaasan*, and the relationship was asymmetrical, producing slight deference from the *okaasan*. But when Etsuko and her family members arrived, the *okaasan*, representing the Katoo *uchi*, shifted to relate to a house which was much more distant—making the relationship much more asymmetrical—than that with the *obasan*'s house. In opposition to Etsuko's household, the *obasan* was now 'close' and the *uchi* boundaries expanded temporarily to include her in the "ground" in opposition to Etsuko's household. During the time she helped the *okaasan* host the more distant guests, the *obasan* was on roughly equal footing with the *okaasan* in relation to the guests. The group boundary had been redrawn so that the asymmetry was between Etsuko's family and everyone else, admitting the *obasan* squarely into the *uchi*.

The nature of figure versus "ground," guest versus host distinctions also allow us to view the humbling act of the *obasan* in allowing herself to temporarily enter an anchor point *that was not hers* as part of a larger system of reciprocity. Her humbling of herself by entering their "ground," is in a broader sense an act of giving deference to the Katoo house by helping *them* give deference to their guests. The *obasan's* anchor point is not the Katoo group, even though she has temporarily 'come into' it. Her 'coming in' is itself a form of reciprocity—in which she is giving more than either objects or actions. She is exchanging her social "ground"—giving up her own "ground" temporarily in order to enter the Katoo *uchi* with the obligations and responsibilities to outsiders that this position implies. This act of temporarily entering another anchor point is very common and constitutes an important kind of reciprocity in Japanese society. This can be seen by the aftermath of the *obasan's* shift. The Katoos, in turn, reciprocated to the *obasan* for her act, by giving her a seat near the top of the table at Shigeto and Etsuko's wedding.[14]

This indicates that the subject of household reciprocity should be approached not only in terms of exchanges like labor and gift-giving, but to include as well the temporary shifting of anchor points, and the kind of giving that this involves. In fact, reciprocity of a variety of exchanges can be viewed within a larger framework of temporary movements between anchor points which, in fact, defines how these other kinds of exchanges are carried out. For example, in the vignettes above, the movement of the *obasan* into the Katoo *uchi* cannot be separated from her physical assistance of helping in the kitchen; in fact, *the latter signifies the former*: her presence in the kitchen (*ura*) in itself signifies that she has temporarily 'come into' the Katoo house, with the connotations of obligations to help that go along with sharing their social "ground."

Implications

Although analyzed separately, the *omote/ura* distinctions discussed in part 1 and the *uchi/soto* distinctions discussed in part 2 were taking place simultaneously, and the deictic anchor point was crucial for both. In a sense, *uchi* and *uchi/soto* organization provides a virtual model of the deictic figure/ground relationships outlined by Hanks (1992). Here, social relationships are indexed through formality/informality as *omote/ura* and these distinctions, combined with the *uchi/soto* indexing, provide the dynamics of guest/host deference, highlighting the guest as "figure" and the host as "background." The group anchor point is required to make these dynamics comprehensible.

Thus relational features specify the deictic relations (for example, as close/distant, immediate/non-immediate, up/down, and so forth), which emerge as "figure." But these "figure" relationships are dependent for their comprehension on the indexical anchor point or "ground," relative to which they are computed (Hanks 1992, 59).

To examine further the way in which deixis is related to *uchi/soto*, we can say that deixis is evident in the organization of Japanese guest/host communication. But we can also turn this around in the other direction to say that the organization of guest/host communication spells out the deictic organization delineated by Hanks. It is this sense of deixis spelling out the organization of *uchi*, and *uchi* in turn spelling out the organization of deixis that exhibits the quality of the snake eating its tail. This circular movement exhibited by the relationship between *uchi* and deixis is fundamental to the constitutive nature of *uchi/soto* (and of deixis); the movement reenacts literally the relationship between all three "levels" of *uchi/soto* I discussed in the introduction to this volume.

For example, the constitution of self and social context is illustrated in the shifting communications of the vignettes. The dynamics of host/guest deference also define an interplay between self and social order, in which each is defined inversely in relation to the other. Thus two-person communication is fundamental to the organization of self, widely defined as relational and interdependent; while the other side of this coin is a social order that is humanly constituted.

In the sense that each is a commentary on the other, self is socially constituted, while at the same time the social order can be viewed as "ordered" by this very process of being constituted. It now seems well worth investigating the possibility of links between the process of being constituted—and with it aspects of social "agency" and "practice"—and deictic organization, which revolves around precisely this process, as is evident in the figure/ground organization of relationships.

As noted in the introduction to this chapter, *ie* organization can be considered as constituted by relationships between *uchi* and *ie*, and elsewhere I have developed these relationships at more length (Bachnik, in press). Just as self and social order can be viewed as constituted by the relationship between *uchi* and *ie*—which takes place in the members' involvement in the interplay of constituting organizational continuity over time (through the mandate of recruiting for the next generation of successors), members are themselves constituted (or given social identity) through their relationships as members in the organization.

Conversely, it may also be possible to view *uchi/ie* relationships as manifesting this very relationship between the constitution of self and social order. In this sense, the relationship between *uchi* and *ie* could be viewed as providing a manifestation of the organizational process (which can only be viewed in process) by which each is constituted. This speaks to agency, pragmatic organization (in Peirce's sense), and practice.

Deictic organization, including both *uchi* and *uchi/soto*, contributes a different focus to *ie* organization, resolving some longstanding problems, and raising many new issues. The common usage of the term "*uchi* in *uchi-no* or *uchi-dewa* referring to one's own people and work place" (Nakane 1970, 120) has been largely interpreted as signifying the importance of "familialism" throughout Japanese society. But although *uchi* designates an aspect of the *ie*, it also specifies an anchor point and 'inside' (in relation to 'outside'). Rather than indicating that virtually every Japanese group is in some way a "family," the widespread usage of *uchi* for groups throughout Japanese society may just as well specify that groups throughout Japanese society *function as deictic anchor points*; thus *uchi-no*, or *uchi-dewa* means *my* group (and anchor point) as opposed to *yours*. The common usage of the term *uchi* indicates that deixis, *uchi/soto* distinctions, and shifting boundaries must also be widely common to Japanese groups.

These distinctions between *uchi/soto*—and the shift in perspective this requires—mean that the *ie* should not be regarded as a self-contained "box" defined by structure, function, form, or responses to economic forces. The distinctions also raise broader questions of the significance of organizations such as the "household." In its replication of the dynamic of the snake eating its tail, both as an organization spelling out that dynamic and as a commentary on the constitution of self and social order by means of that dynamic, the *ie* speaks to issues that are implicit—but crucial—in the organization of social life everywhere.

Notes

1. They include both referential indexes and what Silverstein defines as "pure" indexes, which are "independent of any referential speech events that may be occurring," and "signal the structure of the speech context" (Silverstein 1976, 29–30). One example of pure indexes are deference indexes, which "code sociological relations of personae in the speech situation" (Silverstein 1976, 32). The distinction between referential and pure indexes does not appear pertinent in the Japanese case.

2. Jorden (1962) defines formal forms as "verbals ending in—masu and all of its derived forms . . . and copula forms *desu, desita,* and *desyoo*" (Wetzel 1984, 17).

3. The fieldwork on which this chapter was based was supported by a Fulbright CIES Grant and two renewals, by an NDEA Title VI Fellowship from Harvard University, and by a Kenan Research Grant and a Junior Faculty Development Award from the University of North Carolina, for all of which I am grateful. The subject of indexicality in *ie* organization is more fully developed in a book volume entitled *Family, Self, and Society in Contemporary Japan* (University of California Press, in press).

4. The two vignettes and a part of the *omote/ura* discussion that follows appeared in Bachnik 1989. I am grateful to JAI Press for allowing me to reproduce them. Another discussion of the vignettes appears in Bachnik, in press, and a different version of the vignettes appears in Bachnik 1986.

5. Bateson elaborates these distinctions considerably in his discussion of social communication (1972, 159–339). Ochs (1988) and Silverstein (1976) also develop them in regard to language and culture.

6. It is worth noting that "emptiness" is also a focal point in Japanese aesthetics. Thus the sparsely furnished room in parlor 4, and the importance of 'emptiness' in such aesthetic forms as tea, flower arrangement, art objects, gardens, and architecture, can all be linked to the social/outside/formal end of this continuum, where these art forms are used. The emphasis on form and on content as emptiness, space, or "betweenness," may also replicate form/content at the formal end of the relationship spectrum.

7. Americans, too, use different degrees of formality in language use, in dress, and in gift-giving. We also are able to shift from scene to scene, and we often use distance clines. Yet, culturally speaking, we tend to focus on reference rather than indexing, and to define patterns of action that transcend context rather than shifts differentiating interaction within and between contexts.

8. This axis corresponds to Silverstein's description of "pure" or deference indexes (see note 1). Silverstein assumes propositional referential meaning to remain unaffected by deference indexes. But *omote/ura* affects this meaning as well, indexing what would constitute acceptable discourse topics. In fact, the implications of indexes like *omote/ura* in terms of indexing referential categories would seem quite important.

9. This design idea is Michael Silverstein's (personal communication, 1985); I find his suggestion appropriate.

10. My argument in no way hinges on the generality of the Katoo house design. What it does hinge on is the generality of the formality/informality axis, and this can be demonstrated in other house designs as well. Two-room houses, and even one-room apartments, still have an axis of formality, which is simply less elaborate.

11. For a further discussion of the contrast between normative and indexical approaches to the organization of Japanese social interaction, especially in terms such as *omote/ura*, see Bachnik (1989).

12. There is some disagreement about the universality of the three-person organization of the Indo-European paradigm. "There are always, then, three persons and there are only three" (Benveniste 1971, 195). "All languages have pronominal categories involving at least three persons and two numbers" (Greenberg 1963, 96). But Becker and Oka disagree: "I is not I, you is not you, and we is not we from one language to the next" (1974, 230).

13. The instability of person terms has also been well noted within the *ie*. The terms themselves vary considerably—even from group to group. Reference and addresss within the *ie* is not limited to pronouns, but also includes titles, kin terms, proper names, age-status terms, and zero forms (meaning avoidance of any use of terms) (Befu and Norbeck 1958; Fischer 1964, 1970; Suzuki 1973,

1976, 1977). Finally, two distinct terminologies exist in the *ie*—kinship (as ego-centric) and position (as sociocentric). The stability of person terms in the *ie* is discussed further in chapter 6 of Bachnik, in press.

14. The *otoosan* explained to me that he changed the seating arrangement to move her near the top of the table, because the *obasan* had contributed much—(*iro na sewa ni natta*) including this incident and others during the wedding preparations.

REFERENCES

Bachnik, Jane. 1982. "Deixis and Self/Other Reference in Japanese Discourse." *Working Papers in Sociolinguistics* 99:1–36. Austin, Texas: Southwest Educational Development Laboratory.

———. 1983. "Recruitment Strategies for Household Succession: Rethinking Japanese Household Organization." *Man* (N.S.) 18: 160–82.

———. 1986. "Time, Space and Person in Japanese Relationships," in J. Hendry and J. Webber, eds., *Interpreting Japanese Society: Anthropological Approaches*, 49–75. Oxford: JASO.

———. 1989. "*Omote/ura*: Indexes and the Organization of Self and Society in Japan," in C. Calhoun, ed., *Comparative Social Research*, vol. 11, 239–62. Greenwich, Conn.: JAI Press.

———. 1992a. "The Two 'Faces' of Self and Society in Japan." *Ethos* 20(1): 3–32.

———. 1992b. "*Kejime*: Indexing Self and Social Life in Japan," in N. Rosenberger, ed., *Japanese Sense of Self*, 152–72. Cambridge: Cambridge University Press.

———. In press. *Family, Self, and Society in Contemporary Japan*. Berkeley: University of California Press.

Bateson, Gregory. 1972. "The Logical Categories of Learning and Communication," in *Steps to an Ecology of Mind*, 279–308. New York: Ballantine Books.

Becker, A. L., and I Gusti Ngurah Oka. 1974. "Person in Kawi: Exploration of an Elementary Semantic Dimension." *Oceanic Linguistics* 13(1 and 2): 229–55.

Befu, Harumi, and Edward Norbeck. 1958. "Japanese Usages of Terms of Relationship." *Southwestern Journal of Anthropology* 14: 66–86.

Benveniste, Emile. 1971. *Problems in General Linguistics*. Coral Gables: University of Miami Press. Miami Linguistic Series, 8.

Bourdieu, Pierre. 1977. *Outline of a Theory of Practice*. Cambridge: Cambridge University Press.

———. 1990. *The Logic of Practice*. Stanford: Stanford University Press.

Brown, Roger, and Albert Gilman. 1960. "The Pronouns of Power and Solidarity," in T. Sebeok, ed., *Style in Language*, 253–76. Cambridge, Mass.: MIT Press.

Doi, Takeo. 1973. *The Anatomy of Dependence*. Tokyo: Kodansha Internationl.

———. 1986. *The Anatomy of Self*. Translated by Mark Harbison. Tokyo: Kodansha International.

Duranti, Alessandro. 1986. "The Audience as Co-Author: An Introduction." *Text* 6(3) (Special issue: *The Audience as Co-Author*.) New York: Mouton de Gruyter.

Edwards, Walter. 1989. *Modern Japan Through Its Weddings*. Stanford: Stanford University Press.

Fischer, J. L. 1964. "Words for self and other in some Japanese families." *American Anthropologist* 66(6, part 2): 115–26.

———. 1970. "Linguistic Socialization: Japan and the United States," in R. Hill and R. Konig, eds., *Families East and West*, 107–18. The Netherlands: Mouton.

Friedrich, Paul. [1966]1979. *Language, Context and the Imagination: Essays by Paul Friedrich*. Stanford: Stanford University Press.

Giddens, Anthony. 1979. *Central Problems in Social Theory: Action, Structure and Contradiction in Social Analysis*. Berkeley: University of California Press.

———. 1984. *The Constitution of Society*. Berkeley: University of California Press.

Greenberg, Joseph H. 1963. *Universals of Language*. Cambridge, Mass.: MIT Press.

Hamabata, Matthews. 1990. *Crested Kimono: Power and Love in the Japanese Business Family*. Ithaca: Cornell University Press.

Hanks, William F. 1990. *Referential Practice: Language and Lived Space among the Maya*. Chicago: University of Chicago Press.

———. 1992. "The Indexical Ground of Deictic Reference," in A. Duranti and C. Goodwin eds., *Rethinking Context*, 43–76. Cambridge: Cambridge University Press.

Heidegger, Martin. [1926]1962. *Being and Time*. Translated by John MacQuarrie and Edward Robinson. New York: Harper and Row.

Ikuta, Shoko. 1980. "Ethnography and Discourse Cohesion: Aspects of Speech Level Shift in Japanese Discourse." Masters thesis, Cornell University.

Jakobson, Roman. [1957]1971. "Shifters, Verbal Categories, and the Russian Verb," in *Selected Writings of Roman Jakobson*, vol. 2. The Hague: Mouton.

Jorden, Eleanor H. 1962. *Beginning Japanese*, vols. 1 and 2. New Haven: Yale University Press.

———. 1977. "Linguistic fraternization: A guide for the *gaijin*," in *Proceedings of the Symposium on Japanese Sociolinguistics*, 103–23. Honolulu: University of Hawaii.

———. 1987. *Japanese: The Spoken Language*, Parts 1–3. New Haven: Yale University Press.

Kondo, Dorinne. 1990. *Crafting Selves: Power, Gender, and Discourses of Identity in a Japanese Workplace*. Chicago: University of Chicago Press.

Lebra, Takie. 1976. *Japanese Patterns of Behavior*. Honolulu: University of Hawaii Press.

Levinson, Stephen. 1983. *Pragmatics*. Cambridge: Cambridge University Press.

Lyons, John. 1977. *Semantics*, vols. 1 and 2. Cambridge: Cambridge University Press.

Martin, Samuel. 1964. "Speech levels in Japan and Korea," in D. Hymes, ed., *Language in Culture and Society*, 407–15. New York: Harper and Row.

Merleau-Ponty, Maurice. 1962. *Phenomenology of Perception*. Translated by Colin Smith. London: Routledge and Kegan Paul.

Miller, Roy Andrew. 1967. *The Japanese Language*. Chicago: University of Chicago Press.

Nakane, Chie. 1970. *Japanese Society*. Berkeley and Los Angeles: University of California Press.

Ochs, Elinor. 1988. *Culture and Language Development: Language Acquisition and Language Socialization in a Samoan Village.* Cambridge: Cambridge University Press.

———. 1990. "Indexicality and Socialization," in G. Herdt, R. Shweder, and J. Stigler, eds., *Cultural Psychology: Essays on Comparative Human Development,* 287–307. Cambridge: Cambridge University Press.

Peirce, Charles Sanders. 1931–1958. *Collected Papers,* vols. 1–8. Edited by C. Hartshorne and P. Weiss. Cambridge, Mass.: Harvard University Press.

Rosenberger, Nancy R. 1992. "Tree in Summer, Tree in Winter: Movement of Self in Japan," in N. Rosenberger, ed., *Japanese Sense of Self,* 67–92. Cambridge: Cambridge University Press.

Silverstein, Michael. 1976. "Shifters, Linguistic Categories, and Cultural Description," in K. Basso and H. Selby, eds., *Meaning in Anthropology,* 11–55. Albuquerque: University of New Mexico Press.

Smith, Robert J. 1983. *Japanese Society: Tradition, Self and the Social Order.* Cambridge: Cambridge University Press.

Suzuki, Takao. 1973. *Japanese and the Japanese: Words in Culture.* Translated by Akira Miura. Tokyo: Kodansha International.

———. 1976. "Language and Behavior in Japan: The Conceptualization of Interpersonal Relationships." *Japan Quarterly* 23: 255–66.

———. 1977. "*Hito* as a self-specifier and *otaku, kare* and *kanojo* as other-specifiers," in *Symposium on Japanese Sociolinguistics,* 195–204. Honolulu: University of Hawaii.

Wetzel, Patricia Jean. 1984. "*Uti* and *Soto* (In-Group and Out-Group): Social Deixis in Japanese." Ph.D. dissertation, Department of Linguistics, Cornell University.

Failure to Index:
Boundary Disintegration and
Social Breakdown

Chapter 7

UCHI NO KAISHA: COMPANY AS FAMILY?

Dorinne K. Kondo

Editors' Introduction

In this chapter the collective deictic anchor point again comes into focus, when Dorinne Kondo examines the multiple meanings of *uchi no kaisha*, the "company family." The anchor point in this situation differs from the *ie* of Bachnik's or Rosenberger's chapters, for the Satoo *ie* owns and runs a small business employing thirty full-time workers, which is also included in *uchi*. *Uchi no kaisha* comprises fundamental tensions and ambiguities, for the *uchi* anchor point and its sharing of common "ground" can be redrawn in this "company family" to encompass the company employees within the family *uchi*, or to include the family alone. The anchor point "ground" is constantly shifting because the *uchi/soto* distinctions, and thus the boundaries, can be redrawn in a number of ways—between family and company, between different categories of workers, within the company and between workers and the company president, to name but a few.

These multiplicities of meaning allow for strategic political shifts, and Kondo uses a series of ethnographic dialogues to delineate the redrawing of *uchi* boundaries by the *shachoo*, or company president, and the response of the employees to his delineation of authority. Both president and employees appropriate *uchi no kaisha* to construe different meanings; for example, the employees do so to speak for a more truly familial and caring system, Satoo to emphasize the obligations of loyalty and hard work that the employees owe the company.

Both *shachoo* and the employees consider *uchi* to be crucial—as an informal space where one's inner fillings (*honne*) or informal side (*ura*) can be expressed. Since Satoo-san, as head of both company and family, has most authority and is clearly most *uchi*, he can therefore express intimacy most "authoritatively." If he is *uchi*, the workers are *soto*; he receives indulgence, and they must indulge. Like the *okaasan* in Rosenberger's chapter, they cannot easily counter his authority.

Satoo should balance his authority (and his hierarchical relations) with acknowledgment of the overarching solidarity. He would thereby acknowledge his own submission to the collectivity and balance his authority by allowing them to express *uchi*, or solidarity. Instead, Sato as-

serts his authority arbitrarily on personal whim, using surveillance cameras and microphones for workers—and barking orders over the hidden
microphone in icily polite Japanese. The workers respond by using
uchi—in his absence—to vent their criticism of and outrage against
these practices. Personalized exercise of authority within the *uchi* works
paradoxically, to undermine the *shachoo*'s legitimacy, undermining his
structural position as head of the company. But the workers seem
caught in the same paradox: unable to mount a sustained resistance to
the *shachoo*'s personalism that is not personalized on their part—as a
series of complaints crystalizing only temporarily in isolated incidents.
The shifting ultimately produces an impasse: Satoo maintains control
only through exercising personal power, while the employees' dissatisfaction with his authoritarian style remains unresolved, and Satoo's stature as company president is increasingly undermined.

UCHI NO KAISHA: COMPANY AS FAMILY?

AFTER A DAY off I returned to the confectionery factory in Tokyo, where
I was a part-time worker, and entered a room already alive with activity.
Ohara-san, the chief artisan, sent me to help Hamada-san, one of the
other female part-time workers, with preparing *anmitsu*, a combination
of fruit, bean paste, gelatin cubes, and honey. We were expected to
make hundreds of these and other sweets today, as part of the half-price
sale the owner, Satoo-san, was offering the public. In the midst of cutting gelatin cubes, I queried, "Are they doing a special sale for us, too?"

"Oh, well, yesterday," said Hamada-san conspiratorially, "the *shachoo*[1]
brought down some *leftovers* of the new products, like sour cherry tarts.
They were a mess! Then the *shachoo* offered to sell this '2000 yen value'
for only 500 yen. Not *one* of us bought any. After all, they were all turned
over and broken up. Who would want anything like that?"

By this time Nomura-san had joined us, and she was equally vehe-
ment: "What we want is something you can give as a gift, something that
will keep! Western sweets aren't even pretty in boxes, and they spoil
right away, especially in the summer. All we can do is take them home to
eat, and who can eat that much?"

"I'll bet there's no sale for the employees. There are things you want
and things you don't want, and even if those tarts were free, I wouldn't
take any!" exclaimed Hamada-san.

My co-workers' agitated faces, their frowns, and the fierce tones of
justified anger in their voices were unforgettable.

The memory of this incident set the tone for the entire day and pro-
voked heated discussions of working conditions. Ohara-san, the chief
artisan, brought up the case of Itoo-san, a young man who had recently
quit the Satoos to take a job in a factory subcontracting to Mitsubishi

Heavy Industry. "It must be like going from hell to heaven," he observed. Itakura-san, a woman in her fifties and the oldest part-timer, expanded on Ohara-san's remark, explaining to me how Itoo can now wake up at 8 A.M., since he lives close to work. At the Satoo factory, in contrast, workers who wanted breakfast had to arrive at 7 A.M. for a 7:30 starting time. At Itoo's new, cushy job, the work week is limited to five days, overtime is never more than two hours a day, and workers get double pay if they have to work on holidays. All this was unheard of in the Satoo factory, where people worked six days a week, and overtime regularly surpassed two hours a day.

The conversation turned to wages, and Itakura-san told me that at the Satoo factory, all the "company officers" received no overtime pay.[2] She pointed out that all the artisans kept impressively long hours: even during the slack seasons they worked from 7:30 A.M. until 6 or 7 P.M. "People talk about how hard the Japanese work," the part-timers laughed, "but Ohara-san is a special case. He works about twice the hours of the average person—sometimes even three times the hours—look at the month of March! The artisans work until midnight and get up at two in the morning."

"Plus, no matter how long I work," Ohara-san lamented, "the money is the same. And since the 'officers' have to pay for their own meals, it seems like any extra money goes to food." Screwing up his face, he said he had once refused to become "chief of the factory." But somehow, before he knew it , there he was, a company officer who could no longer receive overtime pay.

"Maybe," I ventured, "it would be better to do without some things like company trips and have the *shachoo* raise salaries," an opinion I had heard from some workers in other companies.

"Are you kidding?" said Nomura-san with great vehemence. "Every company in Japan has a company trip. A company trip is only natural. They have to give us at least that much."

Itakura-san, spurred on by the chief artisan's plaintive narrative, launched into a philippic against the company, the structure of Japanese society, and the corruption of Japanese politicians. Linking the expression of protest to *uchi/soto* contexts and to the *omote/ura* layering of selfhood, she began with the heated observation, "Kondoo-san, your mother and father are Japanese, but a 'pure' American would never understand what Ohara-san is saying. America is a free country, where you can cry if you feel like crying, laugh if you're happy. But Japan's different. Ohara-san is quiet and gentle, and he's so long-suffering that he just takes it."

Another part-timer chimed in. "The factory can't get along without Ohara-san."

"Oh, no," he demurred modestly, "everyone can manage just fine."

172
DORINNE K. KONDO

"But look, nobody can do the special orders except for Ohara-san. And still he's like a slave, to put it mildly."

Itakura-san was becoming more and more vituperative in her condemnations of the *shachoo:* "One of these days, I'm just going to explode, and tell him there are lots of confectioneries in Tokyo, and he'd damn well better watch it. If any inspectors come by, I can tell them about all the violations of the Labor Standards Law—like using kids under eighteen to do all those hours of overtime!"

The part-timers turned their attention from the *shachoo* to politics. "What we need are men like the Meiji politicians. They were selfless; they thought about the welfare of the whole country. The LDP[3] is no good; they're just for the big companies. In Japan, there's too much of a difference between the big companies and the small ones. The big companies are in fine shape; they can give their people lots of vacations, lots of bonuses, lots of benefits. And here we are."

"You know," said Itakura-san, "I was talking to a guy who'd worked here a few years ago. He said that it *used* to be really familylike here, but then the *shachoo* hired a management consultant who charged huge fees, and now the *shachoo* just does as he's told. The consultant doesn't think about the workers; all he thinks about are profits! Money is a dirty thing, isn't it. Now, I don't think the *shachoo* is a bad person—everybody has good and bad points—but sometimes he's really nice, and sometimes he's dishonest."

"What about a union?" I asked.

Laughing, Itakura-san replied, "We'd probably get fired. There's only one president around here!"

Finally, the conversation returned to its starting point, the half-price sale.

"It was so hilarious yesterday! You should have seen the *shachoo*'s face! He couldn't believe we didn't want to buy anything."

The part-timers then began to seek creative solutions. "What would happen," said Nomura-san, "if one day we all decided not to come to work?"

"The factory couldn't get along without us," replied another part-timer.

Hamada-san conceived a plan that included a prominent role for the foreign researcher. "Kondoo-san, maybe *you* should ask the *shachoo* when he'll have a half-price sale for us. I wonder what he'd say then."

"Maybe he'd sell the sweets to you half-price, we could all give you our orders, and then we could come to pick them up at your landlady's place. You'd be the most popular girl in town."

"If he says he's not going to sell anything to you half-price, then you can tell him, 'Well, then, I'll just go someplace else.'"

We were all convulsed in laughter by this time, and I was seriously mulling over the idea of carrying out their plan—but, given the situation, I felt I could hardly jeopardize my relations with the *shachoo* after all his generosity to me. Even more important was my relationship with my landlady, a good friend and exemplary informant, who had provided me with the introductions to the firm. Creating "trouble" in the factory would have called her reputation into question as my guarantor. Nonetheless, in retrospect I wish I had, feigning innocence, asked the *shachoo* about the sale. But "familial" expectations of loyalty in return for benevolence seemed to work vis-à-vis foreign researchers as well as native Japanese—at least in this instance.

UCHI NO KAISHA: CONTESTED MEANINGS

Uchi no kaisha—our company—and a sense that company is family are themes trumpeted loudly in postwar studies of Japanese industry. The company as family idiom is presumably pervasive in Japan, shaping workers' lives and creating disciplined, loyal employees who strive to achieve group goals. Management practices such as lifetime employment, payment of wages by seniority, and quality circles—so goes the explanation—reinforce the family feeling, for a Japanese company is a community of people who share a common destiny (*unmei kyoodootai*).

More recent scholarship has begun to untangle the multiplicities of meaning and the political strands in the notion of *uchi no kaisha* and, by extension, the company as family metaphor. Andrew Gordon (1985) shows how, at various points in history, the management of heavy industry invoked the "beautiful customs" of "traditional" Japan in order to avoid improving working conditions. Most striking, companies extolled the beauty of familialism—a benevolent management caring for loyal and hard-working employees—in order to combat the 1911 factory law. These idioms are open to appropriation by a variety of actors, however, as proponents of the law also invoked the ideology of familistic management, arguing that the "beautiful customs" of familialism would work in tandem with regulatory legislation (Gordon 1985, 68). Mark Fruin (1984) also shows how the Kikkoman family firm articulated an explicitly familial ideology in the wake of the Great Strike of 1927–28, stressing the "spirit of industry" (*sangyoo damashii*) and the common goals uniting managers and workers. Yet "company as family" and attempts to create the sense of belonging implied in the phrase *uchi no kaisha*, our company, are not merely management ruses. Gordon spells out the ways workers also couched their claims to full membership in a discourse of "company as family," arguing that they, too, should belong to *uchi no kaisha*.

The example of the *uchi no kaisha* idiom is particularly eloquent in revealing potential tensions and contradictions in *uchi/soto* discourses. In this volume, Wetzel notes that *uchi* provides a deictic anchor point for the speaking subject, and all the contributors note the tension between authority and solidarity within an *uchi*. But as they also note, *uchi* can designate many different groups—school, company, household, to name only a few. In the context of a family-owned company, the deployment of an *uchi no kaisha* idiom mobilizes fundamental tensions and ambiguities, for *uchi* can have at least two senses: the company as a whole and the owner's household. By extension, *uchi no kaisha* encompasses both the capitalist firm, whose goal is profit-seeking, and the emotional circle of attachment that should constitute "family." Furthermore, as Rosenberger, Bachnik, and Hamabata point out, there are degrees of inclusion, where the househead or housewife who was born in a household is more *uchi* than the in-marrying househead or housewife. In the context of the Satoo confectionery, the *shachoo*, the third-generation successor to the headship of the household and the company, was clearly the most *uchi* member, and the tensions between him and the workers in the Satoo company reveal the tensions animating the *uchi no kaisha* idiom itself.

Given these multiplicities and ambiguities of meaning, my approach would highlight the strategic appropriations, political deployments, ironic twists, and subtle nuances in the *uchi no kaisha* idiom, as it creates and constrains people's lives. At the Satoo company, *uchi* and *soto*, I will argue, create arenas within which protest, resistance, and complaints are structured in culturally specific terms. How the boundaries of *uchi* and *soto* are drawn and redrawn, who is placed in relatively *uchi* or *soto* contexts, and how people play off the tensions inherent in the *uchi no kaisha* idiom, struggling over its meanings, are key questions we must ask. By paying careful attention to the ways the boundaries of *uchi* are drawn, we can see how workers can give a particular spin to the meanings of an idiom, wresting it from the *shachoo* and turning it to their advantage, yet in so doing they create ironies and contradictions for themselves. The discourse on *uchi no kaisha* also intertwines and sometimes strains against other significant idioms and metaphors animating work life in the factory, and the clash of discourses often creates tension and contradiction. These ironies call into question a schema of "hegemony" countered by "authentic resistance," instead drawing attention to the multiplicities, open-endedness, and contradictions that inevitably accompany the crafting of identities and lives within a matrix of power and meaning.

Company as Family in the Satoo Factory

Uchi and *soto* create contexts within which protest, resistance, and complaints are structured in culturally specific terms. Let us begin by laying out some basic features of family firms (household enterprises might be a more accurate term), and the problematic nature of drawing bound-aries between *uchi* and *soto* in the Satoo confectionery in particular.

Chie Nakane captures the distinctive feature of the *ie*, or corporate household: "a personalized relation to a corporate group based on work, in which the major aspects of social and economic life are in-volved" (Nakane 1983, 260). Like the *ie*, the Satoo company was an orga-nized, hierarchically structured entity that involved many aspects of its employees' lives, and served, as I have elsewhere argued, as a locus of hierarchy and duty, a circle of emotional attachment, and a nodal point of identity (Kondo 1990).

Like factories in other countries, the Satoo company was a hierarchi-cally structured organization. Though its hierarchy may seem similar to companies elsewhere, the Satoo company's location within a particular narrative field (cf. Haraway 1989) gives this hierarchical organization a familial resonance it might not otherwise possess in another cultural set-ting. It makes the *uchi no kaisha* idiom especially apt. Take, for example, the structural organization of the company. Perhaps the most obvious cleavage between workers is the distinction between permanent and temporary (so-called part-time) employees—a distinction acquiring in-creased importance in many industrialized countries as the numbers of part-time workers swell. Both the young male artisans who work in the factory and the young women who work in the shop are full-timers, enti-tled to all the benefits I describe below. Part-timers, on the other hand, are structurally marginal, and their rights, duties, and privileges in the company are more attenuated and ambiguous. Bachnik (1983, 177), for example, sees an analogue here between the structurally temporary members of a household, who must eventually leave one day to establish branch households of their own, and the temporary members of a com-pany. In both cases, the sense of belonging is attenuated and the com-mitment expected and benefits accruing to the temporary members will most likely be slight in comparison to the successors/permanent mem-bers. Because the *ie* is basically an enterprise/work organization rather than a unit of kinship (Bachnik 1983), the *ie* and the company can act as templates for one another, in ways not possible in cultures where "household" has different sedimented meanings.

Despite the salience of *uchi no kaisha* as a meaningful cultural con-struct, the Satoo company was in a peculiar and delicate position vis-à-vis its deployment. As in any family-owned firm, the negotiation of the *uchi* and *uchi no kaisha* boundaries are constantly problematic, the two poten-tial strands of meaning creating potential tension. This situation was ex-acerbated by the firm's intermediate size. With a good thirty full-time employees, the Satoo confectionery was somewhat too large for face-to-face paternalistic relations according to "traditional" models. In the old days—indeed, up until the sixties—everyone lived together under a single roof and took their meals together. The firm was smaller then, with only a handful of artisans and two young women who worked in the shop. *Uchi no kaisha* had an immediacy then that it does not now possess. Owners and workers do not live together and no longer take their meals together. Though Mr. Satoo was never really a master working alongside his apprentices, workers who have been with the company for a long time say that he used to be much more of a personal presence on the shop floor. No longer is this the case. Mr. Satoo's activities with the merchants' association, his plans to expand the number of stores, and his business dealings with suppliers and customers keep him away from the factory most of the time. Perhaps the symbol of this new, larger, prosperous—and less familial—Satoo company was the new factory, opened in 1980. A dazzling white, three-story building, it housed the Japanese sweets division on the first floor, Western pâtisserie on the second, and the Satoo family residence on the third. Workers came to the building to work and to work only; they lived either in the company dormitory, a good fifteen-minute walk from the factory, or they rented their own houses or apartments.

As the factory's spatial layout demonstrates, in a family firm the *uchi no kaisha* idiom is of necessity fluid and ambiguous, as the two conflicting senses of *uchi* are brought into play. On one level the *shachoo* and his family occupy the highest positions in the company, and Mr. Satoo himself is the center and key decision maker on most counts. In that sense, there is no doubt who is most *uchi* in the company. In many instances, there is a sharp demarcation between the *shachoo* and his family, and the employees, a demarcation played out in spatial symbolism, the payment of wages, the according of respect and deference, and in working conditions. It is difficult always to maintain the guise of harmonious "familial" relations when, for example, you have installed cameras on the shop floor to check up on your workers. In another sense, though, the company as family metaphor must embrace all workers at least *some* of the time, and the Satoo family attempts to "add a family flavor" (*kazoku no aji o tsukeru*) through a variety of institutional and informal practices. Certainly this is done in order to make work life more pleasant in accordance with meaningful, accepted cultural practices, but it also is intended to make work more efficient and productive, a situation primarily benefiting the *shachoo* and his family. Workers, on the other hand, look to *uchi no kaisha,* the company as a whole, to act as a source of care and respect for their position and their needs. Finally, as we shall see, both *shachoo* and workers define *uchi* as an informal space where one's *honne* 'inner feelings' or *ura* 'informal side' can be expressed. But the lines of demarcation are differently drawn in each case, with workers, in particular, constituting *uchi* as the work group where complaints against the company can be aired with impunity. For the *shachoo*, the whole company can indeed act as his *uchi* for, ordinarily, subordinates must tolerate his outbursts of emotion. The boundaries of *uchi*, then, are contextually defined, replaying and maintaining the tension between authority and solidarity.

Within this narrative field, riven by the contradictions implicit in the notion of company as family, the Satoo family can nonetheless be effective in imparting a family flavor, securing workers' loyalty and promoting identification with the firm (see Kondo 1990). But as we have seen in the incident of the half-price sale, these practices are not carried through in every context. Fixing close attention on certain revealing incidents on the shop floor will allow us to follow out the twists in meaning that provide workers with the arms they can use to counter the *shachoo*'s behavior. Finally, I will argue that the creation of *uchi* and *soto* spheres provides culturally specific means for structuring protest and "resistance," channeling the reappropriations and redeployments of meaning in ways that rearrange, but do not yet fundamentally threaten, the power of Satoo's readings of the idiom.

Strategic Deployments: Uchi/soto *and* uchi no kaisha

Unraveling the implications of the morning's interaction leads us to several observations about the workers' sense of *uchi no kaisha*, their appropriations of the idiom, its intertwinings with other critical discourses, and the expression of discontent and resistance in particular *uchi* contexts.

First, the workers reappropriated the familial idiom of *kazoku* and *uchi* in order to mine its critical potential and, in so doing, created boundaries and definitions for the *uchi*. Itakura-san, for instance, invoked one sense of *uchi* as the company that truly cared for its employees, when she linked the "golden age" of the Satoo company to days when it was "really" *kazokuteki* 'familylike'. The present disregard of the Labor Standards Law, the long hours and low wages, the lack of regard for the part-timers' desires for a half-price sale, were ascribed, in her analysis, to his departure from the truly "familylike" past. The new, more uncaring and exploitative practices she linked to the recent hiring of the management consultant, whose concern was merely for profits and not for the workers. *Uchi no kaisha*, as defined by the management consultant and by the *shachoo*, thus became *uchi* as the Satoo family, not the company as a whole. Itakura-san's sense of *uchi no kaisha* deemphasizes the long-suffering loyalty workers supposedly owe their employers. Rather, employers should more selflessly care for their workers, thinking of the workers' needs with concern and empathy. Purely economic rationality thus becomes an evil in human terms, for it erases human dignity and defines *uchi* too narrowly, as the owner's family. Itakura-san's deployment of the *uchi no kaisha* notion provides her, then, with a richly nuanced critique of what she—or the politically like-minded—might call petty capitalist accumulation.

The discourse on *uchi no kaisha* worked in complicated ways in tandem with other critical discourses. One was a sophisticated leftist political analysis, which was clearly shared by a few of the older, female part-timers. Itakura-san invoked the days of the Meiji Restoration, when politicians worked selflessly for the good of the country. This she contrasted with her comments about the LDP and its connections to big business, and the corruption of today's politicians. Again, "traditional Japan" was represented by an *uchi no kaisha* in which properly familial attitudes were held by owners and managers, who would think not of their career advancement or their profits but for the good of the whole. *Uchi*, in this scenario, again meant the whole company.

In an interesting rearrangement of meaning, the part-timers reappropriated one of the key practices associated with "imparting a family flavor"—that is, the company trip—and claimed it as a right. Itakura-san, Nomura-san, and others emphatically declared that it was only proper and natural that they should, just like other workers in Japan, have their company trip. "That much should be coming to us," was their assessment. No romantic sense of *uchi no kaisha* softened their incisive and determined insistence on their rights to certain benefits. Certainly, no owner I ever interviewed took this perspective on the matter; in the owners' view, they were "giving" the employees a wonderful outing as a culturally appropriate demonstration of their kindness and largesse.

The part-timers' informal, ad hoc remedy for their proximate complaint—the lack of a half-price sale—revealed another way in which *uchi* was defined: as the company work group and the informal context in which discontents could be aired. The part-timers' solution was to call on me, a foreigner and a researcher with a more "official" status, who in some sense mediated between *uchi* and the public sphere. My position as guest, less subject to the owner's complete authority, gave me a potential critical voice that might have been heard outside the confines of the *uchi*, the company work group (cf. Bachnik, introduction to this volume).

It is important to note that the part-timers did take opportunities to register their disapproval of the *shachoo* and his disrespectful treatment. Their refusal to buy the broken-up cherry tarts should not be discounted as an effective act of criticism, for according to their descriptions, the *shachoo* was clearly surprised and taken aback by their actions. My co-workers insisted on their dignity, refusing to accede to the *shachoo's* definition of his offer as a "favor" to them, thus defining the company as a caring *uchi*. The workers' refusal was especially effective because it enacted their disapproval in a way that would not bring down the ultimate penalty of dismissal. Such a strategy reminds us again of the high stakes involved in any act of protest in a more public, formal, *soto* sphere, for union organizing and collective protests were likely to lead to "getting it in the neck" *(kubi ni naru)*, as the eloquent Japanese expression goes. The *shachoo* had the power to impose his reality more exhaustively on others and to enforce his definitions of that reality, and workers who contested his deployments of meaning risked their jobs in so doing. As Itakura-san stated so pithily, "There's only one president here."

What counts as *uchi*, and for whom, are thus matters subject to political struggles. This "classificatory politics" (Stark 1986) shows how different actors can reclaim and redeploy certain idioms in ways they perceive to be just and justifiable (see Joan Scott 1988). The part-timers especially can reappropriate the idiom and subvert the *shachoo's* readings. But it is also clear that his attempts to define the meanings of *uchi* could be more effective, for he had the material means at his disposal to enforce those meanings. And his definitions of *uchi* were sometimes profoundly exclusionary, albeit laced with contradiction.

Wages and Working Conditions: Whose uchi *Is It?*

As the furor surrounding the incident of the half-price sale demonstrated, the battleground most fraught with significance seemed to be that of wages and working conditions, where the lines drawn between *uchi* and *soto* revealed the contradictions and tensions in the notion of *uchi no kaisha:* the company as a whole or the owner's household.

The day after the half-price sale incident, the topic of salaries arose.

"Think about it," said Itakura-san. "We get a raise of ¥20 a year. Over ten years, that's only ¥200." (This was about $1.00 at the exchange rate of the time.)

"Itoo-kun is lucky," said another part-timer. "Over five years here, and his salary went up by only ¥5,000 ($25)! The base pay here is only ¥87,000 ($435)—of course, there's overtime you can add onto that, but to earn ¥10,000 ($50), you've got to work pretty hard!"

"Anyway," said Nomura-san, "they take out money for food and for shoes and for rent and for savings, so all the guys have left is about ¥30,000 ($150) or ¥40,000 ($200) to spend for themselves."

"It's hard work, standing over that hot grill all day!"

Even the timing of payments came under fire. Itakura-san compared the Satoo company unfavorably with larger firms that gave out bonuses at the end of November, so people could use them to buy the ritual end-of-the-year gifts (*Oseiboo*). "Here," she said with considerable irritation in her voice, "they don't give out bonuses until the end of December."

This talk of money provided the prelude for the scene to follow. As he was wont to do, the *shachoo* sauntered in to survey the afternoon goings-on in the factory. Apparently he did not find things to his liking, for his face darkened, and he bellowed, "Look at all this mess! Why don't you people clean things up?" And, as usual, he dashed out in a huff.

Also as usual, he left an uproar in his wake. Yutaka-kun growled, "We're only getting paid to make *okashi*, not to do the cleaning."

"You really do feel like telling him off," said Nomura-san, in assent.

Itakura-san pronounced in her severe way that the *shachoo* should simply decide how much cleaning had to be done on a particular day and have people do it before or after work.

Nomura-san protested, "Most companies have someone who specializes in cleaning."

And I, thinking of the dustballs accumulating in the corners of my six-mat *tatami* room, added, "Plus, there's no end to cleaning."

Money and the monetary idiom provided perhaps the clearest demarcation between owners and workers, the owner's *uchi* and the metaphorical *uchi* of the "company as family." The paltry wages of the part-timers, the low salaries of the young artisans, the lack of overtime provided the chief artisans were subjects of extended commentary, as we have seen. Such injustices highlight the most exclusionary definitions of *uchi no kaisha*, defined as the *shachoo* and his family, who in turn benefit from the workers' labor. One morning, for example, the *shachoo* repeatedly rang the bell of the dumbwaiter, signaling his impatience as he awaited the goods from the second floor to reach him. Kitano-san, a young artisan, commented wryly, "It's hard for the *shachoo*, isn't it—making all that money." Money symbolized above all things the division between owner and worker, between *uchi* as owner's family and *uchi* as the whole company.

Working conditions and workers' control over the work process constituted a similar field of contention, where demarcations were drawn between the owner, who knew little about actual operations on the shop floor, and the workers, presumably his inferiors, who had this knowledge. One day, Teramura-san, who worked on the grill, had to stay at home because of her painful menstrual cramps.[4] Because Itoo, her former co-worker, had left the company, and the factory was generally short-handed, the *shachoo* had no choice but to take over some of the baking himself. Standing over the hot machine all day was apparently no easy task for him, which he duly reported to Teramura-san when she came back. "It was terrible!" he said in wonder. After he left, she said scornfully to us, "It's *his* family's factory; you'd think he'd do this once in a while."

A similiar complaint was lodged by Hamada-san, when the *shachoo* made a new capital investment in a packaging machine. In order to find room for the bulky apparatus, the part-timers' work space had been rearranged in ways that made our work more difficult. No one had bothered to consult us on the matter, and Hamada-san was irritated all day, constantly mentioning how *yarizurai* 'hard to do', 'hard to work with' the machine was, how inconvenient she found the new spatial arrangements, and—the final straw—how implements we used every day were not in their usual places. The can opener had disappeared, and she finally shouted out in frustration, "Why do people who don't know anything put things away in places where we can't find them?" Here again, we were presented with the contradiction of the *shachoo*, whose *uchi* would presumably benefit from the workers' knowledge and expertise, knowing little or nothing about the work process. To add insult to injury, he had not even bothered to consult the workers about matters on which they were expert.

In these examples, the divisions between *uchi* and *soto* were clear, centering around the issues of money, ownership of the firm, and control over the work process. The entire firm was Satoo's *uchi*. Workers pointed out the contradictions underlying this drawing of the *uchi* boundary, however, when they contrasted the ownership of the firm to his actual knowledge about everyday work practices. Despite the fact that it was the *shachoo*'s *uchi*, he knew very little about what the workers went through every day and, as a consequence, he failed to adequately appreciate their contributions. Indeed, he was surprised, when he substituted for Teramura-san, at how hard the work in fact was. Satoo's failure to fully acknowledge his workers was symbolized for them in a variety of ways, including the payment of low wages and failure to consult them about decisions bearing directly on their work. He made no move to draw workers into a more expansive *uchi no kaisha* by according them visible respect for their knowledge and expertise. When the *shachoo* drew the *uchi* boundary narrowly, as *his* family alone, he provided workers with tools of critique as he also, in so doing, reinforced his power base and effectively excluded workers.

Similar tensions and ironies are at play in the *shachoo*'s other enactments of *uchi no kaisha*, most strikingly visible in his exercise of authority. At times he did treat the entire company as his *uchi*, and his actions both define the meanings of *uchi*, strengthening his control, and simultaneously subvert, even as they advance, his purposes.

Owner as Oni

In any work organization, the exercise of authority is a critically important issue. *Ie* structure, at least formally, is constituted through a chain of hierarchical command that buttresses the authority and legitimacy of the *shachoo* and, secondarily, his wife. In *uchi* contexts, Satoo-san sometimes asserted that authority on seeming personal whim, thus keeping workers off guard and reserving for himself a kind of privileged, arbitrary authority, bearing "family resemblances" to the constitution of authority in other so-called paternalistic systems (cf. Genovese 1974; Sider 1986). These moments also sharply drew the lines between *uchi* and *soto*, reinforcing the construction of the *shachoo* as the central *uchi* figure.

The most startling examples were associated with new technologies of power and surveillance: the camera and the microphone. On the shop floor, cameras—much like the ones in American banks—surveyed our day-to-day activities. The Satoos could turn on the monitor in their office at any time. For us workers, this meant that we never knew when a transgression might bring down the wrath of "The Voice." One morning, out of nowhere, it boomed, "Good morning, everyone! As I told you yesterday, uniforms are to be put out today for cleaning. Two of you haven't yet done so. If the uniforms are not downstairs by noontime, I'll have to dock the pay of the offending parties." The icily polite Japanese (e.g., *kinoo mooshiageta yoo ni*), barked out at an excruciatingly high decibel level, was a sure sign that Satoo was holding back his anger. We all exchanged alarmed glances, and a part-timer whispered to me that she thought Kimura-san, one of the young artisans, had been one of those at fault. Needless to say, he slipped out of the workroom early, to take his dirty uniforms downstairs.

Satoo's explosive temper could be loosed in situations where his anger was, in some ways, due to his own lack of foresight. Yet even these eruptions served to buttress his authority. One day, as we were going about our everyday routine, he burst in, face livid, chest heaving. "What's the matter with all of you? Today a customer came into the store and said she'd called the factory to find out how much something cost, and somebody told her it was 130 yen. Then she went to the shop and found out it was really 150 yen. She asked me, 'What kind of company is it, where the workers don't even know the prices of the things they're making?' All of you should know *exactly* how much everything costs! Where do you think your salary is coming from?! Get your act together!" And he dashed out as suddenly as he had dashed in.

Left dumbfounded and open-mouthed for a few minutes, we did not take long to start in.

"What does the guy think? If he wants us to quote prices, he should give us a price list and put it up by the phone!" said Nomura-san, one of the part-timers.

A young artisan muttered in anger about the *shachoo*'s last phrase, "Where do you think your salary is coming from?" "That's what he really wanted to say, so that's why he yelled at us," Yutaka-kun opined.

Itakura-san, the politically savvy older part-timer, also decried the *shachoo*'s egregious behavior. "It's all we can do to just make the stuff and get it to the shop. How can he expect us to know the *price* of everything too?"

Quickly the subject turned to judgments about the *shachoo*'s personal character. "Hot-tempered" was the conclusion.

"Outside, he seems like a nice guy. But he always takes it out on us," said Moriuchi-san, a part-timer. She then cracked, "Maybe the stress was just building up and he had to let it out. He must feel a lot better now!"

Hamada-san, who seemed to get on beautifully with the *shachoo*, surprised me with her observation, "It's because the *shachoo*'s hobby is to mistreat people."

The workers contrasted Satoo's gracious demeanor outside the company in formal, public situations, where he appeared to be the personification of benevolent care, and his unpredictable behavior toward his employees in the confines and "privacy" of *uchi no kaisha*. Clearly, *uchi* was a place where the *shachoo*, too, could express his *honne* 'inner feelings', and his more powerful position gave him a socially recognized platform for the uncensored expression of his anger.

Even the shop manager, who was the Satoo's nephew and the designated successor to the firm, recognized the *shachoo*'s explosive ire. One day I went into the store to buy sweets, and Hiroshi-san asked whether I had been at work that day. "No," I said, "I had to do some interviews." "Well," he said, "the *shachoo* was like this," as he held up his two index fingers, one on either side of his head: the sign of the *oni* 'the horned demon'.

All of these demonstrations of temper would seem to work against the legitimacy of his authority, as it indeed did to an extent. Workers were clearly outraged by his arbitrariness and "unfair" outbursts. Yet, in another sense, this authority could be used to bolster his control over people as he kept them off balance and tied workers' complaints to his "personal" characteristics, requiring them to read his moods—a common occurrence in unequal power relationships (cf. Miller 1976; Kanter 1977). Mr. Satoo himself seemed to think that whenever he did get angry, it was justified, and he apparently took pride in the power of his anger. On my birthday in July, he held a joint dinner party for me and for his daughter Natsuko. During the course of the evening, I found out that his birthday was at the end of June, making us fellow Cancerians according to the Western zodiac. "We Cancerians," Satoo-san said to me with a satisfied air, "are usually quiet, but when we're angry, you'd better watch out!"

Coercive power was the message of Satoo-san's intrusions over the loudspeaker and the angry barrage of words he directed toward his employees. In the *soto* world of other companies and the merchant association, he could reap the benefits of his "familial" care and concern for his employees and, in all fairness, it appeared to be quite genuine. But in an *uchi* setting, the arbitrary exercise of authority left us with the uncertainty of never knowing *quite when* we were being watched or *quite how* the *shachoo* might react. This was especially clear in our vulnerability to his changes in mood—which were, after all, striking: from the jovial, ruddy-faced Satoo-san who joked around with us, to the cold, impassive man who one day handed out pay envelopes ("It would make you feel better if he at least said, 'Thanks for your trouble,' " said the part-timers), to the shouting, livid face wracked by spasms of anger. This meant in effect that authority was personalized and made "familial," linked to personal caprice and character (his hot temper) as much as it was tied to his structural position—a situation possible in any household. Personalized exercise of authority within the *uchi* works paradoxically to undermine the *shachoo*'s legitimacy as it provides workers with the tools of critique. At the same time, it enabled power to resurface in a personal, familial, arbitrary way that resonated with, as it worked against, his structural position as head of the company. Workers' complaints, perhaps like the complaints of family members vis-à-vis a household head, were also personalized, scattered, crystalizing only temporarily in isolated incidents . They could thwart the *shachoo*'s plans to unload his unwanted sweets on them by refusing his offer and, by doing so, they managed to startle him momentarily. Perhaps their refusal even made him reflect on his actions. But more sustained, public confrontation was considerably more difficult. The isolated nature of the protests, combined with the personal nature of the complaints—arising, as they did, from the "very character" of the *shachoo*—discouraged and defused potential, formally expressed opposition, either via the single voice of an intermediary or the collective voice of a work stoppage.

Irony and Multiplicity

Though the boundaries of *uchi no kaisha* created an arena for the exercise of authority and the generative play of power (Foucault 1979, 1980), giving rise to a plethora of creative practices and often creating warm feelings of solidarity and commitment, the contests over the boundaries and the precise meaning of *uchi* were everyday matters at the Satoo company. *Uchi no kaisha,* far from possessing some essential, referential core, was appropriated and transformed by various actors in a multiplicity of creative ways. *Uchi* as the *shachoo*'s family and *uchi* as the whole company provide a constellation of meanings that the *shachoo* and workers, from their contextually specific subject-positionings, deploy. Any of these meanings is necessarily partial and interested, for no *uchi* is ever a single collectivity, and there are always different degrees of *uchi/soto* that can be enforced and enacted, depending on the situation—an argument made by all the papers in this volume. The multiple appropriations of *uchi* in the Satoo factory include the following:

1. For some of the part-timers, *uchi no kaisha* symbolized a return to a Golden Age when employers were truly familial and caring, where *uchi no kaisha* meant the whole company. For owners, *uchi no kaisha* could mean the whole company, but they emphasized instead the obligations of loyalty and hard work *owed* them in exchange for their largesse.

2. In other contexts, *uchi* meant the owner's family—and here, in contrast to the familial idiom, workers invoked the "cold," selfish idiom of economic rationality. Money was a "dirty thing," and the management consultants who worked for profit were working for the owner's *uchi,* not *uchi no kaisha.* Wages and working conditions symbolized the contradictions in the deployment of this sense of *uchi no kaisha,* for the persons who were most *uchi* in fact seemed to know least about the work process in the factory, and revealed their lack of respect for workers by awarding low wages, berating them unjustly, conducting sporadic surveillance of shop floor activities, and failing to improve, indeed exacerbating, already difficult working conditions. The greatest contradiction in the *uchi no kaisha* idiom lay in the *shachoo*'s ability to fire people for whatever reason he pleased, a coercive power that provided the unspoken backdrop to everyday life in the factory.

3. For both *shachoo* and workers, *uchi* was an informal context where complaints and emotions could be expressed with impunity, and where public exposure was unlikely. For workers, the most *uchi* of contexts at the workplace was the work group, where complaints could be voiced, away from the dampening presence of the *shachoo.* For the *shachoo,* the entire company was his *uchi,* a place where his explosions of anger had to be tolerated.

In the end, however, we are left with contradictions and ironies. Though workers subvert the *shachoo*'s readings of *uchi* in their creative redeployments of meaning, they are still not able to subvert in ways that would concretely affect the shape of their lives or that of the *shachoo*. *Uchi* and *soto* thus, finally, create the contexts that culturally mediate the expression of so-called resistance. Until somehow they are able to confront the *shachoo* outside the *uchi* context, using perhaps an "official" voice like the one I might have provided, or banding together collectively to confront him in a more public, *soto* arena, the subversive play of power occurs primarily in one place: *uchi* as work group. And though they creatively and subversively transform the meanings of *uchi no kaisha*, giving it a sharp, critical edge, their invocation of the familial idiom also legitimizes and reproduces it as a culturally meaningful arena of political contest. Equally ironically, the *shachoo* could maximize his personalized imposition of authority within the *uchi no kaisha* in ways that simultaneously undermine and buttress his power.

RESISTANCE?

The transformation of the *uchi no kaisha* idiom leads us, finally, to consider briefly the recent efflorescence of literature on resistance, which focuses on the small, everyday acts of resistance to hegemonic ideologies. Practices heretofore unnoticed or dismissed by grand theory as mere accommodation, false consciousness, or reformism assume a new political weight.

For the people I knew in the factory, the deployment of the notion of *uchi no kaisha* was laced with contradiction, irony, and compromise. No single meaning, no single effect, could be isolated in its pristine abstraction. Workers could invoke *uchi no kaisha* subversively, yet in so doing they also reproduce and legitimize the idiom. The *shachoo* could explode at us, but in so doing he both reinforced his authority and supplied his workers with materials for critique. And different discourses could collide and intertwine: while the *shachoo* might deploy the sense of *uchi no kaisha* as a community with a common destiny, emphasizing his own benevolence in the form of "gifts" such as the company trip, workers shifted the focus to the capitalist organization designed to maximize owners' profits, and to their position as wage laborers who possessed certain rights, when they refigured the company trip as a benefit the company *owed* them. When the *shachoo* marshaled the language of economic rationality and profit-seeking by following his management consultant's suggestions, workers parried with their appropriation of the *uchi no kaisha* idiom, criticizing the *shachoo* for being *inadequately* familial. Such conflicts could reveal the fissures in the discourse of *uchi no kaisha*, where a family feeling fostered in certain contexts could be undercut by practices highlighting the cleavage between the *shachoo* and his family, on the one hand, and the workers, on the other. Given the contradictions, nuances, and multiplicities engendered by any act or appropriation of meaning, how can one account for the lives of my co-workers within the narratives of "resistance" provided in the social science literature? Can the richness of their experiences be adequately captured by those frameworks and, if not, what theoretical moves are necessary so that we can begin to do justice to their lives?

The complexities of deploying the meanings of *uchi/soto*, highlighted by all the papers in this volume, lead us to the difficulties with employing the notion of resistance as an analytic tool. These difficulties appear in exemplary form in two important works that operate within a metaphysics of closure and presence, presuming that human lives can be seen in terms of neat, closed, monolithic, internally coherent categories. These analyses should give us clues that perhaps articulating the problematic of power in terms of "resistance" may in fact be asking the wrong question.

Keeping his focus on the quotidian, a theme animating the new resistance literature, James Scott (1985), in *Weapons of the Weak*, creates a vivid portrayal of peasant resistance in Malaysia. His account argues for an actor-centered, meaning-centered account of everyday acts of resistance, emphasizing the refusal of "the poor" to accept definitions of reality imposed from above. Most central to my argument, he shows the ways Malaysian peasants appeal to a particular, culturally shared idiom of human decency to criticize the actions of the rich. Scott rightfully takes to task those who would limit the definition of resistance to formalized, organized acts, defined by some transcendent political principle.

Still, Scott's analysis relies on uncomplicated notions of human agency and a view of power as simple repression. For example, he argues that power-laden situations drive underground part of the "full transcript" of any special encounter. But the notion of a transcript—a discursive account, more or less hidden, depending on contextually specific power relations—takes on problematic meanings when one considers the kind of self or subject who authors such an account. His less powerful individual who hides the transcript is a consciously intentional, whole, quite uncomplicated self, who holds well-formulated, uncontradictory opinions apart from the dominant ideology. This whole subject's less authentic side is simply a kind of mask, donned for expediency's sake. Nowhere do we find that people like my co-workers can be caught in contradictions, that they simultaneously resist and produce, challenge and reappropriate meanings of *uchi no kaisha* as they deploy the different meanings of the idiom in different contexts. That people inevitably participate to some degree in their own oppressions, buying into hegemonic ideologies even as they struggle against those ideolo-

gies, is a poignant and paradoxical facet of human life given short shrift
in Scott's schema.

Moreover, Scott presumes that power is merely repressive, a mecha-
nism applied from above and outside, which prevents the expression of
authentic resistance. My experiences at the Satoo factory taught me that
power both created and limited definitions and expressions of so-called
resistance. For example, in everyday interactions on the shop floor,
uchi/soto boundaries outline a contested terrain, but also serve as culturally appropriate spaces where resistance could surface. Within the factory, meaning and power are coextensive; this intertwining of meaning
and power creates sets of institutions and disciplinary practices, from
the structure of the company to the designation of the people who
work there as different kinds of selves—*shachoo*, artisans, part-timers—to
everyday interactions such as those I have described in this paper.
Power/meaning *creates* selves at the workplace and, consequently, no
one can be "without" power (Foucault 1979).

In short, the subtleties, multiplicities, ironic twists, and wrenching yet
creative contradictions running through my co-workers' lives—and the
lives of the Japanese people who appear in this volume—cannot be accommodated within Scott's world of resistance. The world of the Satoo
factory is complex and ironic, where no single category, meaning, motivation, or aspect of selfhood can be sifted out from its shifting placement in matrices of power. Multiplicities, tensions, and layerings of
meaning undercut simple resistance at every turn. But as my co-workers
showed me, the factory is also a ludic space, open to creative possiblities
for subversion (Rosaldo 1987; Butler 1989). For Scott, the world is a
simpler place. His rhetoric is animated by a wish for clean-cut, clearly
defined categories that can exhaustively account for the world, but since
reality is messier than that, he is resigned to making do with the messi-
ness. Itakura-san, Nomura-san, Yutaka-kun, even the *shachoo*, would find
this alien territory indeed.

If Scott premises his analysis on a particular notion of the "subject"
and of power, the difficulties with resistance as a category of human action can be seen in Louise Lamphere's (1987) historical and anthropological study of women factory workers in a Rhode Island town. Her
book offers a complex, multistranded analysis, interweaving issues of political economy, class, gender, and ethnicity as they interlace in a particular setting and over time. Based on participant observation fieldwork
in a garment factory and on archival materials, Lamphere's account
gives us richly detailed stories of women's work culture and their strategies of resistance on the shop floor.

What are those strategies? For Lamphere, women workers' actions
can be neatly categorized as resistance, coping, or consent. Resistance

can take the form of various overt or covert acts, from outright strikes and rebellion to less obvious strategies such as socializing new workers to the intricacies of the piece-rate system, and practices creating solidarity among women, such as their efforts to humanize the workplace via baby showers, showing family photographs, and otherwise "bringing the family to work." Coping indicates ways the workers and families adjust to the larger, perceived social environment. Consent is glossed as "acquiescence to a husband's authority or to management policy either because it seems 'right' or because there seems to be no alternative." (338) Certainly, it seems worth distinguishing between different sorts of actions and different degrees of resistance, but there is no indication here that the very act of distinguishing aspects of behavior also suppresses important differences and contradictions *within* the categories one elects to distinguish. The division of social practices into three groups also implies that they are mutually exclusive and temporally and contextually separate, whereas one could equally argue that people consent, cope, and resist at different levels of consciousness at a single point in time, and that social practices can therefore be vexed and complicated, irreducible to three crisply distinct categories. Where within this scheme could we place my co-workers, who both invoke the *uchi no kaisha* idiom in subversive ways, yet feel compelled to express that subversion only in certain contexts? And what of the possibilities for both consent at a certain level and resistance at another? Or what of the *shachoo*, whose exercise of authority, at a single point in time, has paradoxical consequences, both consolidating and undermining his power?

Rather than relying on notions of a whole subject who can authentically resist power, on a notion of power as simply repressive, and therefore on the assumption that a place beyond power exists, or rather than subscribing to a view of social action as divisible into neatly separable categories, I would argue for a more complex view of power and human agency. This approach would see people as decentered, multiple selves, caught in sometimes wrenching contradictions as they craft themselves and their lives. They may rearrange power relations as they appropriate and redeploy cultural meanings, but they can never escape to a romantic place beyond power and therefore beyond contradiction and irony.

In a setting like the Satoo factory, a term like *resistance* seems inadequate at best, for apparent resistance is constantly mitigated by collusion and compromise at different levels of consciousness, just as accommodation may have unexpectedly subversive effects. It seems equally suspect to speak of repressive power, for as Satoo-san has shown us, the strategic deployment of an idiom always produces ruptures and cleavages, so that in most effectively defining the contours of *uchi*—by his anger—Satoo-san also undermines his own purposes, reinforcing the solidarity not of *uchi no kaisha* but of *uchi*, the work group. When he does so, however, he is not mechanically reproducing or undermining configurations of power, for these matrices of power and meaning are to some extent open-ended, with room for play, subversion, change. At the Satoo factory, no deployment of meaning has a single effect; rather, any action produces a multiplicity of sometimes paradoxical and creative effects. Finally, a more complicated view of the agency and selfhood of those who resist would see people caught in contradictions, constructing new arrangements of meaning and power as they craft their lives, but never authentically resisting power to attain some emancipatory utopia (cf. Foucault 1979, 1980; Butler 1987, 1989; Haraway 1989). Perhaps in the end, resistance or a resisting subject should not be the starting point for a politics of meaning. Rather, we should examine the subtle and paradoxical twists in actors' discursive strategies, following the ways meanings are reappropriated and launched again in the continuous struggles over meaning that constitute everday life. For as the papers in this volume demonstrate, it is not a matter of "resistance" as such, but of seeing the tangle of contradictions, ambiguities, and ironies we create for ourselves and are created for us as we forge our lives within shifting fields of power.

NOTES

Elliott Shore, Joan Scott, Judith Butler, Julie Taylor, and Jane Bachnik offered helpful comments on this paper or its former incarnations. Many thanks. Grants from IIE Fulbright, the Social Science Research Council, and the Department of Anthropology, Harvard University, supported the research on which the paper is based. The Rockefeller Foundation funded sabbatical time at the Institute for Advanced Study, allowing me to finish this and other writing projects.

1. Translation note: I have retained the Japanese word *shachoo*, 'head of the company' or 'company president', for lack of a translation that is simultaneously felicitous and accurate. Owner—one obvious choice—calls to mind the distinction between owner and worker, those who possess capital and those who do not. *Shachoo*, both a term of reference and of address, of course implies a hierarchy, where the 'company president' is head of the firm. But he is president of the company, a collectivity of which the workers presumably are a part. *Shachoo*, then, emphasizes hierarchy and the company community, while *owner* highlights the divisions between capitalist and worker.

2. This is common practice in both Japanese and American companies. Company executives are not paid by the hour, but receive a fixed salary with no extra compensation for overtime.

3. Liberal Democratic Party, the conservative party in power 1947–93.

4. According to the Labor Standards Law (*Roodoo Kijun Hoo*), women were entitled to menstrual leaves. Under the new Parity in Employment Opportunity Law (passed in 1985, in effect since 1986), this provision is no longer in force.

REFERENCES

Bachnik, Jane. 1983. "Recruitment Strategies for Household Succession: Rethinking Japanese Household Organization." *Man* (N.S.) 18:160–82.

Butler, Judith. 1987. "Variations on Sex and Gender: Beauvoir, Wittig, and Foucault," in Seyla Benhabib and Drucilla Cornell, eds., *Feminism as Critique*. Minneapolis: University of Minnesota Press.

————. 1989. *Gender Trouble: Feminism and the Subversion of Identity*. New York: Routledge.

Foucault, Michel. 1979. *Discipline and Punish*. New York: Vintage.

————. 1980. *Power/Knowledge*. New York: Pantheon.

Fruin, Mark. 1984. *Kikkoman: Company, Clan, and Community*. Cambridge, Mass.: Harvard University Press.

Genovese, Eugene. 1974. *Roll, Jordan, Roll: The World the Slaves Made*. New York: Pantheon.

Gordon, Andrew. 1985. *The Evolution of Labor Relations in Japan: Heavy Industry, 1853–1955*. Cambridge, Mass.: Council on East Asian Studies, Harvard University Press.

Haraway, Donna. 1989. *Primate Visions: Science, Narrative and Politics in Twentieth-Century Studies of Monkeys and Apes*. New York: Routledge.

Hebdige, Dick. 1979. *Subculture: The Meaning of Style*. New York: Methuen.

Kanter, Rosabeth Moss. 1977. *Men and Women of the Corporation*. New York: Basic Books.

Kondo, Dorinne. 1982. "Work, Family and the Self." Ph.D. dissertation, Department of Anthropology, Harvard University.

————. 1990. *Crafting Selves: Power, Gender and Discourses of Identity in a Japanese Workplace*. Chicago: University of Chicago Press.

Lamphere, Louise. 1987. *From Working Daughters to Working Mothers: Immigrant Women in a New England Industrial Community*. Ithaca: Cornell University Press.

Miller, Jean Baker. 1976. *Toward a New Psychology of Women*. Boston: Beacon Press.

Nakane, Chie. 1983. "*Ie*," in *The Encyclopedia of Japan*. Tokyo: Kodansha International.

Rosaldo, Renato. 1987. "Politics, Patriarchs and Laughter." *Cultural Critique* 6:65–86.

Scott, James. 1985. *Weapons of the Weak*. New Haven: Yale University Press.

Scott, Joan. 1988. *Gender and the Politics of History*. New York: Columbia University Press.

Sider, Gerald. 1986. *Culture and Class in Anthropology and History*. Cambridge: Cambridge University Press.

Stark, David. 1986. "Rethinking Internal Labor Markets: New Insights from a Comparative Perspective." *American Sociological Review* 51:492–504.

Chapter 8

THE BATTLE TO BELONG:
SELF-SACRIFICE AND SELF-FULFILLMENT
IN THE JAPANESE FAMILY ENTERPRISE

Matthews M. Hamabata

Editors' Introduction

In this chapter, Hamabata focuses on tensions between *uchi* and *soto*—intimacy and authority—in the elite Moriuchi *ie*, a household whose family enterprises are international in scale. The case also focuses on the constitution of authority, detailing the tension between emotion (*uchi*) and organization (*soto*), and between self-fulfillment and self-sacrifice. The narrative hinges on a crucial irony: while Grandfather Moriuchi proclaims that self-sacrifice accounts for the five-hundred-year-history of his *ie*, he himself nearly brings that history to an end by his headstrong pursuit of personal goals and lack of self-sacrifice for the *ie*.

The irony of a household where the balance between emotion (*uchi*) and organization (*ie*) has gone fundamentally awry is used to highlight the importance of a balance that is much less visible if the *ie* is functioning appropriately. The lack of *uchi/soto* balance in the Satoo company produces interpersonal conflict and impasse. In the Moriuchi *ie* and household companies it produces organizational conflict and impasse. Hamabata details the origin of the conflict: the downward spiral of the Moriuchi *ie* begins with Grandfather's hubris when he insists on marrying Grandmother, a woman of wholly inappropriate social status, for purely personal reasons. Grandmother contributes to the *ie*'s demise when she treats the relationship in social and economic terms, also for purely personal reasons.

The endless stalemate revolving around their intimate feelings is played out in the social structure of the *ie* and its enterprises. Focusing on succession, which is pivotal to *ie* organization, Hamabata shows how the intrusion of personal desire into a succession choice that *should* be made in terms of the communal good results in the destruction of the communal good—and the *ie*. All the Moriuchi children thus become pitted against one another in a personal struggle to become successor. Internecine strife spreads also among the Moriuchi industries, which begin going bankrupt.

But at another level, because no one had been appointed successor, and no one was in the *uchi*, there *was* no *uchi*—and *uchi/soto* distinctions could no longer be made between the *ie* and its branch organizations. Because none of the children could claim to be successors of either main or branch houses, after Grandfather's death the household altar, the symbolic center of the House of Moriuchi, was left in an empty building. With no living generation—no *uchi*—the *ie* was effectively dead.

The destruction of the Moriuchi *ie* thus hinges on the destruction of these *uchi/soto* boundaries. But the very destruction of this *ie* also demonstrates the importance of balancing *uchi/soto* distinctions in an ordinary organization. Just as Wetzel proposes that *uchi/soto* distinctions are ubiquitous, and far more important, than distinctions of person in language, Hamabata's case demonstrates that balancing *uchi/soto* between personal power and personal sacrifice, between self and collectivity, is crucial in sustaining the organization of family, industry, and religion, all of which intersect in the Moriuchi *ie*.

THE BATTLE TO BELONG: SELF-SACRIFICE AND SELF-FULFILLMENT IN THE JAPANESE FAMILY ENTERPRISE

IN THE EARLY 1980s, I completed approximately three years of fieldwork among elite Japanese in Tokyo, wealthy individuals whose lives were defined by their family enterprises of regional, national, and international scales of operation. Although my time in the field was limited, I had known some individuals for more than ten years prior to engaging in research on their lives. This span of time allowed me to map out life strategies, to see how culture and social structure interacted with personal choice. Indeed, unlike most studies of elites, I did not attempt to untangle interlocking directorates or speculate about the degree to which owners versus managers determine the fate of family-founded enterprises. Instead, I focused on love and commitment, on self-fulfillment and self-sacrifice, on the struggle to find meaning in adulthood.

Coming to terms with the demands of adulthood was not an easy task for men and women in the *doozoku gaisha* 'family enterprise', for life in the *doozoku gaisha* means that emotional and financial investments will, of necessity, become entangled. It is an environment in which the personal often conflicts with the corporate. It is also an environment in which the issue of who belongs in the family and the enterprise, who is allowed to remain "inside" and who is asked to leave, is often resolved in ways both painful and profound. In this battle to belong, sometimes quiet, sometimes noisily public, women and men negotiate and create the boundaries that define the inside, as opposed to the outside, on planes of existence multiple in their human reality: the familial, the economic, and the symbolic.

In families organized as businesses, the question is as simple and as complex as "Who will step into positions of leadership?" This question brings into stark relief the axes of intimacy and authority, around which life in the *doozuku gaisha* is organized. The *uchi* 'inside', defined as the locus of warmth, acceptance, and indulgence, is set within the context of the *ie*, the framework of authority, the organization of individual lives by a formal social order and for a common goal. In everyday parlance, the *uchi* may be conceived of as 'the home', and the *ie* as 'the House'. In the *doozuku gaisha*, this opposition is experienced by individuals as external order versus personal inclination, form versus feeling.[1]

"Authority discourages intimacy," George Homans and David Schneider once wrote (Homans and Schneider 1955, 38). And indeed it does. In the *doozuku gaisha*, concerns intimate present personal dilemmas to individuals, who in their struggle with the responsibilities of adulthood must choose between the personally inclined and the socially informed, between the warmth of the 'home' and the authority of the 'House'. The *ie* 'the House', represents a long line of men and women who have made personal sacrifices for the larger social good. The continued existence of the *ie* represents the difficult choice of form over feeling.

Self-Sacrifice

This choice becomes humanly real in the case of Grandfather and Grandmother Moriuchi, heads of the House of Moriuchi, who successfully transformed a household of former samurai into twentieth-century entrepreneurs. As portrayed by Grandfather Moriuchi in his memoir, the commitment of men to the larger social good, the *ie*, is daunting. Grandfather Moriuchi wrote in *Sincerity*:

> The world around our household completely collapsed. The old feudal estates were abolished at the turn of the century. Not only was our income eliminated but so was our standing in society. If it were not for the Meiji Government, I would have been lord of the province.
>
> My father had to seek work so that we could eat. He gave up the way of the warrior and founded a small manufacturing company. Moriuchi Industries is my castle. By building Moriuchi Industries, I am building Japanese society.

Grandfather commented further on self-sacrifice:

> I know that with the postwar reforms toward democracy, it is unfashionable to praise the ways of our past. But it cannot be denied that our feudal heritage has made us what we are today. The values that made one yield one's full allegiance to one's lord and that made one offer one's unmitigated devotion to one's parents are at the very core of our current economic

success. Loyalty, devotion, and service are part of the spirit of feudal society, a society built on complete self-sacrifice. This spirit is behind every successful undertaking in modern Japanese society.

The continuance of the House of Moriuchi for almost five hundred years of Japanese history, according to Grandfather, is directly attributable to the sacrifice of the personal for the collective, of the individual for the sake of the institution. In *Sincerity*, he carefully documented the individual contributions of men toward the development of the *ie*, of battles won and lost; yet the sacrifices of women, even those of his own wife, go unmentioned. That task was left to women, as they handed down their version of household history, in tales told by mothers to children.

According to women's lore, Grandmother Moriuchi came to the Moriuchi's great house in southern Japan at the age of twelve or thirteen in the company of her mother, who was engaged as a servant. Both mother and daughter came from a high merchant household that had collapsed. Servitude had become their lot in life.

No one could understand why Grandfather insisted on marrying Grandmother, for she was just the daughter of a servant, after all. But insist he did. Given that marriages determine the social status of households, they are to be approached carefully and taken seriously, and given that a "bad" marriage could lower the status of an entire network of affinally related households (Nakane 1967, 158), marriages are the concern of households, not individuals, and ideally ought to be arranged with the careful assessment of each household's economic and political achievements, as well as the temperamental suitability of the individuals involved (Hamabata 1990, 117–41; Vogel 1961). Clearly, Grandfather's headstrong pursuit of an inappropriate marriage presented a problem.

Although it now matters little what Grandmother's origins were, the House of Moriuchi, at the time that Grandfather declared his intentions, dealt with the embarrassment by asking another illustrious *ie* to adopt Grandmother, thereby permitting a suitable marriage. Through the adoption, Grandmother assumed the status of an *ojoosama* 'young lady', which then permitted both houses to arrange a marriage that would allow her to assume the position of the *oyome-san* 'bride' of the designated successor to the headship of the House of Moriuchi.

Despite Grandfather's high regard for the concept of self-sacrifice, he could not give up—for the sake of the House of Moriuchi—his love for a household servant. The Moriuchi *ie*, struggling for its survival in Japan's early industrial period, was highly dependent on this talented and headstrong individual to secure a place for the *ie* in the twentieth century. Thus the House of Moriuchi acquiesced to Grandfather's personal desires and, for this forced choice, a future generation would pay dearly.

Although Grandmother's relationship with Grandfather was sexual, it was, for her, hardly personal. She simply acknowledged that her natal household had collapsed: her marriage to Grandfather would give her a permanent place in a household that seemed to have a future in the new world. Further, through adoption and marriage, she reclaimed lost social status. While Grandfather developed a deep, emotional bond with Grandmother, she sought intimate fulfillment elsewhere, in her relationship with her eldest son, and found it there.

The emotional pattern in which Grandmother's life unfolded is not unusual. In arranged marriages, a bride often arrives as a stranger in her husband's household and is confronted with a cold, if not hostile, environment. Ronald Dore commented: "It is a truism among students of the Japanese family that the strongest tie is often the mother-son tie, that many Japanese women find relief from the emotional aridity of an arranged marriage relationship with an insensitive or domineering husband in a passionate fondness for their eldest son" (1978, 145).[2]

What is unusual in the relationship between Grandfather and Grandmother is that Grandfather was allowed to pursue a marriage for purely personal reasons. He was passionately in love with a woman, who prior to her adoption by an illustrious household, was wholly inappropriate in terms of social status. Grandfather hoped to find emotional involvement and fulfillment in his marriage with Grandmother. Grandmother, however, treated the relationship in purely social and economic terms.

As Grandfather sought intimacy where it could not be found, he became increasingly anxious. Nothing he did was enough to admit him to Grandmother's realm of the deeply personal. Although Grandfather developed something which the women of the Moriuchi household currently describe as an *obusesshon* 'obsession', Grandmother treated Grandfather as someone who simply needed to be managed. Indeed, the women of the Moriuchi *ie* acknowledge that the Moriuchis basked in the good grace of society because of Grandmother's work at managing Grandfather.

Grandmother was always in the shadows, keeping an eye on Grandfather, for he was a tyrant, ill tempered and shrewd, stepping on a lot of sensitive feelings. She would be the one to say good-bye at the door, pressing money and goodwill on those he might have offended. Grandmother's actions were perfect examples of *naijo no koo* 'the good works of a wife'. She repaired any relationship that might have been damaged by her husband's obstinacy. She knew how to evaluate and analyze social situations. She kept *ningen kankei* 'human relationships' going. The women of the Moriuchi household credit Grandmother as an important figure in establishing Moriuchi Industries.

Grandmother was an immensely generous woman, but her open hand tended to irritate her children, for whatever seemed of value to them, she gave away, from cakes to love. It is said that Grandmother took better care of strangers than her own children, the latter resenting the fact that they were assigned nurses who looked after their needs and disciplining.

The one exception was her eldest son, Tetsuo. While the others were given to nurses, she personally looked after his needs. She coddled him. This child not only was the source of emotional fulfillment but he represented her power, as well as the dependence of Grandfather and almost five hundred years of Moriuchi history on that power. Her son would realize her place in the world. He would be the next head of the House of Moriuchi.

Although Grandfather resented his personal dependency on Grandmother, he found his life inseparable from hers. Grandfather's hidden despair was never expressed in any direct way to Grandmother. Instead, it found expression in his dislike, indeed envy, of his eldest son, Grandmother's favorite child. Deep in his heart, Grandfather resolved that his eldest son would never head "his" household or "his" business.

In Grandfather's personal dislike and envy of Tetsuo and in Grandmother's complete and unwavering support of her beloved eldest son lie the fault lines of destruction in the House of Moriuchi. Neither Grandfather nor Grandmother could step away from their personal inclinations. Grandfather's and Grandmother's actions and decisions are seen in stark contrast to the way life in the *ie* ought to take shape. Indeed, the *ie* is a durable social group, made up of positions, not individuals. It moves with the force of the socially informed, rather than succumbing to the weaknesses of the personally inclined.

Hironobu Kitaoji argues that the *ie* is a perpetual social organization: individuals may come and go, but the organization continues in perpetuity in its original form. Unlike the ideal-typical nuclear family, which is highly dependent on the life-cycle of an individual, the structure of the *ie* determines individual participation: only two permanent positions exist within the household, that of household head and wife; children who are not recruited to fill those positions must be placed out of the main household, usually with daughters obtaining memberships in other *ie* through marriage and sons establishing branch households. This is in contrast to the ideal-typical extended family, which accommodates all married sons, their wives, and their children, until the founding generation dies, at which point a single household splits into several, each headed by a son and his family, all once accommodated by one organization. In the *ie*, the individual accommodates the organization and not the other way around (Kitaoji 1971).

Although the *ie* is nominally structured on patriarchal and primo-genitural principles, it is not uncommon for eldest sons to be asked to step aside for younger sons. If all sons are deemed less than fully competent to head a household, a daughter may be asked to remain in the household: she retains the household name and marries a man who is then adopted into the household as a son.[3] If there are no children or if all children are deemed much too incompetent, a fully adult married couple could be brought in to assume permanent positions in the household. There are other strategies, including those that would allow regencies to be established (Kitaoji 1971; Bachnik 1983; Brown 1968; Hamabata 1990, 33–51).

Jane Bachnik commented:

Positional organization means that *ie* succession is not contingent on the maintenance of any specific form for the organization of its successors, and thus allows the widest possibilities for succession options; that the organization should continue takes precedence over how it continues. Positions thus provide flexibility for ensuing succession in the *ie*, because they allow it to be organized pragmatically. 'Position' allows the continuity of the *ie* to be removed (one step) from the disposition of the human successors. They may become ill or mismanage their duties. Positions, not personal relationships, also provide the 'formal' regularity of the *ie*. (Bachnik 1983, 167)

Filling the positions in the *ie*, however, does not occur without human agency.

In ideal terms, even the beloved eldest son would be denied the headship of the main household should he prove himself to be less than competent. Or in the extreme case, all children could be denied the headship if it were deemed necessary for the good of the *ie*. The pain and emotional sacrifice involved in such a decision give profound meaning to life in an institution, which would otherwise be merely corporate. Such sacrifice orders human experience in a way that gives the *ie* meaning as a higher body, to which the individual must be fully committed and from which life gains meaning in and *beyond* the everyday. Such sacrifice allows a higher order, the communal good, to take hold of and direct personal lives.

Neither Grandmother nor Grandfather had the strength to make such a sacrifice. Grandfather could not put aside his personal love for the servant girl for the sake of the House of Moriuchi. He could not give up his feelings of envy and resentment toward his eldest son, feelings that arose because Grandmother spurned his attempts to create an emotionally fulfilling one-ness in their marriage. Grandmother, in turn, highly cognizant of Grandfather's dislike of her eldest son, refused to give her son up for the sake of the House of Moriuchi. Grandmother could have joined in agreement with Grandfather. She could have joined in his decision to place someone else, competent but outside of this emotionally charged nexus of intimacy, at the head of the House of Moriuchi. Instead, Grandmother would do all in her personal power to ensure that Tetsuo would head the main household and assume a position in the center of the House of Moriuchi—no matter what. In direct opposition, Grandfather would do all he could to ensure that Tetsuo was placed outside the main household—no matter what.

Battles Won and Lost

Grandmother Moriuchi died just after seeing her beloved Tetsuo installed as president of the newly established Moriuchi Industrial Design and Construction Company, a *kogaisha* 'child company' or subsidiary. It was a coup for Grandmother, for although she had been able to convince Grandfather to give Tetsuo a titular position and an income as a member of the board of directors of the *oyagaisha* 'parent company' or main enterprise, only the presidency of an important subsidiary would give Tetsuo power, that is, the ability to move both human and material resources. At the age of forty, Tetsuo was finally separated from his mother's firm guidance and protection. He was left to face the future and his father, alone.

Grandfather was not all that displeased with the decision to place Tetsuo in the presidency of a subsidiary, for he convinced himself that it was a routine procedure, carried out according to the organizational principles of branching. Moriuchi Industries had been growing at a rapid pace, moving to dominate a particular industrial sector of the Japanese economy. The main enterprise would be the manufacturing base, and Moriuchi Industrial Design would use that base to move into plant construction: a simple yet effective strategy of forward integration. Later, as high technology became an increasingly important aspect of Moriuchi Industries' products, Moriuchi Science and Technology was established, with the third son, Tasaburo, at its head. Then Moriuchi Properties, with the fourth son, Haruo, as the head, was established to handle the real estate involved in plant sites.

Grandfather's plans for economic development again illustrate the notion that despite its biogenetic morphology, the *ie* is an organization, in which concepts such as "lineage" have little or nothing to do with ordering genealogical relationships. Instead, the concept of "lineage" has been abstracted out of the biogenetic reality of procreation and employed to order social relationships that prove highly adaptable to economic and political pursuits. As Chie Nakane remarked, "Each group is known informally as 'of the line of A' or 'descended' from A, and the word *kei*, signifying 'descent' or 'genealogical relationship', symbolizes the Japanese social system" (1970, 99).

In a system of branching, where a *bunke* 'branch household' is "descended" from a *honke* 'main household', one finds a paired set of vertical relationships in which the branch household is subordinated to the main household. This structure is simply multiplied to create a set of relationships in which access to resources is ordered. For example, in order for the head of the main household to exact a service from a sub-branch household, he must operate through the head of the branch household. Likewise, should a head of a sub-branch household wish to gain access to communal resources not otherwise available to the sub-branch, he must operate through the head of the branch household, who then gains access to those resources through the head of the main household.

To further reinforce the notion that the *ie* is primarily based on corporate or positional rather than biogenetic relationships, Keith Brown noted that although the head of a main household may be a first cousin of the head of a sub-branch household, and only a distant cousin of a branch household head, the relationship between the head of the main household and the branch household is expected to be closer than that between the head of the main household and the sub-branch (1968, 118–19). Positional rather than personal relationships determine the degree of closeness. John Pelzel (1970) noted that households ordered in such a way are likely to be in a relationship that is purely economic and political, for "blood relationships" may not exist at all.

Branching is also part of the system of succession. In ideal terms, sociocentric principles operate, so that the most competent son becomes the successor to the headship of the main household and the main enterprise, while less competent sons establish branch households and subsidiaries. This "lineage" is then maintained by mutual agreement, continuing as long as it is economically and socially viable (Pelzel 1970, 233–39). As Ezra Vogel pointed out, "In business families the selection of someone other than first sons as successors was based primarily on competence and . . . the setting up of branch families to be related to the main families was often done in this context" (personal communication).[4] In the Moriuchi case, however, competence was not the primary issue. Rather, sentiments were behind the organizational developments.

The Moriuchis could have done several things to deal with the issue of succession:

1. The eldest son could have been apprenticed to another family enterprise, where he would have undergone the discipline of training outside his natal household (Kondo 1990, 235–42); should he have proven his merit, he would have been asked to return to head the main enterprise and the main household.
2. Were it discovered prior to or after apprenticeship that the eldest son was less than competent to head the entire *ie*, a branch household and enter-

prise could have been established for him, and another sibling or a non-kinsman would have been asked to head the main household and the main enterprise.

3. Were it discovered prior to or after apprenticeship that the eldest son was less than competent, he could have been given an education in the professions; one informant household, for example, chose to give the eldest son a medical education for precisely the reason of economic and organizational "out placement"; this son's family of procreation was given branch household status.

None of this occurred in the House of Moriuchi because the processes involved in deciding on successorship, on who would be placed in the center of the *ie*, were stalled. Both Grandmother and Grandfather were at emotional loggerheads. The personally inclined reigned over the socially informed.

Sociocentric principles, however, did figure into the strategies that Grandfather and Grandmother developed. Grandmother realized that she would not be able to push through her candidate, as long as Grandfather remained the head of the Moriuchi *ie*. And given her extremely poor state of health, he would likely outlive her. Thus Grandmother latched onto the issue of competency, interpreting the establishment of a subsidiary as a chance for Tetsuo to prove to the public at large that he was worthy of moving back to the main enterprise and establishing himself as head of the main household. She had hoped that publicly visible success would force Grandfather's hand. In this situation the motives were highly personal, yet the strategies were sociocentric.

Given his deep, irrational dislike of Tetsuo, Grandfather had, in his mind, set up a *bunke* 'branch household', as well as a subsidiary; it was a way of fooling himself and acknowledging Grandmother's personal power over him. Because of Grandmother's presence, he was not able to place Tetsuo completely outside the *ie* structure, yet he tried to distance Tetsuo from the very center of the *ie*, the headship of the main household. However, before branching occurred, successorship should have been decided on. Since that did not happen, the subsidiaries were only subsidiaries, economic units that had become separated from familial units.

Although Grandfather had hoped that one of his sons other than Tetsuo would be able to prove his worth by managing a subsidiary, Grandfather was stymied by his personal power over his sons. In fact, it hindered his decision on succession. Because his power over his sons rendered them all absolutely obedient to him, he was never sure if they were equally competent or incompetent: they simply followed his orders. While the company that he founded became known in manufacturing and financial circles as "the peerless Moriuchi," Grandfather became increasingly unsure as to who should assume the helm. The proof of merit involves a certain degree of independence and risk-taking, which none of them was willing to assume for fear of offending Grandfather. In terms of deciding who would succeed him, Grandfather was certain only about one thing: Tetsuo, his eldest son, should never be allowed to assume the headship. It became clear that the Moriuchi *ie* had become the domain of the purely personal.

As Grandfather approached retirement, he arranged for his right-hand man, Satoo-san, to be named the president of Moriuchi Industries. A trusted employee, Satoo-san had a marriage arranged with Grandfather's daughter, Kyooko. Before Grandfather's death at the age of seventy-four, he made it clear that Satoo-san and Kyooko were to assume the positions of household head and mistress. They were, however, to act only as regents.[5] Grandfather was preparing for his death and assuming that through this organizational strategy, the perpetuation of the *ie* would be guaranteed.

If everything were to work according to the highly reliable, sociocentric principles of the *ie*, Satoo-san would decide which of Grandfather's sons would be most worthy of assuming the headship of the House of Moriuchi. After that decision, Satoo-san and Kyooko would abdicate their positions, leaving the main household to establish another with the aid of the main household. Their household would relate to the main household, as subordinate to superior.

Between Grandfather's retirement and his death, Satoo-san and Kyooko came to enjoy the privileges of leadership. Indeed, Kyooko decided that one of her children would step into the position of head of the House of Moriuchi. She hoped that her husband would be able to use the authority of his position to make that possible. While Grandfather was still alive, it did seem as if Satoo-san had that kind of authority, for the Moriuchi brothers did indeed follow Satoo-san's directions. Once Grandfather died, however, it became apparent to both Satoo-san and Kyooko that their authority rested not in their positions but in Grandfather's personage: they were acting in his name, rather than out of their offices.

After Grandfather's death, the entire Moriuchi *ie* was wracked with internecine strife. While Satoo-san maintained that he had been appointed to an office vested with the authority to choose his own successor, the brothers Moriuchi claimed that he was an "outsider," a nonkinsman usurper. Because Grandmother and Grandfather Moriuchi moved with their inclinations and desires, the personal came to play a dominant role in *ie* politics: no longer was it the site of sacrifice that bolstered and gave profound meaning to the offices of household head and mistress, offices that operated with the legitimate exercise of authority because they were ultimately responsible for the larger social good; instead, the personal and the familial were used to undermine the notion of authority vested in the office. Indeed, the personal became the nightmarish source of legitimacy.

Among the moves made that were disastrous to the household as enterprise was Tetsuo's announcement that "his" subsidiary, Moriuchi Industrial Design and Construction, would reduce its purchases of industrial parts from Moriuchi Industries and replace them with purchases from New Nippon Alliances, not only an "outsider" company but a direct rival, which had just moved into the production of heavy machinery. Given his complete lack of control and authority over a major subsidiary's actions, Satoo-san was forced to resign from the presidency of the *oyagaisha* 'main' or 'parent enterprise' of Moriuchi Industries. Satoo-san was replaced by Masao, the second son and the only one to have remained in the main enterprise as an executive and member of the board of directors. (Satoo-san, however, retained his position as regent head of the main household.) Then Moriuchi Properties, headed by Haruo, the fourth son, went bankrupt because it could not meet its obligations in negotiable paper that it had tendered. Because Moriuchi Properties was a *kogaisha* 'child company', or subsidiary, of Moriuchi Industries, there was an absolutely firm expectation that Moriuchi Industries would underwrite the sale of the negotiable paper; however, there were no written agreements to that effect, and Masao, the second son and the new head of Moriuchi Industries, refused to extend financial support to the subsidiary. Then came Tetsuo's forced resignation as president of Moriuchi Industrial Design because of the alleged, then verified, misappropriation of corporate funds for personal use. Further, although Tetsuo's replacement and right-hand man, Fujimoto-san, had planned to purchase back all stocks held by Moriuchi Industries in Moriuchi Industrial Design, thereby establishing complete independence from the parent company, the National Tax Bureau revealed that monies were illegally used by Moriuchi Industrial Design to buy influence at the level of prefectural governments. The scandal brought on Fujimoto-san's resignation, as well as the resignation of the prefectural governors involved. The stock purchase plan was halted. The series of failures and resignations was an embarrassment to the House of Moriuchi. Because each gory detail was covered by the financial press, the world at large could see that personal strife was ruining the *ie* as enterprise and family; the Moriuchi brothers were seen as incompetent managers, driven only by personal concerns.

Meanwhile, throughout this period of strife, which was publicly scrutinized and analyzed, the main residence of the Moriuchi *ie* remained empty, occupied only by the household altar, servants, and ghosts.

A House Devoid of Meaning

As the regent heads of the House of Moriuchi, Satoo-san and Kyooko should have moved into the main residence, which was occupied by Grandfather before his death. However, they refrained from doing so. Instead, they chose to leave it unoccupied and to maintain it, as Grandfather had kept it. It became an odd museum of sorts: a tribute to Grandfather's personal power.

Satoo-san and Kyooko decided to do this for two reasons: first, Satoo-san had been accused by the Moriuchi brothers as being a nonkinsman "outsider," a usurper, and he and Kyooko simply did not have the courage to assume what under normal conditions would have been their rightful place; second, given their weakened official authority, maintaining the main residence as if Grandfather still lived there was a way to keep Grandfather alive, at least in ways conjured by anxious imaginations. Satoo-san and Kyooko were still attempting to exercise authority in Grandfather's name.

The Moriuchi brothers were comforted by this arrangement because, to them, keeping Grandfather's home open and unoccupied meant that a generational change had not occurred: Satoo-san was not "really" the head of the House of Moriuchi; no one was "really" head of the main household; no one was "really" relegated to branch household status; and everyone still had the chance to assume the headship of the main household and the main enterprise.

Furthermore, Satoo-san and Kyooko did not move the household altar, the *butsudan*, the symbolic center of the House of Moriuchi, to their residence. Although the main household is responsible for the daily maintenance of the *butsudan*, and for organizing the rites and rituals of ancestor worship which often revolve around the *butsudan*, Satoo-san and Kyooko decided to leave the household altar in Grandfather's residence. They felt unable to assume the symbolic center of the *ie*. The separation of the household altar from a living and extant household had real meaning: just as sociocentric concerns had been sacrificed for those personal, those symbolic had been sacrificed for those organizational, the sacred for the profane.

David Plath observed that every household is indeed a temple. Living members of the household are solely responsible for maintaining the sacred, for securing the priests, the offerings, and prayers that allow dead members of the household a benign existence as ancestors cum gods (Plath 1964). Further, the rites and rituals, which take place around the household altar, remind living household members of their responsibility to maintain the *ie* as a viable and productive entity (Smith 1974, 123; Plath 1964, 312; Hamabata 1990, 79–82). The rites and rituals of ancestor worship also give profound meaning to life in the *ie*, meaning beyond those of heritage: personal sacrifice for the larger good does not merely mean that an institution is allowed to exist for yet another generation, that one is adding to household history; it means that the limits of personal existence, even death itself, has been transcended in obtaining ancestorhood.

Not everyone, however, is elected to ancestorhood. Death is transcended and ancestorhood obtained only if living members of the household perform the daily, periodic, and personal rites of ancestor worship.[6] There are those who are "stuck in death," neither of this world nor the next, spirit outsiders held suspect and often feared. Herman Ooms commented that the spirit outsiders are those "who have been unable to join some line of ancestors or to start their own" (1976, 69). David Plath noted: "The outsiders form a residual category. They are at the fringes of institutionalization, where conditions of membership are not easy to state with precision. They include all homeless souls who are not regularly affiliated with any household line, or whose line has lapsed" (1964, 304). One could be condemned to the residual category of spirit outsider by allowing the household line to die out, or by not attaining a permanent position in an extant household. In the former case, the souls of the dead have been disconnected from an *ie*. In the latter case, the souls had never been given a chance to connect with an *ie*. The benign existence of ancestors cum gods, then, is tied to the issues of daily life. Living that life in ways merely personal could empty it of ultimate meaning, as the Moriuchis discovered.

Who would have imagined that Grandmother's passionate love for her son could lead to the likely destruction of all meaning in his life? Who would have imagined that Grandfather's deep love of a servant girl could set the stage for destruction in and of the House of Moriuchi? In Grandfather's and Grandmother's actions, the personal was not to be sacrificed for the *ie*. If they had done so, the *ie* would be re-created not only as a durable social group but as a higher order that can give individual lives profound meaning. Instead, the personal came to inform the social in ways manipulative and strategic.

In the self-consciousness that accompanies the manipulation of social form during times of trouble (Swidler 1986), and in the panic over their lack of authority, Satoo-san and Kyooko, the designated "successors," placed the organizational ahead of the symbolic and spiritual order. In an attempt to keep Grandfather alive, at least in fictive terms, they left his residence unoccupied and the household altar in the care of *tanin* 'servant strangers', 'outsiders'. The main residence of the House of Moriuchi simply became a container for symbols devoid of substantive meaning. In real-life terms, the members of the House of Moriuchi, by acting on their personal inclinations, were destroying one another's lives and the entire *ie.* Because the *uchi,* the sphere of the private, the personally inclined, was not sacrificed, the Moriuchis risked the ultimate in self-fulfillment; they lost the possibility of moving beyond their lives as individuals, of participating in something that would allow them to transcend the mere pursuit of material sustenance.

The social should take primacy over the emotional, durable form over transient feeling. The *uchi* should be sacrificed for the sake of the *ie.* In the case of the Moriuchis, the social was sacrificed for the personal and the symbolic and the spiritual for the organizational. In the end, such a situation meant that all members of the House of Moriuchi, living and dead, risked becoming outsiders in the ultimate sense, souls distrusted, feared and, at best, pitied (Plath 1964, 304; Hamabata 1990, 70–75), souls disconnected from the living as the eternal.

Notes

1. Although *uchi* and *ie* form distinct realms of experience, they interact and overlap. As men and women live their lives, the analytic dichotomy between the domestic and the public collapse. As Sylvia Yanagisako and Michelle Rosaldo made clear, economic and political institutions, as well as those familial, are created and re-created by women as they interact with other women, as well as with men, with those whom they see at once as allies and competitors (Rosaldo 1974, 1980; Yanagisako 1979).

2. In the standard virilocal marriage, which is arranged, a young bride finds herself in a structural position of powerlessness. As a stranger in her new household, she speaks with a weak voice. Her husband, from whom she is emotionally distant, cannot serve as an effective ally, for he is torn between the roles of husband and son. The young bride returns to her *uchi,* her home, her relationship with her mother for emotional sustenance (Lebra 1984, 151–52). Further, when her husband's household is in need of a resource, to which it has no easy access, the bride seeks the aid of her natal household (Hamabata 1990, 131–32; Nakane 1967, 153). The dependency of her husband's household on her natal household gives her power in her husband's household. The bride also creates a source of power internal to her husband's household; she creates strong emotional ties with her children (Kondo 1990, 148; Dore 1978, 145; Smith 1983, 71; Lebra 1984, 162–63; Vogel 1963, 231; Lebra 1976, 141; Caudill and Plath 1966), who then serve as her political allies. This relationship extends into her children's adulthood (Smith 1983, 71–72), and that is the relationship that her daughter-in-law, in turn, confronts. For a similar pattern in the Taiwanese household, see Wolf 1972.

It should be noted that in the Japanese household the behavior that leads young brides to create ties between households is not linked to gender per se but to structural position. Men who find themselves in the same structural position as the young bride also resort to the same strategy to enhance their careers in their new households. For an interesting case that most typically involves *muko yooshi* 'male brides', see Hamabata 1990, 150–55.

3. W. Mark Fruin pointed out that in the family enterprise he studied, biological sons needed to provide evidence of merit, such as a graduate degree in economics or business from a Japanese or American university, in order to ensure them top positions in the enterprise. Fruin also made a keen observation about the relationship between natural sons and adopted sons and their styles of management:

> Natural sons and adopted sons are equally esteemed in the performance-conscious Japanese household system; but natural sons, because they have been reared and groomed in the environment of a family business, are perhaps too well informed and too well trained to take chances, to do things differently from their forebears, and generally to experiment with alternate products and processes. Adopted sons by contrast may be less reluctant to try something new; indeed, they may have been anxious to prove their value with new ideas and innovative schemes. The two adopted sons who have been presidents in the postwar era were not adopted until they had completed their university training. (1983, 240–41)

4. There is also the possibility of downward mobility if a family is established as a branch family. For a historical study of branching and mobility, see Hayami 1973, 16–17.

5. The basis of this strategy was outlined by Keith Brown:

> If the head of the household dies leaving an heir who is still too young to take over the management of the household, it may be necessary to bring in someone else to help out, until the heir can manage for himself. This "regent" is frequently a younger brother of the deceased man. Once the regent's services are no longer needed he may be rewarded with a small plot of land and a house in which to establish a new branch household. (1968, 121)

6. For the stages in this transition, see Hamabata 1990, 76. See also Plath 1964 and Smith 1974, 57.

REFERENCES

Bachnik, Jane. 1983. "Recruitment Strategies for Household Succession: Rethinking Japanese Household Organization." *Man* 18:160–82.

Brown, Keith. 1968. "The Content of *doozoku* Relationships in Japan." *Ethnology* 7:113–39.

Caudill, William, and David Plath. 1966. "Who Sleeps by Whom? Parent-Child Involvement in Urban Japanese Families." *Psychiatry* 29:344–66.

Dore, Ronald P. 1978. *Shinohata: A Portrait of a Japanese Village*. New York: Pantheon.

Fruin, W. Mark. 1983. *Kikkoman: Company, Clan, and Community*. Cambridge, Mass.: Harvard University Press.

Hamabata, Matthews M. 1990. *Crested Kimono: Power and Love in the Japanese Business Family.* Ithaca: Cornell University Press.

Hayami, Akira. 1973. "Labor Migration in Pre-Industrial Society: A Study Tracing the Life Histories of the Inhabitants of a Village." *Keio Economic Studies* 10:1–17.

Homans, George, and David Schneider. 1955. *Marriage, Authority, and Final Causes: A Study of Unilateral Cross-Cousin Marriages.* Glencoe: Free Press.

Kondo, Dorinne. 1990. *Crafting Selves: Power, Gender, and Discourses of Identity in a Japanese Workplace.* Chicago: University of Chicago Press.

Kitaoji, Hironobu. 1971. "The Structure of the Japanese Family." *American Anthropologist* 73:1036–51.

Lebra, Takie. 1976. *Patterns of Japanese Behavior.* Honolulu: University of Hawaii Press.

———. 1984. *Japanese Women: Constraint and Fulfillment.* Honolulu: University of Hawaii Press.

Nakane, Chie. 1970. *Japanese Society.* Berkeley: University of California Press

———. 1967. *Kinship and Economic Organization in Rural Japan.* New York: Humanities Press.

Ooms, Herman. 1976. "A Structural Analysis of Japanese Ancestral Rites and Beliefs," in William H. Newell, ed., *Ancestors.* Chicago: Aldine.

Pelzel, John C. 1970. "Japanese Kinship: A Comparison," in Maurice Freedman, ed., *Family and Kinship in Chinese Society.* Stanford: Stanford University Press.

Plath, David. 1964. "Where the Family of God Is the Family." *American Anthropologist* 66:300–17.

Rosaldo, Michelle Zimbalist. 1974. "Women, Culture, and Society: A Theoretical Overview," in Michelle Zimbalist Rosaldo and Louise Lamphere, eds., *Woman, Culture, and Society.* Stanford: Stanford University Press.

———. 1980. "The Use and Abuse of Anthropology: Reflections on Feminism and Cross-Cultural Understanding." *Signs* 5:389–417.

Smith, Robert J. 1974. *Ancestor Worship in Contemporary Japan.* Stanford: Stanford University Press.

———. 1983. *Japanese Society: Tradition, Self, and the Social Order.* Cambridge: Cambridge University Press.

Swidler, Ann. 1986. "Culture in Action: Symbols and Strategies." *American Sociological Review* 51:273–86.

Vogel, Ezra F. 1961. "The Go-Between in a Developing Society: The Case of the Japanese Marriage Arranger." *Human Organization* 20:112–20.

———. 1963. *Japan's New Middle Class.* Berkeley: University of California Press.

Wolf, Margery. 1972. *Women and the Family in Rural Taiwan.* Stanford: Stanford University Press.

Yanagisako, Sylvia. 1979. "Family and Household: The Analysis of Domestic Groups." *Annual Review of Anthropology* 8:161–205.

Chapter 9

WHEN *UCHI* AND *SOTO* FELL SILENT
IN THE NIGHT: SHIFTING BOUNDARIES
IN SHIGA NAOYA'S "THE RAZOR"

MICHAEL S. MOLASKY

> Metaphors may create realities for us, especially
> social realities.
> —George Lakoff and Mark Johnson,
> *Metaphors We Live By*, 1980

EDITORS' INTRODUCTION

In this chapter Michael Molasky focuses on the novelist Shiga Naoya's short story "The Razor," written around 1910. Molasky demonstrates how this story highlights the directional orientations of *uchi/soto* and *ura/omote*. The conflict that enmeshes the main character hinges on his failure to effectively differentiate between shifting realms of *uchi/soto*. In particular, Shiga's story revolves around the third level of *uchi/soto* relations outlined in chapter 1: existential tensions between 'inside' and 'outside' that are manifested in the inability of the main character—who operates a barbershop—to maintain psychic boundaries between *uchi* and *soto*, *ura*, and *omote*.

Molasky shows how "The Razor" is constructed around the very distinctions we are making in this volume. The story amounts to a case study in how physically and socially defined coordinates can impinge on an individual's psychic space. A barbershop with adjoining living quarters affords the reader a glimpse of an *uchi* anchor point which, like the Satoo *uchi*, has multiple perspectives. The *omote* ('front'—that part of *uchi* most accessible to *soto*) of the barbershop is opposed to an *ura* of living quarters ('back'—that part of *uchi* least accessible to *soto*). *Uchi/soto* and *ura/omote* constitute a frame within which both the story and its central figure are stretched to the breaking point. The title of this chapter borrows from the final passage of the story, where the boundaries and the tensions they have come to define are finally dissolved.

As a social order that takes human existence as its starting point—*uchi*—this society is oriented toward organizing principles that thoroughly differ from an approach to social order as a separate, objective *soto*, abstracted from human existence. Human beings and their actual spatiotemporal orientations (as inside/outside distinctions) are crucial to the construction of this order, as are shifts, both within a single context and across different ones. The important place of human beings in the construction of this social order creates the Faustian underside that we glimpse in chapters 7 and 8. Satoo's abuse of personal power produces conflict in interactions within the company, while Grandfather Morioka's inabilities to balance self-will with self-sacrifice result in the destruction of the Morioka *ie* and its large businesses. In this chapter the main character's failure to acknowledge the directional coordinates brings about not personal conflict, or even social destruction, but personal dissolution. When the feverish barber breaks the boundaries that define where he is, he loses awareness of who he is: as *uchi/soto* and *ura/omote* dissolve, so does he, into the undifferentiated world around him. The conflict in this story thus hinges on failure to maintain balance at a level of existential tension, where *uchi/soto* maintains balance between the dualities of life and death.

WHEN *UCHI* AND *SOTO* FELL SILENT IN THE NIGHT: SHIFTING BOUNDARIES IN SHIGA NAOYA'S "THE RAZOR"

SHIGA NAOYA's short story "The Razor"[1] depicts a barber's impulsive murder of a customer who wanders into his shop late one night. A series of irritating events appears to lead ineluctably to the murder, but I will argue that to grasp the full import of these events they must be viewed against the shifting boundaries of *uchi/soto* and *ura/omote*, for the story depicts the barber's relationship to the world in terms of these dualities. "The Razor" delineates the realms of *uchi/soto* and *ura/omote* in their myriad manifestions: physical, social, and psychological. It further reveals how, as interpretations of the barber's lived world, these realms are both "constituted" (by the barber's perceptual vantage point) and "constituting" (of his personal and social reality). In these respects, "The Razor" offers material for a case study of *uchi/soto* and *ura/omote*; conversely, an awareness of the subtle ways in which these dualities are deployed in this late Meiji story is indispensable to fully comprehending the events as they unfold.[2]

In "The Razor," the barber serves as the perceiving body through which the boundaries of *uchi/soto* and *ura/omote* are established. These boundaries are defined most fundamentally in reference to the barber's body itself, for it is through depictions of the barber's physical condition and body position in relation to the surrounding space that the story's events unfold. As Pierre Bourdieu has noted, the interpretation of social space is inescapably mediated by the body: "The house, an *opus opera-*

tum, lends itself as such to a deciphering, but only to a deciphering which does not forget that the 'book' from which the children learn their vision of the world is read with the body, in and through the movements and displacements which make the space within which they are enacted as much as they are made by it" (1977, 90). And Jean Comaroff has remarked in another context that the body mediates not only perception but "all action upon the world" (1985, 6–7). In "The Razor" the barber's actions are constantly frustrated by the debilitating illness that has invaded his body, and his final impulsive act can be partly accounted for by these physical frustrations; at another level, his illness represents one among several intruders that plague the barber and propel him to the murder.

The entire notion of an "intruder" depends on a sense of territory, on a clear awareness of spatial organization and its social dimensions. The organization of space in "The Razor" entails constant shifting between *uchi* and *soto,* as well as between *ura* and *omote,* using the barber as the perceptual anchor point. The barbershop and living quarters are treated together as a place of personal value (*uchi*) in opposition to the undifferentiated surrounding space of the neighborhood (*soto*). *Uchi* is thus distinguished from *soto,* and is further divided into the area constituting the shop itself (*omote,* located in the front) and the living space for the barber and his family (*ura,* located in the rear). From the barber's perceptual locus, the shop belongs to the realm of *soto* when opposed to the living quarters (*uchi*), but throughout most of the story *ura/omote* represents a private/public distinction within the space of *uchi.* Clearly delineated boundaries in "The Razor" begin to blur toward the end of the story, and resolution is achieved only with the total obliteration of those remaining boundaries that prevent the self from merging into the surrounding world.

"The Razor"

"The Razor" takes place (spatial references are inescapable) within an enclosed space (*uchi*), and practically no views of the outside world (*soto*) are provided. A feverish, oppressive atmosphere permeates the story, which opens with the following description: "Yoshisaburo of the Tatsu Barbershop in Roppongi had taken to his bed with a cold. Of all times to be sick, and he hardly ever was, it was the eve of the ceremonies for the imperial ancestors, the peak season for the military trade" (*Zenshuu,* 181; Sibley, 149). Some background information follows: Yoshisaburo is described as a perfectionist so skilled with the razor that in ten years as a barber he has not so much as nicked a customer. Recently, the barber has lost two competent employees, and must now tolerate a pair of lethargic and clumsy apprentices who are left to cope with the increasingly crowded shop as noon approaches. Yoshisaburo's body is heavy with fever, and from his bed, as he envisions the incompetent apprentices struggling to manage the shop, he becomes increasingly irritated. The sliding glass door to the shop rattles loudly each time a customer enters, and the sound of an apprentice's worn wooden clogs dragging across the floor further grates on the barber's nerves.

Explicit and implicit descriptions in the passage locate the story with considerable precision in both time and space. The "ceremony for the imperial ancestors" appears in the Japanese as *Shuuki kooreisai*, which today is known as Autumnal Equinox Day '*Shuubun no hi*'. Temporally, then, both the season and the approximate date are indicated, as is the time of day. The reference here and in other passages to soldiers suggests that the story is set around the time of the Russo-Japanese War (1904–1905).

The story is spatially located *inside* the Tatsu Barbershop, Roppongi, in the Azabu Ward of Tokyo. Although the location is named in this opening passage, no description is provided of the surrounding neighborhood or of the shop's exterior. Moreover, the story contains only one visual description of the world outside, and even this is from the perspective of inside the house. The outside world and surrounding neighborhood are therefore given little identity; they remain relatively undifferentiated space and acquire meaning only in reference to the inner world of the shop and house, which together constitute *uchi* from the barber's perceptual locus.

Another implicit yet vital spatial distinction in the passage is that between *ura* and *omote*. In the story's opening line, the setting is given as a barbershop, yet the protagonist, who is later described as sick in bed, can overhear the activity in the shop.[3] Thus from the story's very outset, spatial orientation is defined in relation to the barber and his perceptions. To establish that the shop and living quarters are located under one roof, the reader must possess a familiarity with Japanese urban architecture of the era. Together the shop and living quarters constitute a place of value and personal reference (*uchi*) which is to be distinguished from the outside world (*soto*). The shop itself is situated in front (*omote*) and the living quarters are in the rear (*ura*). For readers of the Japanese text who possess the requisite contextual knowledge, it is unnecessary to explicitly identify the shop and living quarters as *omote* and *ura*, and these words are not used in the passage. Readers who rely on a translated text, however, require explicit markers, and William Sibley has translated the word for 'shop' *mise* as 'the shop out front' (*Zenshuu*, 182; Sibley, 151).

Since no detailed description of the shop is given at the beginning of the story, the reader is left to imagine a typical, family-operated shop in early twentieth-century Tokyo. The thin sheet of glass in the sliding, wood-framed door rattles whenever it is opened or closed, and the noise reverberates throughout the shop and tiny house. This door serves as the threshold between *uchi* and *soto* or, more specifically, between '*omote*' and '*soto*'. Another door to the outside, connected to the kitchen and known as the '*katteguchi*', is used by family members and "insiders" to enter the living quarters (*ura*) without passing through the shop. To move from inside the shop (*omote*) to the living quarters (*ura*), one must step up.[4] The step, combined with a hanging curtain or sliding door, is another indication of a threshold.

In "The Razor," the shop itself has a dirt floor, and is separated from the private space of the living quarters by a sliding paper door '*shooji*'. Consider the following phrase from a passage describing Oume, the barber's wife, step down from the house (*ura*) to the shop (*omote*): "*Oume wa damatte hangen no shooji o akeru to doma e orite*" ["Without a word, Oume slid open the dividing partition and went down into the shop"] (*Zenshuu*, 184; Sibley, 151–52).

Both language and structured space are cultural systems that routinely embody redundancies, and this short phrase provides us with three different signs denoting a symbolic spatial boundary: the *shooji* ('partition'), *doma* (literally 'dirt space', the profane space of the shop), and the gerund '*orite*' ('stepping down', i.e., into a lower spatial plane). As Mircea Eliade has noted, "The threshold, the door *show* the solution of continuity in space immediately and concretely; hence their great religious importance, for they are symbols and at the same time vehicles of *passage* from the one space to the other" (Eliade 1959, 25). Although Eliade is primarily concerned here with religious dimensions of space, his discussion of threshold and his notion of sacred/profane apply to the secular spatial world of "The Razor." The public spatial plane of the shop is on a lower, metaphorically less exalted level than that of the private living quarters. As if to punctuate this the floor is made of dirt. To move in the opposite direction—from the shop to the living quarters—one encounters the same visible boundaries, but for an outsider (someone not part of the world of *ura*), these symbols serve as reminders that one is about to step into an elevated (sacred) space, and an expression of deference is called for. A redundancy of signs is again evident, for Japanese social protocol demands that shoes be removed, an utterance be offered ('*Ojama shimasu*') reflecting recognition of one's intrusion, and finally a bow is called for: a literal lowering of one's body on entering the elevated space.

As other essays in this volume demonstrate, *uchi/soto* are deictic references grounded in social relations and articulated in specific situations. To the barber, therefore, his apprentices are insiders (*uchi*) with respect to customers (*soto*) but become outsiders (*omote*) when perceived from the private realm of his living quarters (*ura*). The only scene in the story depicting an apprentice in the living quarters describes him as crouched down "on all fours," and although this should by no means be considered typical behavior, the apprentice's posture does symbolize his social status within the private, innermost space of the house (*ura*) (*Zenshuu*, 186; Sibley, 153).

If the organization and interpretation of human space is grounded in the body, then posture—broadly conceived as body position in space— becomes a central element in the constitution of spatial boundaries. "The Razor" begins with the barber, Yoshisaburo, incapacitated, literally on his back. Cultural geographer Yi-Fu Tuan has commented on the symbolic significance of posture: "The human being, by his mere presence, imposes a schema on space," and Tuan further notes that upright posture is generally viewed as dominant and symbolic of control (1977, 16). The inverse of this observation would apply here: the supine posture of the barber emphasizes his helplessness. Later in the story as he struggles to regain control, several passages depict Yoshisaburo's efforts to sit up or stand; other passages describe him dropping exhausted into bed or sinking into a chair.[5] Throughout the story, Yoshisaburo's posture and movements are choreographed in minute detail, and much of the "dramatic movement" in the story centers quite literally on the physical movement of the barber as he struggles to attain a position of control.

The irritations experienced by the barber are not limited to his physical hardships. Yoshisaburo was becoming increasingly annoyed at the clamor made by the rattling door and the dragging feet of his apprentice when the door rattles open once more. This time it is a maid who has brought her employer's razor to be sharpened. After making her request, she closes the door only to open it again moments later and insist that Yoshisaburo, rather than an apprentice, sharpen the razor. The apprentice lamely tries to explain that the barber is ill, but Yoshisaburo interrupts by shouting out his assurance that he himself will sharpen it. No visual description of the woman is given, for the entire exchange is heard, not seen, from Yoshisaburo's location in the back room.

The maid, who enters the inner world of the shop, is depicted as an intruder. This theme of an intruder will return toward the story's end, but it is worth repeating that the entire concept of intruder is contingent on a clear sense of territory, defined here in terms of *uchi/soto* and *ura/omote*. Furthermore, this territory is identified through perceptions that find their locus in the barber's body and body position; as the above passage reminds us, these perceptions are by no means limited to the visual realm.[6] When the maid slides the door closed for the last time, Yoshisaburo curses to himself. This is followed by the passage: "He stretched out his pale, grimy forearm against the silk lining of the coverlet and contemplated it awhile. He was aware of his fever-leeched body as of a dead weight apart from himself. His eyes focused intently on the soot-stained paper dog hanging from the ceiling. It was encrusted with flies" (*Zenshuu*, 183; Sibley, 151). This grim scene demonstrates Shiga's celebrated ability to create a vivid, almost palpable atmosphere in just a few lines. After a description of the pathetic state of the barber's body, the reader's attention is directed to the decoration hanging from the ceiling. The first sentence describing the paper dog reveals that the decoration has been sullied; the short final sentence transforms it into an object of repulsion.[7] The disjunction between the two descriptions is tremendously effective in creating a sense of claustrophobia (the fear of constricting boundaries), for the decoration hanging motionlessly from the ceiling serves as a reminder that even a glance upward provides no relief from the room's oppressive atmosphere.

This atmosphere is intensified by the homology between the barber's body and the surrounding space. As we saw in the story's opening passage, the fever that plagues the barber also permeates the atmosphere; in the present scene, the entire weight of the barber's body is presented as if it were an object apart from himself, and the depiction of his "pale, grimy forearm" followed by that of the "soot-stained paper dog" suggests an analogy between the barber's body and a particularly repulsive object in the room. The separation of the barber from his body also foreshadows the breakdown of boundaries later in the story.

Sibley refers to the visual details in Shiga's work as "almost obsessively sharp" (Sibley 1979, 19), and this impression is supported by descriptions in "The Razor" as well as in other stories, such as *"Abashiri made"* (1908), *"Dekigoto"* (1913), and *"Kinosaki nite"* (1917).[8] Shiga's vivid yet succinct presentation of visual details no doubt contributes to his skill at creating a compellingly tangible atmosphere in his stories. Yet as the preceding passage reveals—with its rattling doors and annoying chatter—Shiga's descriptions are by no means limited to the visual realm. When contrasted with this constant barrage of sound, the pervasive silence in the above scene effectively adds to its morbid atmosphere.

We are soon returned to the world of sound and people as the barber is depicted listening to the lighthearted banter of a few soldiers in the shop. For a short while their small talk provides him with a distraction from the oppressive atmosphere of his room. Then we are given the story's sole visual description of the outside world. The back door to the kitchen is open and Yoshisaburo watches his wife, "bathed in the milky twilight that filtered through the doorway."[9] This is the only scene in "The Razor" that might be construed as pleasant or soothing, and it hinges on the contrast between light filtering in from the world outside (*soto*) and darkness that engulfs the inner recesses of the house (*ura*) where the barber is confined. Yet the light, symbolic of life and activity, fails to reach the barber himself; he is trapped within a space of darkness and silence.

The light and sound that filters in from the outside worlds of *soto* and *omote* tempt the barber to transgress those boundaries that isolate him, and he gets up to sharpen the razor brought in by the woman. Until this time, Yoshisaburo has been in bed, and his supine position has reinforced the depiction of him as powerless, but now he attempts to stand and move into action. Instead, "the effort of raising his leaden body to a sitting position made him dizzy, and he flopped back against the pillow" (*Zenshuu*, 183; Sibley, 151). Throughout the story, the barber's struggle for control is symbolically represented by his body position in space.

Failing to get up, Yoshisaburo rests for a while. Then after several frustrating attempts to make himself heard, he finally succeeds in getting his wife to bring the leather strap from the shop for sharpening the razor. When she returns with the strap, however, Oume must fasten a hook on which to hang it, for razors are normally sharpened in the shop. The barber then sets out sharpening the razor, but his hands tremble with fever and he makes little progress. After about fifteen minutes, his strength gives out and he sinks back into bed and falls asleep.

Two spatial motifs that have already appeared in the story are repeated in this scene. The first is the struggle for self-control as reflected in the barber's body position in space. Again, we see him unable to maintain the vertical posture, which is a spatial metaphor for control, mastery, action. The second motif is the appearance of an intruder and, as mentioned earlier, this depends on a sense of territory—the distinction between private and public space. The black leather strap is quite literally "out of place" in the living quarters. A place's character is conditioned by the kind of human activity performed there (Bourdieu 1977, 90; Lutwack 1984, 47), and something is clearly unnatural about the strap inside the house.[10] On a symbolic level, the strap has invaded the private space of the house and represents a threat to the inhabitants. Pierre Bourdieu in his analysis of the Kabylian dwelling notes that the dark section of the house is associated with illness and with "female" activities.[11] The dark realm of *ura* as delineated in "The Razor" is also clearly imbued with illness (the room is "smothered with fever") and is marked predominantly as female space. Yoshisaburo's frustration derives not only from his lack of control over his own body, but from his confinement to this dark, female realm during working hours. He recognizes his proper place (at that time of day) as out front in the shop.

Unable to resume this position, he has the strap brought in from *omote* in an attempt to redefine the space of *ura* through the distinctly male activity of sharpening the razor. The displacement of this activity signals a series of boundary transgressions that culminates in the ultimate social transgression, murder.

While Yoshisaburo is sleeping, the maid returns for the razor but soon brings it back asking that it be sharpened again. Awakened by his wife at eight o'clock, the barber eats dinner and once more dozes off. Slightly before ten o'clock, he is again awakened to take his medicine. Shiga paints another oppressive scene: "Idle thoughts drifted through his mind. There was an unpleasant sensation of his own warm breath trapped around his face by the coverlet, which he had pulled up to just below his eyes. [The shop had also fallen silent.][12] He cast a listless gaze around him. The black leather strap was still there, hanging from the post, solid, motionless. The lamp gave off a murky, cloying orange light that shone on his wife's back as she sat in a corner nursing the baby. The whole room seemed smothered in fever" (*Zenshuu*, 185–86; Sibley, 152). The "warm breath trapped around his face," the coverlet "pulled up to just below his eyes," the "murky, cloying orange light" that shone on his wife's impassive back, and the black strap that hangs motionless from the post all contribute to the stifling atmosphere of the room, which exudes silence and stillness in its intimation of death. This passage is another instance of Shiga's ability to exploit images that appeal not only to our sense of sight but also to our tactile and aural perceptions. Note that essentially no action is conveyed, and that the silence has spread to the shop, blurring the division between *ura* and *omote*. It is as though during the late hours, the shop returns to the private realm of the house (as would the barber after a full day's work). The homology between self and place is further intensified through personification of the room, for a more literal translation of the final sentence might read, 'It seemed to him that the entire room was suffering with fever' *'Kare wa heya-juu ga netsu de kurushinde iru yoo ni kanjita'.*

There is an inevitable movement toward the abolishment of boundaries in the story, and the final resolution of Yoshisaburo's tension is dependent on such destruction. The razor remains to be sharpened, and it is here that the assistant enters the house and, crouched down on all fours, hands the razor to Yoshisaburo, who is in bed. The barber's wife, concerned about her husband's weakened condition, begs Yoshisaburo to let another barber sharpen the razor but he ignores her. He gets up on one knee (a posture representing only partial control), and for the second time sets out on this task: "After applying the razor to the whetstone awhile, he went back to the leather strap. The slapping sound of the razor against the strap seemed to revive the stagnant atmosphere of the room. In vain Yoshisaburo strained to steady his trembling hand, to adjust himself to the rhythm of the task. Then, suddenly, the hook that Oume had attached to the post came loose; the strap flew off and wrapped itself around the razor" (*Zenshuu*, 187; Sibley, 153). The strap is a catalyst, setting the story in motion again; it is yet another intruder that both breathes life into the room and threatens life. In this sense it portends the appearance of the story's primary intruder.

Oume suggests that they close the shop, and tells the remaining apprentice to go home. The barber impulsively refuses, claiming it is still early. Some small talk ensues, then the door rattles open and a young, stocky workingman enters the shop asking for a quick shave. Oume futilely tries to convince Yoshisaburo to let the apprentice handle the customer, but she soon gives up in the face of her husband's adamant refusal. The customer's manner annoys Yoshisaburo, and the barber is confronted with another series of irritations: the razor is still too dull, his hand trembles with fever, mucus drips unceasingly from his nostrils, the baby cries—and the customer sits in the chair oblivious to it all.

For only the second time in the story, Yoshisaburo is standing and carrying out action. Moreover, he is standing in relation to the sitting customer, acting out his final struggle for self-control. The annoying manner of the customer is depicted in minute detail, thereby solidifying his status as an intruder. This brings us to the following scene:

> After several vain attempts at conversation, the young man had at last been chastened by the barber's unfriendly demeanor and ceased his chatter. By the time the shaving reached the upper part of his face, he had succumbed to his exhaustion from the heavy work of the day and drifted off. Kin [the apprentice] had meanwhile stretched out by the window and fallen asleep. Back inside the house the murmurings of Oume comforting the baby had died away. The stillness of the night spread through the shop and house and all around outside. Only the scraping of the razor was to be heard.
>
> As this new fatigue enveloped him Yoshisaburo's anger and irritation gave way to a feeling of being on the verge of tears. His eyes misted over and seemed about to melt away from the inside with fever. (*Zenshuu*, 191; Sibley, 156)

Almost everyone has fallen asleep. The gentle twilight is long gone, and now the stillness of night has permeated the house and shop. The language used in the original is extremely revealing: "*Yoru wa uchi mo soto mo mattaku shizumari-kaetta*" 'Both *uchi* and *soto* fell perfectly silent in the night'. All other boundaries have dissolved, and the cool world of night, sleep—and by extension, death—is seductively inviting. Only the barber is awake, burning with fever; only the scraping of his razor disrupts the silence. One final boundary remains:

Yoshisaburo was bone tired and at his wits' end. He felt as if poison had been injected into all his joints. He could have thrown everything aside that very second and sunk to the floor. Enough! On the point of calling a halt any number of times, he persisted out of a combination of inertia and obsession.

A soft nicking sound and a sensation of the razor catching against the skin. The young man's throat twitched. A mercurial shudder surged through Yoshisaburo's body from head to toe. At that moment all his physical fatigue, and his paralysis of will as well, were swept away. (*Zenshuu*, 191–92; Sibley, 156)

The tiny cut fuels Yoshisaburo with energy. The fatigue and paralysis are gone; after having been portrayed throughout the story as either on his back or weakly sitting up, Yoshisaburo now literally stands in a position of control. If the desire to obliterate all boundaries that distinguish the self from the surrounding world can be considered a death wish, then the final passage, quoted in its entirety below, constitutes Yoshisaburo's complete surrender to this wish, for destruction of the remaining boundary separating life and death holds out the only promise of peace.

The cut was barely half an inch long. Yoshisaburo stood motionless and examined it. The tiny slit in the skin at first turned a milky white; then a little splurt of pale crimson and the blood began to ooze up. He continued to scrutinize. The color of the blood deepened and a distinct drop formed at the slit. The drop swelled until it burst, and the blood streamed down in a single thin strand. At this sight he was shaken by a violent emotion.

The force of this inner onslaught was doubled by his never having experienced such a sight. His breathing quickened. His whole being came to focus on the bleeding cut. He could hold out no longer.

He changed his grip so that the tip pointed downward and in one swift thrust plunged the razor into the young man's throat. It penetrated the length of the blade up to the handle. The man did not move a muscle.

Presently the blood came gushing out from the deep wound. The man's face rapidly turned an ashen hue.

Yoshisaburo sank into the adjacent chair as though in a faint. All the tension drained out of him. At the same time, the fatigue he had felt before returned with a vengeance. With his eyes tightly shut, his body limp and motionless, he too looked dead. Even the night grew still as death. Nothing moved. The world had fallen into a deep slumber. Only the mirrors looking down from three sides of the room reflected this scene in their cold, impassive gaze. (*Zenshuu*, 192; Sibley, 156–57)

The passage begins with Yoshisaburo standing, staring at the cut. At first the cut appears as a 'milky white' "*nyuuhakushoku*" and becomes 'pale crimson' "*awai beni*" before 'the blood deepened' into a blackish color "*chi ga kurozunda.*" This transformation in color condenses both the passage of time in the story (from daylight to night) and the movement from life toward death.

The barber's "whole being came to focus on the bleeding cut." A more literal translation of the Japanese here would read: 'It seemed as if his entire being were swallowed up by the cut'. "*Kare no zenshin zenshin wa mattaku kizu ni suikomareta yoo ni mieta.*" This literal rendering speaks precisely of Yoshisaburo's desire to be engulfed, or 'swallowed up', by the seductive peacefulness of death. As the boundary between self and other dissolves, murder becomes a form of suicide. The seductiveness of the night, with its deathly stillness, is by this point unbearable. It has seeped from outside into the shop, and has penetrated the depths of the private space of the barber's home. Everyone is quiet, the boundaries between *uchi* and *soto*, *ura* and *omote*, have blurred to the point of dissolution. Now with the opportunity to become part of this world, Yoshisaburo "could hold out no longer."

The story ends with Yoshisaburo sunk into the chair next to the dead man. "With his eyes tightly shut, his body limp and motionless, he too looked dead." Both posture and physical proximity situate the barber in the realm of death. At last, all the tension and fever have drained out of him; he is released to the world in its deep slumber. No boundaries remain as he enters the night, still as death.

NOTES

1. The Japanese title is "*Kamisori,*" and the story first appeared in 1910. Unless otherwise noted, all references are from *Shiga Naoya zenshuu* (Tokyo: Iwanami shoten, 1973), Vol. 1, and English translations are taken from William Sibley, *The Shiga Hero* (Chicago: University of Chicago Press, 1979). Quoted passages from both the original and the English translation will hereafter be noted as "*Zenshuu*" and "Sibley," respectively.

2. *Uchi/soto* as an interpretive pair has been used within Japanese literary studies with differing degrees of sophistication. For two approaches to literature that rely on *uchi/soto* as conceptual categories, see Maeda Ai 1982, and Okuno Takeo 1983.

3. By "bed" I am of course referring to a *futon*.

4. Hence, the phrase commonly used when inviting a guest into one's house: '*O-agari kudasai*' (literally, 'Please step up').

5. Some description of Yoshisaburo's attempt to move from one position to another appears on nearly every page of the Japanese text.

6. Studies in narrative theory have similarly noted the visual bias of terms such as *point of view* and *focalization*, both of which fail to encompass other modes of perception. See the sections on focalization in Shlomith Rimmon-Kenan 1983 and Michael J. Toolan 1988.

7. Sibley's translation here has maintained the rhythm of the Japanese original, the last two sentences of which read: *"Kare wa uttori shita me de tenjoo no susuketa inuhariko o nagamete ita. Inuhariko ni hae wa takusan tomatte ita"* (*Zenshuu*, 183).

8. An English translation of *"Abashiri made"* is now available in a full-length collection of short stories by Shiga Naoya (see Dunlop 1987, 7–15). *"Dekigoto"* is translated by Sibley as "An Accident"; it appears in Dunlop's book as "An Incident." "Kinosaki nite" is rendered into English by both translators as "At Kinosaki." Edward Seidensticker's translation, "At Kinosaki," can be found in Keene 1956, 272–77.

9. 'Milky twilight' is Sibley's translation of *'shiroppoi kumotta yuugata no hikari'*, which might be rendered literally as 'whitish cloudy evening light'. Note that the metaphor 'milky' and the possible association with motherhood, while perhaps implied, is not expressly stated in the original (*Zenshuu*, 136; Sibley, 151).

10. Remember that the barber has been sleeping in the room into which the strap is brought. In American society, this is roughly akin to bringing a toolbox in from the garage and placing it on the bed.

11. The following passage from *Outline of a Theory of Practice* offers a provocative counterpoint to Shiga's mapping of architectural space in "The Razor":

> The opposite wall is called the wall of darkness, or the wall of the invalid: a sick person's bed is placed next to it. The washing of the dead takes place at the entrance to the stable. The low dark part is opposed to the upper part as the female to the male: it is the most intimate place within the world of intimacy (sexuality, fertility). The opposition between the male and the female also reappears in the opposition between the 'master' beam and the main pillar, a fork open skywards.
>
> . . . But one or the other of the two systems of oppositions which define the house, either in its internal organization or in its relationship with the external world, is brought to the foreground, depending on whether the house is considered from the male point of view or the female point of view: whereas for the man, the house is not so much a place he enters as a place he comes out of, movement inwards properly befits the woman. (Bourdieu 1977, 90–91)

12. The sentence in brackets is my translation of 'mise no hoo mo shizumari-kaette iru'. Although omitted from Sibley's translation, it appears in the original *Shirakaba* publication (Shiga Naoya 1910, 85), in Iwanami's 1955 and 1973 versions of the *Zenshuu* (137 and 185, respectively), and in the *Shinchoo* paperback edition (Shiga Naoya 1980, 68). Since there appears to be no textual discrepancy to justify the omission of this sentence from the English translation, I assume this to be a simple oversight in what is otherwise a meticulous and felicitous translation.

REFERENCES

Bourdieu, Pierre. 1977. *Outline of a Theory of Practice*. Cambridge: Cambridge University Press.

Comaroff, Jean. 1985. *Body of Power, Spirit of Resistance: The Culture and History of a South African People*. Chicago: University of Chicago Press.

Dunlop, Lane, trans. 1987. *The Paper Door*. San Francisco: North Point Press.

Eliade, Mircea. 1959. *The Sacred and the Profane*. New York: Harcourt, Brace & World.

Keene, Donald, ed. 1956. *Modern Japanese Literature*. Rutland: Charles E. Tuttle.

Lakoff, George and Mark Johnson. 1980. *Metaphors We Live By*. Chicago: University of Chicago Press. [Epigraph from page 156.]

Lutwack, Leonard. 1984. *The Role of Place in Literature*. Syracuse: Syracuse University Press.

Maeda Ai. 1982. *Toshi kuukan no naka no bungaku*. Tokyo: Chikuma shoboo.

Okuno Takeo. 1983. *Ma no koozoo*. Tokyo: Shuueisha.

Rimmon-Kenan, Shlomith. 1983. *Narrative Fiction: Contemporary Poetics*. New York: Methuen.

Seidensticker, Edward, trans. 1956. "At Kinosaki," in Donald Keene, ed., *Modern Japanese Literature*. Rutland: Charles E. Tuttle.

Shiga Naoya. 1910. *"Kamisori,"* in *Shirakaba* (June): 81–92.

———. 1955. *Shiga Naoya Zenshuu*. Tokyo: Iwanami shoten, Vol. 1, 133–43.

———. 1973. *Shiga Naoya Zenshuu*. Tokyo: Iwanami shoten, Vol. 1, 179–92.

———. 1980. *Seibei to hyootan; Abashiri made*. Tokyo: Shinchoo bunko.

Sibley, William. 1979. *The Shiga Hero*. Chicago: University of Chicago Press.

Toolan, Michael J. 1988. *Narrative: A Critical Linguistic Introduction*. New York: Routledge.

Tuan, Yi-Fu. 1977. *Space and Place*. Minneapolis: University of Minnesota Press.

Chapter 10

UCHI/SOTO: AUTHORITY AND INTIMACY, HIERARCHY AND SOLIDARITY IN JAPAN

Jane M. Bachnik

Editors' Introduction

Just as the papers in part 1 focused on the mutual *construction* of self and social order, the papers in part 2 focus on the *potential for destruction* that is contained within the same dynamic. This chapter explores that potential as manifested in tensions between self and other which can be related to all three levels of *uchi/soto* organization. The tensions can be traced to the interplay between active and passive (*amaeru/amayakasu*), on all these levels.

Bachnik considers the three chapters in this section and adds her own case to illustrate a common point: the humanness of the group leader—whose egotism intrudes in each narrative—produces an imbalance between self-interest and regard for others, the consequences of which are manifested in conflicts at each of the three levels of *uchi/soto* organization. The conflicts revolve around difficulties in delineating hierarchy, authority, intimacy, and solidarity. Hierarchy is too simply defined by Nakane as a "vertical principle," since it requires constant shifts between modes of active/passive communication, as defined in practice.

Thus in Kondo's discussion of the confectionary company, Satoo's humanness results in failure to acknowledge the basis for his authority in *uchi*, the group itself. Bachnik compares Satoo's manipulation of *uchi/soto* boundaries that stymie his workers, with the Katoo *okaasan*'s manipulation of these same boundaries to communicate her dissatisfaction with the authoritarian behavior of the *otoosan*, and to chastise him into mending his ways. Both of these cases deal with inappropriate delineation of hierarchy, and each creates conflicts at the level of interactional context.

But interpersonal conflict ultimately threatens the fabric of social organization, and Hamabata's chapter indicates how this is so, as Grandfather continues to assert personal power while ignoring the overall welfare of the organization, leading to the destruction of both the family and its large-scale industries. Then, Molasky's discussion of Shiga Naoya's "The Razor" indicates how personal hubris—and failure to acknowledge the inside/outside orientations that anchor one's physical, social, and psychic relationships—lead ultimately to destruction of one's very existence. Shiga's focus in this story is as the deepest level of *uchi/soto*—the ontological tensions between dualities—indicating his awareness of how the directional coordinates actually make social life *possible*.

Part 2 adds dimension to the portrayal of *uchi/soto*, and Bachnik now suggests that the shifts portraying tensions—between self and group, self and organization, existence and nonexistence—are crucial to *uchi/soto* organization. Such shifts are essential in comprehending hierarchy group organization, and even conflict in Japan, and they make it possible to turn back once more to the initial focus of "situated" meaning. The lack of "fixed," "unified" perspectives on self and social organization strongly implies that *cultural knowledge* is indexed along with the other situational dimensions, so that the degree to which participants share cultural knowledge as proximate and familiar is included in the gauging of *uchi*. This leads naturally to part 3, which takes up the importance of active/passive dynamics and indexes *uchi/soto* as shared versus unshared knowledge in Japanese grammar.

UCHI/SOTO: AUTHORITY AND INTIMACY, HIERARCHY AND SOLIDARITY IN JAPAN

UCHI/SOTO organization can be viewed as a rich tapestry that is being designed while it is being intricately woven by social participants. The participants start from the collective anchor point of *uchi*, and the process of weaving works by indexing degrees of distance from that anchor point in differentiating *uchi/soto*. They are constantly innovating, since the "weaving" is a social process, involving the constant "construction" of social relationships—and social life—by indexing vis-à-vis the social anchor points. Here the metaphor breaks down somewhat, because the multidimensionality of social life circles around to encompass the weavers, so that what they are weaving also "weaves" them. This is the interplay that exists between self and social life such that each constitutes the other—the one actively (the social participants and their "creation" of social relationships and situations), and the other passively (the "creation" of the participants as social beings by "socialization" in that social order). The dynamic of "active" and "passive" exists at each level, from the interpersonal relations indexing *amaeru/amayakasu*, to relationships between self and social order, even to the conceptualization and relationships between dualities, as included in the conceptualization of the dual sets of terms. What is also noteworthy is that the "patterns" the weavers are weaving into the tapestry *are of this interplay itself*—lending to the whole the quality of a Möbius strip. In other words, the interplay between constituting and being constituted at every level—between self and other, self and society, and the tensions between the dualities—is being played out in the way choices are defined in everyday life, in the organization of relationships, of social contexts, and of social "order." This is even evident in the organization of certain institutions, such as the *ie*.

Relationships are crucial in Japanese society, but this statement involves much more than a truism about social life. In a real sense, not the individual but *the relationship between individuals* is the basic "unit" of Japanese social organization, and this is a general point made about societies characterized by the "interdependent self" (Markus and Kitayama 1991). In the same sense, *the relationship between self and social order* constitutes the organization of social life, defined by the dynamic of *uchi/soto*, along with the other paired terms. And *the relationship between the dual sets of terms*, based on *uchi/soto*, in relating basic tensions that are unavoidable in social life, constitutes the tapestry itself, as a way of being-in-the-world which, as it turns out, *is* the world.

At every level these relationships are constituted by social participants acting in social life—this is the sense of the "tilted" end of the axis, and the deictic anchor point of *uchi*. *Uchi* anchors social relationships, social order, and the basic dualities of the universe, so that one end of the relationship is manifested in social life, as 'us' or 'I'—'our group', as a basic unit of social organization. In the process of relating the two poles of this axis, the participants have a role in the constitution of their social universe.

Yet a human role that includes the potential for creation must carry with it the seeds for destruction, just as the realization of the possibility of choice that God gave to Adam and Eve in the Garden of Eden is the explanation for the human "fall" and the fundamental ambivalence of the human condition in the Book of Genesis (Evens n.d.). If social participants are truly agents in their relationship to social life at any of the three levels discussed, then their potential for *construction* of these relationships must also carry with it the possibility for *destruction* as well. It is now necessary to look more precisely at this possibility.

The Japanese equivalent to the apple in the Garden in this system is personal pride, or hubris, which leads to the use of social power on the basis of purely personal designs for control. The expression of personal power is destructive of society, since self is indexed in relation to society. The more the self operates in purely opportunistic terms, the more the potential for the destruction of others and even for the social organization involved. Finally, this imbalance is ultimately destructive to self as well, since *the organization of self hinges on its relationship with society*.

The evaluation of conflict in Japanese society has been confused because the messages of harmony and consensus communicated by the indexing of *omote, soto,* and *tatemae* have been interpreted as directives admonishing against conflict. But the indexical message of these communications is that conflict is an 'inside' (*uchi*), rather than an 'outside' (*soto*) matter; they communicate nothing about the existence or nonexistence of conflict.

The indexing of different and opposing messages along a spectrum has also confused the issue of conflict because it is viewed as somehow problematic that *ura* does not "agree" with *omote,* or *uchi* with *soto.* But these difficulties occur because referential, rather than indexical, meaning has been the focus. If one looks at social life from the vantage point of indexical meaning, it becomes clear that the arena of greatest conflict for Japanese does not lie in supposed "contradictions" between *omote* and *ura, soto* and *uchi,* which are not, properly speaking, contradictions for Japanese. Rather, *the process of indexing itself* has the greatest potential for conflict, as illustrated by all three chapters in this section.

All the chapters in part 2 deal with an *imbalance* of self in the indexing of *uchi/soto,* or self and society. The imbalances produce all the possibilities for destruction outlined above. This focus on the underside of *uchi/ soto* indexing raises major questions about the organization of hierarchy, including its definition as a "vertical principle." I will now examine relationships between (1) power—as individual self-interest—and hierarchy in Japanese society, and (2) solidarity and hierarchy, considering the three chapters in part 2.

AUTHORITY AND INTIMACY WITHIN THE *UCHI*

Uchi as a deictic anchor point, and the *uchi/soto* dynamic elaborated in dyadic relationships by Rosenberger (this volume), are central to the relationship between personal power, solidarity, and hierarchy in Japanese society. The *uchi/soto* distinctions are necessarily hierarchical, because to *amayakasu* is to be disciplined (*soto*) and allow the other the indulgence of free expression; to *amaeru* is to be spontaneous (*uchi*) and accept the indulgence offered by another. Yet the *amayakasu* giver can also shift the focus to communicate authority, and require the receiver to be controlled, guided, and subordinate. In a sense the tables are turned by this shift, so that the *amakayasu* side of the relationship may *give* deference and be *soto* in the communication of indulgence (for example, the wife in Rosenberger's vignette), or the *amayakasu* side may *receive* deference and be *uchi* in the communication of authority (as with Satoo-san, the company president, in Kondo's narrative). Gender is one factor in this focal shift, but it is not the only one.

The multiple ways in which *amaeru/amayakasu* can be expressed mean that hierarchy is fundamentally ambiguous, because of the shifts between authority and intimacy outlined above. Not only does communication shift between authority and intimacy, but the shifts reverse the direction of giving and receiving deference in *amaeru/amayakasu*. The problem in the Satoo company, as delineated by Kondo, is in the lack of reversal of direction of these shifts. The head of the family-run company, Satoo-san, communicates too often in the authoritarian mode of the *amayakasu* relationship, producing complaints, resistance, and protest from his employees. He fails to implement the shift to communicate indulgence and solidarity—the inverse side of *amayakasu*.

The Satoo firm epitomizes Japanese small-scale family business, and the importance of such firms to the performance of the Japanese economy is increasingly acknowledged (Friedman 1988; Calder 1988). As Kondo points out, the conflict in this company—specifically Satoo's failure to implement shifts between hierarchy and solidarity—revolves around ambiguities in the delineation of *uchi*, which in turn creates constant problems in the indexing of *uchi/soto*. Specifically, the company has grown from a truly small, family-oriented firm to a firm that has more than thirty employees, and is spatially separated from the family. Enterprise has long been closely associated with the *ie*, as Kondo notes: but the fact of the business expansion is not the real cause of this problem. Rather, the problem lies in the way Satoo manipulates the ambiguities of *uchi* caused by the firm's expansion. Satoo is the fulcrum for this ambiguity, since he is the head (or ultimate *uchi* member) of both the family and the business. When he demarcates the family as the locus for *uchi*, the company employees become *soto* in their own workplace.

The ambiguity of the Sato *uchi* can be more precisely delineated if we examine the organization of *uchi* more closely. The organization should be characterized by constant shifts between indexing authority (hierarchy) and solidarity (egalitarianism). There are relative indexes of *uchi/ soto* within the *uchi*, until one reaches the "ultimate *uchi*," comprised, in these chapters, of Satoo-san (the company president and household head); Grandfather (who occupies the same two positions), and the Katoo *otoosan* (the household head).

Satoo-san, as the ultimate in-group member, unfailingly *receives* deference in *amaeru/amayakasu* relationships with employees, and communicates authority in these same relationships. His employees give deference (or indulge Satoo's outbursts), and also submit to his authority. As the epitome of hierarchy, one of the most commonly noted characteristics of Japanese society, the situation might appear to be normal. But the irate objections of the workers in Kondo's narrative to this state of affairs should give us clues that Japanese hierarchy is more complex than a simple "vertical principle" (Nakane 1970).

In fact, the organization of the collectivity as *uchi*, a deictic anchor point, has consequences for the organization of personal power and hierarchy: the group head must *balance* his or her own authority against the backdrop of the group-as-a-collectivity *to which the head is also subordinate* (Smith 1983). Thus the "ultimate *uchi*" position is not an individual per se but an individual against the *uchi* "ground" or anchor point of the collectivity, to use Hanks's terminology (1992). The sharing of the same *uchi* anchor point operates to create a basis for overarching solidarity that can encompass the hierarchy expressed in *uchi/soto*. The basis for this solidarity is that Satoo, as a member of the collectivity, is responsible to the collectivity. In this sense, he must give deference to them as well.

Even the occupant of the "ultimate *uchi*" position does not exercise individual authority over the group, and here is where the organization of power is linked to *uchi/soto* organization. The organization of hierarchy is mitigated by the "common ground" of the anchor point. The authority mode of *amayakasu* communication is potentially divisive, because it splits the members from the group leader. The communication of intimacy or indulgence is what restores the common ground. This is why the leader must shift from communicating authority to indulgence.

The lack of delineation of common ground is precisely the source of conflict in Kondo's study of the small confectionary company. Satoo demands that the artisans work long hours without overtime—selflessly— emphasizing the solidarity aspect of *uchi*, and the anchoring or *uchi* in the family. At the same time, by his arbitrary use of authoritary, Satoo communicates a hierarchical relationship in which he opposes himself to them, placing them outside of *uchi*. This is apparent in his use of surveillance cameras and microphones for workers—barking orders over the hidden microphone in icily polite Japanese. He also demarcates them as *soto* by his focus on his payment of their salary, by allowing them little say in the organization of their workplace, and by having virtually no understanding of their jobs.

His insulting offer to them of badly damaged candies at half-price epitomizes the contradictions of their position: they are not actually *soto*—for as customers they would not be offered badly damaged goods. Nor are they *uchi*—for true *uchi* members would not have to pay for goods that were unsaleable. But Satoo tries to have it both ways: by manipulating *uchi* and *uchi/soto* shifts, he manages to get for his employees the worst of both worlds.

Japanese work-group organizations—even those in large companies— are widely characterized by precisely the kind of shifting that Satoo fails to carry out. Rohlen's (1974) characterization of Japanese work-group organization via constant shifts between pyramid (hierarchical) and circle (solidarity or egalitarian) modes of organization is a commentary on the necessary coexistence of these different modes of organization. Rohlen elaborates these tensions as two fundamental configurations of a group—composed of a formal pyramid and an informal circle. Authority that is not tempered by the informal circle mode is individualistic and devisive, since the leader is splitting himself off from the group by his exercise of authority, which must then be tempered by communication of solidarity.[1] By the same token, these shifts also characterize company failures, as seen in, for example, the Mazda Company (Pascale and Rohlen 1983) and the Moriuchi industries in Hamabata's chapter. One can say that hierarchy is more fundamental than solidarity in Japanese communication—and this may indeed appear to be the case—until one remembers that the basis for hierarchy is the leader's position within the group, which thus "backgrounds" the hierarchical relationships, in the sense of Hanks (1992) discussed in chapter 6, and makes solidarity fundamental as well.

Satoo not only manipulates the boundaries of *uchi* but he also takes advantage of *uchi* communication dynamics which make it difficult for his workers to redress the conflicts he creates. Satoo uses his authority to communicate intimacy to the workers, in the form of negative emotions, such as direct anger, which are commonly regarded as inexpressable in Japanese society. He is here communicating to the workers *as though they are within the uchi*, and they must give him deference in response. Yet at the same time he is denying them one of the most basic dimensions of *uchi* communication—the collective solidarity that puts him on the same "ground" as his employees—and effects a deference shift, from hierarchy to solidarity, without which intimacy is incomprehensible. Even though they acknowledge *uchi* to Satoo, he fails to acknowledge *uchi* to them.

In so doing, Satoo also puts his employees in a true double bind. The very dynamics of the deference mode prevent the workers from getting him to effect the communication shift they require. Even if the workers are justified in resenting his arrogant behavior they cannot communicate their difficulties when they lack the very circle mode that would allow them the reciprocity to do this. Once again, they are inside the circle in terms of their obligations to Satoo, but outside in terms of his obligations to them. Yet Kondo notes that Satoo is undermining his own authority by acting this way, and that he is building enormous resentment among the workers.[2]

Such *uchi/soto* conflicts are not limited to a small enterprise that has outgrown its family. The family itself (*ie*) is characterized by some of the same conflicts. To illustrate these conflicts within *uchi* I will present another case from the same Katoo family discussed in chapter 6.[3]

Handling an Obstreperous Household Head

The *otoosan* 'father' in the Katoo household is highly regarded by virtually everyone he knows, and is extremely adept at maintaining relationships. In-group relations are usually smooth between both the *otoosan* and *okaasan* 'the mother', 'the *otoosan*'s wife', and between them and their children. The house members are probably exceptional in the degree to which their relationships work well. Yet at times even this *otoosan* became *iji warui* 'cantankerous' or, to put this another way, he allowed his personality to interfere with his running of the household, and put the members under considerable strain. At other times the *otoosan* thought we were impeding his running of the household with *our* personal idiosyncrasies or whims. The methods of dealing with these two kinds of personal impediments, however, were quite different: the *otoosan* could lecture the rest of the household to *shikkari suru* 'get your acts together', while the rest of us, if we wanted to communicate similar sentiments to him, had to resort to entirely different means of expression.

As the most *uchi* member, the household head, the *otoosan* was able to command us directly: *"Shikkari suru!"* In turn we gave deference to him, or we indulged him; we were disciplined and he was spontaneous—allowing even his direct outbursts of displeasure and anger. But what happened if he abused his position and became egocentric and autocratic?

One particular spring the *otoosan* decided to get his driver's license— a belated decision, since he was fifty-five at the time and nearly everyone else in the area, including me, had gotten a car. For a period of six weeks while he was going through his training, virtually no other topic of conversation was heard in the house. All this time he sat in the *kotatsu* (the low table with a charcoal warming fire beneath it). Here the *otoosan* traced practice routes on a map of his practice course at the school where he was learning to drive, memorizing the exact order of the driving routines he had to follow. The rest of us sat in the *kotatsu*, where we once joked, held discussions, gossiped, and even sang, but now were reduced to watching in numbing boredom as the *otoosan* traced and retraced his routes around his imaginary driving course endlessly, day after day, week after week. Clearly things had gotten out of hand.

When the *otoosan* finally got his license, and with it, a car, I fervently hoped that the subject of driving would cease to be the focus of the entire household. But it was not to be. After a couple of weeks of driving, on his way home from work the *otoosan* hit a post and knocked the side mirror off his car. Then, while it was in the garage being fixed, unbeknownst to me, he borrowed my car. While driving the same route, he hit another post and knocked the mirror off *my* car. When I arrived back at the house, the *otoosan* muttered cryptically that he had done something wrong in driving my car, and had had to buy another mirror for it. And he repeatedly pointed out that it had cost 1,500 yen (approximately $5.00 at that time).

For the *okaasan* this was simply too much, and speaking privately to me in the kitchen, she commented on the *otoosan*'s behavior: "I can't believe how angry and puffed up *'ibatte ite'* he is, even though he did this whole thing himself. To absolutely *never* admit that he's the one who's wrong and *never* to apologize even in the tiniest way—why he's completely off the wall! *'Chittomo jibun ga warui to iwanai de zenzen sumimasen to iwanai de taihen okashii yarikata desu'*. It was clear that she opposed the *otoosan* on this issue, but it was also clear that she could not express her opposition directly to the *otoosan*—at least not in the way she had to me.

Two weeks later the *yooshi* 'adopted husband' from next door came over in the evening to escape from a difficult domestic situation, namely, his wife. He was a frequent visitor, and he and the *otoosan* would often use the occasion to drink sake together. This time the *yooshi*—named Ishihara—was, as usual, complaining about his wife—"She's always saying I'm nagging her" *'itsumo urusai, urusai to iu n desu'*—and the *otoosan* was going on, as usual, about his driving lessons. Someone mentioned that I had a driver's license, and the *otoosan* responded that this was only an international driver's license and that I was really a bad driver *'heta na unten desu yo'*.

Then the *okaasan* entered the conversation. Only now she was airing her complaints with the *otoosan* in an absolutely direct manner—just as she had spoken to me in the kitchen—and the list was even longer now than it had been two weeks ago. She began by stating that the *otoosan* was very egocentered *'wagamama'* and thought only about himself: *'jibun no koto kiri kangaeru hito'*. At this point I could not resist adding that it was strange how he smashed up my mirror and then called *me* a bad driver. "It certainly is," the *okaasan* agreed.

The *okaasan* proceeded on in great detail—no matter what happened, she said, the *otoosan* would absolutely *never* admit he was in the wrong—and *that* is the problem! *'chittomo gomen nasai to iwanai—da kara komaru'*. She thought he should certainly have apologized when he drove my car into a post, but instead he got uppity and became angry at what *he himself* had done. I sensed that this had been a source of conflict for the *okaasan* for quite a while and that she had had no opportunity to express her annoyance to him.

I realized that the forthright manner of the *okaasan*'s complaints about the *otoosan* was in part because she could present them in the guise of "telling it to the *yooshi*" from next door. In front of a *soto* person, the *otoosan* could not respond to the *okaasan* in the same manner she spoke about him (that is, critically), for it was no longer the same kind of communication situation. The existence of a *soto* person had changed the Katoo's relationships within the *uchi*. Before the *okaasan* had had to indulge the *otoosan*; now they were both *uchi*, indulging a *soto* guest. Like the *obasan* in the vignettes in chapter 6, the *otoosan* had shifted from the position of indulgee to indulger (from self-expression to self-discipline), and he was now sharing a vantage point that was symmetrical with the *okaasan*. And to make the guest, who is escaping a difficult domestic situation, feel more comfortable, the *okaasan* was giving him an earful about the difficult domestic situation in her *own* household. The *otoosan* now had to maintain a joking good humor, in sympathy with his wife's efforts—for he was indulging the guest now too. But the *okaasan* had made her point. And her strategy was surprisingly effective; it brought an end to the *otoosan*'s discussions of his driving, and complaints about the accident.

In fact, the adopted husband (Ishihara) is in exactly the same situation as the *okaasan* because, as an adopted husband, his situation is comparable to the wife in certain ways—specifically, the *amaeru/amayakasu* relationships within his house are reversed.[4] He must be more self-disciplined, while his wife can be more spontaneous—for she is living in her natal home with her parents. This means that he, rather than she, is supposed to be circumspect in what he says, and he, rather than she, cannot manifest his anger at his wife's criticism of him. He has come to the Katoos to do exactly what the *okaasan* is doing in venting her problems to him—escape from uncomfortable relationships within the *uchi*.[5] When his wife came over later on to collect him, he proceeded to complain about her to the Katoos, in the same way that the *okaasan* had complained about the *otoosan* to him.

Ishihara's quarrel had less dimension than that of the *okaasan*, since his consisted largely of repeating variations of a single theme: *"urusai, urusai to iu n desu"* 'She's always saying I'm nagging her'. And what happened next dispelled any doubt I might have had that the two of them were not aware of what they were doing.

"I really wish you would do *one* thing for me," the *otoosan* now spoke plaintively. "Just *one* thing. If you would just make me a *small* bottle of sake when I come home at night." But the *otoosan* actually never drank sake at home unless there were visitors.

"Because when I go out drinking and come home drunk *'yopparachatte kaette kitara'* the thing I would *really* like most is one small bottle of sake." But, in fact, the *otoosan* rarely came home drunk. The *okaasan* agreed immediately with the *otoosan*'s request, leaving me wondering why she had suddenly switched to a position of compliance. She added that her father "had always wanted to drink a little bit more sake when he came home and my mother always fixed it for him."

Then I grasped what was going on. The *otoosan* and *okaasan* were attempting to assist Ishihara in *his* quarrel. They had switched roles and were playing the parts of the Ishihara couple, trying to get the message across that the Ishihara wife should be more attentive to her husband's needs. When I asked afterward, the *otoosan* confirmed to me that these were indeed their intentions. Unfortunately, the subtleties of this part of the conversation were lost on the Ishihara adoptive husband, who by now had consumed so much sake that he merely persisted in alternately mumbling and shouting *"urusai urusai, URUSAI to iu n"* 'Nag, nag, NAG is all she says I do!' at his wife.

The *okaasan* found a solution for her inability to confront the *otoosan* directly by using *uchi/soto* and communicating her *uchi* problem to a *soto* person. We could say that in shifting her communication from *uchi* to *soto*, she dislocated reference and address, communicating indirectly *about* her husband instead of directly *to* her husband. The *otoosan* became an onlooker to the tirade against his misdeeds, since he was the subject of reference but not of address.

But we can be more precise than the use of reference and address terminology in this situation, since these terms are dependent on the individually defined deictic anchor point discussed in chapter 6. Since Japanese person is based on a collectively defined anchor point, then group boundaries, and distinctions between two kinds of others—those within and outside one's group—are crucially important. The group boundary is signaled by *uchi/soto* distinctions, which translate into the directional deference discussed in the vignettes in chapter 6 in guest/host behavior.

Within the *uchi*, reference and address are also differentiated—since one is more deferential in face-to-face behavior than when speaking about someone to others. Satoo's employees were deferential to him in speech and interaction; but their behavior shifted markedly when he was not present and they spoke *about* him. Outside reference and address and inside address can thus be grouped together as deferential, and juxtaposed to inside reference, a distinction that is made in kinship terms (where one set of deferential terms corresponds to the first grouping, while a set of familiar or humbling terms corresponds to the second). This distinction is also crucial in verbs for giving and receiving, and in the ubiquitous distinctions of deference (Wetzel, chapter 3). Thus when in-group members communicate *about* other insiders *to* outsiders, the "inside others" must be humbled in the same way as the self.

In the situation recounted above, the *okaasan* ingeniously makes use of the humbling required when speaking *about* the in-group *to* the out-group, by using this opportunity to embed her criticisms of the *otoosan* in the humbling-of-in-group required by the guest's presence. In so doing, the *okaasan* not only manages to vent her criticisms of the *otoosan* but accomplishes this in a way that is beyond reproach because she is conforming fully to directional deference.

As in-group members, the part-time (*paato*) workers in Kondo's company have the same kind of difficulty in expressing their criticisms to Satoo-san directly about being asked to buy the damaged tarts at half-price. In response, they jokingly ask Kondo, as the "outside insider," to approach Satoo-san to request that he sell her undamaged tarts at half-price, under the guise that she is buying them for herself. She will then transfer the tarts back to the employees at her landlady's place. The employees use Kondo to turn the tables on their dilemma of being neither truly *soto* nor *uchi* but reaping the disadvantages of both, because her position is exactly the opposite of theirs.

As an "outside insider" Kondo can approach Satoo-san and ask him to sell her undamaged tarts at half-price, because as an American researcher who is only temporarily working in the company, he must respond to her with deference. They are aware that as an insider she would be able to request an "inside" discount, and that as an outsider Satoo-san would be required to treat her with deference, thus making it hard to refuse her.

The Katoo couple's abrupt shift from the indirect airing of their own quarrel, to playing the Ishihara couple's roles in the guise of "assisting" them with *their* quarrel indicates their awareness that the Ishiharas were trying to use *uchi/soto* in the same way that they were. The Katoos' shift is an inversion of the shift the *okaasan* had made to air her grievances about the *otoosan*. She aired her actual quarrels under the guise of "telling it to the *yooshi*." The Katoos aired the Ishiharas' quarrels as if *they* were quarreling with each other. The *okaasan* aired an *uchi* matter by conveying it to a *soto* person; the Katoos aired what was really a *soto* quarrel for them *as if* it were an *uchi* matter. But the crucial point in both the above quarrels and in Kondo's narrative of the half-price conflict is that the parties within the collective anchor point use strategic shifts to direct their grievances outside—from *uchi* to *soto*; or to shift themselves temporarily outside the anchor point to air their dirty linen and redress their conflicts, when they are unable to do this appropriately inside.

EMOTIONS AND SOCIAL CONFLICT: THE HAMABATA CASE

To turn now to Hamabata's case, we find a fuller elaboration of the tensions involved in balancing self-interest with self-sacrifice for the greater good of the collectivity. The reproduction of the *ie* over time is one of the most widely acknowledged aspects of *ie* structure. What Hamabata is discussing, however, is another aspect of the *ie*—human, and "nearly bursting with passionate love, anger, deep disappointment, envy, nurturing care, with all the exalted and sullied aspects of human nature and human emotion" (1990, 162). The human aspect is not only a significant aspect of the *ie*, but as discussed in chapter 6, the organization specifically includes it as one of its two named facets: *uchi* and *ie*.

Ie is the realm of "structure," of goals and order existing beyond the individual, and greater than the individual, involving continuity over time; *uchi* is the realm of the personal and emotional—the realm of human existence *in time*. The negotiation of authority, particularly that of the household head, and the shift between hierarchical and egalitarian modes, marks the arena of intersection of these two facets. The head of the group must therefore balance his own personal agenda against the goals of the collectivity—which include managing the *ie* and its enterprise(s) so that the organization continues through time. In effecting the balance between personal and social realms, the balancing of personal versus collective agendas by the group head is literally crucial to keeping the organization from destruction, as we see in this case.

The case hinges on a crucial irony: while Grandfather Moriuchi proclaims that self-sacrifice accounts for the five-hundred-year history of his *ie*, he himself nearly brings that history to an end by his headstrong pursuit of personal goals and his virtual lack of the very quality he advocates in his management of the *ie*. To explain Grandfather's conflict more precisely, each generation of successors is required to provide for *ie* continuity by recruiting the next generation to succeed them. While the household members usually have emotional ties which lead them to recruit within *uchi*, by selecting one of their own children—and preferably the oldest son—the requirement to continue the *ie* means that if the son is incompetent, or inadequate in other ways, they must pass him over and recruit an outsider to succeed the *ie*. Recruitment to household succession thus clearly demonstrates the tensions between self and society discussed at the beginning of this chapter.[6]

The intrusion of personal desire into a succession choice that *should* be made in terms of the communal good results in the destruction of the communal good—along with the *ie*. In failing to recruit a successor for the next generation grandfather gains enormous personal power in the Moriuchi *ie*. But his personal power is at the expense of the collective organization of the *ie*, and its continuity over time. Grandfather creates a situation after his death where the *ie* still exists—but in the bizarre form of an empty house with bankrupt industries, inhabited only by the ancestor shelf. The living members of *uchi* have ceased to exist, since Grandfather has recruited no successor, and the *ie* becomes an empty shell.

Hamabata details the origin of this conflict: the downward spiral of the Moriuchi *ie* begins with Grandfather's hubris when he insists on marrying Grandmother, a woman of wholly inappropriate social status, for purely personal reasons. Grandmother contributes to the *ie*'s demise when she treats the relationship in social and economic terms, also for purely personal reasons. The endless stalemate created by these differing perspectives on their own relationship is played out in the imbalance between *uchi* and *ie*. When Grandfather creates branches (and subsidiary companies) without first selecting a successor, the boundaries between *uchi* and *soto* become hopelessly blurred. *Soto* could not be defined without *uchi* being defined first; no one could be recruited *outside* the *ie* until someone had been recruited *inside* it. None of the siblings could consider themselves "branch" households (since they were all potential successors to the "parent" household). There appeared no way out of this impasse.

All the Moriuchi children thus become pitted against one another in a personal struggle to become successor. Moreover Grandfather's failure to recruit a successor means that the relationships between the siblings could not be carried on as usual but that all had to be kept in check by Grandfather himself. Grandfather kept all the potential recruits in a situation analogous to the workers in Dorinne's confectionary company, constantly under the watchful eye of Satoo's cameras and microphones. The adult children who should have been heads of their own households had to defer to Grandfather like the employees of the candy company had to defer to Satoo's rages and arbitrary coldness. Their deference resulted in a mirroring effect—since they always appeared to accept Grandfather's definition of the situation, he could learn little about their underlying feelings, or even their potential talents as successors. Grandfather also managed to pit each child in competition against all the others, so that they seemed perpetually unable to deal collectively with the situation. This prevented them from accomplishing the strategy of overriding Grandfather—by acknowledging the collectivity with its potential to encompass Grandfather and his personal usurpation of power.

This case is reminiscent of King Lear, in the way that Grandfather's lack of providing a successor (just as Lear's lack of providing a successor) unleashes a fury of twisted personal emotions that threaten to engulf the kingdom itself. The inability to delineate *uchi* also reveals how much the facets of social existence—from economic to religious—are dependent on *uchi/soto* distinctions.

LIFE VERSUS DEATH: SHIGA NAOYA'S "THE RAZOR"

As developed by Molasky's insightful commentary, Shiga Naoya's short story focuses on personal control as well—but here the conflict actually revolves around the third level of *uchi/soto* organization, namely, the indexing of relationships between dualities. The conflict is not abstract but existential, as is clear by the way the story opens. The main character, Yoshisaburo, lies ill and helpless in bed, in the living quarters just in back of his barbershop. Since the barbershop is an *ie* enterprise, house and shop are under the same roof. He finds himself in exactly the reverse of his normal situation. A perfectionist so skilled that he has never nicked a customer in ten years, and a person who is rarely ill, he now lies overcome with fever, helplessly listening to his incompetent apprentices, and unable to rise from bed and direct their work on a busy holiday. He is supine, rather than upright; 'inside' the house (*uchi*), rather than 'outside' in his shop (*soto*); helpless and being waited on, rather than exerting his authority as manager of the shop; he must *amaeru* (be cared for), rather than *amayakasu* (exert authority).

The story revolves around Yoshisaburo's struggle to right the balance, reassert his authority, and once more become an active agent in social life. His difficulty lies in the way he attempts to accomplish this. The razor is crucial in the story, as it signifies the potential for destruction that lies in even a seemingly innocuous miscalculation. The barber ultimately violates the razor-edge balance between construction and destruction, between life and death, because he fails to balance the tensions between self and world at their most basic level—where the directional coordinates of *omote/ura* and *uchi/soto* signify these distinctions.

As the master of a shop, Yoshisaburo should be controlling the apprentices and *giving* deference to his customers. Yet bedridden and incapacitated with fever in his family quarters, he is *receiving* deference or indulgence. He is caught within these two conflicting sets of directional coordinates, as illustrated by the repeated intrusions of the maid, who insists that Yoshisaburo sharpen her employer's razor, which intrudes into the *uchi* space. Yoshisaburo compounds the intrusion, and further violates the same balance by attempting to assert control, insisting that he *will* sharpen the razor—in the face of the patent impossibility of his being able to do so.

Like Faust, Yoshisaburo has attempted to assume powers beyond his control. The conflict for him is thus between the successful assumption of his powers and what he views as helpless impotence. Initially he fails in his attempts to assert his self-control and sharpen the razor within the *uchi* of his living quarters. With darkness and silence, the division between *uchi/ura* and *soto/omote* blurs, as the shop returns to the private realm of the house.

At this moment a customer enters the darkened shop, and here Yoshisaburo attempts to resume control, again through sheer self-will, by refusing to close the shop, refusing to let the apprentice shave the customer, and attempting to exert control himself. He rises, goes into the shop, and begins to shave the customer. "The gentle twilight is long gone, and now the stillness of the night has permeated the house and shop. 'Both *uchi* and *soto* fell perfectly silent in the night' " (Molasky, p. 218). The boundaries are dissolving, and the world of silence, and by implication death, are inviting the barber, as Molasky comments.

At this point the barber, now burning with fever and barely managing to carry on, nicks the customer's neck slightly with his dull razor. This galvanizes him into action; all his physical fatigue leaves him, and fueled with energy, he rises to a position of control. He now attempts to obliterate the boundaries that distinguish self from the surrounding world. "[I]n one swift thrust [he] plunged the razor *into* the young man's throat. It *penetrated [in]* the length of the blade up to the handle . . . Presently the blood came gushing *out* from the deep wound" (Molasky, p. 219).

This vignette brings us full circle back to the introduction to this volume: from waking *into* the world to dissolution and dying *out from* it; from reaching *into* the medicine cabinet, and taking *out* the toothpaste, to plunging the razor *into* the young man's throat and watching all the tension drain *out of* him, thus ending up in a mirror-image pose of the dead customer. In fact, the drama revolves around the *undoing* of the main character, closely linked to the unraveling of his relationship to his context. But these are simply two sides of the same coin, hinging on a razor-edge of balance. In attempting to assume control when it is clearly beyond him, Yoshisaburo destroys what he would create, with the ultimate result of self-annihilation. In "The Razor," Shiga merely exaggerates dynamics that should be recognizable to anyone. The problem here is also hubris—completing the circle begun by Kondo's and Hamabata's chapters which detail respectively the destruction of interpersonal relationships and social structure. Shiga's final image of the barber, sunk into a chair in the mirror image of the dead customer, conveys the consequences of failure to acknowledge the basic coordinates of inside and outside, front and back, up and down.

REASSESSING *UCHI/SOTO:* TOWARD A SITUATED SOCIAL ORDER

Shiga Naoya's narrative about the barber naturally takes us back to the starting point of the volume, making it useful to chart our progress in relation to the problematic issues delineated in the introduction. The "relational" self and "situated" social order, the "vertical principle," embedded "points of view," and "shifting"—the five issues outlined there—represented different facets of the same problem: how can those aspects of context that are particular, situated, embedded—or identified with "uniqueness"—be identified with general "principles" or patterns that *transcend* context? What kind of an "order" (and "self") do they represent? Does this order avoid linguistic or cultural relativity, and if so, how?

The response to this problem constitutes a shift in focus to indexical or situated meaning, and the organization of *uchi/soto*. A word is necessary here about the relationship between indexing and *uchi/soto*. The indexical (inside/outside) meanings in *uchi/soto* are linked with the clusters of polarized meanings for "self" and "society" so that the organization of "self" and "social order" is produced through indexing of inside/outside coordinates. But this linkage works both ways. The indexing that produces an "interdependent" self can be seen simultaneously as the producing of an "interdependent" self *that exemplifies the organization of indexing*. The ways in which self and society are mutually constitutive can also be viewed as a *dynamic that exemplifies the organization of pragmatic meaning in social life*, which must be viewed through social practice. This quality of the snake eating its tail is exemplified by the organization of *uchi/soto*, and Japanese social organization, and it seems basic to the organization of indexing. In this way *uchi/soto* organization also exemplifies the organization of indexical meaning.

I will now briefly explicate *uchi/soto* organization and the organization of indexical meaning, as two sides of the same coin. In this volume *uchi/soto* is depicted as a continuum gauging multiple indexing, or "mapping" (Ochs 1990), between an engaged, intimate, spontaneous perspective (*uchi*) and a detached, disciplined, ordered perspective (*soto*). One end of the continuum is anchored (literally) in social life, as the collective deictic anchor point or *uchi* (Wetzel). The other end is detached from social life as *soto* 'other', 'distant', or 'ordered'. The configuration is not simply an axis, but a tilted axis, with one end embedded in the social life of actual participants and the other end detached, abstracted, or general.

This indexing, in turn, maps communication in a number of different modes—bowing, greetings, use of space, gift-giving, choice of topics, dress, food presented to guests, and so on. The Katoos are indexing degrees of self-expression, intimacy, spontaneity, informality, content, and "behind-the-scenes" affairs for self/group, in opposition to the degree of social constraint (or self-discipline), and attention to appearance, politeness, and form. The first level of *uchi/soto* organization moves outward from self (and group) along a continuum from self (and group) to outsiders and strangers.

The entire range of this communication defines the Japanese self, which is thereby related in multiple ways to context. Self is simultaneously indexed vis-à-vis *specific* others; yet the way this is done involves a more *general* ordering of the *organization* of self versus the *organization* of social order. Thus *soto* has two senses—a particular, located instance of "other" as, for example, in the appearance of the Katoo guests. *Soto* is also "other" in the sense of a social order of a generalized, abstract nature, which contrasts with a specific situation and engaged experience.

The tilted axis, then, creates two sets of inverted relationships: between self/society and engagement/detachment. The *uchi* pole consists of an engaged, experienced, detailed, individuated perspective, centering on the embedded perspective of "self" (and group) on society; versus the *soto* pole as abstracted, generalized, "ordered" perspectives, which include general social perspectives on the self.

The tilted axis is a means of indexing not only social relationships but relationships between the *poles* of self and society at another conceptual level. The indexing of actual engaged human perspectives in social life (*uchi*) with organizational facets that transcend context and exist over time (*soto*) produces the dynamic of the "situated" social order, and the "relational" self, which mutually constitute each other. The interplay between these two facets constitutes self and social life, as well as the organization of the *ie*, through what we might term *relationships between agency and structure* (Bachnik, in press).

What I have termed *levels* are interconnected, so that each level encompasses all the others as well. A third level, which relates the poles themselves, can include virtually any terms that can be identified as polar dualities. These are then linked by indexing them vis-à-vis inside/outside dimensions. For example, knowledge is commonly indexed along inside/outside dimensions—not only in Japan but in virtually every society. As Ochs puts this: "Epistemological dispositions refer to some property of participants' beliefs or knowledge . . . for example, the source of their knowledge or the degree of certainty of their knowledge. These two dispositions are directly indexed in all languages, are central dimensions of all communicative events, and are central constituents of other dimensions of communicative events" (Ochs 1990, 296).

Culturally, it is crucial to index the degree to which we share cultural knowledge with others, along the dimensions of familiar versus unfamiliar, and the degree of sharedness or "we-ness"/ These in fact correspond to some of the earliest examples of *uchi/soto* categories in Japanese history, as Quinn details in chapter 2. The dimensions being gauged in assessing the degree of "otherness" as shared/nonsharedness include proximate, familiar, assumed information versus distant *un*familiar, *un*assumed information. This kind of indexing is extremely basic to *uchi/soto*, and to Japanese social life, with its marked differentiation between 'outside' guest and 'inside' host. For example, the two sets of guests who were simultaneously visiting the Kato house in chapter 6 differed markedly in respect to "otherness." The Katoos had a thin degree of shared knowledge with Etsuko's family because of their lack of mutual experience; it was their first meeting. They had considerable shared knowledge with the *obasan*, who had grown up in the Katoo house and had been kept informed about the affairs of that house, even after she had married out. In fact, the degree of her shared knowledge was the basis for the *obasan*'s shift within the *uchi*, in opposition to Etsuko's family. The degree of shared knowledge was the initial basis for indexing in these situations; everything else was mapped upon this. The indexing of shared knowledge thus encompasses what I have outlined about *uchi/ soto* so far.

For Japanese, beliefs and attitudes can be indexed along a "certainty scale," the "certain" pole of which is 'inside', *uchi* knowledge: firsthand, personally experienced, detailed, and individuated. Experience is an important component of *uchi* knowedge, which is the sort of knowlege one gets from being a member of the household. This contrasts with knowledge of a more removed, or *soto* 'outside' kind: secondhand, detached, communicated from others, and more generic. The point is that "knowledge" here is not defined in "either/or" terms but along a scale that prioritizes shared experience (as *uchi*) and fades into more remote, secondhand information (as *soto*). Knowledge can be closely related to the shifting boundaries of the house itself, so that *uchi* knowledge is not confined only within *uchi* boundaries but shades outward through people like the *obasan*, who have been married outside. Knowledge is commonly indexed for familiarity—or degree of sharedness—so that a single house has numerous other households with whom it shares partially overlapping knowledge, and constantly indexes sharedness.

In this sense "uniqueness" can be viewed as a claim about the prioritizing of *uchi* knowledge over *soto*, rather than a claim about culture, race, or general knowledge. Only "we" occupy "this" deictic anchor point, which is a unique locus. And the anchor point can expand or contract as the "we" expands or contracts according to the discourse vantage point. Each household in the region I worked in considered itself unique, in opposition to *every other household*. But this was a focus that emphasized the degree to which insiders shared, and outsiders could not share, the common 'ground'. The degree of shared/nonsharedness is a dimension of inside/outside that is indexed at every guest/host encounter by virtually every kind of *uchi/soto* communication.[7]

The epistemic focus on *uchi* as certain, familiar, experiential knowledge versus *soto* as more removed, secondhand, and detached can also be related to issues of cultural unity versus linguistic/cultural relativity.[8] Rather than a unified, monolithic perspective on culture, the *uchi/soto* perspective is pluralistic and dynamic. Each of the uniquely anchored groups gauges the degree of cultural knowledge its members share with each of the other groups in the process of constituting and being constituted by the intricate social tapestry that is *uchi/soto.*

NOTES

1. As Rohlen notes: "One of the most common phrases used to describe good relations in the group is *matomari ga aru* 'the group is drawn together', 'it has unity'. A major dimension of Japanese popular thought about small groups is represented by the contrast between this state and its opposite, . . . *bara bara* 'scattered', 'fragmented', or *matomari ga nai* 'lacking unity' " (1974, 93). "There is no sense in describing the group as having but a single structure. Each activity and context calls forth slightly different arrangements based on a combination of the two principles, and the group finds it normal to shift from one to another . . . one key to maintaining an efficient office is to make frequent, but orderly, shifts from one arrangement to another so that the spectrum of relationship possibilities within the group, official and personal, may be realized" (1974, 106).

2. Christena Turner (1987) details similar dynamics in a conflict within a union attempt to take over a dying company. In this account the union officials appear to be fully aware, and taking strategic advantage of the difficulties members have in confronting them from within the *uchi.*

3. See chapter 6, note 3.

4. To explain Ishihara's conflict, two successor positions exist in the household in each generation, for a male and female who are married. Recruitment takes place at the time of marriage; the preferred strategy is to recruit a male (son) from within the ie, and a female (wife) from outside (Bachnik 1983). The recruitment strategy that occurred in the Ishihara household worked in the opposite way: the female (Ishihara's wife) was recruited as a daughter from the *ie,* and a male (Ishihara) was recruited from outside at marriage. This is why Ishihara's position is analogous to that of a wife, and why this produces gender conflict (Kitaoji 1971; Bachnik, in press; Hamabata 1990).

5. This is consistent with other accounts of the *yooshi* (Befu 1962; Kitaoji 1971; Bachnik 1983).

6. For further discussion of these tensions in recruitment see Hamabata (1990), Bachnik (1983; in press).

7. Smith notes (1983, 93) that "one of the major tasks confronting the new bride is learning 'the ways of the house' (*kafuu*) of her husband." He then adds: "On the face of it, this is an extraordinary claim. What are the ways of the house? Does the inner working of every household in Japan really differ so drastically from that of all the rest that a new recruit can possibly find it so difficult to master it?" (1983, 93).

8. On this subject Gumperz and Levinson (1991) also propose a focus on indexing: "One keystone in the arch [of addressing these issues, specifically

through a focus on relating grammar to language use] [is] the phenomenon of deixis or indexicality, whereby words like *I, now, here,* polite pronouns, and so on have their interpretations specified by the circumstances of use . . . and *thus to wider social organization"* (1991, 614; emphasis mine).

References

Bachnik, Jane. 1983. "Recruitment Strategies for Household Succession: Rethinking Japanese Household Organization," *Man* (N.S.) 18: 160–82.

———. In press. *Family, Self, and Society in Modern Japan.* Berkeley: University of California Press.

Befu, Harumi. 1962. "Corporate Emphasis and Patterns of Descent in the Japanese Family," in R. J. Smith and R. K. Beardsley, eds., *Japanese Culture: Its Development and Characteristics*, pp. 34–41. Chicago: Aldine.

Calder, Kent E. 1988. *Crisis and Compensation: Public Policy and Political Stability in Japan, 1949–1986.* Princeton, N.J.: Princeton University Press.

Evens, T.M.S. n.d. "All about Eve: An Anthropological Reading of the Feminine Principle in Genesis 2–3." Unpublished manuscript.

Friedman, David. 1988. *The Misunderstood Miracle: Industrial Development and Political Change in Japan.* Ithaca: Cornell University Press.

Gumperz, John J., and Stephen C. Levinson. 1991. "Rethinking Linguistic Relativity." *Current Anthropology* 12(5): 613–22.

Hamabata, Matthews. 1990. *Crested Kimono: Power and Love in the Japanese Business Family.* Ithaca: Cornell University Press.

Hanks, William F. 1992. "The Indexical Ground of Deictic Reference," in A. Duranti and C. Goodwin, eds., *Rethinking Context: Language as an Interactive Phenomenon.* Cambridge: Cambridge University Press.

Kitaoji, Hiranobu. 1971. "The Structure of the Japanese Family." *American Anthropologist* 73, 1036–57.

Markus, Hazel Rose, and Shinobu Kitayama. 1991. "Culture and the Self: Implications for Cognition, Emotion, and Motivation." *Psychological Review* 98(2): 224–53.

Nakane, Chie. 1970. *Japanese Society.* Berkeley and Los Angeles: University of California Press.

Ochs, Elinor. 1990. "Indexicality and Socialization," in G. Herdt, R. Shweder, and J. Stigler, eds., *Cultural Psychology: Essays on Comparative Human Development*, pp. 287–308. Cambridge: Cambridge University Press.

Pascale, Richard and Thomas P. Rohlen. 1983. "The Mazda Turnaround." *Journal of Japanese Studies* 9(2): 219–63.

Rohlen, Thomas P. 1974. *For Harmony and Strength: Japanese White-Collar Organization in Anthropological Perspective.* Berkeley: University of California Press.

Smith, Robert J. 1983. *Japanese Society: Tradition, Self and the Social Order.* Cambridge: Cambridge University Press.

Turner, Christena Linda. 1987. *Breaking the Silence: Consciousness, Commitment, and Action in Japanese Unions.* Ph.D. dissertation, Stanford University.

PART THREE

Language as a Form of Life:
Clines of Knowledge as Clines of Person

Chapter 11

UCHI/SOTO: TIP OF A SEMIOTIC ICEBERG?
'INSIDE' AND 'OUTSIDE' KNOWLEDGE
IN THE GRAMMAR OF JAPANESE

CHARLES J. QUINN, JR.

"What is character, but the definition of incident? What
is incident but the illustration of character?"
—Henry James, *The Art of Fiction*

"Language enters life through concrete utterances
(which manifest language) and life enters language
through concrete utterances as well."
—M. M. Bakhtin

EDITORS' INTRODUCTION

In this final chapter, Charles Quinn argues that structure in language is
partly a product of the lived world, a world where, in Wittgenstein's
words, "Language is a form of life." Quinn picks up the argument from
chapter 10, and studies the indexing of epistemology in the Japanese
language. In the language's major grammatical categories, the principal
options for expression index knowledge, beliefs, and attitudes along a
scale of familiarity. At the more certain pole of this scale Quinn finds
knowledge of an *uchi* 'inside' sort: firsthand, perceived directly, detailed, familiar, and individuated. This contrasts with knowledge of a *soto*
'outside' sort, which tends to be externally mediated or secondhand,
less detailed, less familiar, and generic. Quinn's chapter pulls this volume together by demonstrating the remarkable consistency between
the organization of *uchi/soto* in language and in social life. It is hoped
that the chapter's position here, at the end of the volume, makes it
more accessible to nonlinguists and readers who do not speak Japanese,
since it echoes themes and arguments they have by now come to know
in an *uchi* kind of way.

Quinn examines the grammatical categories of (in)transitivity, aspect,
and modality, as well as a pair each of clause nominalizers and locative
particles. In each case, expression in Japanese is very much (although
not exclusively) a matter of choosing between two opposed perspectives,

one of which construes its subject matter as 'inside', the other, as 'outside'. For example, acts under volitional control are most typically expressed as transitive predicates, which is to say as change structured in terms of mutually distinct agents, who control the change referred to, and undergoers, which change. Events that simply "happen," by contrast, are typically intransitive in form, with an undergoer, but no controlling agent of change. The logical structure of transitive predicates is thus more complex than that of the intransitives. If transitive predicates most typically express a familiar, phenomenologically detailed, *uchi* kind of world, intransitive predicates tend to express a less familiar, less detailed world, where change occurs outside our control, without observable source or agency. This *soto* world extends to a horizon where there is no observable change at all, where the most typical expression is "atransitive"—the domain of adjectival and nominal (+ copula) predicates. The similarity of this (in)transitive version of *uchi/soto* to that of self (the world we control) and society and the natural world beyond (the larger, outside world where our control ends) is striking.

The association of transitivity and intransitivity with these two kinds of change, one more "known" or "knowable" than the other, motivates their use in indexing social deference. In Japanese, honorific deference toward an out-group person is regularly expressed by applying an intransitive conversion to the verb that expresses the honored person's act. This effaces the notion of agency, in what amounts to respectful avoidance. While indirection or avoidance is a major strategy for honoring a referent in many languages, so too is its opposite, drawing near. That is, symbolic avoidance of an out-group referent is complemented by the practice whereby insiders emphasize their agency in acts they direct toward outsiders. The verb denoting this humbly put act undergoes a transitive conversion, which highlights the notion of agency and, thus, the willingness with which the act is undertaken. The agent in this case is the speaker or someone in her *uchi* group. These two indexical uses of prototypical intransitive and transitive structures closely parallel the guest-host and *amaeru/amayakasu* forms of deference already discussed by Bachnik and Rosenberger.

Choice of clause nominalizers *no* and *koto* corresponds regularly with a distinction between information that is firsthand, perceived, or otherwise engaged, 'inside' knowledge (*no*), on the one hand, and generic information to which the speaker is not necessarily committed, on the other (*koto*). The locative particles *ni* 'in/at' and *to* 'with' likewise differ in several constrastive uses according to whether the relation established is natural and unremarkable or contingent and somehow problematic. Finally, several ways of converting an engaged, experienced perspective on a predicate into a detached, observed one are discussed.

Quinn concludes that this differentiation of engaged/detached and un/familiar is the most widely indexed epistemological distinction in the Japanese language.

This chapter links up with the major themes of the volume in other ways, too. Quinn notes, for example, how little coherence we find when we conceive of person in Japanese in terms of the discrete reference of "pronouns" like *watashi* 'I', *anata* 'you', and *kanojo* 'she'. There is much more systemic coherence to an analysis that construes person in Japanese as an evidential cline, an indexical field extending out from *uchi* into *soto*. After suggesting how knowledge is indexed in an *uchi/soto* cline, Quinn interprets this as a congruent cline of person. Moreover, this *uchi/soto* cline corresponds functionally to what is expressed as grammatical person in most Indo-European languages—a fact little remarked on, considering its consequences for both spoken and written communication. As Quinn concludes, "It is no exaggeration to say that this mutual indexing with reference to *uchi/soto* parameters is how people, together, create their selves" (p. 286). All the other papers in the volume depict the same cline. An individual's self is but the *uchi* that develops every time it is distinguished against a *soto* of social other and social order. Without engaging the *soto*, one can grow no *uchi*. "Incident" and "character" are as interdependent in life as they are in fiction, and the form of social life called language plays a central role in making us the people we are. For Japanese people, the nature of the parallel distinctions they practice in social intercourse, index in grammar, and refer to in words means that the creation of a self is for them very much a matter of *uchi* and *soto*.

UCHI/SOTO: TIP OF A SEMIOTIC ICEBERG? 'INSIDE' AND 'OUTSIDE' KNOWLEDGE IN THE GRAMMAR OF JAPANESE

The Indexing Implicit in Grammatical Expression

Such uses of the words *uchi* 'inside' and *soto* 'outside' as those surveyed in chapter 2 of this volume, and the network of concepts they manifest, are but the tip of an iceberg with a broad beam and a deep draft. This essay attempts to sound that draft, by examining some ways in which the linguistic organization of information in Japanese is structured along lines that are, as I see it, very much a matter of opposing an *uchi* to a *soto*.[1] To change the metaphor, in considering *uchi* and *soto* in their roles as common nouns, we have in fact examined but one household in a large, extended family of homologously related phenomena.[2] The household to be surveyed in this paper is not that of individual words but rather meanings that function either below the level of the word (in the form of derivational or inflectional morphology) or above it (in the form of syntactic constructions, the components of which are individual words). Each of these meanings, in its own way, indexes information as either *uchi* or *soto*, relative to the domain of use, so that an *uchi/soto* opposition—engaged/detached, proximal/distal, and so forth—informs the construction of meaning in a wide variety of different communicative contexts, from the social one already examined in the chapters that precede this one, to the most basic grammatical relations in a clause-in-use.[3]

What does it mean to "index" information? Lyons's definition (1977, 106) is straightforward: a sign "A" indexes some other information "C" when "the occurrence of A can be held to imply the presence or existence of C." To say that a pair of contrasting signs or forms index information "in an *uchi/soto* manner" means, then, that while one of them evokes the presence of meanings associated with *uchi* in various contexts (e.g., familiarity, proximity, inclusion, certainty, control, etc.), the other evokes meanings conceptually associated with *soto* (unfamiliarity, distance, exclusion, uncertainty, lack of control, etc.). The main contention of this chapter is that an *uchi/soto* distinction, far from being limited to social or spatial deixis, indexes differences of an epistemological kind, too, as a function of the meanings of certain pairs of grammatical devices, which contrast along just these lines. To put it simply, the semantics of one grammatical form display some feature(s) common to other *uchi*-type contexts (such as control or familiarity), while an alternative form shows features typical of *soto*-type contexts (such as lack of control or unfamiliarity). The idea is that in their actual *use*, these grammatical devices serve to index information in an *uchi/soto* manner, in addition to whatever other functions, representational or relational, they accomplish. While this argument could be strengthened by extending its analyses beyond the level of the sentence, it will not do so, but will focus instead on how intrasentential devices—morphemes, phrases, words, constructions—function to index various kinds of information or knowledge in an *uchi/soto* way.[4] Of course, in each context, the 'inside/outside' schema will be realized in a somewhat different way; the particular "content" that is configured in terms of *uchi/soto* will differ as the domain or level of signification differs. It is the 'inside/outside' nature of the *relation* that is decisive, not the contents.

Grammatical devices that index such *uchi/soto* distinctions include (but are not limited to) (in)transitivity,[5] aspect, and modality, two clause nominalizers (*no* and *koto*), and a pair of particles (*ni* and *to*). In each case, it seems, the language provides resources to express two opposed perspectives, one of which views its subject matter as 'inside', the other as 'outside'. In the domain of interpersonal relations, for example, the difference is *social*—in-group/out-group—and such instances are examined variously in several chapters of this volume. In the domain of epistemic modality, beliefs and attitudes can be indexed along a certainty scale, the surer pole of which is knowledge of an *uchi* 'inside' sort: firsthand, perceived, engaged, detailed, and individuated. This contrasts with knowledge of a more removed, or *soto* 'outside' kind: secondhand, detached, communicated from others, less detailed, and generic.

If we examine the (in)transitivity of the clause (as we do in later sections below), prototypical transitivity entails, among other *uchi*-like concepts, a volitional control over the act denoted. Conversely, intransitivity most typically associates with, among other *soto*-like concepts, less control. This reaches its extreme in stative (e.g., adjectival) predicates, which denote no change and are consequently atransitive. Furthermore, the detail of a highly transitive clause, such as *tsubusu* '[someone] crushes [something]', with its volitional agent, undergoer, and change imposed on the undergoer, exceeds the detail expressed in a corresponding intransitive clause like *tsubureru* '[something] is crushed', which includes an undergoer of change but lacks an agent. Now, in actual communication, the greater phenomenal detail of the transitive clause indexes a higher degree of knowledge on the part of a speaker/writer who articulates such a clause. In realis—roughly, nonhypothetical—modality, this amounts to an indexing of greater certainty. The knowledge and certainty, of course, are attributed even if the speaker/writer lies. In this way, to use a bare, (in)transitive predicate is also to index *evidentiality*, or degree and kind of one's knowledge. The detail in stative clauses like *aru* '[something] exists' is less than in intransitives like *tsubureru*, since not only an agent but change, too, is missing. The actual use of a stative clause indexes a still lower degree of knowledge. Thus the detail with which a clause structures and represents a situation can be located on a continuum extending from transitive (greatest detail) to intransitive (less) to atransitive, or stative (least), and this degree of detail can be interpreted as indexing greater or lesser knowledge on the part of the person who speaks or writes that clause. In Japanese, this supports a further distinction. Since describing another's action as something fully known indexes familiarity with that person, deferential expression speaks of such action in the grammar of less detail. (See below: (In)transitivity as Social Index: Ideational as Interpersonal.) The indexical effects of semantic structure obtain when a speaker or writer addresses a clause to an audience, but they are invisible unless the clause is construed *in use*, that is, in relation to the participants in communication. Grammar can thus have its indexical functions, *if* we consider grammar as a feature of live utterances.

Although limitations of space preclude a full treatment, other basic grammatical devices index similar *uchi/soto* distinctions in knowledge.

Among these are clause nominalizers *no* and *koto* and the particles *ni* and *to*. In the nominalization of clauses, Japanese provides the option of /clause + *no*/, which indicates that the information expressed is nearby, accessible, and is the ground against which the figure of new, recently distant information is presented. The contrasting option, /clause + *koto*/, simply converts the clause into a common noun. The first option thus marks the epistemological status of that information as given, assumed, or somehow established, while the second does not. Information that is placed with particles *ni* 'in/at' and *to* 'with' also differs in a parallel way, in that while semantic relations established with *ni* tend to be unremarkable, natural, enduring, and essential, those established with *to* tend to be problematic, products of human deliberation, temporary, and accidental. The last predicative index of *uchi/soto* taken up is the morphological differentiation of an internal, engaged point of view from one that is external and observed. The latter is created by adding some form of *aru* 'be' as the final operator on a predicator. Just as there is no social *uchi* without a *soto*, no "humble" without an "honorific," there is none of the high detail of controlled acts without the lesser detail of noncontrolled events and states, no known information without "news," no assured 'in/at' location without location approximated in terms of 'with', and no engaged vouching without detached observing. As much as these categories differ in content, each distinguishes a speaker's or writer's choice of an 'inside' perspective from an 'outside' one.

Distinctions of an *uchi/soto* sort inform meaning-making in Japanese to such an extent that we may speak of *uchi/soto* as a *metapattern*, a pattern of patterns that informs the structuring of the world on a number of different planes of signification. It is a good example of what Pierre Bourdieu calls *habitus*—a disposition or tacitly known way of acting which is itself reshaped every time it shapes a new context. But if *uchi/soto* is such an ingrained way of construing things in Japan, the question arises as to what extent people living there are beholden, inured, or otherwise predisposed to seeing their world in these terms and not others—a question of linguistic relativity. The question is worth addressing briefly, if only to neutralize the potential for misunderstanding that this phrase has demonstrated in the past.

The idea of linguistic relativity has recently been taken up anew and somewhat redefined. This is, in part, the consequence of a growing body of research that depicts language and thought as activities that are *situated*, that is, developed and maintained in an historical and ongoing matrix of cultural activities.[6] In this perspective, both language and thought are *expected* to display homologies with those larger cultural frames, in a kind of four-part (biological-cultural-cognitive-linguistic) harmony. A syncretic scenario of this sort is a far cry from the crude "linguistic determinism" attributed—unfairly, I think—to Benjamin

Whorf, since it is not language that "determines" cognitive consequences, but rather that language, with cognition, emerges at the interface of biological inheritance and sociocultural practice, personally embodied while socially situated. This interface is alive today with interaction between social and cognitive psychologists, philosophers, anthropologists, and linguists, who are addressing questions of linguistic relativity anew.[7]

While in the present instance, it seems quite reasonable to say that *uchi/soto* informs or even constrains the expression of meaning in Japanese, it is difficult to extend the claim directly to cognition. The *uchi/soto* habitus may or may not inform the structure of cognition in an overarching, general way (if cognition indeed has such an overarching structure). But insofar as the major expressive options of (in)transitivity, aspect, and modality index information along *uchi/soto* lines, this distinction may well constrain "thinking-for-speaking," the on-line kind of thought in which people frame, on the run, what they are about to say.[8] It is something like this kind of "thinking in the language" that takes foreign learners of any language so long to develop. To use indexical expressions coherently requires knowledge of "the social relations in which one stands to those with whom one converses."[9] Accepted ways of referring to oneself, to others, and to actions and events—the list goes on—are typically keyed to the parameters of deixis as a culture practices it. Thus if a foreign culture and its linguistic practices differ enough from one's own to require anchoring one's language acts in new indexical grounds, one will feel significant differences in those aspects of thinking—such as point-of-view—that accompany communication, and they *will* be constrained by culture and language. This chapter attempts to delineate some previously unremarked aspects of indexicality in Japanese, to demonstrate that *uchi/soto* indexing is considerably more than just a matter of the social deixis of donatory ("giving") verbs or the spatial deixis of demonstrative pronouns, in that it is tacitly practiced whenever individuals use one of the major structures of predication[10] to express themselves. From such a perspective, there is an unavoidable indexicality right in the choices made within categories like (in)transitivity, so that the pragmatics of communication are no mere "postsyntactic" add-on, but a basic dimension that grounds the very significance of structure.

CONCEPTUAL GROUNDING: FROM WORDS TO GRAMMAR

Wetzel and Sukle (this volume) have explained how, in the give and take of communicating in Japanese, *uchi/soto* deixis is essential to recognizing and maintaining certain roles sanctioned by society. As their studies suggest, it is the social domain with which *uchi* and *soto* are most readily associated as concepts, and this is the "tip of the iceberg" of my

TABLE 1
Lexical *uchi* vs. *soto*, Regular Conceptual Contrasts

UCHI : SOTO =

INDOORS : OUTDOORS

CLOSED : OPEN

EXPERIENCED : OBSERVED

HIDDEN : REVEALED

BOUNDED : UNBOUNDED

LIMITED : LIMIT-IRRELEVANT

SACRED : SECULAR (Cf. imperial palace vs. outer buildings, outer shrine vs. inner
              shrine at Ise, etc.)

SELF(-VES) : OTHER(S)

LINEAL FAMILY : EXTRALINEAL FAMILY

FAMILIAR : UNFAMILIAR

"US" : "THEM"

PRIVATE : PUBLIC

INCLUDED : EXCLUDED

KNOWN : UNKNOWN

INFORMED : UNINFORMED

CONTROLLED : UNCONTROLLED

ENGAGED : DETACHED

EARLY/PRIMARY : LATE/SECONDARY

title. My own survey of *uchi*- and *soto*-based expressions in chapter 2 attempted to reveal their presence as an organizing principle in other aspects of Japanese life, through the lexicons of social, psychological, temporal, and spatial domains, in which certain contrasts and correspondences emerged, as listed in Table 1.

Now, if people in Japanese society have for so long oriented themselves in their spatial, social, and psychological worlds in an *uchi/soto* manner, chances are that this distinction may have found its way into differences and relations expressed in other, nonlexical structures of their language, too. If one major function of a predicate, for example, is to represent experience, the question arises as to whether the orientational habitus of *uchi/soto* might not somehow be indexed in the grammar of predication. I should like to suggest that distinguishing between an 'inside' and an 'outside' is, in fact, a feature of the grammatical categories basic to predication in Japanese, as they are used in communication. For (in)transitivity, aspect, and modality, for clauses nominalized with *no* or *koto*, for nouns placed with *ni* or *to*, and in other grammatical distinctions as well, the choice is between alternative forms and perspectives, which index contrasting qualities like controlled versus noncontrolled, engaged versus detached, experiential versus secondhand, or subjective versus objective. I do not claim that the predicate categories of (in)transitivity, aspect, and modality can be reduced to or captured in all of their multifunctionality by concepts like 'insideness' and 'outsideness', or even that such features are what is most basic or characteristic about any one of them. I do believe, however, that the major expressive options available in each category, which is to say semantic differences signaled by regular structural (morphological or syntactic) contrasts, can be understood in terms of an inside perspective that is opposed to an outside perspective. In other words, in addition to their representational and logical functions, these structures have *indexical* functions, which distinguish an *uchi* from a *soto*.

Conditions that produce this indexical effect arise when the meanings of two alternative forms contrast in ways congruent with those opposed in Table 1. Such parallel symbolic contrasts have natural potential for indexical uses. Again, the particulars differ with the category: (in)-transitivity functions are not the functions of modality. But the presence of an *uchi/soto* indexicality across such different grammatical phenomena relates categories and structures that are usually assumed to be unrelated. If such homologies be admitted, they have theoretical import for the nature of linguistic structure (lexico-grammar), since they can only be explained in a world where linguistic form is open to a complex interaction with life—social and individual, physical and psychological. The practice of *uchi/soto* indexing across these categories suggests that structure in language is partly a product of the lived world of human beings, that, in Wittgenstein's words, language is a "form of life."

One of the first questions to consider, then, is how or why grammatical forms might have a representational kind of significance, in addition to their more relational or "logical" significance. The short answer is that, over time, the latter often emerges out of the former; the conceptual side of a grammatical construction or morpheme follows from its origins in a lexical item or combination of lexical items.[11] This idea is perhaps most convincingly argued with the lexical and morphological composition of syntactic constructions in which the concepts represented by the participating morphemes and words can clearly be seen to help determine the meaning of the construction as a whole. Some of the grammatical uses of the word *uchi* examined in chapter 2, such as *ame ga furanai uchi ni kaeroo*, literally, 'Let's go home in the interval during which it doesn't rain' (= 'before it rains'), illustrate this phenomenon rather well. Grammatical constructions like this one are the product of expressing a negative state in time (-*nai*) as an *uchi* 'inside'. For all its productivity, the construction is really just another context in which the word *uchi* contributes a meaning of 'inside'. Representational or symbolic bases of grammatical constructions are clearest when (as in these examples) a collocation constructed of spatial terms is applied in another domain. As Whorf once put it:

We can hardly refer to the simplest nonspatial situation without constant resort to physical metaphors. I "grasp" the "thread" of another's arguments, but if its "level" is "over my head" my attention may "wander" and "lose touch" with the "drift" of it, so that when he "comes" to his "point" we differ "widely," our "views" being indeed so "far apart" that the "things" he says "appear" "much" too arbitrary, or even "a lot" of nonsense. (1956, 146)

If grammatical structure is viewed as one feature of a communicative ecosystem, it seems preferable to assume that, until proven otherwise, structure *is* related to acts of meaning. In an ecological conception of grammar, meaning is a constant factor in grammatical structure over the life of a language community.

The relation between meaning and structure need not be simple and one-to-one to hold true. As physiology and environment are to anatomy, for example, so is communication embodied in social life to linguistic structure. An ecological theory of grammar is *motivated* in that it seeks to explain form by relating it to life—to larger systems that are social and conceptual. "Motivation may best be thought of as 'systemic redundancy'—redundancy as defined by the overall structure of the grammar and conceptual system taken together," writes George Lakoff (1987, 538). Lakoff's point that there are radial structures[12] in the lexicon was noted in chapter 2's survey of expressions based on the terms *uchi* and *soto*. In the aggregate, those examples illustrate how a single concept provides such redundancy when it informs the structuring of a variety of otherwise unrelated domains. Whence such links? The aspects of motivation enumerated by Lakoff emerge from the basic human cognitive proclivity for abduction,[13] whereby, through tropes like metaphor, metonymy, synecdoche, and irony, a term already in use is applied in a new domain. Just as pairs of words like *uchi* and *soto*, *hairu* 'enter' and *deru* 'emerge', *ireru* 'insert' and *dasu* 'take out' can be analogically related in a metapattern of 'inside' versus 'outside', so too might pairs of grammatical form/meaning composites share in a similar metapattern. If such concept-based creativity is not usually thought to affect the grammatical resources of a language, this may be because not enough of us have taken the trouble to look.

If concepts expressed lexically *are* in fact used in creating and re-creating grammatical form, the most likely way for this to happen would be by analogy, whereby social and conceptual habits developed and maintained lexically are put to work in grammatical expression as well. The lexical and grammatical dimensions of Japanese may be indexed against the *uchi/soto* axis by a common, analogically established grounding in the same conceptual values. Since grammatical distinctions often involve different perspectives—temporal, epistemic, and otherwise—on the information that they relate, it seems possible, even likely, that in

Japanese some of these might be indexed in an *uchi/soto* kind of way. If, as John DuBois (1987) and others argue, "Grammars code best what speakers do most," there should be some *uchi/soto* homologies in the grammar of Japanese.

For the purposes of this study, the functions of a grammatical structure will be identified as the relations it enters, when used, with a variety of contexts: *interpersonal* (involving people present to the communicative act as well as others they might refer to), *epistemic* (beliefs and attitudes held about information being communicated), *informational* (assumed versus newly introduced content), and *ideational* (the "what" referred to, representational content, and the internal relations of its component parts).[14] These four contexts provide complementary ways to describe the meanings into which a structure enters.

INDEXING (UN)FAMILIARITY: (NON)CONTROL AND (IN)TRANSITIVITY

Grammatical options that offer an *uchi*- or a *soto*-oriented perspective can be found at the heart of the predicative system, in its verbal, adjectival, and nominal predicates. *Uchi* and *soto* differences are indexed first of all by the language's three varieties of predicators: verbs, adjectives, and /noun + copula/. (The term *predicator* will refer to verbs, adjectives, and /noun + copula/ combinations, and will include whatever derivational suffixes [e.g., passive, causative, negative, *-rashii*, etc.] might attach.) Adjectives (e.g., *atsui* 'is hot') and copular predicators (e.g., *kyooshi da* 'is a teacher') typically express conditions or relations that are not under volitional control, but just "are." The verbal predicator class, on the other hand, is mixed. Some verbs (e.g., *heru* '[something] decreases') represent noncontrolled events, while others express volitionally controlled actions (e.g., *herasu* 'reduce [something]'). With many Japanese verbs, this semantic distinction is expressed in strikingly regular morphological distinctions. Thus the available predicative options distinguish on two major structural levels—word class and verb class—between the expression of (1) situations that are under control or possessed of a source, and (2) those that are not. It is fair to say that the most regular options in Japanese predication divide the world into controllable, typically human acts at one extreme, and noncontrolled, nonhuman situations at the other. For verbs, in fact, the controlled/noncontrolled distinction has a long history in native Japanese philology and linguistics.[15] While the control/noncontrol parameter applies to all types of predicators, even main-verb uses of the 'be' verbs *iru* and *aru*, another parameter comes into play within the subcomponent of the verbal system that distinguishes between transitive and intransitive verbs.

"Transitive" and "intransitive" traditionally refer to contrasting types of verbs, distinguished on the basis of the number of entities (arguments) implicated in the event or act denoted by the verb. For example, a verb like *kau* 'buy' relates a changed argument (undergoer) to a volitionally acting argument (agent) in a social act (*kau*) whereby the former moves into the possession of the latter. Anyone who can use the verb *kau* (or the English verb "buy") knows that these roles, related in this way, define this act. The type of (in)transitivity exemplified by *kau* is one among several. Transitive verbs assume two arguments, typically an agent, or controlling source of the act, and an undergoer; intransitives assume one argument, an undergoer, which is sometimes also a self-determined agent (as in *iku* '[someone] goes'). Transitive and intransitive verbs, then, can be described with reference to (1) the systemwide parameter of the presence or absence of a controlling source, and (2) the (in)transitivity-specific roles of agent and undergoer. Any study of the Japanese verbal system will refer in some manner to these two parameters. Indeed, the analyses of Jacobsen (1982) and Jorden (1987–1990) take such an approach. Jacobsen's parameters are "dynamic" versus "nondynamic," on the one hand, and transitive versus intransitive, on the other. Jorden's are "operational" (volitional) or "affective" (nonvolitional) and transitive or intransitive. These parameters correspond, respectively, to the controlled/noncontrolled and (in)transitivity parameters of the present analysis. For both Jacobsen and Jorden, the really fundamental semantic distinction in the Japanese verbal system is the one of control/noncontrol. Jorden's treatment goes so far as to point out that the operational/affective distinction applies not only to transitive and intransitive verbs but to every predicator type in the language, including stative verbs, adjectives, and /nominal + copula/ combinations. The control feature of this distinction thus applies beyond verbs for acts or events occurring in time, to the major stative verbs, *iru* 'be' (contingent, controlled) and *aru* 'be' (unmarked).[16] The single argument implicated by stative *aru* would be an inert "existant," as in *Nagoya ni aru* '[It]'s in Nagoya', while with *iru* (e.g., *Nagoya ni iru* '[S/he]'s in Nagoya') it is a self-controlled participant in that state. While *aru* cannot be marked for potential with the suffix *-(rar)e* ('can, be able to'), *iru* can,[17] as in *Amari nagaku i-rare-nai* '[I] can't remain long', or *mite i-rare-nakatta* '[I] couldn't stand to watch'. Since stative predicators do not involve an argument undergoing any change, they can be called *a*transitive. The control/noncontrol opposition thus distinguishes the two main stative verbs of Japanese, in addition to verbs expressing acts and events. Not surprisingly, it is with predicators expressing the occurrence of some change that the parameter of control/noncontrol is most highly developed. This distinction is manifested nowhere so fully as in

TABLE 2
Paired Transitive/Intransitive Verbs

dasu 'take/put out X'	*madowaseru* 'confuse X'	*sageru* 'lower X'
deru 'X comes out'	*madou* 'X becomes confused'	*sagaru* 'X lowers'
kawakasu 'dry X'	*chirasu* 'scatter X'	*morasu* 'let X leak'
kawaku 'X dries'	*chiru* 'X scatters'	*moreru* 'X leaks'
nasu 'make/form X'	*utsusu* 'move X'	*toosu* 'let X pass'
naru 'X becomes'	*utsuru* 'X moves'	*tooru* 'X passes through'

the language's many etymologically related pairs of transitive and intransitive verbs.

The paired transitive and intransitive verbs[18] share a single root, for example, *tsubureru* '[something] gets crushed' and *tsubusu* '[someone] crushes [something]'. These verbs have the same root but differ in their derivational morphology. As in the pair *tsubusu/tsubureru*, one member represents a change as a controlled act with a source, while the other member represents the same kind of change as an event that simply "happens." The member of the pair exemplified here by *tsubusu* is transitive, with distinct agent (a "crusher") and undergoer (the item "crushed"), while its partner (e.g., *tsubureru*) is intransitive, with a single argument involved, as undergoer (the entity "crushed"). In the maximally contrastive, prototypical pair—such as *tsubusu/tsubureru*—the transitive member is volitionally controlled, its intransitive partner non-controlled. Both members of the pair assume an argument that undergoes the process signified by the verb's root, but the degree to which that argument is affected by this process will vary from pair to pair. The main difference is that in the transitive instance (e.g., *tsubusu*), the process has its origins in a controlling source that is unaffected by the process, while the intransitive (e.g., *tsubureru*) is unspecified for source. Insofar as it has been manipulated, the transitive undergoer is more affected than the intransitive undergoer. Some additional examples are given in Table 2.

The last three pairs listed in Table 2 are representative of a subclass of transitive/intransitive pairs in which the intransitive member (*naru*, *utsuru*, *tooru*) is also used to refer to volitional acts in which the single argument is at once undergoer and controlling source in that act. In this usage, the entity that 'becomes' something, 'moves' or 'passes through' somewhere does so voluntarily. The fact of such uses precludes a blanket characterization of all paired verbals as transitive-with-controlling-source versus intransitive-without-controlling-source. For the entire corpus of paired verbs, the opposition is most commonly one between a single-argument (intransitive) predicate and a two-argument (transitive) predicate, which *tends* to correlate the feature of having but a single argument (i.e., intransitivity) with less control and the feature of having two arguments (i.e., transitivity) with more control. Again, contrast between two paired verbs is maximal when they differ along both the control and argument parameters.

As argued by Hopper and Thompson (1980), (in)transitivity is primarily a matter of *affectedness*, the degree or "the intensity with which the action is transferred from one participant to another," and for Japanese, as for other languages, it is the presence of a cluster of related features, such as telic aspect,[19] perfective aspect,[20] a thoroughly affected undergoer, and a volitionally acting human source, among others, that makes a predicate prototypically transitive. But as they point out, each feature may not be of equal importance in every language. While control or volition is but one of ten parameters Hopper and Thompson list for indexing an expression's transitivity on a scale from high to low, in Japanese it is a crucial distinction even for the two major stative verbs *aru* and *iru*. In fact, the control/noncontrol parameter has its counterparts elsewhere in the grammar of Japanese, too, as will be seen. For now, the structure of the ideational field represented in the predicators of Japanese can be roughly outlined as in Table 3. The continuum is a simplified adaptation of the (in)transitivity universals of Hopper and Thompson (1980).

If we view (in)transitivity in Japanese as a range within this continuum, the transitivity, intransitivity, or atransitivity (= stativity) of an individual predicator becomes a matter of degree, according to how it matches up against the features listed at either pole. Those verbs that cluster closest to the transitive pole involve two arguments, an agent and an undergoer of change. The quality of being affected makes the undergoer more of an integral participant in the change named by the verb than the unaffected agent. On the extreme right, at the atransitive pole, are stative verbs such as *aru* 'be (unmarked)' and *iru* 'be (contingent)', although since *iru* is often used to express location that is taken up deliberately or temporarily (as in /-te iru/), it would classify over all as less atransitive than *aru*. Other stative predicators align at the right pole, such as adjectives (*atsui* 'is hot') and /noun + copula/ composites (*zasshi da* 'is a magazine').

At the left, maximally transitive pole, we find predicators like *tsubusu* '[someone] crushes [it]' (transitive partner to *tsubureru*), or *sageru* 'lower [something]' (cp. intransitive *sagaru* '[something] comes down'). But just as a few intransitive pair partners are used with a reflexive, volitional undergoer (e.g., *tooru*) so, too, are some transitive partners used to describe events with nonvolitional sources (*ashi o itameru* 'injure one's leg',

TABLE 3
The (In)transitivity Continuum in Japanese

Transitive Pole	Intransitive Zone	Atransitive Pole
+Source		−Source
+Control		−Control
+U(ndergoer)		−U(ndergoer)
+Change in U		−Change in U

←——————————————————————————————————————→

Default Predicator Type:		
(transitive verbs)	(intransitive verbs)	(stative verbs)
		(adjectives)
		(/NP + copula/)

tsui o nasu 'form a pair'). In both these cases, however, the undergoer is part of or identical with the implicit "agent" (the owner of the leg and the members of the pair), which makes them less typically transitive. Specifying different contexts by, for example, using *dasu* with *jishin* 'earthquake' as its controlling "agent" reduces the transitivity of that predicate (*jishin wa shishoosha o takusan dashita* 'the earthquake produced many dead and injured'). The "inherent" (in)transitivity a verb is said to possess is thus the default context(s) of use we assume for it. Through all this adaptability, however, the general tendency holds: for transitive members of transitive/intransitive pairs, volitional contexts are the norm, and nonvolitional contexts are marked, or off-norm.

Even in those few pairs where both verbs are restricted to volitional contexts, such as *doku* 'get (oneself) out of the way' (transitive partner *dokeru* 'get [something] out of the way'), *utsumuku* 'face down' (transitive partner *utsumukeru* 'put [something] face down'), or *hagemu* 'strive' (transitive partner *hagemasu* 'encourage'), a reflexive change is opposed to a change imposed on another. The paired verbs still differ along the control parameter, but the scope of control is greater for the second member of each pair. A similar reflexivity also characterizes the less transitive member of pairs of transitive verbs that describe putting on clothes, as Jacobsen (1982) has observed. One member of these pairs refers to the reflexive act of putting something on oneself (e.g., *kiru* 'put on [the trunk of the body]', *kaburu* 'put on [the head]'), while the more transitive partner is used in referring to putting things on others (*kiseru* 'put on [someone else's] body', *kabuseru* 'put on [someone else's head]'). Even in off-norm pairs in which the less transitive member describes an act that is always under volitional control, the more transitive member invariably denotes an act that involves the exercise of greater control, insofar as it involves bringing about the same change in or on a participant other than the agent.

The paired verbs are therefore best and most generally described not in traditional transitive/intransitive terms as one-argument/two argument pairs but as pairs of verbs representing higher-control versus lower-control change. Both members of the paired sets will typically have an undergoer in which some change occurs. In maximally differentiated pairs, like *tubusu/tubureru*, the transitive partner, with its distinct agent, undergoer and imposed change, offers greater phenomenological detail in its ideational representation of the world. The intransitive partner, with its single, typically passive undergoer of uncaused change, is a less detailed rendering of experience. Finally, atransitive predicates constructed of stative verbs (which denote no change), are the "still life" of verbal predication—the least phenomenally detailed of all.

There can be little doubt that the transitive-to-intransitive subrange within Table 3's larger transitive-to-atransitive field is the most heavily populated region in the land of Japanese verbs; stative verbs are by comparison very few. The most highly structured set of verbs, the transitive/intransitive pairs of Table 2, can be thought of as occupying the center of that transitive-intransitive subrange. What differentiates them so regularly is most often the degree of control involved. If this difference is placed against the list of conceptual oppositions found in the various contexts in which the words *uchi* and *soto* are used (reported in chapter 2 and repeated as Table 1 above), some interesting parallels are apparent. The transitive prototype, in which process and change come about under identifiable, deliberate control, amounts, in Japanese folk taxonomy, to an *uchi* kind of concept cluster. And in the same idiom, the most typical intransitive paired verb, for which the same phenomena (processes of change) are construed as *out* of human control and *lacking* identifiable sources, may be said to describe change in a *soto* kind of world.

This is the first step of our argument: that the lexical pairing of transitive and intransitive verbs in Japanese is another instance in which two complementary perspectives on an otherwise similar situation are grammatically distinguished: (1) an act controlled by its source, which in the prototypical case produces change in some entity other than that source, and (2) an event in which change occurs, but for which, in the prototypical case, source and control are irrelevant. In every pair, even the most peripheral, the minimal distinction is between more and less control. Furthermore, acts undertaken volitionally are logically and phenomenologically more complex than events that just happen; they represent the nearer and more knowable side of experience. They are the building blocks of an *uchi* kind of world. A world in which things simply happen, on the other hand, is a world to which we must occasion-ally resign ourselves, with expressions like the atransitive, stative *shikata ga nai* 'there's nothing to be done', literally, that a controlled way to act (*shi* 'doing' + *kata* 'way, manner') 'does not exist' (*nai*). This is the grammar of a world 'out there', in which control is lacking, the grammar of *soto*.

If "grammars code best what speakers do most," it seems likely that congruent semantic distinctions might be expressed elsewhere in the grammar of Japanese. Might not related verbal categories, such as as-pect (the temporal contour of a state or event) or epistemic modality (belief, (un)certainty, etc.), reveal a similar conceptual distinction in the patterning of their use? We will look at these categories after further exploring the ins and outs of (in)transitivity.

PROSTHETIC (IN)TRANSITIVITY: "VOICE" OR "VALENCY" CONVERTERS

As the *iru/aru* pair of stative verbs shows, an *uchi/soto* kind of ideational opposition is not limited to transitive/intransitive pairs of etymologi-cally related verbs. In fact, the same perspectival distinction distin-guishes two contrastive verbal suffixes usually referred to as "causative" (*-(s)aseru*) and "passive" (*-(r)areru*).[21] These will here be called *causative* and *middle*, since the Japanese passive is better understood as a contex-tual variant of what is basically a middle voice—a representation of a change as sourceless and noncontrolled. These two suffixes can, among other things, convert a lexical verb of the opposite (in)transitivity to ei-ther a typically transitive (volitionally caused) or intransitive (noncon-trolled, sourceless) representation. For example, intransitive, nonvoli-tional *tsubure-ru* 'be crushed' is converted into a transitive by suffixing the causative *-(s)aseru*, yielding *tsubure-saseru* '[someone] causes [some-thing] to be crushed'. The prosthetic *-(s)aseru* restructures the predi-cate so that an agent role is added, a causer of the 'crushing' that affects the undergoer. This prosthetic (or, more commonly, "derived") *tsubure-saseru* suggests a causation that is less direct—perhaps from a distance and instrumentally mediated—than lexical *tsubus-u* '[someone] crushes [something]'. The basic transitive *tsubus-u* is the normal, unmarked way to express a caused crushing; the transitive derived with *-(s)aseru* ex-presses a marked, off-norm variant of the same type of change.

Conversely, transitive, volitional *tsubus-u* 'crush [something]' can be converted to intransitive *tsubus-areru* 'be crushed' with middle suffix *-(r)areru*. This derived intransitive expresses a situation in which the sub-ject is no longer the controlling agent of *tsubus-u* but instead the non-controlling undergoer of a 'causing to be crushed'. While the transitive base (*tsubus-*) in *tsubus-areru* 'be crushed' implies the presence of an agent, there is no such implication with the lexical intransitive *tsubure-ru* 'be crushed'.

While the causative derivation adds the participatory role of a volitional agent to a predicate, the middle voice derivation shunts the causing agent aside and re-presents an erstwhile act as an *event*, that is, centered on a single undergoer that lacks control. In other words, while the role of an external agent is added to the predicator with the *-(s)aseru* derivation, the *-(r)areru* derivation refocuses the predicate so that its agent role is effaced and the undergoer becomes the main, focal argument. In *kuruma wa tsubus-are-ta* 'the car was crushed', for example, the 'car' that undergoes 'crushing' is the main argument in focus; the crushing agent, while tacitly present in the transitive base *tsubus-*, is effaced. If expressed, it is indicated obliquely, as source, with *ni* 'in/at': *kuruma wa sensha ni tsubus-are-ta* 'the car was crushed by a tank'.

It is also possible, with the middle derivation, to create a second, indirect undergoer, external to the event itself. Thus *Suzuki-san wa, kuruma o tsubus-are-ta* 'Suzuki underwent/suffered the crushing of (his) car' or *Suzuki-san ga kuruma o tsubus-are-ta* 'It was *Suzuki* who underwent/suffered the crushing of (his) car'. Suzuki is affected by the crushing but not so directly as his car is; in English we might say 'Suzuki had his car crushed' or 'It was Suzuki who had his car crushed'. In this case, the primary undergoer *kuruma* 'car' is marked as it would be marked in a normal transitive predicate, with accusative particle *o*, and the secondary undergoer (the adversely affected *Suzuki-san*) is marked like the subject of a normal intransitive predicate. When, as in the last example, the primary (direct) and secondary (indirect) undergoer are distinct, the interpretation is invariably that the secondary undergoer is adversely affected by what happens to the primary undergoer. This indication of involvement in an event outside one's control is the point of such derivations. The most common secondary undergoer in actual discourse is probably the speaker, who usually goes unmentioned, as in *kuruma o tsubus-are-ta* '[I] underwent/suffered the crushing of [my] car'. Thus might the so-called adversative or suffering passive of Japanese be characterized as an "out-of-control" passive with a wider-than-usual scope: one undergoer (e.g., the 'car') directly undergoes change and the other (e.g., the speaker) is indirectly affected by that change, which for him is a noncontrolled event.

While derived transitivity and intransitivity are more marked—semantically more complex and pragmatically more specialized—than their lexical cousins, the causative and middle suffixes contrast and complement each other in ways similar to the paired verbs. In other words, the contrast of change that involves greater control with change that involves less control finds highly patterned expression not only in pairs of transitive/intransitive verbs but also in this pair of derivational suffixes (-(s)ase-ru and -(r)are-ru), which restructure a verb's perspective on the situation to which it refers. Much has been written about the causative and middle derivations and their various uses, but for the purposes of this argument it is enough to note the conceptual parallels with the pairs of transitive and intransitive verbs. Both the paired verbs and the paired suffixes, as representatives of prototypical transitivity and intransitivity in Japanese, serve an ideational function that distinguishes between an *uchi* perspective and a *soto* perspective: controlled situations, with known sources and caused effects, versus uncontrolled changes for which the source is nonexistent, unknown, irrelevant or, at best, offstage. The grammar of controlled/transitive acts and uncontrolled/intransitive events also serves to index an *uchi/soto* distinction in the social domain, but before that, let us examine one more epistemological index of controlled 'insides' and less controlled 'outsides'.

ASPECT: TWO KINDS OF PERFECT

Aspect[22] refers to the temporal contour of a predicate's ideational representation of a situation.[23] A particular temporal contour may be associated with an individual lexical predicator (a verb, an adjective, or /nominal + copula/) and such arguments as are assumed or specified for it. For verbs, aspect can be expressed inflectionally (e.g., -(r)u for imperfective; perfective -ta for realization) or in a way that involves both derivation and syntax. With Japanese verbs, the basic aspectual markings are imperfective -u ("unrealized"), perfective -ta ("realized"), /-te + iru/, which is interpreted as progressive (action underway) or *perfect* (a state in effect), depending on factors such as the aspect of the verb-plus-arguments complex it subsumes, and other features of the represented situation. Another perfect, limited to verbs expressing controlled acts, is formed with /-te aru/. Unlike most verbal predicates, the temporal contours of individual Japanese adjectival and nominal predicates are stative ("the way things are"); verbal predicates for the most part represent some change in time, whether it comes as a controlled act or a noncontrolled event (stative verbs excepted).[24] As an expression of a state that results from change, the Japanese perfect is limited to verbal predicators that denote change; it would be redundant with stative verbs, adjectival, and nominal predicators, since these in themselves do not refer to change.

In Japanese, the perfect expresses a state that results from an act or an event, and like acts and events expressed by the paired transitive/intransitive verbs, or the causative and middle conversions, the perfect, too, comes in controlled and noncontrolled varieties. Perfects that result from controlled, mostly transitively expressed acts differ in form from those that result from noncontrolled, mostly intransitively expressed events. What we can call the controlled perfect is formed by adding *aru* 'be' after the gerund or "*-te* form" (a perfective infinitive) of a verb used to refer to a volitionally controlled act. This perfect is functionally complemented by a noncontrolled perfect, which is formed with the gerund (perfective infinitive) of the verb used to refer to a noncontrolled event; this gerund is followed by *iru* 'be' (contingent).

For example, *doa ga akete aru* 'a door is/has been opened' is based on controlled *doa o akeru* '[someone] opens a door', while *doa ga aite iru* 'a door is open' is based on noncontrolled *doa ga aku* 'a door opens'. Each perfect results from either a volitional act (*aketa* '[someone] opened [it]') or a sourceless event (*aita* '[it] opened'). Aspectual adjustments like these perfects *adapt* the temporal contour of a lexical predicator with its arguments, and provide a way to restate, for example, an event (e.g., *kawat-ta* '[it] changed') as a state (*kawat-te iru* '[it] is changed/different'), or an act (*ire-ta* '[someone] inserted [it]') as a state (*ire-te aru* '[it] is/has been inserted'). In this last example, the point of view typically shifts to that of the undergoer, the item 'inserted', consistent with the reduced control that usually follows when an act produces a state.

While the controlled perfect with *aru* is based most often on transitive verbs, and the noncontrolled perfect with *iru* is most common with intransitive verbs, this is because volitionally controlled acts are most typically represented as transitive verbs, just as noncontrolled events are primarily expressed by intransitive verbs. A few intransitive verbs are used in the *-te aru* perfect, but all of them represent *volitional* acts, as in *juubun ne-te aru* '[I]'ve got enough sleep'. The distinguishing parameter for the two perfects is volitional control (or its lack), not the number of arguments.

Within the *aru* perfect (e.g., *tsubushi-te aru* '[it] has been crushed'), different degrees of control can be indicated, depending on which grammatical relation the undergoer—the 'crushed', in this case—is marked for. When the undergoer is marked with *ga* (*akikan ga tsubushi-te aru* 'the empty cans are crushed'), the stative whole governed by *aru* is attributed to it, and the predicate is staged from the undergoer's point of view. If, on the other hand, it is marked with *o* (*akikan o tsubushi-te aru* '[I] have the empty cans crushed'), the 'crusher' remains engaged in the state her act has produced, and the predicate's point of view is not surrendered to the undergoer. Both versions, however, retain the mark of caused origins in the transitive gerund *tsubushi-te*.

Controlled, *-te aru* perfects are used in a variety of contexts, to a variety of ends, but all of them are tinged with the controlling agency of the underlying volitional verb, such that the state described is understood to have been *put* that way by *somebody*. This perfect is employed to describe things that have been purposely put in a state of readiness, such as doors being opened at a hall (*akete aru*) or outside lights being turned on in anticipation of a guest's arrival (*tsukete aru*), among other uses. In sum, the *-te aru* perfect expresses a condition that is the product of an intended, controlled act. That condition is, not surprisingly, often goal-oriented and, being contingent on an external, volitional source, is more open to sustained control (indexed by an *o*-marked undergoer) and implicitly less objectlike than conditions that result from noncontrolled events. Prototypically transitive *-te aru* perfects express conditions that are a rather *uchi* kind of state to be in, while prototypically intransitive *-te iru* perfects are simply states that have "come about."

Variation on the periphery is consistent. While *-te aru* perfects are limited to volitional, mostly transitive verbs, and *-te iru* perfects are mostly the province of intransitive verbs, "hybrid" transitive perfects in *-te iru* do occur, such as *te o poketto ni irete iru* '[S/he] has [her] hands in [her] pockets' (controlled, transitive *ireru* 'insert'). There are also intransitive perfects in *-te iru* which express states that result from volitional acts, such as *Nihon ni itte iru* '[S/he]'s gone to/is in Japan'. A consequence of the reflexivity in perfects like *te o poketto ni irete iru* and *Nihon ni itte iru* is that, since the agent is one with the undergoer, s/he remains in direct control of the state. Such *controlled* intransitive perfects contrast with *non*controlled intransitives like *te wa poketto ni haitte iru* 'The hands are in the pockets' (based on noncontrolled, intransitive *hairu* 'go/fit into').[25] This clause might describe a doll or a painting of someone,[26] in which the hands are not under control, but is an oddly static way to describe a live person holding her hands in her pockets. Control is of course also present in *te o poketto ni irete aru* '[I] have [my] hands in [my] pockets', which might be said on having concealed one's hands for some anticipated trouble. When the verb refers to a controlled act, the *-te aru* perfect is more likely, especially if the resultant state prepares one for something. Transitive perfects like *te o poketto ni irete iru* share with their more common *-te aru* counterparts (and intransitive perfects like *Nihon ni itte iru*) an element of volitional control, which is missing in the perfects of prototypically intransitive verbs, such as *tsuburete iru* 'is crushed'.

Even allowing for borderline hybrid cases, then, *-te aru* perfects refer to the results of controlled acts, with identifiable, agentive sources, whether the verb is transitive or intransitive. And perfects based on verbs used to refer to noncontrolled, agentless events, with no specifiable source, use only *-te iru*. The distinction expresses the same conceptual contrast that motivates other major categorical structurings of the Japanese verb: transitive/intransitive paired verbs like *tsubusu/tsubureru*, less/more transitive "clothing" pairs (*kiru* 'put on [oneself]' versus *kiseru* 'put on [another]'), and the paired (in)transitivity converters, causative suffix *-(s)aseru* and middle *-(r)areru*. Also, as mentioned earlier, the two primary stative verbs of the language, *iru* 'be (contingent)' and un-marked *aru* 'be', regularly contrast in regard to volitional control when used as main verbs. Incidentally, in earlier Japanese, the perfective (today expressed with *-ta*) also distinguished between realization caused by a controlling source (inflecting suffix *-tsu*) and a sourceless, "middle" kind of realization (inflecting suffix *-nu*).[27] In the predication of Japa-nese, then, volitionally controlled acts and sourceless events are regu-larly opposed to each other in lexical structures (paired transitive/in-transitive verbs), derivational structures (paired suffixal (in)transitivity converters), and syntactic combinations (the two perfects). The index-ing of this semantic difference remains relatively constant across all three kinds of structure, and is a basic function of the grammatical cate-gories of (in)transitivity and aspect in Japanese.

To sum up, this regular and highly patterned distinguishing of con-trolled situations with a volitionally acting source from noncontrolled, sourceless situations is conceptually congruent with distinctions drawn by many lexical expressions based on the words *uchi* and *soto*. Con-trolled, volitional, agent-instigated or maintained acts and states belong to the world of the familiar and the human, where agency is an issue and is knowable: the world of *uchi*. The two-argument transitive verb, with its distinct agent and undergoer, is a tool well adapted to expressing the kind of phenomenal detail that we access in nearby and familiar sur-roundings. Uncontrolled, nonvolitional, sourceless events and states, on the other hand, constitute a world "out there," *soto*, and the lexical, deri-vational and syntactic tools for expressing such events typically present no more than bare outlines, which do not bother with sources or causes. We might compare this difference in detailing to the difference between a frontal view of a moving object in broad daylight and the same glimpsed in black-and-white silhouette. In the expressive resources of the Japa-nese verbal system, then, construing, representing, and communicating the world ideationally tends, more or less, to index two complementary perspectives on experience, which can be coherently characterized as either *uchi* or *soto* in orientation. The *uchi/soto* indexing in Japanese (in)transitivity and aspect suggests that indeed "grammars code best what speakers do most."

(IN)TRANSITIVITY AS SOCIAL INDEX: IDEATIONAL AS INTERPERSONAL

Patricia J. Wetzel (1984, this volume) has discussed the expression of social indexing in a class of donatory verbs that distinguish whether the giver and the receiver share the same social 'inside' or stand 'outside' each other. This kind of social indexing is more generally (not just in giving and receiving) accomplished by using one or the other of the language's (in)transitivity types, for their distinction of acts from events. One major type of deferential indexing of a human referent by a speaker in Japanese ("honorific" in Jorden 1987–1990)[28] is regularly expressed with noncontrolled, intransitive forms. Another, contrasting type of deference ("humble" in Jorden 1987–1990) is expressed with controlled, transitive forms. These uses of intransitive and transitive grammar remind us that in Japanese, social indexing is ideational, part of the world-as-represented. As a medium for the expression of social indexing, the (in)transitivity structures we shall review here constitute yet another instance in which social and conceptual habits—in this case, *uchi/soto*—interface with grammatical categories.

Honorifically deferential verbal complexes like *o-dashi ni naru* 'put/ take [it] out (subject exalted)' or *das-are-ru* 'id.' are intransitive conversions of transitive verbs, in this case, plain[29] *dasu* 'put/take out'. *O-dashi ni naru* is derived by prefixing a polite *o-* to the plain verb's infinitive ("INF"), *dashi*, and then marking this *o-dashi* with particle *ni* as the goal of *naru* 'become': /*o*-INF *ni naru*/. If this sounds roundabout, it is; the deferential construction thereby produced means, literally, 'honored putting/taking out comes about'. Such an expression is less direct—we might say "less knowing"—than *dasu* '[someone] puts/takes [it] out' because its outermost structure (*ni naru*) does not include a place for an agent of the act. Indirection or avoidance is a major strategy in many languages for expressing a deference that exalts the referent.

The conversion of the verb *dasu* to the complex *o-dashi ni naru* constitutes an externally intransitive staging of a transitive act; the periphrastic restructuring of the predicator effaces the notion of agency, in a gesture of avoidance. It is a partially intransitive staging because the undergoer retains its marker *o* (typical in controlled predicates), instead of being marked with *ga*, which would create a thorough conversion to noncontrolled form. Consequently, in the sentence *tegami o o-dashi ni narimasu* '[someone exalted] will put out (= send) a letter', the undergoer *tegami* is marked as it would be if the verb were controlled, transitive *dasu*, despite the embedding of this act as goal in the intransitive syntax of /goal + *ni* + *naru*/. Using the agentless frame of such honorific conversions constitutes a rhetorical move of the sort Erving Goffman characterized as "avoidance ritual," "those forms of deference which lead the actor to keep at a distance from the recipient (of the deference, CJQ) and not violate . . . 'the ideal sphere' that lies around the recipient" (1956, 481).[30]

The same kind of deference is also expressed by the middle suffix *-(r)areru*. As noted earlier, *-(r)areru* reframes a controlled verb as a noncontrolled intransitive, an event structure that is not oriented from the point of view of its agent. Thus, *das-areru* 'putting/taking out happens' (from controlled, transitive *dasu* 'put/take out') expresses deference toward the agent by the same metaphor that motivates *o-dashi ni naru* '[polite] putting/taking out comes about'. Whether the conversion is syntactic in form or derivational, deference is expressed by applying an outer frame associated with unknown or no agency.

Effacing agency from the ideational frame is what we might call a grammatical "figure," and does not mean there is no agent. It is also rather different from simply not mentioning the agent. Agents, even those deferred to, can be mentioned, as in *Kore wa goshujin ga o-dashi ni natta n desu yo* 'This *your husband* put out (= contributed), you know'. While the verb in this sentence wears the raiments of noncontrol, its agent is not only mentioned but singled out, as *goshujin* '[honored/out-group's] husband'. The point of the mention of *goshujin* and its marking with particle *ga* is to identify the 'contributor'; *o-dashi ni natta* 'has written' is thereby attributed to him. Such identification of an agent is motivated by *informational* constraints, which arise in discourse, and are functionally distinct from the ideational world of acts, events, states, and participants. Since the honored referent is the would-be agent in the ideational frame, it is removal of this *role* that is suggested by the outer framing of the predicator with a form associated with no agency or no known agent. To use such a predicate is, in Durkheim's (1953) phrase, to express deference by means of a "negative" rite of avoidance.[31]

The other kind of deference expressed in today's Japanese, humble deference, employs the converse of the honorific avoidance strategem. Humble deference is routinely expressed by a kind of *transitive* conversion, which focuses on agency instead of effacing it. As in the honorific conversion with *naru*, the infinitive of the plain verb is prefixed with polite *o-*, so that for *dasu* 'put/take out', infinitive *dashi* becomes polite *o-dashi*. This polite noun is predicated with the verb *suru* 'do, perform, cause to happen', yielding *o-dashi suru* 'perform putting/taking out [for out-group]'. In contrast to honorific /*o*-INF *ni naru*/, where the outer frame's predicating verb is *naru* 'come about, become' (a prototypical intransitive), humble /*o*-INF *suru*/ is predicated with *suru* 'do, perform, cause to happen', a verb that is paired contrastively with *naru* in a variety of other expressions that contrast acts with events (e.g., /—*koto ni suru*/ '[someone] decides to—' versus /—*koto ni naru*/ '[it] comes about that—'). Neither the honorific /*o*-INF *ni naru*/ nor the humble /*o*-INF *suru*/ conversion occurs with all verbs. In the humble case, for example, the operation involves a volitionally controlled verb.

If the ideational frame imposed with /*o*-INF *ni naru*/ effaces the notion of agency and is thus deferential by avoidance, then humble /*o*-INF *suru*/ expresses its deference in a form that is precisely the converse, by saying *suru* 'perform/cause to happen' of a volitional infinitive marked for politeness. Expression of the control indicates that the polite act (*o-*INF) is willingly undertaken (*suru*). In that it "regularly implies a definite involvement of the referent (= the beneficiary), representing activities that are performed by the speaker *for* that person" (Jorden 1987–1990, 1:177), this conversion expresses the deference Durkheim called "positive." Goffman described such deferential behavior as "presentational ritual," an act "through which the individual makes specific attestations to recipients concerning how he regards them and how he will treat them in the on-coming interaction. . . . presentational rituals specify what is to be done" (1956, 485).

While an expression of volitional control is quite to the point in humble deference, mere mention or nonmention of the agent is not at issue here, either. *Watashi ga*, in *watashi ga o-kaki shimasu* '*I*'ll write it [for out-group]' serves to identify the agent of the 'writing'. But again, the agent would be mentioned in this way for informational reasons, which have to do with communicative needs at a specific point in a discourse. The polite *o*-infinitive of a volitional verb, plus the use of *suru* in the sense of 'perform, do', creates a predicate that focuses on a controlled act directed outward from the *uchi* to *soto*, and not on the individual identity of the agent.

In this way, structures associated with the notion of a controlling agent (or its lack) are put to work in the expression of social indexing. The key parameter is a controlling source. Referents deferred to and those deferring can be one person or several; what matters is *position* with regard to a boundary. Deference is paid by the speaker's side, or speaker's *uchi*, to the speaker's *soto*, in two ways. Honorific deference is expressed with an intransitive figure, an ideational frame lacking in agency, which is elsewhere used to express events in the natural world, where causes of things are often beyond our ken and control. Acts of the nonspeaker, *soto* side, however volitional they actually are, are reframed from the speaker's *uchi* as agentless events. Humble deference takes the opposite strategy, and employs an ideational frame that expresses the act taken with respect to the outside as polite and performed willingly.

Thus agency is alternatively played down or played up, depending on which side of the speaker's boundary—her own (*uchi*) or the other's (*soto*)—the control of the act is located. The values and attitudes implicit in the two frames—intransitive, noncontrolled *naru* or the volitional infinitive plus transitive, controlled *suru*—align with *uchi/soto* oppositions already pointed out, namely, a less controlled, less familiar, detached, and observed world versus a more controlled, more familiar, engaged, and experienced one. The *structures* of these deferential conversions were apparently adopted for their semantic association with *uchi/soto* distinctions perceived and practiced in social life. In the expression of deference, grammar is put to work symbolically:[32] agency-effacing structure when referring to acts taken by people on the *soto* side, and agency-focusing structure when actions are offered by *uchi* people to *soto* people. Either way, the boundary is inside/outside.

INDEXING EPISTEMOLOGY IN THE NOMINALIZATION OF CLAUSES

The "knownness" of what a nominalized clause expresses is regularly indexed by a pair of contrastive morphemes, *no* and *koto*. A chapter in Kuno, for example, described the difference in terms of "concrete events" versus "abstract concepts" (1973, 221).[33] A subsequent study by Lewis Josephs (1976) characterized the difference as "direct" versus "indirect" semantic marking, and an article by Noriko Akatsuka explained the distinction by relating it to a larger one of "Ego" versus "nonEgo" (1978, 203). Taken together, these analyses differentiate *no*-clauses from *koto*-clauses in terms of concepts that amount to a rather *uchi/soto* kind of opposition, as we have characterized it: experienced, direct, proximate, concrete information (*no*), on the one hand, opposed to unexperienced (hearsay, effects observed), indirect, removed, abstracted information (*koto*), on the other. The difference is clear in examples like these, from Kuno (1973, 213; some glosses changed):

1. Otooto   o   butsu NO o   kono me de   mita.
   younger brother ACC hit   fact ACC these eyes INST saw
   'I saw him hit my little brother with my own eyes.'
2. Nihongo ga muzukashii KOTO o   mananda.
   Japanese ID is difficult   fact   ACC learned
   'I found out that Japanese is difficult.'

Akatsuka's insight is that "where the speaker's own mental state is at issue, *no* seems to be much more natural than *koto*. Also, *koto* seems to become much more natural when an internal feeling of somebody other than the speaker is at issue" (1978, 189–90).

   While clausal complements nominalized with *no* comprise established, familiar information from a particular discourse, clauses nominalized with *koto* can be considered names of categories in the generic world of what might be called *possible* discourse. Clauses nominalized with *no* express information that has a place in someone's particular world—knowledge that has been, so to speak, handled, and is accessible by simply pointing. *No*-type facts are facts that, for the speaker at a particular nexus in a particular discourse with a particular audience, are assumed to be *referable*. This means information that is "there," established already, in the realm of the familiar, things that are known to have happened, been decided on, talked about, and so forth. Referable information does not include, for example, unsupported, timeless statements of identity, like *Kujira wa hoonyuu-doobutsu de aru NO 'that whales are mammals' (Kuno 1973, 221–22).[34] On the other hand, if this same copular proposition of identity (Kujira wa hoonyuu-doobutsu de aru) is embedded under the "quotative" complementizer to and governed by the verb iu 'say', a referable fact is created and no is quite natural, as illustrated in Kujira wa hoonyuu-doobutsu de aru to iu NO wa 'that it's said that whales are mammals'. It seems to me that, in short, no is an indexically grounded deictic nominalizer, which both marks information and points to it as already established and given in the discourse under construction. While statements of definition, such as 'is a mammal', do not qualify, saying or claiming something about an identity relation is readily indexible.[35]

Nominalization of a clause with koto, on the other hand, makes the ideational picture that the clause paints into a category name, a common noun. Koto-facts are types, not particular tokens. Koto presupposes nothing other than that the clause modifying it describes a kind of situation, which is thereby referred to as such. The nominal phrase produced by koto is a nonce nominal, created on the spot, and entails no indexicality. This is not to say that koto cannot be used with information known by the speaker to be established fact but rather that it does not mark that information as such. While koto creates a generic type, then, no tends to the specific and familiar, even in the quasi-generic Sushi o taberu NO ga suki da '[I] like eating sushi'. What one "senses" or "realizes" (in Kuno's and Akatsuka's terms) is familiar information, and people will therefore usually mark it with no (e.g., the objects of verbs of perception, like miru 'see', or Akatsuka's verbs of internalized knowledge). Information that is describable but not the known product of a familiar discourse, such as doubted information and statements that establish identity ('the whale is a mammal'), information removed from one's own experience, or knowledge just acquired (oishii koto! '[How] delicious!' or information appropriated from without in activities like manabu 'learn') will usually be marked with koto.

The accessible quality in information that is indexically referable supports a characterization of no complements as pointing to information familiar not just to the speaker but to the speaker-with-the-hearer. The world of no factuality is uchi: information that is personally familiar, established in particular, accessible discourses. In contrast to such evidentially proximate information, information that is still unfamiliar, or recently received, say, by channels other than the speaking subject's senses, is more likely to be classed as type, not token, with nominalizer koto. Koto facts are new, recently unfamiliar, and less established, that is,

epistemically more *outside. No* and *koto* serve similar information-distin-
guishing functions with similar *uchi/soto* epistemic nuances in other
contexts, too, which unfortunately cannot be examined here. Ray (1989)
provides a broader survey.

LOCATIVE FIGURES: THE EPISTEMOLOGY OF
PLACING INFORMATION 'IN' AND 'WITH'

The term *localist(ic)* refers to "the hypothesis that spatial (more specifically, "locative") expressions are more basic, grammatically and semantically, than various kinds of nonspatial expressions" (Lyons 1977, 2:718;
cf. Anderson 1971, 1973; Jackendoff 1983, 188–211). This is so, it has
been argued, because spatial expressions show the greatest degree of
extension to other domains, and because of the centrality of spatial imagery in human cognition (cf. Miller and Johnson-Laird 1976, 375). The
point has been made, for example, that "nearly every preposition or particle that is locative in English is also temporal," and "those prepositions
that have both spatial and temporal use developed the temporal meaning later in all instances" (Traugott 1975). With regard to aspect, there
are expressions like "be IN a state of bliss," "be ON cloud nine," or even
the progressive "be working" (presumably derived from "be AT working"; cf. "is a' workin' " [Lyons 1977, 2:719]). As Lyons has noted, "There
are many languages in which the aspectual notions of progressivity or
stativity (and more especially, contingent stativity) are expressed by
means of constructions that are patently locative in origin" (Lyons 1977,
2:719; cf. Anderson 1973; Comrie 1976).

In Japanese, not only has the copula *d(e)a(ru)* apparently evolved from
a locative expression but the language has throughout its history utilized a pair of epistemically contrastive copular expressions, which were
extensions of, I believe, contrastive locative constructions. These copular expressions are made, respectively, with particles *ni* 'in/at' and *to*
'with, in the company of'. *Ni* and *to*, moreover, show the same epistemic
contrast in a considerable variety of other contexts of use, too, although
not every use of *ni* contrasts with some use of *to*. The perspectives
indexed by *ni* and *to* differ as the consequence of their meaning as
symbols, specifically placing a referent 'in/at' (*ni*) or 'with' (*to*) some
other information. While limitations of space prevent presentation of
a full argument for this idea, I would like to outline it briefly, for consideration as another instance of *uchi/soto* indexing of knowledge in
grammar.[36]

Just as the many uses of *ni* (e.g., location, goal, source, manner, copular) can be seen to cluster around a basic context that is locative in the
sense of 'in/at' a static, unmoving place, the uses of *to* (e.g., accompaniment, manner, quotation, conditional, copular) can be understood as

related to a central meaning of accompaniment. With *ni*, one entity ("Y") or process is related to another ("X") by occupying its locus, whether that is construed temporarily, permanently, previously, or at some future time—the possibilities are limited only by context. If Y is located 'in/at' X, it is likely to share the same outer boundary with X. If Y is related to X in a relation mediated by *to*, however, Y does not co-occupy an identical locus but rather takes a position alongside, that is, *outside* X. The consequences of this simple difference are perhaps clearest in the copular uses of each particle, discussed briefly below. Like other oppositions that contrast in an *uchi/soto* way, *ni/to* opposition is not limited to the spatial; it has figured in structuring more abstract domains, too, notably copular predication.

EARLIER COPULAR COMPLEMENTS WITH *NI* AND *TO*

At an earlier stage of the language's history and in certain written registers today, complements of the unmarked 'be' verb (*ari* = present-day *aru*) were linked to it with *ni* and *to*, to produce alternative expressions, which inflected for the most part as the verb *ari* did. The paradigm for each is conventionally represented by the unmarked indicative forms *n(i)ari* and *t(o)ari*. *N(i)ari* is the ancestor of today's unmarked copula *d(e)a(ru)* (< *nde aru* < *ni te aru*), as well as of the *na* with which adjectival nouns link to their head noun, as in *shizuka na heya* 'a quiet room' (earlier *shizuka naru heya*). Parentheses here enclose vowels that surfaced when the expression was decontracted into its component parts of /particle + *ari*/, to meet metric demands of verse, or to mark the *ni* or *to* complement for focus: *X nari* 'is (an) X' might be clefted with identifying particle *zo* into *X ni zo aru* 'is an X [is what it is]'. The contracted *tari* is not attested in the earliest texts and was limited to the function of ascribing some observable quality to a referent, but like *n(i)ari*, it is also uncontracted when the *to*-marked complement is in focus as, for example, in *X to mo aran mono* 'a person even of the stature of X', an idiom still current.

The difference between placing a copular complement with *ni* and placing it with *to* amounts to a distinction between identification and characterization.

1a. kimi N(I)aru hito[37]
    'a person who is a lord'
1b. kimi T(O)aru hito
    'a lordly/lordlike person'

While (1a) identifies the unmentioned referent as 'a person' who actually *is* a 'lord', (1b) locates the referent approximately, in terms of accidents. If the *ni*-based copula is interpreted localistically, as placing a referent 'in' or 'at' the category *kimi*, and the *to*-based copula as placing him 'with' that category, the received interpretations seem to follow naturally enough. The distinction these alternative copular expressions draw certainly has an *uchi/soto* flavor: *n(i)ari*'s familiar "things as they are" identification versus *t(o)ari*'s brand of less certain, accidental "things as they seem to be" approximation.

Samuel Martin has referred to these two copular devices of earlier Japanese as the "objective copula" (*n(i)ari*) and the "subjective copula" (*t(o)ari*), and explains that whereas *n(i)ari* means " 'it is,' " *t(o)ari* means " 'it is seen/heard/thought/felt/said to be (or: as)' " (1975, 754).[38] Martin's glosses are consistent with the localistic interpretation of *ni* and *to*, including the idea that *to* expresses the *approximation* of an identification.

Yamada Yoshio (1922, 115) ascribed the different nuances of *n(i)ari* and *t(o)ari* to the particles *ni* and *to* in each. He says that while the former asserts (*dantei*) that something is 'internally' (*naimenteki*) so, the latter expresses a quality that is 'externally apparent' (*gaibooteki*). But how or why do *ni* and *to*, when combined with *ari*, produce these nuances of 'internal' and 'externally apparent'? Yamada does not say. His characterization resembles Martin's (1975, 237–38) description of the *ni* in *n(i)ari* as an "objective essive," which contrasts with the "subjective essive" *to* (of *t(o)ari*). "Essive" presumably refers to the copular roles *ni* and *to* play as individual particles in interclausal, coordinate conjunction, where they function as suppletive "infinitives" for *n(i)ari* and *t(o)ari*, respectively, as in this example, from *Taketori monogatari* (tenth century):

2. Ware wa tsuki no   miyako no   hito   NI-te,   chichi haha   ari
   I   RF moon GEN capital GEN person LOC-PFinf father mother be
   'I am a citizen of the lunar capital, AND have a father and a mother.'

Even if *ni* and/or *to* was derived from a lost 'be' verb, as some scholars think, it seems likely that each had been adapted to use as a locative particle before being put to work in copular predication.

Why or how, then, should the components in *n(i)ari* combine to express an "internal" or "objective" link, and those in *t(o)ari* as an "external" or "subjective" link? To my mind, the most coherent answer sees each as based on a locative construction, by which a referent X is located 'in' a category X (X *n(i)ari*) or 'with' it (X *t(o)ari*). In this view, placing a referent 'in/at' a certain locus (with *ni* and *ari*) serves to identify something or someone in a wide variety of ways, from metaphors of the "ontological," "A *is* B" sort (cf. Lakoff and Johnson 1980, 25) to the very context-dependent, loose sense of utterances like *boku wa unagi da* 'I'm the eel' (spoken in a restaurant, ordering eel). This unmarked iden-

TABLE 4
Two Locative Figures as Contrasting Copulas

	In = Essential		With/Accompanying = Contingent
(A wa)	X ni ari		X to ari
referent A is	in/at X	alongside	X
Nominal X is an ──→ attribute of the referent A (Yamada 1922), that is,	"internal"	or	"external"
	X's "location" is given as it is assumed to exist, independent of interpretive acts:		X's "location" is given as estimated by speaker, approximated in an interpretive act:
	Unmarked copular relation consubstantial, metaphorical		*Marked* copular relation contiguous, metonymic

tification expresses a relation taken to be full but unremarkable and unproblematic in its context of use. Using *to* and *ari*, on the other hand, places a referent 'with' or 'in the company of' a category, and describes it in a marked, provisional, contingent, somehow less established kind of way. The relationship between the referent and the category 'with' which it is placed is not identity but rather approximation or accidence, and is in this sense more of a metonymy (specifically, simile—'is *like* X') than a metaphor ('is X'). A *to*-marked copular relation is not treated as holding on its own but as overtly maintained by the interpreting speaker. In fact, the complex of nuances expressed in *any* predicate complement with *to* carries the nuance of an overtly interpretive act. The differences in perspective implicit in these two earlier copular expressions, then, can be related to the contrast between the two localistic figures on which they are based, as illustrated in Table 4.

The two different meanings that Yamada has defined in terms of perspective ('internal' versus 'externally apparent') may have emerged from each of these locative schemata by what has been called "invited inference."[39] That is, if a referent is placed 'in/at' (*ni*) a nonspatial category, this would invite the inference that the relation is analogous to the spatial, in a way that is relevant to the context, in particular, to the present referent. In (3) below, for example, the referent is *yoru kotsumi* 'flotsam that washes up (on the beach)', and this is related to *kai* 'sea-shells' by means of *ni* and *ari*-. The inference invited by such an otherwise anomalous semantic combination is that the 'flotsam' pertains to 'seashells' in a locative relation other than the physically spatial.

3. . . . yoru   kotsumi kai   NI   ARI-se-ba . . .   (*Manyooshuu* 4396)
        wash up flotsam shells LOC be-FACT-COND
    'if the flotsam washed ashore were seashells', . . .

Such inference is invited under one of the most basic conventions of communication, which H. P. Grice has called "relevance," and which might be expressed as "When communicating, say things that somehow fit together and make sense."[40] Once this particular inference—that *n(i)ari*-related things relate in a way not limited to the physically spatial—becomes conventionalized, a distinct copular use of *n(i)ari* has emerged. The metaphor may then be "dead," but its form and the kind of relation it created live on.

The genius of the copula is that the relation it establishes is loose and pragmatic, not tight and mechanical. Copular /X *n(i)ari*/, like today's /X *da*/, merely identifies the referent 'in/at' category X, in a relation that makes sense in the circumstances at hand. If the categorization of the referent is, on the other hand, an impression, a rough approximation, or otherwise problematic and still challengeable, the referent is placed alongside, *with* that category. This might account for the frequent use of *to*, and not *ni*, in attributing unfamiliar—indeed, foreign—nouns as modifiers of other nouns, in the early (Nara and early Heian periods) marking of sutras written in Chinese to be read off as Japanese. The same process of a conventionalized invited inference may have produced the copular uses of *t(o)ari* as well.

Copular *ni* and *to*, then, distinguish between "things-located-in/at" (the assumed relation, unproblematic) and "things-located-with" (approximate, challengeable), and contrastive localistic figures are the source, it seems, of both Yamada's interior/exterior characterization and Martin's objective/subjective reading. A localistic account of copular *ni* and *to* is consistent with all the present-day, noncopular contexts of each. For *to*, these include the reporting of communication ("quoting"), describing the manner in which something moves, sounds, appears, strikes, or affects one (e.g., with many of the mimetic words in which Japanese abounds), and irrealis hypotheticals, such as classical *yuku to mo* 'even supposing [she] goes' (cf. the fossil *sukunaku to mo* 'at least'). There is also the contrastive pair *X to shite mo* 'even supposing [it] to be X' and *X ni shite mo* 'even given [its] being X', which differ in just this regard: what is marked as hypothetical supposition with *to* is marked as presupposed fact with *ni*.

In general, *ni*'s uses, including the copular one, index unmarked and accepted ideational relations, while *to*'s uses index relations that are contingent, for the nonce, not yet internalized, and challengeable. Epistemologically speaking, the established, unremarkable relations indexed with *ni* are familiar and certain, that is, *uchi*-type knowledge, of the sort we identified with clause nominalizer *no*. A relation that is entertained for the nonce or as an approximation, on the other hand, is reminiscent of that converter of clauses to nonce common nouns, *koto*; like *koto*, *to* does not commit the speaker to the factuality of its complement. There are obvious parallels with the epistemological stances indexed by the prototypical transitive and intransitive verbs and the causative/middle derivations. Volitionally caused, transitive change is well known, familiar enough to be articulated in the detail of two or more arguments; *ni*-related information is unremarkable, "things as they are," as they are assumed to *be*. A proportion suggests itself: as controlled, transitive change is to nonvolitional, sourceless, intransitive change, so too is known, unremarkable, unproblematic knowledge to less known, less sure, and less committed information. With *ni*, we place things as they are known to be; with *to*, as they are assumed, conjectured, guessed, or about to be. The metapattern, whether for the verbs, *no* and *koto*, or *ni* and *to*, is *uchi/soto*.

To be sure, not every use of *ni* contrasts with every use of *to*; nor is the converse true. But there are significant numbers of contexts of contrastive use, in which consistently analogous distinctions recur. A summary of systematic tendencies in the ways *ni* is conceptually opposed to *to* would make note of points such as the following. *Ni* marks steady, stable reference points, in which referents reside, from which they emerge, into which they enter. These meanings are relatable, by various extensions, to a basic sense of static location. *To*, on the other hand, marks accompaniment, a relation in which both referents remain outside each other. Nor does accompaniment obtain in stillness; it is a relation most typically taken up on the move, for the duration of the activity or attention indicated by the governing predicate. In terms of the structure of verbal predicates, while *ni* marks both arguments (in the sense of case roles predictable from the verb itself, such as a buyer and a bought for *kau* 'buy') and adjuncts (information less inherent to the meaning of the verb, such as time when or manner), *to* tends toward marking adjuncts and complements. In other words, *ni* relations are more typically relevant to the internal semantics of a predicate than are *to* relations. The low commitment to factuality indexed by *to*'s ("quotative," etc.) use with interpretive verbs is yet another sense in which the relation it creates is less indicative of "the way things are."

From one perspective, *to* relations can be said to be closer to home, *uchi*, since they are marked as the products of human interpretation, things as we place them; by contrast, *ni* places things where *they* are, in themselves. Thus the characterization of *to*-based copular predicates as "subjective" and their *ni*-based counterparts as "objective." However, from an epistemological perspective, *ni* is clearly the indicator of *un*marked—known, normal, unremarkable, expected—relations, which is the way we generally *assume* things to be. The "objective" world is but the taken-for-granted world. *Ni* relations are "objective" *because* they are familiar; they are that well known. *To* relations are subjectively tentative, unestablished, and challengeable, but for these very reasons are *soto*. *To*-mediated information has not yet "come inside." From either point of view, however, the difference remains constant: an 'inside' opposed to an 'outside'.

INTERNAL AND EXTERNALIZED POINT OF VIEW IN JAPANESE PREDICATES

A number of recent research initiatives in linguistics have investigated the idea that a predicate structures its ideational representation of experience from a particular perspective. Whether a predicate represents something executed in society or only in the imagination, it has a point of view, a fact that has structural consequences. Research that teases out point of view from the grammar of predication has been done by scholars working in the framework of cognitive grammar, such as Ronald Langacker and his associates (e.g., Langacker 1987, Lindner 1987), as well as by others whose work is identified more with syntax per se, such as Ann Borkin (e.g., Borkin 1984) and Susumu Kuno (e.g., Kuno 1987).[41] The discussion to follow will not concern itself, as much of this research does, with the theoretical consequences of covert point of view in different kinds of predicates. The phenomenon we shall examine is, for one thing, overtly present and, for another, distributed widely in Japanese. For all of that, however, it has not been discussed as a single phenomenon, to the best of my knowledge, perhaps because its various instantiations have not been regarded in the framework of a larger, unifying concept. The absence of a larger unifying concept is another way of saying that these phenomena were not perceived as having theoretical significance. The phenomenon in question is the change effected in a predicate's point of view when additional morphology, most notably some form of *aru* 'be' (earlier *ari*), is attached as a superordinate operator. While the outline and colors of that picture are sharpest at an earlier stage of the language, an overview of the phenomenon as it obtains today will suffice for present purposes.[42]

Expression in Japanese has long distinguished in a highly developed and regular way between information that is the product of personal experience and information that is not firsthand knowledge, a distinction I am suggesting is of the *uchi/soto* sort. For example, in the present-day language there is a constraint on the present-tense ("here-and-now") use of adjectival predicates expressing perception and emotion, such as *atsui* 'is hot' and *sabishii* 'is lonely', so that these forms are typically used by a speaker in describing present states s/he experiences, feels, and knows firsthand, but not in asserting how another person feels.[43] To say that another 'feels the heat' or 'is lonely', these plain imperfective forms are typically subordinated to an epistemic modal, such as the tentative copula *daroo* (< *de aroo* < *ni-te arau* < *ni-te ara-mu*) in *atsui daroo* 'must be hot' or the suffix *-rashii*, in *sabishii-rashii* 'is apparently lonely.' Without the modal interface, to assert *atsui* of another is to assert it *for* her, in effect to present an interior monologue—possible but rare in most everyday genres of speech.

Similarly, the desire to do something is routinely expressed by the person experiencing the desire with the adjectival suffix *-tai*. Formally, predicates ending in *-tai* are adjectival, and like those just cited above, are routinely used in questions directed to others, but not in statements asserting others' present desires. When referring to others, the *-tai* statement typically ends in a modal, such as one of those just mentioned (*daroo*, *-rashii*, etc.), or is replaced by the "exteriorizing" verbal suffix *-tagaru* 'act in a wanting-to-X manner' (probably a lexicalization of < *-taku aru*, the infinitive of *-tai* plus *aru* 'be'). The perspective created by X-*tagaru* is "observed from without"; like *daroo* (and probably *-rashii*), *-tagaru* is derived with a form of *aru* 'be'.

Those forms that in present time frames refer to the speaker's perceptions index an *internal* or *experienced* perspective on the sensation or feeling that they name and predicate. Without exception, however, each of them can be transformed so as to express an *external, detached,* or *observed* perspective, by bracketing the form with another signal that says the sensation it refers to 'exists'. Whether this takes the form of *-rashii*, tentative copula *daroo*, noun *yoo* 'appearance' plus copula *da*, suffix *-tagaru*, or reporting . . . *to iu* 'says . . . ,' the effect is the same: to present the felt sensation into the outer world, where it can be spoken of as if observed. Out here, a nonexperiencing speaker can observe and comment on the condition predicated. *Aru* in these derivations has a basically presentative, "third-person" kind of 'there is' function.

A related phenomenon is the distinction between verbal derivations for "proposing," such as *ikoo* 'Guess I'll go/Let's go' and the "tentative," which adds a copula inflected in the same way to the imperfective of the verb: *iku daroo* '[someone] will probably go'. While *ikoo* refers minimally to the speaker's going ('Guess I'll go'), it can include the second person(s) as well ('Let's go'). But it is generally not used to refer to third parties, that is, those not present to the utterance, or speech act.[44] Usage of the *ikoo* form indexes a boundary between the speaker and all others (the 'I guess I'll go' use) or a boundary between people involved in the act (speaker and addressee[s]) and all others, as in the 'Let's go' use. *Iku daroo* complements these: in present time reference, it applies to nonspeaker referents, either the second person or a third party, but not the speaker. Either way, the boundary indexed distinguishes between an inside and an outside, and the speaker is the minimum in-group. A similar distinction is indexed by /clause X + *hazu*/ and /clause X + *tsumori*/, which mark "X" as a nonpersonally established expectation or a personally established expectation, respectively: *Kau hazu da* 'It's expected s/he/they'll buy [it]' contrasts with *Kau tsumori da* 'I/we expect to buy [it]'.

The epistemological distinction in all cases—adjectives of sensation and their exteriorizations, *ikoo* and *iku daroo*, *tsumori* and *hazu*—is between proximate information and information that is as yet outside one's present sphere. This also is the fundamental existential difference Emile Benveniste (1966) observed to hold between first and second person, on the one hand, and third person, on the other. First person and second person come with the privilege of ostensive reference; in many languages, they are formally distinguished with deictic terms of reference. Third person, by comparison, is simply "the rest of the world," that is, what is "not you or I." In Japanese the difference that is primary—and more basic than first, second, and third person, or singular versus plural—is that of *uchi/soto* 'inside/outside'. Even when *-tagaru* or *daroo* is used by the speaker of himself (as when describing some distant experience, such as a childhood memory or a guess about one's future), the perspective is detached, viewed from without:

1. Ano koro wa itsu mo Amerika e   iki-TAGATTE ita.
   that time RF always   America DIR go-want-being was
   'Back then, [I] was always wanting to go to America.'
2. Boku mo yahari   furikaette   tanoshikatta to   omou
   I   IF as expected looking back was fun   QUOT think
   DAROO ne.
   COPtent CONF
   'I'll probably look back, too, and think it was fun, you know.'

In present-time, here-and-now use, however, it is only the addressee in the speech act who is "variable," that is, who can be included inside with the speaker, or addressed outside.

From such regular distinguishing of information according to whether it is or is not the product of one's own experience emerges a speaker-centered indexical field or "cline of person" (see below) that is culturally quite Japanese. Japanese linguistic behavior, as manifested in the forms thus far discussed, recognizes and maintains a boundary in this field by separating an experienced, engaged, enclosed area of first-hand, more certain knowledge from an external, detached, open, and less directly known realm that the knower faces or beholds, rather than dwells in. Insofar as it is knowledge and belief that use of these linguistic forms indexes, the indexing is epistemic.

The same kind of inside/outside boundary is also present in the structure of the *ko-*, *so-*, and *(k)a-* paradigm of demonstrative pronouns, determiners, and adverbs in Japanese.[45] The vowel /o/ is common to forms whose use is grounded in presence at the utterance, that is, *ko-* 'speaker/here/now' and *so-* 'addressee/right there/just now'; these share a position that removed (= third person) *(k)a-* referents do not.[46] Whether the reference boundary separates speaker from addressee (*ko-* versus *so-*), or whether it joins referents who are speech-act participants (speaker-with-addressee, *(k)(s)o-*) while separating them from nonparticipant referents (*(k)a-*), each of these stances distinguishes an inside from an outside. The boundary separates the speaker's inside from an outside, whether the inside includes or excludes the addressee. It is this distinction, *uchi/soto* in shape, that corresponds functionally to the grammaticized person of the Indo-European languages—a fact curiously little remarked on, considering its consequences for the both spoken communication and the interpretation of texts.

CONCLUSION: PERSON AS EVIDENTIAL CLINE

It is sometimes said that there are no personal pronouns in Japanese, or that there is no grammatical category of (first, second, third) person. This is true enough if one defines pronouns as morphologically related terms that come in paradigmatic sets, as in English (I, my, mine; you, your, yours, etc.), German, or the Romance languages. Nor is there subject-verb agreement of person or number in the Japanese clause. But this hardly precludes expression of the same or similar functions in other ways. After all, deictic or indexical reference is the most basic kind of reference we humans practice. First, there is the highly developed set of deictic words in Japanese (which are, of course, also used anaphorically), the paradigm of *ko-*, *so-*, and *(k)a-* words discussed above. Whether nouns (*kore*, etc.), adnominal determiners (*kono, konna*, etc.), or adverbs (*koo*, etc.), the *ko-*, *so-*, and *(k)a-* words correspond, and rather closely, to perspectives expressed grammatically by first, second, and third person in languages which have that category. Their proximal (*ko-*), mesial (*so-*), and distal (*(k)a-*) structure even matches the demonstrative paradigm in Romance languages. In addition to this three-way perspective, there are the distinctions like those drawn between simplex predicators (e.g., *ikoo* 'Guess [I]'ll go/Let's go') and complex predicators that have been exteriorized by adding some form of *aru* 'be' to the simplex (e.g., *iku daroo* '[someone] will probably go'), and evidentials like *tsumori* and *hazu*. Each of these formal differentations—*ko-*, *so-* versus *(k)a-*, simplex versus complex predicators, and *tsumori* versus *hazu*—indexes information that is grammaticized as person in other languages. They remind us that to define the cline of person only in terms of pronouns like "I, you, he/she/it" and subject-verb agreement is to miss much about the way that cline can be structured. While we have to be careful not to impose the categories of our language in the analysis of others, at the same time we must not assume that if we cannot find words like "un(e)/le/la," "a(n)/the," "s/he," and "il/elle" in a language, it therefore "does not have definite/indefinite," or that it does not "have" person.

In charting a referential map for genuinely distant languages, it can be more revealing to begin by examining the expression of similar discourse functions than by looking for similar words or morphology, such as personal pronouns or person-number inflections. As A. L. Becker and I Gusti Ngurah Oka noted:

> While person appears to be a universal semantic dimension of language, structures of person and linguistic manifestations of person—particularly personal pronouns—differ from language to language. Language students and linguists have to learn that I is not I, you is not you, and we is not we from one language to the next. Within a language family, however, these differences may not be so great as across genetic boundaries. (1974, 230)

Much of the coherence of natural language, they wrote, is structured in this indexical continuum:

> A central thread—perhaps *the* central thread in the semantic structure of all languages is the cline of person, an ordering of linguistic forms according to their distance from the speaker. Between the subjective, pointed, specific pronominal "I" and the objective, generic common noun, between these poles the words of all languages—words for people, animals, food, time, space, indeed words for everything—are ordered and categorized according to their distance—spatial, temporal, social, biological, and metaphorical—from the first person, the speaker. The cline of person also underlies most linguistic systems as well as words, systems of deixis, number, definiteness, tense, and nominal classification among others. (1974, 229)

The notion of a cline, a gradient range or field, is helpful in taking an evidential perspective on the category of person, which works particularly well when analyzing a language like Japanese: how evident, that is, near to or distant from the speaker and audience, is a given piece of information? Evidentiality can be understood as "knowability," a perceived or felt proximity or distance between oneself and the information one would communicate to another. We can relate informational and epistemologically significant linguistic marking to evidentiality by saying that they *index* evidentiality. Information with high evidentiality is proximate and readily accessible (ostensive, deictically or anaphorically referable); evidentiality is low when the information in question is distant in time, in space, culturally, or conceptually. In mapping the cline of person in Japanese, the trick is not to think of person as a collection of discrete words like *watashi* 'I', *anata* 'you', and *kanojo* 'she' but to conceive of it as an evidential cline, an indexical field extending out from a socially constituted *uchi*, the minimum instance of which is an individual speaker. This *uchi* and its evidential cline are defined only in contrast to a *soto*, and the particulars of that definition will differ as communicators and occasions of communication differ.

The way in which a given language structures its cline of person will be, in part, constrained by the way it represents and structures other dimensions of experience. In Japanese, the cline is as coherent as it is in large part because of the indexical power of a rich collection of evidential suffixes and nouns. In the present-day language, indexing of evidentiality is the principal function of such devices as /clause X + *yoo*/ 'a semblance of X', /clause X + *mitai*/ 'id.', /stem X + *soo*/ 'looking as if to X', /X-*rashii*/ 'is apparently X', and /X *ni chigai nai*/ 'no doubt is X'.[47] In addition to these nominal, derivational, and syntactic devices, there are also the indexical functions of *no* and *koto*, *ni* and *to*, of lexical predicators like (in)transitive verbs, adjectival predicators of sensation and emotion, and of the other forms we have examined. Learning the cline of person as it is expressed in Japanese is part of the larger task of learning to index evidentiality in that language, those informational and epistemic handles placed on or implicit in the ideational meaning of words and constructions. Indexicality is, at bottom, largely a matter of evidentiality.

Uchi/soto coordinates are not the only ones by which Japanese people position themselves or structure their experience. Nevertheless, as the chapters in this volume together demonstrate, they capture in a coherent way how people stand together or apart, here or there, to index their world spatially, temporally, socially, and epistemologically. The same coordinates inform the way people shape their psychological worlds through interaction with an environment, as Shiga Naoya (and Michael Molasky, this volume) has shown us. It comes as no surprise, then, that there are lexical and grammatical contrasts in Japanese that index the same orientational difference. Speakers index analogous distinctions of an engaged/detached sort in the three predicate categories of (in)transitivity, aspect, and modality, in the nominalization of clauses with *no* and *koto*, in the many contrastive uses of *ni* and *to*, and in the semantically motivated use of controlled and noncontrolled (in)transitivity structures for social indexing. Whether manifested lexically or grammatically, and whether they serve the purposes of social indexing (Sukle's and Wetzel's chapters, this chapter) or evidential indexing (this chapter), the parameters look to be congruently *uchi/soto*.

It is no exaggeration to say that this mutual indexing with reference to *uchi/soto* parameters is how people, together, create their selves. The indexing in one's acts, linguistic and otherwise, of where one stands, with whom one stands, what one knows and does not know, in other words, constitutes who one is: a self emerges as it is indexed in social activity. This is true regardless of whether the anchoring grounds of this indexing change over time, as they must, and whether the self is one's own or another's. In the words of M. M. Bakhtin: "The spirit, mine as well as the other's, is not a given, like a thing (like the immediate object of the natural sciences); rather, it comes through expression in signs, a realization through 'texts', which is of equal value to the self and to the other."[48] Social "incident," to paraphrase Henry James, is not only "the illustration of character" but also the *constitution* of character. The notion of a self indexed in communication with others is not the unchanging, inviolate ego of Western folk ideology, to which we are enjoined to "above all be true," but it is certainly closer to life as it is lived.

Perspectives gained from the phenomenological detail of ethnographic study, in particular from folk categories like *uchi/soto*, can alert a student of a distant culture to differences and regularities s/he might otherwise not look to see. We need to look carefully, because "I is not I, you is not you, and we is not we from one language to the next." In the context of the phenomenological detailing of the analyses that precede this one, I have offered what I take to be evidence that, thanks to the human cognitive propensity for abduction, analogy, and tropes, grammatical constructions will develop along lines conceptually congruent with perceptual and social interaction. As the philosopher said, language is "a form of life."

NOTES

1. This research was supported in 1990–91 by a Seed Grant from Ohio State University, a Fulbright Research Grant administered through the Japan-U.S. Educational Commission, and a Research Grant from the Social Science Research Council, for which I am most grateful. Thanks to co-editor Jane Bachnik for her insightful suggestions on several drafts of this chapter, and to my wife Shelley for her critical comments and encouragement.

2. Bateson (1979, 250) defines "homology" in biology as "a formal resemblance between two organisms such that the relations between certain parts of A are similar to the relations between corresponding parts of B. Such formal resemblance is considered to be evidence of evolutionary relatedness."

3. That is, a clause as enacted or performed, not just as a formal object.

4. It would be possible, for example, to study the distribution of transitive, intransitive, and stative clauses in the subordinate and main clauses of a narrative, and describe how these function to ground some information while highlighting other information as figure, as the story develops. See Paul Hopper (1979, 1983, 1985), Hopper and Thompson (1980), and Talmy 1978.

5. *(In)transitivity* will be used as a cover term for the full range of transitive (typically, two arguments: subject = agent, direct object = undergoer) and intransitive (typically a single argument: subject = undergoer) predicates.

6. See, for example, Vygotsky 1978; Wertsch 1985, 1991; Bakhtin 1981; Bruner 1990; Ochs 1990, 1992; Schieffelin and Ochs 1986; Rumelhart, McClellan, et al. 1986; Haiman 1985; or Clancey and Roschelle 1991 (their notion of "situated cognition," in particular).

7. See the report by Gumperz and Levinson on a 1991 conference, "Rethinking Linguistic Relativity," *Current Anthropology* 32(5):613–23.

8. The term is Dan Slobin's; cf. Gumperz and Levinson 1991, 615–16.

9. Mühlhäusler and Harré (1990, 16).

10. For the purposes of this paper, a *predicate* minimally includes a *predicator* (verb, adjective, /noun phrase + copula/), which typically relates one or more arguments (nouns) to itself and to one another. A predicator (*yoogen* in Japanese) is a verb, adjective, or the /noun phrase + copula/composite.

11. See the work of Talmy Givón (1979, 1984), the papers in Traugott and Heine (1991), Fillmore et al. (1988), and Sweetser 1990.

12. *Radial structure* is typical of natural (evolved) categories, which have a central, prototypical core and noncentral extensions, "which are not specialized instances of the central subcategory, but rather are variants of it" (Lakoff 1987, 91). Extensions are motivated by the central model and certain general principles of extension, which are basically abductive and analogical in nature (e.g., metaphor, metonymy). As an example, consider the Japanese classifier *-hon* (cf. Lakoff 1987, 104), which in its central sense refers to rigid, long, thin objects, such as pencils, umbrellas, and dried fish. The same category, however, also includes such varied phenomena as hits in baseball and shots in basketball (both of which have a long, thin trajectory), casette tapes (which when unwound are long and thin), telephone calls (which travel over long, thin wires), and others. Lakoff argues that the same kind of central model-plus-extensions structure is to be expected in grammatical categories as well, which is to say that they will have their prototypical exemplars and their extensions. On prototype effects in general, see Rosch 1975 and Rosch and Lloyd, eds. 1978.

13. In Charles Peirce's sense of the term, *abduction* is the process of grasping new phenomenon B by assuming it can be understood in a way similar to that whereby we understand known phenomenon A.

14. Three of these terms—*interpersonal, informational,* and *ideational*—are adapted from the functional linguistic theory of Michael Halliday (e.g., Halliday [1985]), in which any linguistic unit-in-use relates to three kinds of context:

ideational (reference-and-predication, the elements of a scene as we would relate them in a proposition), *textual* (status of that ideational meaning as information in an ongoing text, or discourse: is it at issue? assumed? and so on), and *interpersonal* (status of the utterance as a link between speaker and audience: is it interrogative, declarative, intimate, distant? and so on). I have substituted "informational" for Halliday's "textual," to refer to distinctions such as given versus new, referred-to versus presented, focused versus not focused, and so on, and have added *epistemic* to Halliday's original three; this amounts to separating out one aspect of his "interpersonal" function, since the interpersonal can be understood to include the personal, that is, the speaker's knowledge, beliefs, and attitudes toward the information being communicated. Epistemic values are related to informational values in that both are based on the kind and degree of *evidence* available to the speaker or writer; epistemic and informational values thus represent different functions of what is called *evidentiality* (cf. Chafe and Nichols, eds. 1986). Evidentiality is also gauged by the speaker/writer with an eye to what s/he assumes the addressee(s) to know. For proposals similar in spirit, see Jakobson (1960) or Becker (1982).

15. As Jacobsen (1982) points out, Motoori Haruniwa's (1828) distinction between *onozukara* 'in and of itself' and *mizukara* 'self-determined' verbs is virtually identical with the categories employed by Gonda (1884) and that drawn between *shodooshi* 'place verbs' and *noodooshi* 'action verbs' by Mikami (1972).

16. Both *aru* and *iru* are finite forms (as is the English "is" or "are" but not "be"); each is imperfective and can mean, depending on context, 'is', 'are', or 'will be'. Unless the context is also cited, they will be glossed as 'be'. *Aru* can be understood as the default verb for existence, and is used most often of inanimate referents, but also of animates when simple existence is the issue ('having' siblings, for example) and special resultant states (the *-te aru* perfect of verbs of volitional control, examined below). *Iru*, by contrast, is used as a main verb in expressing contingent, mutable states, such as the existence (in a location) of animate, mobile creatures; when attached to the perfective infinitive (gerund) of a verb, it expresses resultant states or sustained activity, depending on whether that predicate as a whole is punctual or nonpunctual.

17. The quasi-literary potential derived from the verb *u* 'gain, obtain' occurs with *aru*, as in *ari-uru koto da* 'It's a possible thing', or *Sonna koto wa ari-enai* 'That sort of thing is not possible'. The use of this potential is limited, by and large, to collocations like these two, and has an epistemic nuance of likelihood or the lack of it (cp. /X + *hazu*/ 'likelihood that X').

18. Jacobsen (1982) lists almost four hundred such pairs of verbs.

19. Predicates with "telic" aspect are understood to have an *endpoint*, as in *tsukuru* 'make [something]'; *oyogu* 'swim' is thus *atelic*.

20. "Perfective" in present-day Japanese is expressed with *-te/-de* (the "gerund," a perfective infinitive) and *-ta/-da* (conclusive), and signals *realization*. Anything more specific than this seems best interpreted as the product of the semantics of the situation of use and of the clause.

21. The optional consonant comes into play with vowel stem verbs.

22. The term *Aktionsart* is used to refer to the temporal characteristics represented in a single lexical item or predicate (with unmarked arguments only), in

contrast to "aspect," which is often used to refer to changes in this basic temporal contour. A single term, *aspect*, will be preferred here, and distinctions made by means of qualifiers, for example, "lexical aspect," "derivationally converted aspect," and so forth, as necessary.

23. Aspect also serves to index discourse-level distinctions, such as the foregrounding and backgrounding of information in narrative, and it has been said of several narrative traditions that a plot line tends to be developed with human-instigated action, expressed in transitive verbs and perfective aspect. Stative predicates, whether verbal, adjectival, or copular, tend to provide background or narrative commentary (Hopper 1979, inter alia). There is indeed something *uchi/soto* about the near/removed, action/stasis, shown/explained contrasts of these functions, but it can hardly be unique to Japanese narrative.

24. Some theorists of aspect would exclude the notion stative from aspectual status but states, too, can be more stable or less stable in time, and are grammatically related to change in a variety of aspectual categories.

25. When used in the frame /V-*te iru*/, many transitive verbs produce a progressive ('in the process of -ing') meaning. The subset of transitive verbs that refer to punctual change (e.g., *ireru*), however, resemble intransitive verbs in the kind of change to which they refer, and in the /V-*te iru*/ frame can produce a perfect meaning, as in the 'has her hands in her pockets' example. However, these can also be contextualized so as to express repeated action, as in *Ringo o ikko ikko hako ni irete iru* 'S/he is putting the apples in boxes, one by one'.

26. Thanks to Mari Noda for these examples.

27. The story of these suffixes is more complex than this, since each was also used in the expression of tense and modality, but perfectivity seems to belong at the core of each family of meanings (Quinn 1987, 317–58).

28. *Deferential* is used in the sense of Jorden's (1987–1990, parts 1–3) term *polite*, which includes both *honorific* and *humble.*

29. *Plain* is used in the same sense as in Jorden (1987–1990), of predicates in which no deferential (= her term *polite*) distinctions are drawn.

30. Goffman's study is informed by Emile Durkheim's earlier distinction (1953, 1954) between *positive* (drawing near) and *negative* (withdrawing from) rites, both of which can express deference. See the following note.

31. While "negative" rites involve avoidance or keeping one's distance, "positive" rites involve a drawing near. Deference can be expressed with either. What Durkheim observed of religious sentiments applies, *mutatis mutandis*, to social relations, too: "The sacred object inspires us, if not with fear, at least with respect that keeps us at a distance; at the same time it is an object of love and aspiration that we are drawn toward. Here, then, is a dual sentiment which seems to be self-contradictory but does not for all that cease to be real" (1953, 48; quoted in Goffman 1956, 500).

32. Friedrich's (1986, 32) "language-intensive symbolism."

33. Kuno (1973, chap. 18) and Akatsuka-McCawley 1978 consider *to* against *no* and *koto*, and show that *to* involves least epistemic commitment from the speaker. Cf. the account of *to* offered below.

34. Cf. also (Kuno 1973, 222) *John ga jussai de aru *? no wa tashika desu* 'It is certain that John is ten years old'. In a prototypal account, these would be central for *koto*, but peripheral for *no*.

35. Historically speaking, this use of *no* as a nominalizer and complementizer of clauses (/clause *no*/) seems to have been analogically modeled after the phrasal deictic /N$_1$ *no*/ '(the) one(s) identified with N$_1$'. /N$_1$ *no*/ itself was probably a synecdochic ("part-for-whole") abbreviation of loose, pragmatically interpreted noun phrases of the form /N$_1$ *no* N$_2$/ 'N$_2$ identified with N$_1$', much as in English, "John's" is used as an abbreviation of "John's X," to refer to some known entity relating to John. Both deictic /N$_1$ *no*/ and its source /N$_1$ *no* N$_2$/ historically predate the deictic nominalization of clauses with *no*. See Quinn 1987, chap. 8.

36. Quinn 1992 includes a survey of the basic uses of each particle as presented in Jorden 1987–1990; see also Miyajima 1972, 688.

37. The form *n(i)arU* is the attributive or adnominal form; the usual citation form is the imperfective indicative *n(i)arI*. Likewise, for attributive *t(o)arU*, the citation form is *t(o)arI*.

38. Martin has also collected a set of present-day examples of copular *to aru* (*to atte, to areba,* etc.); cf. Martin 1975, 1002.

39. On this idea, see Carey 1990 and the references cited therein.

40. Grice 1975 proposes that it is a mutually assumed "cooperative principle" that makes communication possible, and elaborates this principle in terms of several conversational maxims, one of which is to "be relevant." We "expect a partner's contribution to be appropriate to the immediate needs at each stage of the transaction" (Grice 1975, in Davis 1991, 309).

41. Two studies of related phenomena in Japanese grammar, which complement much of what is reported here, are Kamio 1990 and Tokunaga 1986.

42. The parameters of this distinction are outlined for the language of the Nara and Heian periods in Quinn 1987, 545–71.

43. Pointed out in Kuroda 1973.

44. Except for the archaic *soto* ("third person") use of *-(y)oo* in certain written styles (*Soori mo deyoo* = . . . *deru daroo* 'The P.M. too will attend').

45. This paradigm includes seven sets of forms based on the same three perspectives (the fourth, interrogative member of each set is given last): (1) nominal *kore, sore, are, dore;* (2) adnominal *kono, sono, ano, dono;* (3) typological *konna, sonna, anna, donna;* (4) manner *koo, soo, aa, doo;* (5) locative *koko, soko, asoko, doko;* (6) directional *kochira, sochira, achira, dochira;* (7) elegant directional *konata, sonata, anata, donata.*

46. The use of /(k)a-/ forms to refer to referents known to both speaker and addressee can be understood as following from a *(k)a-* referent's being equally accessible to both in the prototypical case, as when used to refer to something in their shared visual field. The *k-* deictics are today lexicalized (e.g., *kanojo* 'she [known to us]') or stylistically archaic (e.g., *kanata* 'far side, over there').

47. In the language of the Nara and Heian periods, such evidentials existed in paradigms of inflecting derivational suffixes.

48. Quoted in Todorov 1984, from an article in Bakhtin 1979 (284).

References

Akatsuka (-McCawley), Noriko. 1978. "Another Look at *no, koto,* and *to*: Epistemology and Complementizer Choice in Japanese," in J. Hinds and I. Howard, eds., *Problems in Japanese Syntax and Semantics,* 178–212. Tokyo: Kaitakusha.

Anderson, John M. 1971. *The Grammar of Case: Towards a Localistic Theory*. New York: Cambridge University Press.

———. 1973. *An Essay Concerning Aspect*. The Hague: Mouton.

Aoki, Haruo. 1986. "Evidentials in Japanese," in W. Chafe and J. Nichols, eds., *Evidentiality: The Linguistic Coding of Epistemology*, 223–38. Norwood, N.J.: Ablex.

Bakhtin, Mikhail. 1979. "Problema texta v lingvistike, filologii i drugikh gumani-tarnykh naukakh. Opyt filosofskogo analiza" (The problem of text in linguistics, philology, and the other human sciences: An essay in philosophical analysis), in *Estetika slovesnogo tvorchestva* (The aesthetics of verbal creation), 281–307. Moscow: S. G. Bocharov.

———. 1981. *The Dialogic Imagination: Four Essays*. Translated by C. Emerson and M. Holquist. Austin: University of Texas Press.

Bateson, Gregory. 1979. *Mind and Nature*. New York: E. P. Dutton.

Becker, A. L. 1982. "Beyond Translation: Esthetics and Language Description," in H. Byrnes, ed., *Contemporary Perceptions of Language: Interdisciplinary Dimensions*, 124–38. Washington, D.C.: Georgetown University Press.

Becker, A. L., and I Gusti Ngurah Oka. 1974. "Person in Kawi: Exploration of an Elementary Semantic Dimension." *Oceanic Linguistics* 13: 229–55.

Benveniste, Emile. 1966. *Problèmes de Linguistique Générale*. Paris: Gallimarde. English translation: *Problems in General Linguistics*. Translated by M. E. Meek, 1971. Coral Gables, Fla.: University of Miami Press.

Borkin, Ann. 1984. *Problems in Form and Function*. Norwood, N.J.: Ablex.

Bourdieu, Pierre. 1977. *Outline of a Theory of Practice*. New York: Cambridge University Press.

———. 1990. *In Other Words*. Stanford: Stanford University Press.

Bruner, Jerome S. 1990. *Acts of Meaning*. Cambridge, Mass.: Harvard University Press.

Carey, Kathleen. 1990. "The Role of Conversational Implicature in the Early Grammaticalization of the English Perfect," *Proceedings of the 16th Annual Meeting of the Berkeley Linguistics Society*, 371–80. Berkeley: Berkeley Linguistics Society.

Chafe, Wallace and Johanna Nichols, eds. 1986. *Evidentiality: The Linguistic Coding of Epistemology*. Norwood, N.J.: Ablex.

Clancey, William, and William J. Roschelle. 1991. "Situated Cognition: How Representations Are Created and Given meaning." To appear in a special issue of the *Educational Psychologist*.

Comrie, Bernard. 1976. *Aspect*. New York: Cambridge University Press.

Davis, Steven, ed. 1991. *Pragmatics: a Reader*. New York: Oxford University Press.

DuBois, John W. 1987. "The Discourse Basis of Ergativity." *Language* 63 (4): 805–55.

Duranti, Alessandro, and Charles Goodwin, eds. 1992. *Rethinking Context: Language as an Interactive Phenomenon*. New York: Cambridge University Press.

Durkheim, Emile. 1953. "The Determination of Moral Facts," in *Sociology and Philosophy*, 35–62. Translated by D. F. Pocock. Glencoe, Ill.: Free Press.

———. 1954. *The Elementary Forms of the Religious Life*. Translated by J. S. Swain. Glencoe, Ill.: Free Press.

Fillmore, Charles J., Paul Kay, and Mary Catherine O'Connor. 1988. "Regularity and Idiomaticity in Grammatical Constructions: The Case of *Let Alone*." *Language* 64 (3): 501–38.

Friedrich, Paul. 1986. *The Language Parallax: Linguistic Relativism and Poetic Indeterminacy.* Austin: University of Texas Press.

Givón, Talmy. 1979. *On Understanding Grammar.* New York: Academic Press.

————. 1984. *Syntax: a Functional-Typological Introduction,* Vol. 1. Philadelphia: John Benjamins.

Goffman, Erving. 1956. "The Nature of Deference and Demeanor." *American Anthropologist* 58: 473–502.

Gonda, Naosuke. 1884. "Gogaku Jizai," reprinted in part in Shimada Masahiko 1979. *Kokugo ni okeru jidooshi to tadooshi* (In-transitive and transitive verbs in Japanese). Tokyo: Meiji Shoin.

Greenberg, Joseph H. 1978. *Universals of Human Language,* Vol. 4: *Syntax.* Stanford: Stanford University Press.

Grice, H. Paul. 1975. "Logic and Conversation," in Steven Davis, ed., *Pragmatics: a Reader,* 305–15. New York: Oxford University Press.

Gumperz, John, and Stephen Levinson. 1991. "Rethinking Linguistic Relativity." *Current Anthropology* 32(5): 613–23.

Haiman, John, ed. 1985. *Iconicity in Syntax.* New York: Cambridge University Press.

Halliday, M.A.K. 1985. *An Introduction to Functional Grammar.* London: Edward Arnold.

Hinds, John, and Irwin Howard, eds. 1978. *Problems in Japanese Syntax and Semantics.* Tokyo: Kaitakusha.

Holenstein, Elmar 1976. *Roman Jakobson's Approach to Language.* Translated by C. and T. Schelbert. Bloomington, Ind.: Indiana University Press.

Hopper, Paul J. 1979. "Aspect and Foregrounding in Discourse," in Talmy Givón ed., *Syntax and Semantics,* Vol. 12: *Discourse and Syntax,* 213–41. New York: Academic Press.

————. 1983. "Ergative, Passive, and Active in Malay Narrative," in *Discourse Perspectives on Syntax,* 67–88. New York: Academic Press.

————. 1985. "Aspect between Discourse and Grammar: An Introductory Essay for the Volume," in Paul Hopper, ed., *Tense and Aspect: Between Discourse and Grammar,* 3–18. New York: Academic Press.

Hopper, Paul J., and Sandra A. Thompson. 1980. "Transitivity in Grammar and Discourse." *Language* 56 (2): 251–99.

Jackendoff, Ray S. 1983. *Semantics and Cognition.* Cambridge, Mass.: MIT Press.

Jacobsen, Wesley. 1982. *Transitivity in the Japanese Verbal System.* Bloomington, Ind.: Indiana University Linguistics Club.

Jakobson, Roman. 1960. "Closing Statement: Linguistics and Poetics," in T. Sebeok, ed., *Style in Language.* Cambridge, Mass.: MIT Press.

Jesperson, Otto. [1924] 1965. *The Philosophy of Grammar.* New York: W. W. Norton.

Jorden, Eleanor H., with Mari Noda. 1987–1990. *Japanese: The Spoken Language,* Parts 1, 2, 3. New Haven: Yale University Press.

Josephs, Lewis S. 1976. "Complementation," in Masayoshi Shibatani, ed., *Japanese Generative Grammar,* Vol. 5: *Syntax and Semantics,* 307–69. New York: Academic Press.

Kamio, Akio. 1990. *Joohoo no nawabari riron: gengo no kinoo-teki bunseki* (The theory of territory of information: A functional analysis of language). Tokyo: Tai-shuukan Shoten.

Kuno Susumu. 1973. *The Structure of the Japanese Language.* Cambridge, Mass.: MIT Press.

————. 1987. *Functional Syntax.* Chicago: University of Chicago Press.

Kuroda Shigeyuki (S-Y). 1973. "Where Epistemology, Style, and Grammar Meet: A Case Study from Japanese," in S. Anderson and P. Kiparsky, eds., *A Festschrift for Morris Halle,* 377–91. New York: Holt, Rinehart and Winston.

Lakoff, George. 1987. *Women, Fire and Dangerous Things: What Categories Reveal about the Mind.* Chicago: University of Chicago Press.

Lakoff, George, and Mark Johnson. 1980. *Metaphors We Live By.* Chicago: The University of Chicago Press.

Langacker, Ronald. 1987. *Cognitive Grammar,* Vol. 1: *Theoretical Prerequisites.* Stanford: Stanford University Press.

Lindner, Susan. 1987. *A Lexico-Semantic Analysis of Verb-Particle Constructions with UP and OUT.* Ph.D. dissertation, University of California, San Diego.

Lyons, John. 1977. *Semantics.* 2 vols. New York: Cambridge University Press.

Martin, Samuel E. 1975. *A Reference Grammar of Japanese.* New Haven: Yale University Press.

Miller, George A., and Philip N. Johnson-Laird. 1976. *Language and Perception.* Cambridge, Mass.: The Belknap Press of Harvard University Press.

Miyajima Tatsuo, ed. 1972. *Dooshi no imi yoohoo no kijutsuteki kenkyuu* (Descriptive research on the meaning and usage of verbs). Report no. 43 of the National Institute for the Study of Japanese Language. Tokyo: Shuuei shuppan.

Morson, Gary S., and Caryl Emerson. 1990. *Mikhail Bakhtin: Creation of a Prosaics.* Stanford: Stanford University Press.

Motoori, Haruniwa. 1828. *Kotoba no kayoimichi,* reprinted in part in Shimada Masahiko. 1979. *Kokugo ni okeru jidooshi to tadooshi* (Intransitive and transitive verbs in Japanese). Tokyo: Meiji Shoin.

Mühlhäusler, Peter, and Rom Harré. 1990. *Pronouns and People: The Linguistic Construction of Social and Personal Identity.* Oxford: Basil Blackwell.

Ochs, Eleanor. 1990. "Indexicality and Socialization," in G. Herdt, R. Shweder, and J. Stigler, eds., *Cultural Psychology: Essays on Comparative Human Development,* 287–308. New York: Cambridge University Press.

————. 1992. "Indexing Gender," in A. Duranti and C. Goodwin, eds., *Rethinking Context: Language as an Interactive Phenomenon,* 335–58. New York: Cambridge University Press.

Quinn, Charles J. 1987. *A Functional Grammar of Predication in Classical Japanese,* 3 vols. Ann Arbor, Mich.: University Microfilms.

————. 1992. "Giving Spoken Language Its Due" (review/article on Jorden with Noda 1990). *Journal of the Association of Teachers of Japanese* 25 (2): 224–67.

Ray, Yuko. 1989. *Unity in Variety: Family Resemblance in the Use of Japanese NO.* M.A. thesis, The Ohio State University.

Rosch, Eleanor. 1975. "Cognitive Representations of Semantic Categories." *Journal of Experimental Psychology: General* 104: 192–233.

Rosch, Eleanor, and B. B. Lloyd, eds. 1978. *Cognition and Categorization.* Hillsdale, N.J.: Lawrence Erlbaum.

Rumelhart, David E., James L. McClelland, and the PDP Research Group. 1986. *Parallel Distributed Processing: Explorations in the Microstructure of Cognition.* 2 vols. Cambridge, Mass.: Bradford Books/MIT Press.

Schieffelin, Bambi, and Eleanor Ochs. 1986. *Language Socialization across Cultures.* New York: Cambridge University Press.

Sweetser, Eve. 1990. *From Etymology to Pragmatics: Metaphorical and Cultural Aspects of Semantic Structure.* New York: Cambridge University Press.

Talmy, Leonard. 1978. "Figure and Ground in Complex Sentences," in Joseph H. Greenberg, ed., *Universals of Human Language*, Vol. 4: *Syntax*, 625–49. Stanford: Stanford University Press.

Todorov, Tsvetan. 1984. *Mikhail Bakhtin and the Dialogical Principle*, Vol. 13: *Theory and History of Literature.* Translated by Wlad Godzich. Minneapolis: The University of Minnesota Press.

Tokunaga, Misato, 1986. *Affective Deixis in Japanese: A Case Study of Directional Verbs.* Ann Arbor: University Microfilms International.

Traugott, Elizabeth Closs. 1975. "Spatial Expressions of Tense and Temporal Sequencing." *Semiotica* 15: 207–30.

Traugott, Elizabeth Closs, and Bernd Heine, eds. 1991. *Approaches to Grammaticalization.* Vols. 1 & 2. Philadelphia: John Benjamins.

Vygotsky, Lev S. 1962. *Thought and Language.* Cambridge, Mass.: MIT Press.

———. 1978. *Mind in Society: The Development of the Higher Psychological Processes.* Cambridge, Mass.: Harvard University Press.

Wertsch, James. 1985. *Vygotsky and the Social Formation of Mind.* Cambridge, Mass.: Harvard University Press.

———. 1991. *Voices of the Mind: a Sociocultural Approach to Mediated Action.* Cambridge, Mass.: Harvard University Press.

Wetzel, Patricia J. 1984. "Uchi and Soto ('In-group and Out-group'): Social Deixis in Japanese." Ph.D. thesis, Cornell University.

Whorf, Benjamin L. 1956. *Language, Thought and Reality.* Cambridge, Mass.: MIT Press.

Wittgenstein, Ludwig. 1958. *Philosophical Investigations.* Translated by G.E.M. Anscombe. New York: Macmillan.

Yamada Yoshio. 1922. *Nihon bunpoo koogi.* Tokyo: Hoobunkan.

INDEX

References to tables are in italics.

abduction, 53, 70, 70n.13, 256, 287; defined, 287n.13; and radial structure of categories, 287n.12

Abu-Lughod, Lila, 19

active/passive dynamics, 94–95, 223–24. See also *amaeru/amayakasu*; engaged/detached distinctions.

acts (controlled), vs. events (noncontrolled): 248, 251; in causative and middle derivations, 263–65; as expressed in (in)transitive paired verbs, 258–63; as social index, 268–72; vs. states, 257; in two perfects, 265–68; in two perfectives, 268

addressee, 76, 114–15, 119, 121, 136, 147, 159, 282

adjectives, 257, 265, 287n.10

adulthood, 193–94

aesthetic arts, 99, 163n.6; affectedness, 260; and social indexing, 271–72

agency, 4–5, 16–17, 22, 144, 145, 155, 161, 187–90, 198, 240, 248; and household organization, 144–45; and structure, 4, 5, 16–17, 22, 144. See also *uchi/soto*

agent, 29, 237, 247, 269–70; effaced, 248, 268–70; focused/emphasized, 248, 270–71; and undergoer, 258–64, 268

Aitchison, Jean, 69n.7

Akatsuka, Noriko, 272, 289n.33

Allen, Donald E., 78

amaeru/amayakasu, 88–89, 94–99, 103–9, 157, 223–24, 226–27, 248; and hierarchy, 80–99; and gender, ch. 4. See also *uchi/soto*

analogy, 256; and abduction, 53, 65–66, 286; across domains, 42; and radial structure of categories, 287; and (re)creation of grammatical devices, 256–57

anaphora, 76, 78–79, 283

anatomical, 65; anatomy, 256

ancestor worship, 204–6, 211

anchor point, 26–27, 29–30, 44, 73, 143–148, 156–60, 224, 226; collectively defined, 73, 75, 144–45, 156, 159, 228; deictic, 12, 26–27, 47, 73, 75–84 passim, 143–48, 155–62 passim, 169, 173–74, 233, 239;

deictic indexing of, 12, 146; as frame-of-reference, 148, 152–53, 159–60; and group organization, 162; and household organization, 143–46, 155–60; and indexing of self, 156–57; and shifting boundaries, 80–84, 159–60; symbolic, 44–45; as *uchi*, 73–76, 79–84 passim, 143–62 passim, 169–90 passim, 271; as zero point, 44, 253. *See also* deixis: and ground; *uchi*

Anderson, John M., 274

Araki, Hiroyuki, 4, 9

architecture, 154, 212–14; and doors, 213; and illness, 221; and thresholds, 213

argument, 258, 287. *See also* (in)transitivity; roles: in predicate

Aristotle, on metaphor, 41

aru/iru, 260, 263, 265, 280–81

aspect, 247, 254–55, 260, 263, 265–68, 274, 289n.23; as grammatical device, 250, 253, 254; related to (in)transitivity, 260, 265–66, 268; and *uchi/soto* values, 268, 286

atransitivity, 258, 260, 262

authority: 89–98, 169–74, 177–90, 226–38; abuse of, 228–29, 230–31; and *amaeru/amayakasu*, 226–27; axis of, 91, 194; conflicts over, ch. 7, ch. 8; and deictic anchor point, 228–29; as discipline vs. spontaneity, 88–89, 94–95, 226; and hierarchy, 88–89, 91–95, 103; indexing of, 102–4, 227, 229; and inside/outside orientations, 88–96; and intimacy/solidarity, 94–95, 174–77, 227–34, 242n.1; and power, 102–4, 226; and resistance, 174, 186–90; within *uchi*, 169–90 passim, 226–34; and *uchi/soto*, 88–95, 181, 184, 202–3, 226–29, 230–34; and ultimate *uchi* position, 228–29

avoidance ritual, 269, 270

avoiding refusal, 137, 139

ba (frame of reference), 7, 9, 31, 156

Bachnik, Jane M., 3–37, 66, 75, 91, 105, 143–66, 174, 175, 178, 198, 223–43

Bakhtin, Mikhail, 6, 18, 22, 247, 286

Barthes, Roland, 108

Bateson, Gregory, 13, 15, 65
Becker, A. L., 15–16, 17, 25, 284
Bedouins (Egypt), 19
Befu, Harumi, 106
Ben-Ari, Eyal, 11
Benedict, Ruth, 74, 99
Benveniste, Emile, 26, 282
body, 210–11, 214, 215; control of, 217; as deictic anchor point/ground, 49–50, 60–61, 211, 214; as indexical origin, 40, 60; as mediating, 211; and orientation, 40–41; and perceiving, 210, 214; separated from self, 215. *See also* self
Bolinger, Dwight, 40, 41, 69n.3
Borkin, Ann, 280
boundaries, 41, 42, 47–48, 53, 59–60, 74, 184; and body, 49–50, 214; breakdown/dissolution/blurring of, 210–11, 215, 217–20, 236–38; as central feature of *uchi* schema, 60–61; constricting, 215; as fluid/rigid, 73; group, 73, 148, 157–60, 174, 177–81, 233; of *ie*, 148, 157–60; and life and death, 210, 219–20; manipulation of, 223, 231–34; negotiation of, 169–90; and position, 271; private/public, 211; self/other, 159–60; shifting, 75, 148, 156–60, 175, 210–11, 217; signaling of group, 115; spatial, 213, 216; spatial as symbolic, 213–14; as variable, 282–83. See also *uchi/soto*
Bourdieu, Pierre, 4, 5, 18, 22, 210, 216; and *habitus,* 39, 68n.2, 145, 252
branching, 199–201, 207n.4
Brenneis, Donald L., 5, 20
Brown, Keith, 198, 200
Brown, Penelope, 83, 114, 136, 140
Brown, Roger, 84, 103, 159
Bruner, Jerome S., 18, 70n.10
Burtt, E. A., 21
business, 51–52, 173–77, 192–203
Butler, Judith, 188, 190
butsudan (ancestor altar) 204. *See also* ancestor worship; household
Bybee, Joan, 70n.14

Calder, Kent E., 227
causative, 263–64, 267–68, 268. *See also* (in)transitivity: prosthetic
character, and incident, 247, 249, 286
choodai, 120–21, 123, 132–33, *133*
Cicourel, Aaron V., 20
circles, 52, 229

Clancy, Patricia, 76, 78–79
clause-in-use, 250, 251, 287
clause nominalizers *no* and *koto,* as grammatical devices, 247–48, 250–53, 254, 272–74, 279, 285–86
cline: of distance, 28; evidential, of person, 15–17, 25, 30–31, 249, 283–86
close/distant, 153–55, 160, 285
coevolution, 65
cognition, 75, 253, 280, 287n.6
collocation, 40, 67, 69n.3; defined, 69; uses of *uchi/soto* in, 40
Comaroff, Jean, 211
communication, 20, 241
competence, 200–201
compound words, 40, 54–55, 56, 60, 70n. *See also* lexicon
Comrie, Bernard, 274
concepts, associated with *uchi/soto,* 38–39, 64, 66–67. *See also* values
conflict, 30, 224; avoiding, 114–15; over authority, ch. 7, ch. 8; and between authority (hierarchy) and solidarity (intimacy), 228–34; over indexing, 169–90, 192–206, 209–20, 226–38; internecine, 202–3; interpersonal, 195–203; between life and death, 209–20 passim, 236–38; Japanese, reevalutation of, 225–26; between self-interest and self-sacrifice, 192–206 passim, 234–36; within *uchi,* 169–90 passim, 226–34, 242nn.2–4, between *uchi* and *ie,* 193–206 passim; between *uchi* and *soto,* 226, 234–36
Confucianism, 21
constitutive: language as, 135, 140; nature of deixis, 161–62; *omote/ura* axis as, 154–55; relationships between self and social order as, 5, 14–15, 17, 22, 29–30, 144–45, 161–62, 210, 224–25, 239–40; relationships between self and society as, x, 4–5, 17, 23, 224–25, 239. *See also* agency; practice
container schema, 47–48, 59, 61
context, 4–6, 8–10, 12, 17–18, 91, 163n.7; anchorage in, 19–20, 238; as constitutive of social life, 4, 239–40; and deixis, 8, 12, 26–28; epistemic, 257, 283; and hierarchy, 8; ideational, 257; and indexical meaning, 5, 6–7, 10–17, 24–27, 28; and indexing, 11–17, 89–99, 146–60 passim; informational, 257; and inside/outside orientations, 20, 22–27; interactional, 28,

30; and interdependent self, 4, 17–21; interpersonal, 257; and language, 30; multileveled relationships to, 89–109 passim; negotiated social definition of, 114, 128–29, 140; organization of, 8–10, 238–40; and organization of self and society, 3–5, 8–10, 224–26, 238–40; and public meaning, 19, 20, 28; and shifting, 9, 15; and situated social order, 5, 8, 10, 23, 146, 238–42; and situationally defined self, 5, 8–10, 239; and *uchi/soto*, 27–31, 38, 41–43, 44, 89–109, 174, 186, 250; and wrapping, 4–5, 13; and uniqueness, 238; and verbs, 257, 261–62. *See also* agency: and structure; deixis; indexing

contingent: copular expressions with *to*, 275–80; states, 274

contrasts, between *uchi* and *soto, 254,* 255

control, 19, 201, 214, 217, 237–38, 251, 257, 262; of change, 247, 261–62; experimental, 128; vs. noncontrol, 253, 257; and the perfect, 266; and posture, 214, 216–19; self-control and lack of, 216; volitional, 247, 251, 257

control/noncontrol, 258–59, 265–69

Cooper, William E., 43

copular complements, 274–80, *277,* 281

corporate enterprises, 49, 51

Crapanzano, Vincent, 11, 16

daroo/deshoo, 134, 281; and style-shifting, 127, 282–83

dasu (put/take out), 67, 269

death, 202–6, 219–20, 236–38

deference, 213, 227, 229, 237, 251, 269; and communication of person, 147, 156–57; conventional indexing of, 248, 268–72; defined, 269–72, 289; directional axis of, 147–48, 155–62 passim, 176, 233–34; guest/host, 148–55, 157–62; and inside/outside distinctions, 147, 157–62

deictic center, 75, 79, 83. *See also* anchor point; deixis

deictic organization, 17, 144, 157, 160–61. *See also* deixis

deictic projection, 60–61, 85n.2, 85n.8

deictic references, 214, 282

deictic terms, as shifters, 12, 75

deixis, 12–13, 17, 25–27, 74–75, 79–84 passim; defined, 26–27, 75; and directional deference, 80–84, 157–60; and ground, 146–48; and guest/host communication,

161; and *ie*/household organization, 143–62 passim; and indexing, 12, 242–43n.8; and language organization, 73–85 passim; lexical, 44, 253; and organization of *uchi/soto,* 80–84 passim, 143–48, 161–62; and point of view, 8–10, 27–28; and pragmatic/situated meaning of, 12–14, 79–80, 145; projected, 60–61; and self and social organization, 17, 144–45; and situated social order, 145; and situationally defined self, 145; social, 79–80, 84, 144–45, 253. *See also* anchor point; indexing; *uchi*

derivation, 263–64, 265, 269, 270

destruction: of communal good, 235; of existence, 223–24, 237; of family, 192–206; of industry, 203; of life, 224, 236–38; by personal hubris, 225; potential for, 225–26; of social order and self, 30, 169–246; as underside of creation, 225. *See also* conflict

detail: in expression of index of familiarity, 251; and (in)transitivity, 248, 262, 268

determiners (*ko, so-, (k)a-*), 283, 290n.45; and personal pronouns, 78

DeVos, George, 74

dictionaries, 25, 42–43, 60, 69n.7

differences, 153, 174, 250, 272–73

directional orientations, 3, 6–8, 18, 147, 224, 237

directives, 126, 128, 130, 132, 134, 137, 138, 139; defined, 115; distribution of, 131; sociolinguistic meaning in, 119–23; speech acts as, 113–15

dislike, envy, 197, 198, 201

distance: axis of, 147; and formality/informality, 147, 150–55; indexing of, 147–48. *See also* formal/informal; *omote/ura*

distancing strategy: in families, 134–40

Doi, Takeo, 4, 6–7, 8, 9, 27, 74, 94

domains: of experience, 39, 41, 44; of human experience, 38, 42; (non)domestic, 48–51; of purely personal, 202, 235–36; quantitative, 43; semantic, 84; of signification, 250; social, 38, 41, 43; spatial, 38, 41, 43, 45–47, 56–57; temporal, 53–54; of *uchi/soto,* 42–43, 254

doozoku gaisha, 193–206 passim

Dore, Ronald, 196

dualisms, 20–23, 29–31, 32n.14, 224–26, 240–42

dualities, 19, 21–24, 28–29, 97, 210, 224–25, 236–38, 240

Dubisch, Jill, 101, 108
DuBois, John, 257
Dumont, Louis, 95, 97
Duranti, Alessandro, 4, 17, 20, 144
Durkheim, Emile, 270, 289nn.30–31
dynamic/nondynamic, 258

Edwards, Walter, 7, 28, 102, 145
Eliade, Mircea, 213
ellipsis, 76, 78–79
embodied, 60–61, 253
empty/full, 152, 163n.6
engaged/detached distinctions, 25, 28–29,
    91, 94, 239–42, 249–50, 252, 254, 280–90;
    and scale of familiarity/certainty, 247
epistemic: defined, 257, 288; distinctions
    29–30, 241–42
epistemology: and epistemic modality, 251;
    indexed by absence vs. presence of *aru*,
    280–83; indexed in clause nominalizers
    no vs. *koto*, 272–74; indexed in derived
    (= prosthetic) (in)transitivity, 263–65;
    indexed in lexical (in)transitivity, 251;
    indexed with locative particles *ni* vs. *to,*
    274–80; indexed in perfect aspect, 265–
    68, 272–74; indexing of, 247, 249–50,
    254–55; as scale of familiarity, 247
Evens, T.M.S., 21, 225
evidential cline of person. *See* cline; person
evidentiality: as basis of indexicality, 285;
    and cline of person, 284–85; defined,
    251, 285; hearing vs. seeing, 214;
    indexed, 251, 286; relation to informa-
    tional and epistemic functions of lan-
    guage, 285
experience: experiential vs. second-hand,
    254; representation of, 254. *See also*
    evidentiality
extension: and radial structure of catego-
    ries, 287; of word use across domains, 42
external world: and self, 286; and society,
    23, 248

face-threatening acts, 114–15
facilitation: and *soto*, 101; and *uchi*, 101, 102
familiarity: epistemological, 29, 30–31, 224,
    240–42, ch. 11; indexing of, 151–52, 251;
    social, ch. 5. *See also* knowledge; *uchi/soto*
family: company as, 173–90 passim; de-
    struction of, 192–207, 223; directives
    used in, 129–40; organization, 143–62
    passim. See also household; *ie*

family enterprise, 169–90, 192–206 passim,
    211–13
Farmer, Ann, 76
field, indexical, 249, 285
figure/ground, 14, 26, 246–48, 157–61,
    252
Fillmore, C. J., 26
Fischer, John L., 9
folk categories, 286
foreground/background, 146–48, 157–60
form: direct, 12, 126, 127, 133, 141n.3, 147;
    distal, 119–20, 122–23, 132–33, 138–40,
    141n.3, 147, 284; distant, 125, 126, 127,
    128, 133–34, 138–39; distant, defined,
    120, 141n.3; distant, used within nuclear
    family, 134–40; distant vs. distal, 120;
    first-person, 76, 78, 282, 283; grammati-
    cal, 239, 255, 256; honorific, 79, 80–83,
    85, 85n.4, 85n.5, 119, 132, 136, 140, 157,
    269–71, 270, 289; humble, 79, 121, 132,
    138, 140, 157, 159, 233, 269, 270–71, 289;
    polite, 80–82; second-person, 78, 282,
    283; third-person, 282, 283; variations in,
    153, 154
formal/formality. See *omote*
formal/informal, 22, 23, 95, 141, 143, 147–
    52, 153, 154, 163n.10. *See also* form: di-
    rect; form: distal; form: distant
form of life, language as, 247, 255, 286
Foucault, Michel, 184, 188, 190
fragment, 122–23, 126
frame: bounded, 47; group, in Japanese so-
    ciety, 7, 11–12, 145; ideational, 270–71;
    substitution of, 53–54; *uchi/soto* 'inside/
    outside', 38. See also *ba*
Friedman, David, 227
Friedrich, Paul, 159, 289n.32
Fruin, Mark, 173
futokoro, 49, 52

Garfinkel, Harold, 20
Geertz, Clifford, 18–19
gender relations, 89–109 passim, 110n.5;
    and age, 104–7; conceptions of power in,
    99, 101–4; in data collection, 118; in fam-
    ily, ch. 4; and hierarchy, 95–96, 108; in-
    dexing of, 88–109 passim; and meaning,
    107–9; metaphysical orientations in,
    101–2; and position, 104–7; shifting in,
    97–98
Genovese, Eugene, 182
Gergen, Kenneth J., 18

Gerlach, Michael, 7
Giddens, Anthony, 4, 5, 18, 22, 145
Gilman, Albert, 84, 103, 159
giri (social obligation), 27
giri/ninjoo, 6–7, 27, 146; and indexical meaning, 11
glosses, 146, 153, 189
Goffman, Erving, 78, 92, 269, 270, 289n.30, 289n.31
Goodwin, Charles, 4, 17, 20
Gordon, Andrew, 173
grammar: constructions, 54–55; ecological view of, 256; grammatical devices as indexes, 39, 250; grammatical indexing of *uchi/soto* values, ch. 11; motivation of grammatical form, 256; representational significance of grammatical devices, 255, 272, 274; semantics of, 250
grammatical devices, 39, 250–53, 255, 269, 272, 274, 285
Grice, H. Paul, 278
ground, 45, 73, 146–48, 155–62 passim, 228, 241; body as deictic/indexical, 60–61, 211, 214; as deictic anchor point, 45, 46–48; and figure, 14, 26, 146–48, 157–61, 252; as pragmatic meaning, 14; as *uchi*, 45–56, 147–48, 155–62. *See also* anchor point; *uchi*
group: as anchor point, 26–27, 29–30, 44, 143–62 passim, 224; boundaries, 73, 148, 157–60, 174, 177–81; in-group/out-group, 74, 143, 174, 177–83; as organized deictically, 143–44, 155–56; reference point, 73, 80–84
guest/host relationship. *See* relationships: guest/host
Gumperz, John J., 14
Guy, Rebecca F., 78

habitus, 4, 22, 39, 59, 65–66, 145, 252–54; defined, 39, 68–69n.2; and *ie* organization, 145; *uchi/soto* as, 39, 40, 59–60, 66, 252, 254
Hall, John W., 21
Hamabata, Matthews M., 6, 7, 174, 192–208, 195, 206, 229, 234–36; and precise variability, 154; and self, 28, 145
Hamada, Morio, 76
Hanks, William F., 6, 12, 20, 26, 146–48, 159, 228, 229; and deictic organization, 17, 144, 157, 160–61; and *habitus*, 68–69n.2

Haraway, Donna, 175, 190
Hardacre, Helen, 7
hare/ke, 145
Harré, Rom, 27
hazu, 282, 284
hegemony, 174, 187
Heian period, 42, 278
Heidegger, Martin, 4, 5, 18, 20, 22, 145
Hendry, Joy, 4–5, 11, 13, 16
Herbert, Jean, 100
Herzfeld, Michael, 108
hierarchy, 8, 95–99, 108–9, 169, 175, 182, 223, 226, 228; and age, 104–7; and *amaeru/amayakasu*, 88–99; ambiguity of, 89, 226–27; and authority, 88–89, 91–95, 103, 227–28; and context, 88–109 passim; contradictions, 8; as difference, 108–9; and discipline vs. spontaneity, 88–89, 94–95; and gender, 95–109 passim, 224; as indexed, 88–109 passim, 227; and metaphysical meaning, 99–102; and power, 89, 102–4, 226; and relationships, 102–4; and shifting, 95–99, 226–29; and social practice, 17; and solidarity, 95–96, 227; and *soto* contexts, 96; tensions in, 94–97; and *uchi/soto*, 88–109 passim, 227; within *uchi*, 169–90 passim, 226–34. See also *amaeru/amayakasu*; *uchi/soto*
Hinds, John, 76, 78
Hoji, Hajime, 76
Homans, George, 194
home, 48, 58
homology, 65, 215, 217, 252, 255, 257, 287, 287n.2
honne (inner world of feelings), 6–7, 27, 169, 176, 183; and *tatemae*, 6–7
honorific, 119, 120, 132; defined, 85n.5, 85n.9, 136, 269; distinguished from more general sense, 85n.4, 85n.5; vs. humble, 81–83, 139–40, 269–72, 289n.28
Hopper, Paul J., 260, 287n.4, 289n.23
household, 7, 31n.5, 42, 47, 49, 61, 96, 104, 110n.10, 140, 162; and ancestor altars, 203–4, 205; branch, 200, 204; corporate, 51, 175; and deicitc anchorpoints, 143–46, 155–60; head of, ch. 8, 230–34, 235; main, 199–202, 204; meanings of, 175, 249; positions in, 197–99, 206n.2; recruitment to succession, 197–201, 235, 242n.4; shifting boundaries in, 157–60, 276–79; spatial organization of, 152–54; as temple, 204–6. See also *ie*

humble, 120, 121, 132, 138, 157; acts, as
    reciprocity, 259–60; defined, 269; vs.
    honorific, 81–83, 139–40, 157, 269–72,
    289n.28
Husserl, Edmund, 20

"I": as indexical reference point, 12, 26, 27,
    75, 144, 156, 271, 284; of Indo-European
    language, 73
icons: diagrammatic, 45; and sign system,
    24, 44–45; as symbolism in lexical use, 45,
    47
ideational, 262, 268–69, 273; defined, 257,
    287–88; perspectival, 279–80
ideology, 75
ie, 143–60 passim, 175, 195, 197–98, 203,
    237; and ancestors, 204–6; as anchor
    point, 143–48, 155–56; and continuity,
    202, 235; and death, 205; defined, 145; as
    defining self and social order, 146, 161;
    and deixis, ch. 6; and durability, 197;
    human aspects of, 234–35; and indexing,
    ch. 6; and marriage, 195–96, 206n.2; and
    meaning, 204–6; organization and, 146–
    48, 182, 199–200, 225, 234, 240; and or-
    ganization of person, 156–57; politics of,
    202; shifting boundaries of, 144, 156–60;
    spatial design of, 154; succession, 197–
    201, 235; succession conflicts, 202–6,
    235, 242n.4; symbolic center of, 204; as a
    temple, 204–6; and uchi, 26, 27, 31n.5,
    ch. 6, 192–206, 206n.1, 234–35; women
    and, 195–96
ikoo, vs. iku daroo, 281–82
Ikuta, Shoko, 147
Ilongot, 19, 70n.12, 99, 110n.5
imbalance, in indexing self vs. society, chs.
    7–10
imperfect, as term equivalent to imperfec-
    tive, ch. 5
(im)perfective, 265, 268
incident, and character, 247, 249, 286
inclinations, personal, 201, 206
inclusion, degrees of, 174
independent self, 4, 18, 21–22, 32n.13. See
    also self
indexes, 4, 12; and agency, 155; contrasted
    with symbols and icons, 24–25, 70n.10;
    defined, 10–13, 23–26, 250; of epistemol-
    ogy in grammar, ch. 11; as evolved from
    symbols, 44–45, 70n.11; organization of,
    24–27; Peirce's focus on, 24; referential,
    145, 162n.1, 283, 286; as rules of use,

155; and uchi/soto organization, chs. 1–6,
    11
indexical meaning, 3–6, 10–17, 22, 60–61,
    114, 145, 160–62, 239–42. See also deixis;
    meaning; pragmatic meaning; situated
    meaning; wrapping
indexical signs: parameters of, 11–12; sym-
    bolic sources of, 70
indexical uses: motivated by symbolic val-
    ues, 70; of signs, defined, 70; of uchi/soto
    schema, 44; of a word, 44
indexing, 3, 10–17, 147–62 passim; and
    agency, 4, 5, 16–17, 22, 144, 155; con-
    flicts over, chs. 7–9, 223–38; defined,
    ch. 1, 250; deictic, 146–48; in guest-host
    communication, 148–55, 157–60; and
    hierarchy, 96, 226–27; indexical terms,
    146; inside and outside of Japan, 17–22;
    and interdependent self, 18, 20–22; of
    knowledge, 152–53, 240–42, ch. 11; of
    language/self/social order, 5, 14–15, 17,
    22, 25, 29–30, 225, 226, 232, 249, 268,
    286; organization of, 238–42; process of,
    5, 12, 23, 226; referential, 146–47; and
    relational self, 5, 9–10, 17–18; and sign
    system, 24, 44, 70n.10; and situated social
    order, 5; of social behavior, 44, 140, 271;
    and social context, 5; of social relations,
    248–60, 268–72; two kinds of, 146–7;
    and wrapping, 13. See also constitutive;
    meaning
inference, invited. See invited inference
informal/informality, 147, 152
information, 151, 240, 285; accessibility of,
    53; epistemology of, 274–75, 282, 285;
    expressed, 119; indexing, 250, 253; refer-
    able, 272–73
information(al), 250; defined, 257, 287–88
inside, 3, 5, 42, 53, 212, 229; and emotion,
    19, 93; and giver and receiver, 268; and
    informality, 152–53; meaning of, 6–7.
    See also uchi
inside/outside orientations, 3, 6–7, 18, ch.
    8, 224, 237–38; as axes, 25–27, 100, 107,
    146–47, 194, 225; and cartesian dualities
    between self and world, 19, 21–22; and
    directional deference, 147, 156–57; as
    emotion vs. social life, 19; as engagement
    vs. detachment, 25, 28–29, 91, 94, 239–
    42, 285–86; and evidential cline of per-
    son, 15–17, 25, 30–31, 249, 283–86; and
    giving/receiving, 160, 268; and indepen-
    dent/interdependent organization of

ont.)

+/− *aru*) of predicator, *so* anchor point; deixis; per-

deference, 147–48; and in- negative/avoiding/honor- 0, 269–72, 289; polite style vs. 81, 289n.29; positive/drawing ble, 270–72, 289; strategies, 270–71, 289; terms, 79; wrap- anguage, 4–5

s. attribute, 74; household, 197– tion and social/psychological on, 217; privileged, 53; relative to ndary as deference, 271; relative ame, 56; vs. shape, 61; situational,

fice, 116–21. *See also* Shinjuku Cen- Post Office

re, 214, 217. *See also* control r, 184–90, 206n.2, 237; abuse of, 182– 225–32, 235–36; and authority, 102– of Grandmother, 196, 201; personal ubris, 197, 201–3, 225, 235; and rela- ionships, 102–4; sacred, 101, 102, 107 actice: 4, 5, 15, 22, 145, 223, 239; catego- ries and social praxis, 65; and constitu- tion of self and social order, 17; of deixis in a society, 253. *See also* constitutive

pragmatic meaning, 10–17, 22, 79–80, 145, 239; cultural focus on, 11, 14; and perfor- mative meaning, 14; vs. semantic mean- ing, 10–17. *See also* deixis; indexical meaning; indexing; meaning

pragmatics, 31n.8, 79, 102, 115, 117, 253; defined, 79; predicate categories, 254– 55; and positive politeness strategies, 270–71, 289. *See also* meaning: pragmatic

predicates, 122–23, 251, 254, 257–65, 280– 83, 287n.10; defined, 119, 141, 287; ex- tended, defined, 141n.4; stative, 251, 258. *See also* paired verbs; verbs

predicators, 284, 287n.10; defined, 257, 265, 287; lexical, 265–66; stative, 258, 262, 263, 265; *yoogen*, 287

primogeniture, 198, 235

principles: cooperative, 290; structural, 8, 9; vertical, 8, 10, 31n.7, 227, 238

projection, deictic, 44, 60–61, 85

pronouns, 12, 15, 32nn.9–10, 45, 156, 249, 253, 283–84

prosthetic (in)transitivity. *See* (in)transi- tivity

prototype, 60

prototypical (in)transitivity, 248, 251, 259– 62, 265, 267, 279

prototypically "nouny," 68

proverbs, ch. 2

proximal-distal semantics, 28, 43, 250, 284

public/private, contexts/space, 39, 66–67, 120, 193, 213, 216

Quinn, Charles J., Jr., 24, 38–72, 84, 240, 247–94

radial structure, 256, 287n.12

railroad station, 116, 118–21, 123. *See also* Sugamo National Railway Station

rashii, 281–82

Ray, Yuko, 274

realis (nonhypothetical) modality, 251. *See also* irrealis

reference, 147, 233, 277, 283; and address, 147–223; by nominal vs. by verb, 80; non- referring expressions and, 76; speaker and addressee, 76, 147, 233; to *soto* 'out- group', 83; and speaker/self, 15, 76; to *uchi* 'in-group', 83

reference points, deixis and deictic, 12, 26, 155

referential indexes, 146–48, 162n.1, 283, 286; and relational features, 146; two necessary points of, 146

regencies, 198, 202, 204, 207n.5

register: and indexical messages, 150–51; shifting, 113–14, 124–40; and social vs. pragmatic variables, 117

relationships: and age, 104–7; between agency and structure, 4–5, 16–17, 22; and *amaeru/amayakasu*, 88–109, 157, 223–24, 237; as basic "unit" of Japanese social or- ganization, 225; and conceptions of power, 99, 101–4; and Confucianism, 21; between constituting and being consti- tuted, 224; between construction and de- struction, 225; between dualities, 21–22, 29–30, 224, 236; gender, ch. 4, 195–97; guest/host, 30, 148–55, 157–62; indexi- cal, 11–13, 24–26, 224, 240; between indi- viduals, 225; and in-group/out-group dis- tinctions, 74, 96, 114, 140, 230, 233; and meaning, 20; between self and context, 12, 18, 22–23, ch. 4; between self and so- cial order, 5, 22–23, 225–26; between self and society, 5, 17–19, 22, 23, 74; shifting, 105–6, 240; between *uchi* and *soto*, 27; be-

self, 4, 18–19, 20–22, 225, 239; indexical meaning of, 11, 44, 102, 147, 238–39, 254, 280; toward knowledge, 240–42, ch. 11; as linked, 27; as located, 27; and rela- tions between self and social order, 22, 146, 161, 225–26, 239–40, 248; and rela- tionships between self and society, 20, 22–23, 28, 145, 272; in societies other than Japan, 18–19, 20; and we-ness/oth- erness, 240–42. *See also uchi/soto*

interdependent self, 4, 8, 20–22, 32n.12, 225. *See also* self

internal world: and self, 23. *See also* inside/ outside orientations

interpersonal, defined, 257, 287–88

intervals, 53–54, 55, 59

intimacy, 129–40, 192–96; and authority, ch. 4, ch. 8, 223–24, 226–34; axes of, 91, 194; and *uchi*, 226–29. *See also uchi/soto*

(in)transitivity, 247, 254–55, 260, *261*, 286; as continuum, 260–61; defined, 287; grammatical devices of, 250, 251, 253, 269, 287n.5; as index of *uchi/soto* knowl- edge, 248, 253, 262–65; as phenomenal (descriptive) detail, 248, 262; prosthetic (derived), 251, 258, 263–65, 268–72; pro- totypical, 262; vs. stative/no change, 247, 262; symbolic use of, 248; as (un)con- trolled, 247, 262–65

intruder, 211, 214, 216, 218, 221

invited inference, 277–78

invited reference, 277–78

ireru (put in, insert, accept), 67

irony, 235, 256

irrealis (hypothetical) modality, 278. *See also* realis modality

itadaku, 138–39

Jackendoff, Ray S., 274

Jacobsen, Wesley, 258, 261

Jakobson, Roman, 6, 12, 75, 146

James, Henry, 286

Java, 18, 70n.12, 99, 110n.5

Jesperson, Otto, 12, 75

Johnson, Mark, 6, 40, 59, 69n.5, 276

Johnson-Laird, Philip N., 274

Jorden, Eleanor H., 120, 147, 258, 269, 270

Josephs, Lewis, 272

kabuto (helmet), 49, 52

Kanter, Rosabeth Moss, 183

Katoo household: conflict with househead,

230–34; discussion of vignettes, 150–55, 158–60; guest vignettes, 148–50; house design, 154; indexing of shared knowl- edge, 241

Keeler, Ward, 18–19, 99

kimono, 4, 13, 49, 101, 150

Kirkpatrick, John, 19, 20

Kitagawa, Joseph, 100

Kitaoji, Hironobu, 197, 198

Kitayama, Shinobu, 4, 15, 17, 18, 225

knowledge, 241, 285; degree of sharedness of, 29, 152–53, 224; as engaged/de- tached, 28–29, 91, 94, 240–42, 252, 254, 280–90; familiar/unfamiliar, 29, 240–41; indexing of, 29–31, 240–42, ch. 11; and inside/outside dimensions, 240; in Japa- nese grammar, 224, ch. 11. *See also uchi/ soto*

Kondo, Dorinne K., 7, 84, 169–91, 226–29; and organization of self, 28, 145; and re- lationships, 105, 175, 177; and self, 9–10

kotatsu, 90, 92, 230

koto. See clause nominalizers *no* and *koto, no/ koto*

Koyré, Alexandre, 21

kudasai, 119–20, 124–25, 132–33, *133*, 136– 37

Kuno, Susumu, 76, 272, 280, 289n.33, 289n.34

Kuroda, S.-Y., 76, 77

Kurylowicz, J., 26

Labor Standards Law, 172, 177, 190n.4

Lakoff, George, 40, 52, 59, 69n.5, 256, 276, 289n.12

Lamphere, Louise, 188

Langacker, Ronald, 280

language: culturally defined perspective of, 7; as form of life, ch. 11; and hierarchy/ power/authority, 84; ideology of, 11; re- lation to social life, 84, ch. 11; situated, 252–53; situationally defined, 84; use, 10

language-intensive symbolism, 282, 289n.32

Lave, Jean, 13, 14

LDP (Liberal Democratic Party), 172, 177

Leach, Edmund, 16

Lebra, Takie, 4, 7, 8, 9, 31n.6, 84, 104; and Japanese relationships, 11–12, 94; and organization of self, 28, 91, 145, 156

levels: of individual, 96, 103, 107; of rela- tionship, 96, 103, 107; reversal of, 97; of social reality, 23, 28–29, 210; of *uchi/soto* organization, 23, 28–29, 223, 240

Levinson, Stephen C., 27, 79, 83, 114, 136, 140, 144

Levi-Strauss, Claude, 108

lexicalization, 54–55, 262, 263

lexicon, 68, 115; broader use of *uchi* than *(so)to*, 39, 42, 44, 61; mental, 69

Liberal Democratic Party. *See* LDP

Lindner, Susan, 280

linguistic relativity, 53, 252, 287

lived focus, on social life, 4, 22, 145; on language, 247

localistic hypothesis, 274

location, spatial, 42, 45–48, 145, 211–12

locative particles, 247–48, 252, 254, 274–80, *277*, 285

Lock, Andrew, 19

logical complexity, 248, 262

Luckmann, Thomas, 21

Lutwack, Leonard, 216

Lutz, Catherine A., 17, 19, 20

Lyons, John, 6, 12, 26, 75, 77, 145, 250, 274

McClelland, James L., 52

Malaysia, 187

mana, 99, 107

Manyooshuu, 43, 69n.9

mapped terms, 153, 239, 284

Markus, Hazel Rose, 4, 15, 17, 18, 225

marriage, 195–96, 206n.2

Martin, Samuel, 77, 78, 80, 147, 275, 278

Mazda Company, 229

meaning: complementary description of, 257; core, 103, 107; creative aspect of, 14; cultural, 11; and domain of use, 250; dynamic, 97; expression of, 253; as a form's use in language, 40; and groups, 103, 174, 177, 186; indexical, 4, 5, 6, 16, 104, 226, 239; and individuals, 103; literal, 41, 69; making, 252; performative, 14; and power, 188; pragmatic, 9–17, 31n.8, 94, 109n.2, 145, 239–42; private, 18; public, 20; as public, 144; referential, 10–11, 14–16, 226; as relation to multiple contexts, 257, 287–88n.14; and relationships, 91, 94, 103; semantic or propositional, 10–11; semantic or referential, 10–11, 14–16; situated, ix, 3–6, 10–17, 22, 145, 160–62, 224, 239–42, 252–53; situational, 4, 10, 84, 145, 239; and structure, 256; and words, 249–50; as wrapping, 45

meditation, 99, 100

Me First Principle, 43

Meiji Restoration, 172, 178

Merleau-Ponty, Maurice, 4, 5, 18, 20, 22, 145

messages, relational (indexical), 151, 153

metapattern, 65–66, 252, 256, 279

metaphor, 41, 49–50, 55, 65, 68, 69n.5, 256, 265, 277–78, 286; Aristotle on, 41; company as family, 173, 176, 180; denatured, 41; of gender, 101; for power of universe, 100; as source of new meanings, 41, 270; spatial, 216; of weaving, 224

metonymy, 49, 58, 65, 256, 265, 277, 286

middle (passive) suffix, 169, 263–64, 268. *See also* (in)transitivity

middle voice, 263–64, 268. *See also* (in)transitivity: prosthetic

Mikami, Akira, 80

Miller, George A., 274

Miller, Jean Baker, 183

Miller, Roy Andrew, 76, 77, 80, 147

Miyaji, Yutaka, 76

moat, 47, 61

modality, 247, 254–55, 286; epistemic, 251, 257, 288; as grammatical device, 250, 251, 253, 263, 281; realis, 251

modifiers, in data collection, 118–19

Molasky, Michael S., 66, 84, 209–22, 236, 238, 285

Moriuchi household, 194–206, 235–36

morphemes, 56, 61, 119, 250, 255, 272

morphology, 69, 70n.14, 115, 199, 250, 257, 259, 280, 284

motivation, in grammar, 256

Mühlhäusler, Peter, 27

Mukhopadhayay, Carol, 109

Myers, Fred R., 20

Nakamura, Hajime, 21

Nakane, Chie, 7, 8, 9, 32n.7, 227; and *ba* (group frame), 11–12, 156; and groups, 26, 74–75, 155, 199; and *ie/uchi,* 7, 31n.5, 175; and marriage, 195; and organization of self, 28, 80, 146–47; and workplace, 51, 162

Nara period, 42, 278

negotiation: of context, 114, 128–29; interpersonal, 114; of social definition, 128–29, 140

New Nippon Alliances, 203

ni, 274–75

Nietzsche, Friedrich Wilhelm, 22

ningen kankei (human relationship), 196

ninjoo (personal feelings), 27; and g 67

ni/to, 247–48, 250, 252, 254, 274–80, 286. *See also* copular complements, locative particles

noh theater, 55, 59

no/koto, 250, 252, 254, 272–73, 279, 286, 290n.35. *See also* clause nominalizers *no* and *koto*

/nominal+copula/ predicator, 257, 265, 287n.10

nonspatial related to spatial expressions, 274–75. See also *ni; to*

Nyamwezi (Tanzania), 97

obasan (aunt), 149–50

Ochs, Elinor, 6, 13, 25, 153, 239, 240

Ohnuki-Tierney, Emiko, 7

Oka, I Gusti Ngurah, 15–16, 17, 25, 284

okaasan (mother), 90, 93, 96, 104, 105, 149–50, 223, 230–34

omote, 147, 151, 151–54, 209–14; of barber shop, 211–13; as 'front', 27, 43, 66, 147, 151, 153, 154; indexing of, 226; as produced by participants, 154–55

omote/ura, 6–7, 8–9, 27, 31n.4, 66, 146, 147, 158, 163n.8; axes of, 147, 150–55, 237; and distance, 147, 154; and indexical meaning, 11; physical manifestations of, 154–55, 210–16; psychological manifestations of, 210; relation to *uchi/soto,* ch. 9; and self, 171, ch. 9; and shifting boundaries, 210–11; social manifestations of, 210

oni, 38, 182–84

Ooms, Herman, 205

orientation(al) expressions, 40–41; directional, 209; indexing of, 106; projected orientation, 40; relational, 40–41; spatio-temporal, 210

Ortner, Sherry, 108

Oshima, Shin: and anaphora, 76

ostensive reference, 282

otaku (your), 26, 156–57

otoosan (father), 90, 96, 98, 104, 149, 223, 230–34

outside, 3, 5, 42, 53, 56–61, 212, 229; and formality, 152–53; and giver and receiver, 268; meaning of, 6–7; and power, 19. See also *soto*

outside insider, 234

304

(points of view,
morphology
280–83. *See a*
spective
polite(ness): a
dexing, 13;
ific, 136, 1
plain style
near/hu
114, 115
ping in
position:
98; loc
definit
a bou
to a f
74
Pelzel,
Peng, F
perfect a
trolled,
uchi/soto
term equiv
kinds of, 26
267–68
perfective aspe
performative mea
ing; meaning; p
person: and anapho
76, 235; and ellipsi
cline, 15–17, 25, 30,
ical, 76, 249, 282–84;
inside/outside distinc
57; instability of terms,
zation of, 15–17, 25, 30,
sim, 249, 284; as problema
and pronouns, 76–79; and
power and solidarity, 84, 159
15; as shifters, 75; and *uchi/so*
tions, 80–85, 147, 156–57
personal pronouns, 12, 15, 25, 30,
84, 103, 159, 283
perspective, 281; indexed differently
predicate, 262–68, 280–83; indexing
29; shifting of, 9, 255, 286
Pharr, Susan, 108
phenomenology, 5, 20, 22
physical orientations, 3, 39–40, 210–11,
214, 220
Plath, David, 204, 205, 206
points of view, 8–10, 17, 27, 28, 238, 252,
253, 280; as deixis, 12; indexed by

tween unity and diversity, 29; vertical, 200

relativity, 8, 41, 239, 252; cultural, 29, 239, 241–42; linguistic, 252–53, 287

relevance, 278; defined, 290n.40

resistance, 174, 186–90

Rice, Phillip, 108

Rohlen, Thomas P., 228–29

roles: of participant, 76; in predicate, 253, 270; shifting, 97–98, 226, 233. *See also* argument

Rosaldo, Michelle Z., 19, 20, 112

Rosaldo, Renato, 19, 188

Rosenberger, Nancy R., 7, 88–112, 129, 130, 174; and *amae,* 74, 84; and dyadic relationships, 226; and gender, 84, 101; and organization of self, 28, 91, 146

Ross, John R., 43

Rumelhart, David E., 52

Russo-Japanese War, 212

sacred/profane, 64, 99–101, 146, 204, 213, 254

sacrifice, 194–98, 206; and conflict, 198, 202–6, 223; self-sacrifice, 194–95, 198–99, 200, 234–36

Saito, Mamoru, 76

Samoa, 18, 70n.12, 99, 110n.5

Satoo firm, 169–90, 223, 226–29

schema: container, 47–48, 59, 61; flexible, lived, 38; locative, 277; tight, 52; *uchi/soto,* and indexing, 44

Schneider, David, 194

Schutz, 20

Scott, James, 187–88

Scott, Joan, 179

self, 3, 5, 11, 239; cline of, 15–17; and context, 9–10, 15–17, 20, 99; contextually defined, 5, 9, 18, 239; decentered, 189–90, 249, 286; as defined within collectivity, 28, 145–46, 155–57; as defined in practice, 15, 249, 286; destruction of, 236–38; and hubris, 195–96, 201–3, 225, 228–29, 230–31, 234–38; imbalance of, vs. society, 193–206, 226–38; independent, 18, 21–22, 32n.13; as indexically defined, 5, 239–40, 249, 286; and indexing, 225–26, 239–42, 249, 286; individual, 18, 210; interdependent, 4, 18, 20–22, 32n.12, 225, 239, 249, 286; organization of, 28, 75, 80, 91, 145–47, 239; and pragmatic vs. referential meaning, 15, 156; relational, 4, 5, 9–10, 17–18, 28, 238, 240, 249, 286; self-

interest vs. self-sacrifice, 192–206, 234–36; shifting, 15, 18; situationally defined, 10, 145, 146, 157, 188–89, 232; and social order, 3–31 passim, 146, 161, 225–26, 239–40, 248; socially defined, 9, 16, 249, 286; and society, 3–31 passim, 99, 102–4, 144, 156, 225, 226, 248–49, 286; as *uchi,* 6, 143, 146–48, 155–57; and world, x, 23

semantic meaning, vs. pragmatic meaning, 10–17

semantics: proximate (also: proximal)-distal, 38, 43

sets, bounded, 54–55, 59

shachoo (company president), ch. 7

Sheldrake, Rupert, 69n.2

Shibatani, Masayoshi, 83

shifters, 12, 75, 146

shifting, 9–10, 15, 18, 91, 97, 224–30, 238; between authority and intimacy, 226–29, 230–34; and context, 99; between discipline and spontaneity, 88–98; of distance, 125, 224; in gender relations, 95–101; group boundaries, 73, 75, 80–84; in hierarchy, 95–97; as pragmatic meaning, 12; of roles, 97–98, 226, 233, 253; strategic, 234; between *uchi* and *soto,* 88–109 passim; and work-group organization, 228–29

Shiga Naoya, 209–20 passim, 236–38, 285

Shinjuku Central Post Office, 114, 116

Shintoism, 99–100, 107

Shore, Bradd, 18, 99, 101

Shotter, John, 18

Sibley, William, 211–19

Sider, Gerald, 182

signs: arbitrary quality of symbolic signs, 45; indexical use of, 70; redundancy of, 213; symbolic use of, 70

sign system. *See* sign types

sign types, 24, 44, 70; according to Peirce, 44–45, 70; over time, 45; as perspectives, 44

Silverstein, Michael, 6, 10, 11, 14, 16, 17, 145, 146, 155

Singer, Milton, 7, 24

situated meaning, ix, 3–6, 10–17, 22, 145, 160–62, 239–42, ch. 11; and context, ix, 5, 6–7, 10–17, 24–27, 28; defined, 4, 8, 238, 252–53; and deixis, xi, 12–14, 17, 25–27, 74–75, 79–84 passim, 145; and hierarchy as negotiated, x, ch. 4, 227; and indexing, ix, 3, 10–17, ch. 6, 239, 250–51; linking of emotions and social

(situated meaning, *cont.*)
  practice, xi; and situated social order, 4,
    5, 8, 10, 238–42; and situationally
    defined self, 4–5, 9–10, 17–18, 23, 28,
    146, 238, 240; and social life as consti-
    tuted, x, 5, 14–15, 17, 22, 29–30, 210,
    224–25, 239–40; and *uchi/soto, omote/ura,*
    ix, 29–31; and wrapping, x, 4–5, 13, 23.
    See also deixis; indexical meaning; index-
    ing; meaning; pragmatic meaning; self;
    social order
situationalism, 7–8; as indexing, 12
Slobin, Dan, 287n.8
Smith, Robert J., 4, 8, 9, 15, 21, 28, 75, 145,
  156, 204, 228
social deixis, 79–80, 84, 85n.4, 144–45,
  268–72. *See also* deixis; indexing
social life: organization of, 146–47, 224;
  perspectives on, 14–15, 109; and practice, 15, 161, 253. *See also* social order
social order, 3, 21; and authority, 8; con-
  ceptualizing, 17; context of, 15, 28; as indexically defined, 5; organic, 4; organization of, 225, 239; and self, 3, 146, 161,
  225–26, 239–40; shifting, 4, 8; situated, 4,
  5, 8, 10, 23, 146, 238–42; situationally defined, 4, 8, 17, 238. *See also* agency; *soto*
society, 3, 5; meanings for, 11; processes of,
  103; as outside, *soto,* 6; and self, 99, 102–
  4, 144, 156, 225, 226
sociocentric principles, 200–202, 204
sociolinguistics, 84, 115
solidarity, 103, 169, 174, 229. See also *uchi/
  soto*
soto, 3, 5, 6–7, 27, 146–47, 216, 237, 268; addressee as, 121–25, 128, 134, 140; and
  amayakasu, 94–109 passim; and authority, 91; as customers, 214; and deixis, 84,
  253; and detachment, 28; and discipline,
  92; domains of, 56–61, 254; and formality, 96, 147, 179; as general, 28; grammar
  of, 263; and group definition, 91, 96; hierarchy, 96; history of word, 42–43; indexing of, 226; knowledge, 241, 247–49;
  less defined than *uchi,* 60; and neighborhood, 211–12; as orientational expression, 40, 262, 281; as other, 240; and out-
  group, 115–17, 119–20, 124, 155–62; partitive (bounded subsets) of, *59;* and
  points of view, 27; psychological/attitudi-
  nal domains of, *58,* 58; public, outer, 28;
  as Shinto manifestation of bound energy,

100–101; social domains of, *58, 59,* 59,
  253; social order, 239–40; spatial domains of, 56, *57,* 58; terms modified by,
  63–65; two senses of, 240
sound: heard vs. seen, 214; and silence, 215,
  217, 219–20; sound/silence and light/
  darkness, 215–16; and *uchi/soto,* 215
source, controlling, 258–59, 262
space: defined by human/social activity, ix,
  49, 216, 218; and domains, 49–50, 53, 55,
  255, 274–75, 278; indexing of, 152–54;
  and localist(ic) hypothesis, 274–75; public and private contexts of, 39, 66–67, 120,
  213, 216; religious dimensions of, 213;
  situationally defined, xi; social space and
  time of day, 217; undifferentiated, 212
spatial boundaries, 47–50, 214
spatial expressions, 274–75
speaker, 114–15, 119, 121, 136, 157, 159,
  271–72, 285
speaker-addressee, relationship of, 110–20,
  129, 140
specification: with *choodai,* 119, *120, 121;* in
  data collection, 118–19; degree of, *120;*
  with *kudasai,* 119, *120, 121;* lack of, 119,
  120, 123; type of, *121*
speech: careful, 120; casual, 120, 123; register, 151
Stark, Werner, 21, 179
Straus, Erwin, 18
structure, 145, 240, 255–56, 271; contradictions in structural principles, 8. *See*
  agency: and structure
style. *See* form
style shifting, 124–28, 133; and negotiation
  of social definition, 128–29; within the
  nuclear family, 135–40; social definition
  and, 128–29; at vegetable market, 124–25
style switching. *See* style shifting
subject: deletion of, 83; implicit in verb
  form, 83; not specified, 83; of sentence
  triggers polite marking, 82, 85
subjective: vs. objective, 254; vs. objective
  essive, 276–78
subordination: in gender relations, 93, 96,
  102, 108
subsidiary company, 199, 201, 203
succession, household, 197–201, 205, 236,
  242n.4; and branching, 199–201; conflicts, 202–6; and enterprise, 199–203,
  207n.3
Sudnow, David, 14

Sugamo National Railway Station, 114
Sukle, Robert J., 84, 113–42, 253, 286
Suzuki, Kenji, 101
Suzuki, Takao, 9, 76
Swidler, Ann, 205
symbols: in lexical usage, 45, 47, 108, 272; as origin of indexes, 70n.11, 255–57; significance of grammar and, 255; and sign system, 24, 44, 70n.10; spatial, 176, 216; and *uchi/soto* schema, 44; and uses of a word, 44; and uses of signs defined, 70
synecdoches, 47, 52, 65, 256
syntax, 54, 115, 255, 265, 268, 270

tama, 100, 107, 110n.7
tatemae, 27, 226
tatemae/honne, 6–7, 11, 27, 146; and indexical meaning, 11
Tcherkezoff, Serge, 97
telic aspect, 260, 288n.19
tensions: in *amaeru/amayakasu* relationship, 94–95; between authority and solidarity, ch. 4, ch. 8; basic to human existence, 21; between context and relationships within context, 89–99; existential, 209–10; in gender relationships, 93–95, 96, 102, 103, 108, 109n.1; in hierarchy, 94–97; between ontological dualities, 21–22, 29–30, 224; between self and group, 224, 229, 242n.6; between self and other, 223; between self and society, 21–22
thinking-for-speaking, 253, 287n.8
Thompson, Sandra A., 260, 287n.4
tilted axis, 28, 29, 225, 239–40
time and space, 53–54, 145, 212
to (outside), 40, 42–44, indexical use of, 44
to (particle 'with'), 289n.33; contrasted with *ni,* 274–80; copular uses today, 290n.38; in earlier copula, 275–78. See also *ni/to*
Tokugawa shogunate, 52
transitivity. *See* (in)transitivity
Traugott, Elizabeth Closs, 69n.6, 274
trope, organizational, 68, 256, 286
tsubusu/tsubureru, 259, 262, 267
tsumori, 282, 284
Tuan, Yi-Fu, 214
tu and *vous,* 103, 159
Turner, Christena Linda, 242n.2

uchi, 3, 5, 6–7, 146, 148, 155, 237; addressee as, 123, 125; as agency, 26; and *amaeru,*
94–109 passim; as anchor point, 27, 73–76, 79–84 passim, ch. 6, ch. 7, 228–34; and associated values/concepts, 64, 254; authority and solidarity within, 169–90, 226–34; and *ba,* 28, 156–57; boundaries of, 144, 156–60, 177, 184–85; bounded sets of, 52, 53–54, *54;* conflict within, 169–90, 226–38; contradictions in discourse, 173–77; as deictic anchor point, 12, 26–27, 73–76, 79–84 passim, ch. 6, ch. 7, 228–34; and deixis, 25–28, 75–76, 84, 155, 161–62, 253; domains of, 45–56, 254; and engagement, 28; as epistemological realm, ch. 11; in expressing temporal intervals of, *53,* 53–54; and family, 49, 51, 91, 104–5, 135, 140, 173, 178, 185; and groups, 174, 177, 178, 186, 190; history of word, 42–43; as home, 48, 58, 194; and identity, 74, 175, 206, 268, 273; and *ie,* 27, 143–60 passim, 194, 234–35; indexing of, 44, 106, 143–62 passim; and individual self, 91, 206; individual within collectivity, 26–27; and informality, 91, 147, 176, 178, 185; informal situation and, 89–94; and in-group, 115, 119–20, 155–62 passim; as inside, 28; as insiders, 214; and intimacy, 91–169; and knowledge, 240–42, 247–49; as locus for self, 28; and *no,* 273; as orientational expression, 40, 281; and *otaku,* 156–57; as particular/specific, 28; partitive (bounded subintervals/subsets) of, 55–56, *56;* and person, 76–79, 156–57; and personal, 211, 235; psychological/attitudinal domains of, *50,* 254; psychological domains of, 49–50; as shared cultural frame of reference, 148; as Shinto manifestation of generative energy, 100–101; social domains of, *48,* 48–49, *51,* 51–52, 253, 254; as social space, 49, 216; social usage of, 42; as socially negotiated, 124–40; spatial domains of, 45, *46,* 47, 53, 254; as speaker, 75–76, 80–82, 114, 121, 155, 271; taxonomy of, 45–56, 262; terms modified by, 63–65; two meanings of, 25–28, 145–46; and *uchi-no,* 155; ultimate *uchi* position, 227–28
uchibutokoro, 49, 52
uchiki (shy), 41
uchi no kaisha, 169–90 passim
uchi/soto, 3–31 passim, 237; and address, 147, 233; agency/structure, 4–5, 22, 240;

(*uchi/soto*, cont.)
and *amae*, 84; and *amaeru/amayakasu*, 88–99, 94–99, 103–9, 158, 223–24, 226–27, 232, 240; authority/discipline vs. solidarity/intimacy, 25, 91, 94, 103, ch. 8, 227, 232; as axis, 25–27, 91–93, 100, 107, 146–47, 194, 225; and boundary distinctions, 74, 75, 81–84, 115, 140, 148, 157–60, 174–81, 192–99; conflicts and, 226, 230; and context, 3–31 passim, 262; continuum of, 91, 92, 94, 96, 97, 103, 104, 106; as creation/destruction of self and society, 205, 225–26; defining person, 5, 9, 15–16, 156–57; in degree, as continuum, 128–29; and deixis, 12, 161; delineation of, 3–31 passim, 236; destruction of *ie* and family firms, 192–206; dichotomy of, 118, 140; directional deference, 155–60; discourses, 173–74; and dyadic relationships, 88–106 passim; dynamics of, 91, 225, 226, 229; emotional self/social order, 161, 195–97, 200–203, 239–40; engagement/detachment, 240; in family life, 88–89, 129–40; figure/ground distinctions, 159–60; fluidity of, 97–98; and gender, 84, 92–94, 101, 114; group boundary distinctions, 157, 174; guest/host relationships, 157–61; *habitus* of, 39, 59, 68; and hierarchical relations, 91–97, 103, 175; and hierarchy, 97–98; history of words, ch. 2; ideational indexing of, 268, 279–80; in *ie* organization, 143–62 passim; and indexing, 10–27, 39, 114, 147, 226, 250–52, 255, 265, 268, 274, 286; indexing of shared/unshared knowledge, 224, 240–41; and in-group/out-group boundaries, 114, 155–62; inside/outside, 3–5, 6–7, 22–28; and interdependent self, 18; and intimacy, 125; and knowledge, 240–42, 247–86 passim; and *kudasai/choodai*, 121, 132, 133; and language, 75, 84, 114–40; and levels of social reality, 28–29, 240; as lexical resource, 38, 39–72; lexical summary of, 40, *64*; lifeway of, 39; and linguistic behavior, 73–84; linguistic manifestations of, chs. 2, 3, 5, and 11; and meaning, 187, 253; as metapattern, 65–66, 252, 256, 279; metaphysical meanings of, 99–102; opposition of, 249–50, 272, 275; organization of, 3–31 passim, 224, 236, 239; and organizational conflict, 192–206; partitive do-

mains of, *63*; physical manifestations of, 210; and power, 99–104; and power and resistance, 186–90; predicative indexing of, 252, 254, 268, 285; problems in delineation of, 7–10; and processes, 100, 108; psychological manifestations of, ch. 9; as reciprocity, 157–60, 164n.14; and reference, 147; and reference and address, 81–82, 233; and sacred power, 99–101; schema of, 44, 64–66, 250; and shifting, 91, 228, 233; and shifting boundaries, 210–11, 233, 283; and Shinto powers, 100–101; signaling, 115; social domains of, *63*; and social life, 91–93, 107, 115, 272; social manifestations of, 210; spatial domains of, *62*; and strategic shifts in communication, 124–40, 232; and symmetry/asymmetry distinctions, 159; vocabulary of, ch. 2; word order of, 43, 54. *See also* inside/outside orientations
undergoer, 247, 251, 258. *See also* (in)transitivity
uniqueness, 238, 241. See also *uchi/soto*: indexing of shared/unshared knowledge
universe, power of, 99–100, 101
(un)marked, 56, 59; and marked strategies, 136
ura, 6–7, 9, 27, 43, 66, 154, 176, 211–12; as close, 153; and everydayness, 153; and female space, 216–17; in house design, 154; and insidedness/context/informality, 152; and living quarters, 211–13, 214, 216

values: concepts associated with *uchi/soto*, 38–39, 55–56, 254; as implicit in verbs of entry and exit, 38–39; summarized, 63–67
variation: socially vs. pragmatically motivated, 117; sociolinguistic, 114
vegetable market, 114, 116–17, 122–28, 134–35
verb class, 257
verbs, 257, 265, 270, 287n.10; brief, 106; centripetal, 80, 100; as a class of predicator, 257; deferential, 269, 289n.28; deictic nature of, 80; directional/deictic nature of giving and receiving, 80–81; distant marking of, 125; donatory, 253, 268; of entry and exit, 38–39, 66–67; finite, 288n.16; of giving and receiving, 73, 80–81, 83, 87, 141n.6, 268–69; intransitive,

38–39, 66–67, 258–65, *259*; (non)cen-
tripetal, 80; paired transitive and intransitive, 258–62, 288; and politeness in Japanese, 82–83; signals from, 115, 125, 134;
stative, 258; suffixes of, 263; transitive,
38–39, 258–65, *259*. *See also* (in)transitiv-
ity; paired verbs; predicates
vertical principle: contradictions in, 8,
32n.7, 223, 227, 238–39; and hierarchy,
226
vignette: confectionery factory, 170–73,
179–80, 182–83; family evening at home,
89–91; obstreperous household head,
230–31; two sets of guests, 148–50; waking up, 6, 40
Vogel, Ezra F., 195, 200
volitional/nonvolitional, 260–63, 266, 270–
71
Vološinov, Valentin Nikolaevic, 6, 18, 22
Vygotsky, Lev Semenovich, 5, 18, 22,
287n.6

watakushi (speaker), 76
Watson-Gegeo, Karen Ann, 20

Waugh, Patricia, 108
Wetzel, Patricia J., 73–87, 119, 173, 233,
253, 268, 286; and meanings of *uchi*, 25,
27, 147, 156, 239; and self, 9, 144, 157
White, Geoffrey M., 17, 19, 20
Whitman, John, 76
Whorf, Benjamin, 253, 255
Wittgenstein, Ludwig, 20, 40, 255
Wolff, Jonathan Hart, 76
word class, 257
word order, and world order, 43
world: as lived, 247, 286; interpreted in values associated with *uchi* and/or *soto*, 66–
67, 248, 262–63, 268, 273–74, 285–86
wrapping, x, 4–5, 13, 23, 31n.2; and indexical meaning 11–13

Yamada Yoshio, 276–78
yooshi (adopted husband), 202, 204–6, 231–
34

Zenshuu (Shiga Naoya), 211–19
zero point, 44, 47, 70n.11. *See also* anchor
point; ground